FAMILY COMMUNICATION

Cohesion and Change

Second Edition

Kathleen M. Galvin
Northwestern University

Bernard J. Brommel
Northeastern Illinois University

Scott, Foresman and Company
Glenview, Illinois   London, England

Acknowledgments

pp. 14, 18–22. Excerpts from *Family Worlds* by Robert D. Hess and Gerald Handel. Copyright © 1959 by The University of Chicago. Reprinted by permission.

pp. 13–17. From "Circumplex Model of Marital and Family Systems: 1. Cohesion and Adaptability Dimensions, Family Types, and Clinical Application" by David H. Olson, Douglas H. Sprenkle, and Candyce Russell in *Family Process*, Vol. 18, No. 1, March 1979. © 1979 by Family Process, Inc. Reprinted by permission.

pp. 117–21, 267–68. From *Inside the Family* by David Kantor and William Lehr. Copyright © 1975 by Jossey-Bass, Inc., Publishers. Reprinted by permission.

All other acknowledgments follow the index, constituting a legal extension of the copyright page.

Library of Congress Cataloging in Publication Data

Galvin, Kathleen M.
  Family communication.

  Bibliography: p. 304.
  Includes index.
  1. Family—United States. 2. Interpersonal
communication—United States. I. Brommel, Bernard J.,
1930–   . II. Title.
HQ734.C2515 1986   306.8′7   85-11983
ISBN 0-673-18174-X

1 2 3 4 5 6 - MPC - 90 89 88 87 86 85

To my family: The Galvins, Wilkinsons, Nicholsens, and Sullivans, plus the special friends I consider as my family.

KMG

To my children; Michaela Ann, Brian, Debra, Brent, Brad, Blair; with thanks to my dad Bill, Grace Laird, Vic Silvestri, Florence Cairo, Alice and Mary Frances Hanrahan, and Wayne and Winifred Jones. A special thanks to Perry Rudman, a divorce lawyer who believes in divorce only when communication completely fails. His referrals of couples for counseling have provided valuable insights into the communication theories in this book. And thanks to the couples, too.

BJB

An Instructor's Manual for *Family Communication: Cohesion and Change* is available through a Scott, Foresman representative or by writing to: Speech Communication Editor, College Division, Scott, Foresman and Company, 1900 East Lake Avenue, Glenview, IL 60025.

Preface

Family Communication: Cohesion and Change evolved in response to the need for a textbook that examines the family from a communication perspective. It is for students and teachers of family-related courses in communication, psychology, sociology, counseling, home economics, theology, and health. Historically, family interaction has received attention within a medical and therapeutic perspective. Only recently have scholars turned their attention to interaction within functional families, with the past decade witnessing growing interest in ordinary family interaction processes within all of the social sciences. Current scholarship is examining the role of communication in both short- and long-term relationships, such as those found in marriages, families, and cohabiting couples. This text presents an overview of these issues.

The basic premise of this book is that communication undergirds family functioning. Using a systems approach, we consider in depth the communication processes within the family as well as the extent to which they affect and are affected by the interdependence of family members. The focus of the text is descriptive rather than prescriptive, because we believe that description provides the understanding necessary to the eventual development of valid prescriptions. We recognize the vast range of family types and life-styles. Within this diversity, however, we examine how family members typically perform primary family functions—regulating cohesion and adaptability—and secondary family functions—developing appropriate family images, themes, boundaries, and biosocial beliefs.

The first three chapters of the book establish the foundation for what follows by presenting basic communication concepts, a framework for analyzing family communication, an explanation of how specific family meanings develop, and illustration of the role of one's family-of-origin in establishing communication patterns. Later chapters explore communication issues related to basic family interaction: relationship development, intimacy, roles, power, conflict, developmental stages, and adjustment to unpredictable crises. The final chapters focus on the physical and temporal contexts for communication patterns and on approaches toward the improvement of family communication.

Throughout the book we present first-person examples and quotations that complement and expand upon the content and make direct application of the ideas, thereby piquing students' interest and involvement in the issues. Thus, the book contains a combination of research and experience. Except for name changes, all examples are true.

Many persons contributed to the completion of this edition. We received valuable feedback on manuscript drafts from Mary Anne Fitzpatrick, University of Wisconsin, Madison; Arthur Bochner, University of South Florida; and Sandra Schrader, University of Connecticut. We are indebted also to the following people who provided feedback on the first edition: Sandra S. Collins, Joseph DeVito, Pat Goehe, James M. Harper, Jackson R. Huntley, Gary G. Konow, Sheila McNamee, John O'Brien, Don Orban, and Lucille Pederson. Our students provided insightful commentaries and examples. Todd Fry, Marcy Velick, and Joyce Dolmas typed the manuscript; Pamela Cooper provided organizational support. Charles Wilkinson supplied numerous examples from his family practice, and Northeastern Illinois University provided a faculty research grant for development of the text.

We are grateful to the Scott, Foresman editorial staff: Barbara Muller and Louise Howe for their supportive encouragement and guidance through the writing stages and Debra DeBord for directing us through the final stages as painlessly as possible. To our families we express our gratitude for their exceptional patience and moral support, even when we wrote about them in these pages!

Finally, this book comes from our own commitment to and enthusiasm for teaching family communication. Unlike most other academic courses, students bring their personal experiences to the course content and, thus, start with considerable insight and knowledge of the subject. The result is a variety of teaching and learning methods and experiences that continue to educate us, as well as the students, about how families function and what it means to be a member of a family.

Kathleen M. Galvin
Bernard J. Brommel

Contents

Chapter 1

Introduction to
Family Communication

Families: We are born into a family, mature in a family, form new families, and leave them at our deaths. Family life is a universal human experience. Yet, no two people share the exact same experience. Our lives are shaped by family experiences.

"My family remains my schoolhouse. From those people, I learned to love music, fight for the underdog, save my money, treasure autumn walks, and tickle unmercifully. I also learned how to love and how to fight. Sometimes I learned by good examples; other times I learned what not to do. Now I carry my family with me as I live out the lessons of childhood in the process of creating my new family. At this point, I'm very grateful that I grew up in a good 'school.'"

Because the family is such a powerful influence in our lives, we need to examine families and their interaction patterns thoroughly in order to understand ourselves better as members of one of the most complex and important parts of society. Therefore, as you read this book, you will examine a subject you already know something about, since you have spent your life in some type or types of family arrangement. Yet, since you have lived in only one or a small number of families, your experience is limited compared to the range of possible family experiences. Your reading should expand your understanding of many types of families.

This book will present a framework for examining communication within families; by the end of the text, you should be able to apply this model to an unknown family and understand it as a communication system. We also hope that you will apply what you learn to your own family or to the family you will eventually form, in order to improve communication among its members.

Throughout this book, you will find some material written in the first person and set off from the text as quotations. These examples, provided by friends, students, and clients, illustrate many of the concepts in the chapters. These statements should motivate you to apply the material to your own experiences in order to understand it more completely. Some material may remind you specifically of your own family experiences, while other material may seem quite different from your background, since people relate to each other very differently within what is called a "family."

As an introduction to family communication, this chapter will discuss families, the communication process in general, and the relationship between the two. This discussion will create a framework for understanding the rest of the book.

FAMILIES: DESCRIPTION AND STATUS

What images come to your mind when you hear the word "family"? How would you define the term? Although "family" is a word we use frequently, reaching agreement on its meaning is much more difficult than you might suspect. In the following section, you will see the complexities inherent in the term "family."

Description

There is no single complete, widely agreed-upon definition of the term "family." Traditionally, families have been viewed according to *consanguine*, or blood, ties and *conjugal*, or marital, ties. Accordingly, Laing (1972) suggests that we identify as families, "networks of people who live together over periods of time, who have ties of marriage and kinship to one another (3)." Fitzpatrick and Badzinski (1984) suggest the only universal family type is a small kinship-structured group whose primary function is the nurturing socialization of newborn children.

Emphasizing the generational aspects of families, Terkelsen (1980) suggests that a family is a "small social system made up of individuals related to each other by reason of strong reciprocal affections and loyalties, and comprising a permanent household (or cluster of households) that persists over years and decades" (23). Kramer's (1980) definition is a workable model. He defines "family" as a "group of people with a past history, a present reality and a future expectation of interconnected transactional relationships. Members often (but not necessarily) are bound together by heredity, by legal marital ties, by adoption or by a common living arrangement at some point in their lifetime" (43). Clearly, this definition emphasizes the personal, connected relationships among family members, instead of relying solely on blood ties or legal contracts as the basis for a family.

In contemporary society, family diversity abounds. One indication of the complexities of today's families may be found in a review of current literature, which includes such categories as large, extended blood-related families, formal communal groups, stepfamilies, single-parent families, gay-parent families, and families of various races and economic situations. This book's authors represent two very different family orientations. One grew up on an Iowa farm in a family of nine children, married, fathered six children, divorced, and is now a grandfather. The other grew up in New York City as an only child. After her parents died, she acquired an adopted family with three siblings. Currently, she is married and raising three children, one of whom is adopted. Although blood relatives are important, each also has friends who are considered family members.

You may have grown up in a small family, large family, three- or four-generation household, or communal family. Your brothers and sisters may be blood related, step, or adopted. Some of you may be single parents, stepparents, or foster parents. Whereas some of you may have experienced one long, committed marriage, others may have experienced divorce, death, desertion, and remarriage. No simple pattern exists.

There are many categories of families. We will use a rather simple one. In this book, the term "family" refers to a wide range of people-combinations encompassed within the following styles of family formation: the two-parent biological family, single-parent family, blended family, extended family, and partners without children. These are not discrete categories; some families may belong to more than one.

A *two-parent biological family* consists of two parents and the children who are from the union of these parents. Thus, blood ties and the original marriage bond characterize this type. Although frequently thought of as "typical," this type of family no longer represents the majority of types.

A *single-parent family* consists of one parent and one or more children. This formation may include: an unmarried man or woman and his or her offspring; men

Single-parent families are one of many forms.

and women without partners through death, divorce, or desertion, and the children who remain; single parents and their adopted or foster children.

The *blended family* style consists of two adults and their children, all of whom may not be from the union of those two parents. Families may be blended through the remarriage of adults whose spouses have left, a situation that brings the children into new family ties. Families may also be blended through the addition of adopted or foster children. Many of us have witnessed the common pattern in which a natural family becomes a single-parent family for a period of time, after which certain members become part of a stepfamily.

Although an *extended family* usually refers to that group of relatives living within the surrounding city or nearby area, it may be more narrowly understood as the addition of blood relatives, other than the parents, to the everyday life of a child unit. For example, this may take a cross-generational form, including grandparents who live with a parent-child system or who take on exclusive parenting roles for grandchildren.

"I grew up in an extended family. My great-grandparents were the dominant figures. Most of us lived with our grandparents at one time or another. There were six different households in the neighborhood I grew up in. My great-grandmother, referred to as 'Mother,' babysat for all the kids while our parents were at work.

"There are also people who were informally adopted in my family. My mother and one of my cousins were raised by their grandmother, even though their parents did not live there. In my family, no one is considered half or step. You are a member of the family, and that is that."

Another variation of the extended family is the *communal family,* a couple or a group of people, some of whom are unrelated by blood, who share a commitment to each other, live together, and consider themselves to be a family. Formal examples of these family types are found in a kibbutz or in religious organizations, whereas other communal families are informally formed around friendship or common interests or commitments. Two families may share so many experiences that over time both sets of children and parents begin to think of each other as "part of the family."

Although we usually think of families as having children, *partners without children* may form their own familial unit as an outgrowth of their original families. Although their numbers are small, some married couples are choosing to remain childfree, while others remain childless due to infertility. Homosexual partners may also be included in this category, as long as the partners consider each other as family members. Partners without children continue to serve as children to the previous generation and as siblings and extended family members to other generations, while at the same time providing loyalty and affection to one another.

As we talk about families in this book, we will take a broad, inclusive view; therefore, if the members consider themselves to be a family, we accept their self-definition. Generally, we will refer to networks of people who live together over long periods of time bound by ties of marriage, blood, or commitment, legal or otherwise, who share future expectations of connected relationship. Such a definition encompasses countless variations and numerous interaction patterns.

It is important to distinguish between two types of family experience—current families and families-of-origin. As you well know, families in combination beget families through the evolutionary cycles of coming together and separating. Thus, each person may experience life in different families starting with his or her family-of-origin. *Family-of-origin* refers to the family or families in which a person is raised. The family in which you grew up is your family-of-origin. Satir (1972), noted family therapist, stresses the importance of the family-of-origin as "the main base against and around which most family blueprints are designed." She suggests: "It is easy to duplicate in your family the same things that happened in your growing up. This is true whether your family was a nurturing or a troubled one" (200). As you will discover, family-of-origin experiences are crucial in the development of communication patterns in newly-formed or current families.

Another concept central to understanding the family is its systemic nature. Although the next chapter will explore in detail the family as a system, let us examine this concept briefly. Each individual is a part of an overall *family system* and affects, and is affected by, that system. Therefore, you cannot fully understand a person without knowing something about his or her family. For example, an individual's behavior may appear strange, but if you understand the whole family context, your perceptions may change. Many individuals' behaviors are more understandable when viewed within the context of the human systems in which they function, since this understanding enables us to know the environment and the other people who influence individual family members. Thus, the environment and kinship serve as contexts in which family systems are shaped.

Within a system, the parts and the relationship between them form the whole; changes in one part will result in changes in the others. So, too, in families. Satir (1972) describes a family as a mobile (119). Picture a mobile that hangs over a child's crib as having people instead of elephants or sailboats on it. As events touch one member of the family, other members reverberate in relationship to the change in the affected member. Thus, if a member of your family gets a raise, flunks out of school, marries, or becomes ill, such an event affects the surrounding family system, depending on each person's current relationship with that individual. In addition, because family members are human beings, not elephants or sailboats, they can "pull their own strings." At some point, a family member may choose to withdraw from the family and, by pulling away, force other members into closer relationships. Thus, as members move toward or away from each other, all members are affected.

Status

In order to understand family interaction more completely, we need to examine the current status of family life in America. No matter how old you are, you have lived long enough to witness major changes in your family or in the families around you. Although research figures shift constantly and various sources provide slightly different numerical data, the overall point is clear—the American family has undergone dramatic changes in the twentieth century. Reports of census data attest to the scope of such change (*Current Population Reports*, March 1983; *Abstract of the United States*, 1984).

The incidence of divorce has risen rapidly throughout this century, up 700 percent since 1900. This figure also reflects the longevity of persons in today's society. In earlier times when more people died at a younger age, many unsatisfactory marriages were ended by death rather than divorce.

The current divorce rate affects children greatly. Experts estimate that four out of ten children born in the 1970s will live in a single-parent household for part of their childhood. And, the recent rate of divorce continues to rise. For example, in 1960, 2 percent of males over eighteen and 3 percent of females over eighteen listed themselves as currently divorced. In 1970, the figures had risen to 5 percent for men and 7 percent for women. In 1982, 6 percent of men and 8 percent of women listed themselves as currently divorced. Clearly this population shifts as most individuals remarry.

At this time, remarriage rates are high and most divorced individuals will form a new partnership. About five out of six men and three out of four women remarry after a divorce. About half of these remarriages occur within three years of the divorce.

Also at this time, we are witnessing the rapid rise of single-parent systems. In 1970, 11 percent of children under age eighteen lived with their mothers, 1 percent with their fathers, and 85 percent with two parents. In 1982, 20 percent of children under eighteen lived with their mothers, 2 percent with their fathers, and 75 percent with two parents. The remainder were cared for in an institutional setting. These rates are rising in part because more children are entering life as part of a single-parent system. Whereas in 1960 approximately 5 percent of births occurred to unmarried women, by 1982 that figure had risen to 18 percent.

Recent census data indicate that the number of unmarried-couple households is growing rapidly. Such households are defined as "two unrelated adults of the opposite sex sharing living quarters with or without children present." There were 1,891,000 unmarried-couple households in 1983—more than three times the number in 1970. Although during the 1970s this type grew rapidly, the amount of growth in the 1980s has been comparatively small. In 1983, unmarried couples represented one in twenty-five of all couples (married and unmarried).

Although census figures on gay-male and lesbian couples are not available, Blumstein and Schwartz (1983) included such couples as a significant part of their study. They suggest that, until the 1970s, gay men and lesbians were a fairly invisible part of the American population. In the late 1960s, the Kinsey Institute found that 71 percent of its sample of gay men between ages thirty-six and forty-five were living with a partner. Other studies in the 1970s and 1980s point toward the desire for couple relationships within the gay male or lesbian community (Weinberg and Williams, 1974; McWhirter and Mattison, 1984; Majors, 1983; Johnson, 1984).

As household interpersonal structures are changing, the actual size of households has shifted downward. For example, in 1960, approximately 40 percent of all households had four or more persons; in 1970, the percentage dropped to 37, while in 1982, 28 percent of all households had four or more members. Some of this shift is attributed to economic pressures and the increasing number of working women, factors which contribute to a lower birthrate.

Other factors, such as economics, are affecting the ways in which families relate. There is an increasing number of two-paycheck couples. Approximately 62 percent of married couples have two incomes, not necessarily from two full-time positions. This is up from 50 percent a decade ago and 40 percent in 1960. Young two-career couples are becoming a larger segment of the twenty- to thirty-year-old age group. As more dual-employed couples emerge, the United States is witnessing a phenomenon of "latchkey children" who return from school hours before a parent returns from work, and who are expected to contribute to the successful running of the household. Younger children may spend many of their waking hours with babysitters or in day-care centers, encountering their parents only a few hours a day.

All these changes are occurring against a backdrop of longer life expectancy. Persons born in 1960 have a life expectancy of 69.7 years, while those born in 1982 have an expectancy of 74.5 years. The male expectancy is 70.8 years, whereas the female is 78.2 years. When you consider that most people marry before the age of thirty, a continuous marriage might well be expected to last forty to fifty years.

Finally, we need to recognize the effect of ethnicity on family functioning. Within the past decades, two forces have combined to bring ethnic issues to the attention of family scholars. First, the overall ethnic composition of U.S. families is changing as the number of black, Hispanic, and Asian families increases. Second, scholars are recognizing the long-term effect of ethnic heritage on family functioning.

American society represents a wide diversity of ethnic and cultural groups. A 1984 analysis of voting-age Americans reported that an estimated 2.6 percent of the American population over age eighteen is Jewish, while 11 percent is black. There are 2.5 million Asian-Americans over age eighteen and over three million Hispanics. Mexican-Americans comprise the second largest U.S. minority with over 6.5 million persons, while over 50,000 Puerto Ricans live on the U.S. mainland. The 1.8 million Native Americans also reflect a growing population. Although immigration from Europe is limited, the United States continues to receive new families from Western and Eastern Europe (*U.S. News and World Report*, 1984). Although generalizations about cultural groups must always be accompanied by an indication of their many exceptions, a consideration of family ethnicity provides one more perspective from which to examine communication patterns.

It is important to consider ethnicity in families because, contrary to popular myth, Americans have not become homogenized in a "melting pot"; instead, various cultural/ethnic heritages are maintained across generations. In her overview of studies in family ethnicity, McGoldrick (1982) points to the increasing evidence that ". . . ethnic values and identification are retained for many generations after immigration and play a significant role in family life and personal development throughout the life cycle" (3). She maintains that second-, third-, and even fourth-generation Americans reflect their original cultural heritage in life-style and behavior.

Ethnicity may affect family life through its traditions, celebrations, occupations, values, and problem solving. McGoldrick goes so far as to say the definition of "family" differs across ethnic groups. Whereas the dominant "WASP" definition focuses on the intact nuclear unit, black families focus on a wide kinship network, and Italians function within a large, intergenerational, tightly knit family which includes godparents and old friends. The Chinese are likely to include all ancestors and descendants in the concept of "family" (10). Each of these definitions has an impact on communication within the family.

The changes of the past hold many implications for the ways in which family members relate to each other and which family members relate to each other. Throughout this book, we will attempt to provide examples and information which reflect the changing family life-style.

WHAT DO WE MEAN BY "COMMUNICATION"?

"My sister and I have a long history of intimacy. Since early childhood, we have shared unique communication behavior. Gail refers to me as 'Sis,' 'K. C.,' or 'Coops.' I, in return, call her 'Kitten,' 'G. K.,' or 'Li'l Coops.' As a result of doing many activities together, we acquired the duplex nickname of 'The Coop Sisters.' She and I have always shared some type of personal jargon. This ritual began with our secret language of 'witchtalk.' Witchtalk meant saying the exact opposite of what one really meant. Now, in our current jargon, a romantic relationship is official only if one has been kissed by the male, and "the bone" refers to a male who is sexually exciting. We also share a peculiar handshake, which can be interpreted as meaning 'I agree with you 100 percent' or 'I can identify with you.'"

In this book, we are exploring the family as an interaction system, concentrating on the mutual influence between communication and family development: (1) how communication patterns affect family relationships and (2) how those relationships affect communication. In order to do this, we have to examine the general communication process and then apply it to family situations. Within the framework of common cultural communication patterns, each family has the capacity to develop its own communication code based on the experiences of individual members and the collective family experience. Most of us develop our communication skills within the family context, learning both the general cultural language and the specific familial communication code. Since most of us take our own backgrounds for granted, you may not be aware of the context your family provided for learning communication. For example, on a simple level, you may have learned "funny" words for familiar things, such as "official" or "the bone" (described in the preceding quotation); on a deeper level, you have learned particular ways to express feelings of affection or conflict. People in other families may have learned these things differently.

The Communication Process

Communication may be viewed as a symbolic, transactional process, or to put it more simply, the process of creating and sharing meanings. In saying that communication is *symbolic*, we mean that symbols are used to transmit messages. Verbal behavior, or words, are the most commonly used symbols, but the whole range of nonverbal behavior, including facial expressions, eye contact, gestures, movement, posture, appearance, and spatial distance, are also used symbolically. Objects and ideas can also be symbols, or *referents*. Families may use kisses, special food, toys, or poems as symbols of love. Although symbols allow us to share our thoughts on the widest range of possible subjects, the symbols must be mutually understood for the meanings to be shared. For example, if family members do not agree on what activities are "fun," how much is "a lot" of money, or which behaviors imply anger, there will be confusion. If meanings are not mutually shared, messages may not be understood.

To say that communication is *transactional* means that when people communicate, they have a mutual impact on each other. In short, you do not originate communication, you participate in it (Watzlawick et al., 1967). Thus, in communicative relationships, all participants are both affecting and being affected by the others. It does not matter how much more talking one person appears to do; the mutual impact remains the same. The focus is placed on the relationship, not on the individual participants.

A transactional view of communication and systems perspective of the family complement each other, since both focus on relationships, which take precedence over individuals. A communication perspective focuses on the interaction of two or more persons. Accordingly, from a systems perspective it is nonproductive to analyze each individual separately because of the integrative nature of the system. Each individual communicates within the context of a system, and each communication act reflects the nature of those relationships. As two people interact, each creates a context for the other and relates to the other within that context. For example, you may perceive a brother-in-law as distant and relate to him in a very polite but restrained manner. In turn, he may perceive you as formal and relate to you in an even more distant and polite manner.

"My father and brother had a very difficult relationship with each other for many years, although each of them had an excellent relationship with everyone else in the family. Dan saw Dad as repressive and demanding, although I would characterize him as serious and concerned. Dad saw Dan as careless and uncommitted, although no one else saw him that way. Whenever they tried to talk to each other, each responded to the person he created, and it was a continual battle."

In this example, knowing Dan or his father separately does not account for their conflictual behavior when they are together. Each influences the other's interaction. Each creates a context for the other and relates within the context. It is as if you say to another: "You are sensitive," or "You are repressive," or "You are shiftless," "and that's how I will relate to you." The content and style of the messages vary according to how each sees himself or herself and how each predicts the other will react. As well as taking the environment or context into account, the transactional view stresses the importance of the communicator's perceptions and actions in determining the outcome of interactions.

Thus, the relationship pattern, not one or another specific act, becomes the focal point. Our perception of one another and our subsequent behavior can actually change the behavior of the person we see. A mother who constantly praises her son for his thoughtfulness and sensitivity, who notices the good things in his efforts, may change her son's perception of himself and his subsequent behavior with her and other people. On the other hand, a husband who constantly complains about his wife's parenting behavior may lower her self-esteem and change her subsequent behavior toward him and the children. Thus, in communication relationships, each person (1) creates a context for the other, (2) simultaneously creates and interprets messages, and (3) affects and is affected by the other.

To say that communication is a *process* implies it is continuous and changing. Communication is not static; it does not switch on and off but, rather, develops over time. Process implies change. Relationships, no matter how committed, change constantly, and communication both affects and reflects these changes. The passage of time brings with it predictable and unpredictable crises, which take their toll on family regularity and stability. Yet, everyday moods, minor pleasures, or irritation can shift the communication behaviors on a day-to-day basis.

As each day passes, family members subtly renegotiate their relationships. Today you may be in a bad mood and people adjust to that with you; tomorrow adaptations may be made around your brother's great report card. Next week a major job change may affect all your relationships. Over time, families change as they pass through stages of growth; members are born, age, leave, and die. As you will see in the chapters on family development and change, communication patterns reflect these developments in family life.

As we said earlier, communication may be viewed as a symbolic, transactional process, one of creating and sharing meanings. Let us now examine the ways in which meanings develop.

Meanings and Messages

How does a person gain a set of meanings? Basically, our perceptions of the world, which affect our meanings and messages, result from our filter systems, which reflect our past experiences and the current situation. You might say we have lenses, or filters, through which we view the world. This filter process involves physical, social, and individual factors (Bandler and Grinder, 1975, 8–12). These factors combine uniquely for each individual and determine how that person perceives and interacts with the world in general, and more specifically to the surrounding family system. Although this sounds like a very singular process, as we talk about communication events, we must remember the transactional perspective. Each communicator constantly affects and is affected by the other; thus, perceptions occur within the context of a relational system and are constantly influenced by that system.

Development of Meanings. Our physical state based on our human sensory sytems—sight, hearing, touch, taste, and smell—constitutes the first set of filters. Our perceptions are also filtered through the social system or the way we use language, our accepted ways of seeing things, and all the socially agreed-upon conventions that standardize parts of our world. We come to share some common meanings for our verbal and nonverbal symbols with those around us. We may share some very general experiences with many people we encounter and much more specific experiences with a smaller group of people. For example, with some persons we share only global experiences, such as cultural background, including language, geographic area, customs, beliefs, and attitudes. With others, we may also share the specific and narrow experiences of living together in the house at 6945 Osceola Street and learning to understand each other's idiosyncrasies.

Our social experience frames our world. The language we speak limits and shapes the meanings we can ascertain. For example, Eskimos have over twenty words for snow; therefore, they have many more ways of perceiving this substance than most other Americans. The current pressure to use nonsexist language reflects a belief that women have formed less-powerful images of themselves due to the emphasis on the masculine in pronouns and other words. Proponents of change believe perceptions of women will be altered by the new use of language. Our current language limits our ability to discuss easily certain new family relationships such as "my stepmother's sister" or "my half brother's grandfather." As language adapts to such variations, we will be able to speak more clearly of such individuals. Yet, although language may limit our meanings, we are capable of broadening such perspectives by learning new languages, opening ourselves to new experiences.

Thus, the overall culture affects perceptions and meanings, but the immediate groups to which one belongs exert a strong influence on an individual's perceptual set. The family, school, office, and friendship group all provide contextual meaning and influence the way we give meaning to the sense data we receive. If giving a handmade gift is considered a special sign of caring, a knitted Christmas stocking may be valued, but an expensive necklace will not. Being a member of the Thurman family, a farmer, a square dance caller, a volunteer fireman, or a church elder provides context for giving meaning to the world for the individual and for a small segment of people who surround that person.

Although physical and social systems provide the basic general filters, specific constraints upon an individual influence that person's meanings and his or her interpretation processes within the larger society. Individual constraints refer to all the representations we create for our meanings based on our own personal histories. Although some of us may have similar histories, each person develops a unique way of dealing with sensory information and, thus, an individual way of seeing the world and relating to others in it. Two members of the Thurman family may share being farmers, square dance callers, firemen, and church elders, yet they will respond differently to many situations. For example, many brothers and sisters disagree on the kind of family life they experienced together. One declares, "I had a very happy childhood" versus a sibling's statement, "I would never want to go through those years again." For each of us, specific events and people affect our meanings. A creative third-grade teacher and the summers at Aunt Mary's all contribute to our response to the world, yet are influenced by others' responses.

"My sister Diane was considered the 'problem child' in our house. As far as experts can determine, her emotional difficulties stem from an unknown trauma when she was three, when they suggest she was rejected by my parents at a time when she needed love. The reality was that Diane functioned as a scapegoat for all of us. Although Diane and I are very close in age, we had different experiences in our family because of the way she perceived the family and was perceived by its members."

As family members, we also share many similar perceptions with the other family members who have learned to see the world in similar ways.

When we talk about communication, we are dealing with symbolic acts to which we assign meaning through our transactions with the people around us. The meanings emerge through the use of symbolic acts as our interactions give us information on how to interpret the symbols. After each encounter with a person or object, we become better able to deal with similar situations, and our behavior takes on certain patterns. The greater the repetition, the greater the probability of the assigned meaning.

After you have functioned within a family system, you become comfortable with your ability to handle the symbols, mainly because you are able to interpret them on all levels and feel that you really understand them. As a child, when you heard your mother yell "Johnny" or "Elizabeth-Marie," you were able to tell from her tone of voice just what to expect. Today, you can sit at dinner and hear your younger sister say, "I just hate that Ernie Johnson" and know that she is really falling in love.

Levels of Meaning and Metacommunication. Communication of meaning occurs on two levels: the content level and the relationship level. The *content level* contains the information, while the *relationship level* indicates how the information should be interpreted or understood. The relationship level is more likely to involve nonverbal messages. When your mother says, "When are you going to pick up those clothes?" she is asking an informational question, but there is another level of meaning. It is up to you to determine if, by her nonverbal tone, she is really questioning at what time of day you will remove the articles, or if she is telling you to get them out of there in the next thirty seconds.

Metacommunication occurs when people communicate about their communication, when they give verbal and nonverbal instructions about how their messages should be understood. Such remarks as "I was only kidding," "This is important," or "Talking about this makes me uncomfortable" are signals to another on how to take certain comments, as do facial expressions, gestures, or vocal tones. On a deeper level, many couples or family members have spent countless hours talking about the way they fight or the way they express affection. Metacommunication serves an important function within families, because it allows members to state their needs, clarify confusion, and plan new and more constructive ways of relating to one another.

The ways in which people exchange messages influence the form and content of their relationships. Communication among family members shapes the structure of the family system and provides a family with its own set of meanings. Although we have used many family examples in describing the communication process, we have not explored the role of communication within the family. In the following section, we will examine the role communication plays in forming, maintaining, and changing family systems as families perform core functions.

COMMUNICATION PATTERNS AND FAMILY FUNCTIONS

When you come into contact with other families, you may notice how their communication differs from that of the families in which you have lived. Ways of relating, making decisions, sharing feelings, and handling conflict may vary slightly or greatly from your own personal experiences. Each family's unique message system provides the means of dealing with the major functions that give shape to family life. In other words, communication provides form and content to a family's life as members engage in family-related functions. We may define a *function* simply as something a system must do if it is not to break down (Cushman and Craig, 1976). We will examine two primary family functions and four supporting functions that affect and are affected by communication.

Primary Functions

In their attempt to integrate the numerous concepts related to marital and family interaction, researchers Olson, Sprenkle, and Russell (1979) have developed what is known as the *circumplex model* of marital and family systems. Over the past five years, the model has evolved to include three dimensions: (1) cohesion, (2) adaptability, and (3) communication. The two central dimensions are family cohesion and family *adaptability*, which are perceived as the intersecting lines of an axis. The third dimension is family *communication*, a facilitating dimension that enables couples and families to move along the cohesion and adaptability dimension (Olson and McCubbin, 1983). The complete circumplex model was developed to describe various types of families.

In this text, the concepts of cohesion and change form a backdrop against which to view communication within families. From this perspective, two primary family functions involve:

1. Establishing a pattern of cohesion, or separateness and connectedness.
2. Establishing a pattern of adaptability, or change.

Cohesion.   From the moment you were born, you have been learning how to handle distance or closeness within your family system. You were taught directly or subtly how to be connected to, or separated from, other family members. Cohesion implies "the emotional bonding members have with one another and the degree of individual autonomy a person experiences in the family system" (Olson et al., 5). In other words, a family attempts to deal with the extent to which physical or psychological intimacy is encouraged or discouraged.

"When I got married, I tried to reserve a psychological space that was just mine— something that would keep me from being so involved with my husband that I could not separate one from the other. I was afraid that if anything happened to him, I would not be able to cope unless I could keep from sharing everything with him. Over the past five years of my marriage, I've changed my mind, because I began to believe that I was only cheating the two of us out of the best relationship we could have. I realize that David is willing to love me as fully as possible, so I've grown to take the risk to respond as fully as possible. It still frightens me, though."

The issue of cohesion has been identified by many scholars from various fields as central to the understanding of family life. Family researchers Kantor and Lehr (1976) view "distance regulation" as a major family function; family therapist Minuchin (1967) talks about "enmeshed and disengaged" families; sociologists Hess and Handel (1959) describe the family's need to "establish a pattern of separateness and connectedness."

Cohesion in a family affects and is affected by the communication among members. It is through communication that family members are able to develop and maintain or change their patterns of cohesion. A father may decide that it is inappropriate to continue the physical closeness he has experienced with his daughter now that she has become a teenager, and he may limit his touching or playful roughhousing. She may become angry, find new ways of being close, develop more outside friendships, or attempt to force her father back into the old patterns. A husband may demand more intimacy from his wife as he ages. He may desire more serious conversation, make more sexual advances, share more of his feelings. His wife may ignore this new behavior or engage in more intimate behaviors herself.

Families with extremely high cohesion are often referred to as "enmeshed"; members are so closely bonded that individuals experience little autonomy or fulfillment of personal needs and goals. "Disengaged" refers to families at the other end of the continuum in which members experience very little closeness or family solidarity, yet each member has high autonomy and individuality.

Disengaged Families	Cohesion	Enmeshed Families
Low		High

Specific issues used to examine the degree of family cohesion are "emotional bonding, independence, boundaries, time, space, friends, decision making, and interests and recreation" (Olson et al., 6). Throughout this book, we will look at ways families deal with issues of coming together or staying apart and how they use communication in an attempt to reach their desired cohesion level.

Cohesion is not a permanent state, however. A family does not come together and stay there, as is evident from the previous examples. Hence, we must account for change within a family's life.

Adaptability. When you think of the changes in your own family over the past five or ten years, you may be amazed at how different the systems and its members are at this point. A family experiences changes as it goes through its own developmental stages and deals with crises that arise in everyday life, such as adapting to the marriage or job transfer of one of its members.

Adaptability may be viewed as "the ability of a marital/family system to change its power structure, role relationships, and relationship rules in response to situational and developmental stress" (Olson and McCubbin, 62). The researchers see family power structure, negotiation styles, role relationships, relationship rules, and feedback as central to the concept of adaptability.

Each human system has both stability-promoting processes (morphostasis) and change-promoting processes (morphogenesis) to maintain itself. Such systems need periods of stability and of change in order to function. Families that regularly experience extensive change may be considered chaotic. Due to total unpredictability and stress, they have little opportunity to develop relationships and establish common meanings. On the other extreme, rigidity characterizes families that repress change and growth.

Rigid Families	Adaption	Chaotic Families
Low		High

Family systems constantly restructure themselves as they pass through predictable developmental stages; marriage, pregnancy, birth, parenting, and the return to the original couple all represent major familial changes. Likewise, when positive or negative stresses arise involving such issues as money, illness, or divorce, families must adapt. Finally, family systems must adapt both structurally and functionally to the demands of other social institutions as well as to the needs of their own members.

"*My son and daughter-in-law adopted an older child and had to adapt their communication patterns to accommodate her. Although lying was forbidden in their family when they adopted Shirley, they had to reassess this position, because she had learned to lie for most of her life. My son and daughter-in-law had to learn to be more tolerant of this behavior, particularly when she first joined the family, or they would have had to send her back to the agency.*"

Communication is central to the adaptive function of a family. Any effective adaptation relies on shared meanings gained through the family message system. Through communication, families make it clear to their members how much adaptation is allowed within the system and regulate the adaptive behaviors of their members and the system as a whole. Variables that affect this family function include: family power structure (assertiveness and control), negotiation styles, role relationships, and relationship rules and feedback (positive and negative). Olson et al. hypothesize that, where there is a balance between change and stability within families, there will be more mutually assertive communication styles, shared leadership, successful negotiation, role sharing, and open rule making and sharing (13).

Adapting the work of Olson et al., we can visualize the mutual interaction of adaptability and cohesion within families by placing them on an axis (see Figure 1–1a). By adding the extremes of cohesion (disengagement and enmeshment) and adaptability (rigidity and chaos), we can picture where more or less functional families would appear on the axis (see Figure 1–1b).

Figure 1–1 _____
Family Cohesion/Adaptability Axes

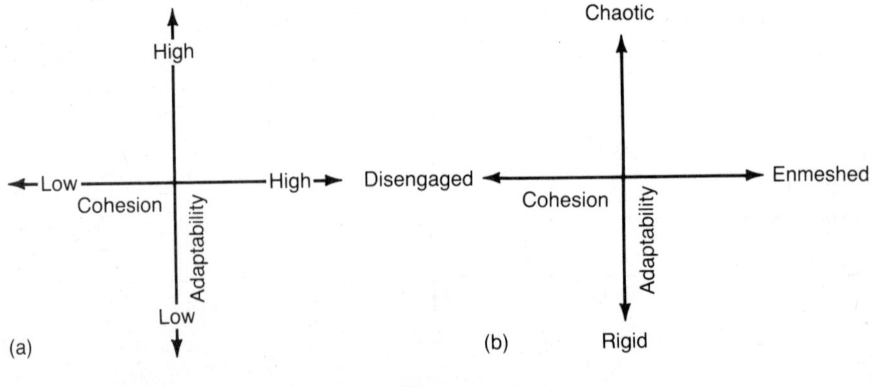

The central area represents balanced or moderate levels of adaptability and cohesion, seen as a highly workable communication pattern for individual and family development, although there may be instances when a different pattern could aid a family through a particular developmental point or through a crisis. The outside areas represent the extremes of cohesion and adaptability, less workable for consistent long-term communication patterns.

Most well-functioning families are found short of the extremes, except when they are under high levels of stress. In those situations, placement at the extreme may serve a purpose. If a family is faced with the loss of a member through death, a highly cohesive communication pattern may be critical for mourning purposes. In Figure 1–2a, at the time of a family death, members may find themselves at point Y. Such a family may be experiencing extreme closeness among remaining members but chaos in terms of dealing with the changes in roles or in everyday activities.

As another example, a family with an acting-out teenager may find itself shifting from point X to point Z on the axis, as the adolescent demands greater freedom and less connectedness from the family and forces changes upon the system (see Figure 1–2b).

The situation in the following quotation may be graphed as three moves (Figure 1–2c).

"During one period of my childhood after my parents' divorce, my mother took a series of part-time jobs with variable hours, and my father left the state. My brother and I depended upon ourselves and the neighbors for whatever we needed. The family was very fragmented, and due to money and health problems, we never knew what would happen from day to day [point A]. After my mother seemed to straighten out her life a bit, we were able to do more things as a family and to get closer to each other again. Life was still pretty unpredictable [point B]. Finally, my mother married again, and we now live a very predictable life-style, but it has allowed us to get closer to each other again. We are a somewhat dull but close family [point C]."

If you think about periods in your family life, you should be able to envision how the family shifted from one point to another on the cohesion-adaptability axis.

Figure 1–2
Application of Family Cohesion/Adaptability

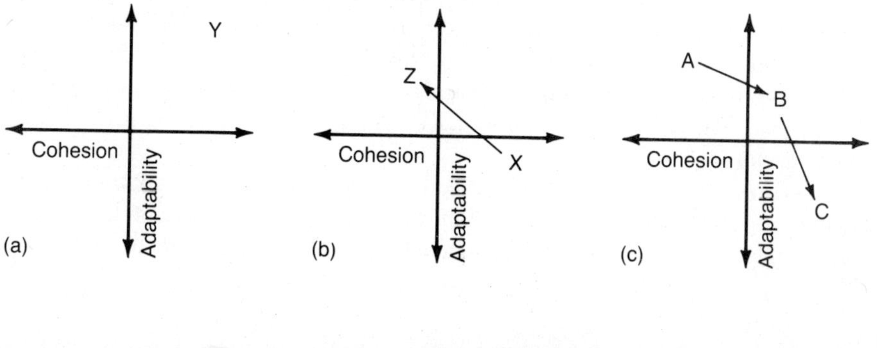

Because we are talking about the whole system, you may find certain members who would be graphed in a different place if they were to be pictured individually. We are attempting to represent the group on the axis. Throughout the text, we will use the cohesion/change framework as a backdrop for understanding family communication.

Although the issues related to cohesion and adaptability/change are viewed as the primary functions, these functions do not provide a complete picture. There are additional family functions—supporting functions—that contribute to the understanding of family interaction.

Supporting Functions

There are four supporting functions which, in conjunction with cohesion and adaptability, give shape to family life. Hess and Handel identify five processes, or family functions, which interact with the development of a family's message system. Because one of these processes relates to cohesion, we will list only the remaining four. The supporting family functions include:

1. Establishing a satisfactory congruence of images.
2. Evolving modes of interaction into central family themes.
3. Establishing the boundaries of the family's world of experience.
4. Dealing with significant biosocial issues of family life, such as gender, age, power, and roles. (4)

Each of these processes interacts with a family's point on the cohesion/adaptability axis and influences a family's communication pattern.

Family Images. If you had to assign *images,* or mental pictures, to certain family members, what would they be? Would your father be a teddy bear who is warm, soft, and lovable? Would he be a general—organized, military, distanced? Or would his image combine some of these qualities? Every family operates as an image-making mechanism. Each member develops images of what the family unit and other family members are like; these images determine his or her patterns of interaction with the others. Images are one's definitions of people as objects of one's own action or potential action. A person's image of his or her family embodies what is expected from it, what is given to it, and how important it is (Hess and Handel, 7–8). Thus, the image has both realistic and idealized components that reflect both the imagined and the imaginer. In reflecting upon family image, people have provided the following examples: circus, flower, broken wagon wheel, nest, corporation, schoolroom. One couple described their family as a "seesaw, because we are able to balance each other well and be flexible in allowing the kids to move between us. But if a crisis hits and we have to move in new patterns, such as sideways, we run into problems."

If two people's images of each other are congruent and consistent for a period of time, a predictable pattern of communication may emerge in which both are comfortable. If a mother sees her son as a helpless and dependent creature, she may exhibit many protective behaviors, such as keeping bad news from him. If the son's image of his mother is as a protector, the congruence of the images will allow harmonious communication, but if the child sees his mother as a jailer, conflict may emerge. If one child sees the mother as a jailer and the other sees her as an angel, the lack of consistent images held by family members may result in strong alliances among those with congruent images. A husband and wife are likely to experience conflict if one sees the family as a "nest" involving nurturing, emotion, and protection and the other sees it as a corporation involving a strong power structure and good organization. Yet, since complete consensus is improbable and change inevitable, the patterns will never become totally predictable; the level of congruence relates to the effectiveness of communication within the family.

Family Themes. As well as having images for the family and for every member, each family shares themes—or takes positions in relationship to the outer world that affect every aspect of its functioning. A *theme* may be viewed as a pattern of feelings, motives, fantasies, and conventionalized understandings grouped around a particular locus of concern, which has a particular form in the personalities of individual members (Hess and Handel, 11).

Themes represent a fundamental view of reality and a way of dealing with this view. Through its theme, a family responds to the questions, "Who are we?" and "What do we do about it?" Sample theme issues which some families value include the following: physical security, strength, dependability, inclusion, and separation. To demonstrate the viability of themes in a family, we view them as statements that actualize the values more specifically:

1. We have responsibility for those less fortunate than we are.
2. You can depend only on your family
3. You can always do better.
4. We are not quitters.
5. You have to work for what you get.

Themes relate directly to family actions, thereby allowing us to surmise a family's themes by watching its actions. Living according to a theme necessitates the development of various patterns of behavior, which affect (1) how members interact with the outside world, (2) how they interact with each other, and (3) how they develop personally. For example, a family system with the theme of "We have responsibility for those less fortunate than we are" might be a flexible system open to helping relationships with non–family members and may accept temporary family members, such as foster children, who have problems. Yet, it may be difficult or impossible for such a family to accept help from an outside source because of its own self-definition as helper. Members may tend to put themselves and other family members second as they deal with outside problems. Following the classic line of the shoemaker's children without shoes, a mother who lives according to this theme may spend hours working at an adolescent drop-in center for the community and be unaware of the problems her own teenage children are having because of the outward focus of the family life. Young members may grow up learning to minimize their problems and may not have much experience expressing painful feelings. Yet, they may learn to willingly self-sacrifice for those less fortunate and may be very empathetic and attuned to the needs of others.

> "I grew up with a family theme related to success. Our real theme might be stated: 'We must uphold the Roland name through our successes.' Subthemes would include 'Rolands will do well in school,' 'Rolands do not quit,' and 'Rolands play to win.' As you can well imagine, this affected communication, because when you did well you got lots of positive reactions, support, and praise. When you did not do well, it was clear that you had disappointed the family. The best communication happened after you won something."

Family themes may be complex and subtle. They may involve beliefs that are not immediately obvious. It is important to identify a family's main theme(s) in order to fully understand the communication behavior of its members.

Boundaries. As well as developing images and themes, families create *boundaries*, limits for how members may act. We can imagine boundaries as the limits of a particular territory or as a separation of two territories. Boundaries are barriers to the exchange of material, information, and values. All families establish some boundaries as they restrict their members from encountering certain physical and psychological forces. Most frequently, family boundaries regulate access to people, ideas, and values.

Some family boundaries are *permeable,* or allow movement across them, and others resist movement. Certain families permit or encourage their children to make many different kinds of friends, explore alternative religious ideas, and have access to new ideas through the media; such permeable boundaries permit new ideas, people, and values to enter the family. Conversely, some families retain rigid control of their children's activities to prevent them from coming into contact with what the family considers "undesirable." Extremes of such behavior result in the creation of rigid boundaries around the family system.

> "Although we are close to our parents, my sister and I can do anything that most other young people in our area are allowed to do. My cousins from Greece live in a different world. They are not allowed to date, even though they are sixteen and seventeen. Their parents do not want them to go away to college, and they will be expected to live at home until they are married. They constantly hear that 'good Greek girls would not do that.' There are far stricter boundaries on what they are allowed to experience than what I can do."

Yet, no matter how set family boundaries are initially, they will vary according to the personalities of the members, types of experiences to which members are exposed, and freedom each member has to create his or her own value system.

Although the family unit system may set strong boundaries, a strong, self-assured person may challenge rigid or stereotyped thinking about certain issues and reject the traditional boundaries set for him or her. An intensely emotional or sensitive child may comprehend things never imagined by other family members. This child may push far beyond the geographic limits or aspirational levels held by other family members. As a Kentucky mountain girl becomes an unmarried San Francisco novelist, she may have to cross most of the family's accepted boundaries regarding place, aspiration, and position. Such actions represent a threat to the family value system that stands as one guardian of its boundaries. This type of action may result in decreased meaningful communication as the gulf between the two worlds continues to widen.

Most families experience boundaries between generations, which establish subsystems of generational hierarchy. Generations establish their boundaries based on behaviors appropriate for that subsystem (Wood and Talmon, 1983). For example, parents usually provide nurturance and control for their children. It is unusual for children to extensively nurture or control their parents unless they have become aged and ill. In two-parent families, the marital subsystem represents a critical entity in the functioning of family life. In most families, husbands and wives share unique information and give each other special emotional and physical support. Children are not allowed to share in all aspects of the marital dyad. Many types of conflict may arise if the system's interpersonal boundaries, particularly the marital boundaries, are too permeable and children or others are expected to fulfill part of the spouse role. For example, troubled families, such as those with an alcoholic spouse, may experience shifts in the marital boundary. If an alcoholic husband cannot provide the interpersonal support needed by his wife, she may co-opt one of the children into the marital subsystem by expecting the child to act as an adult confidant and emotional support. When boundaries are inappropriately crossed, roles become confused and pain may result for all members.

Interpersonally testing or forcing boundaries may involve deep emotional conflicts, which could be resolved through the increased growth of all family members or by the severing of bonds with specific members who eventually leave the system. Each of you has experienced resisting boundaries or having persons challenge your systems boundaries with positive or negative results. Your family relationships may have eventually become stronger or certain relationships may have suffered. Thus, the physical and psychological boundaries set by each family strongly influence the kinds of interpersonal communication that can occur within the system.

Biosocial Issues. All families operate in a larger sphere that provides conventional ways of coping with biosocial issues, but each family creates its own answers within the larger framework. Hess and Handel identify the following as included within biosocial issues: male and female identity, authority and power, shaping and influencing children, and children's rights (17–18).

All people are faced with sexual identity issues while growing up and/or while forming their own family systems and raising children. Sexual identity and physical development issues affect styles of interaction and vice versa. A family that assigns responsibilities based on a member's sex operates differently than one that uses interest or preference as the basis for assigning responsibilities. If physical stature automatically determines duties and privileges, the interaction will be different than in a setting where physical development is only one factor among many by which privileges are awarded and duties are appropriate to males and females.

Other value decisions in the social sphere relate to the use of power within the family structure. To what extent are leadership, decision making, and authority issues resolved according to traditional sex and role configurations? Families negotiate the use of power within the system, and members may find themselves in the renegotiation process for much of their lives. The social sphere also involves attitudinal issues related to roles and responsibilities which may be exemplified in parent-child relationships. Parent-child interactions reflect the mutually held attitudes. If a parent sees a child as a responsibility to be dispensed with at a given age, the interactions will be immensely different than if the parental attitude reflects a prolonged responsibility for his or her offspring, perhaps far beyond the years of adolescence. The extent to which a child is permitted privacy, physical or psychological, also reflects a biosocial orientation.

"For the first eleven years of life, my stepson Travis was raised in a household that catered to his every need. He was encouraged to be dependent and to remain a little boy in many ways. His mother Martha could not have more children, so she doted on him as her only child. When I married Martha, my two children came to live with us. They had been raised to be self-sufficient and independent. I have found myself becoming very impatient with Travis and pushing him to act like my children. Martha and I have had many fights over the children's responsibilities."

The development of images, themes, boundaries, and responses to biosocial issues interacts with the functions of cohesion and adaptability. Flexible families will experience greater variety in images, themes, boundaries, and responses to biosocial issues than will rigid ones who allow little adaptability. These responses also affect the family's acceptable level of cohesion. For example, a family with fixed boundaries and themes related to total family dependence will develop extremely high cohesion in contrast to the family with themes of service or independence and flexible boundaries. This entire process rests with the communication behaviors of the family members. Communication, then, is the means by which families establish their patterns of cohesion and adaptability, based at least partially on their interactions in the development of images, themes, boundaries, and responses to biosocial issues.

A FRAMEWORK FOR EXAMINING FAMILY COMMUNICATION

To analyze the family as a system, we could take numerous approaches, such as looking at a family as an economic, political, or biological system. Since our concern lies with the interaction within and around the family, we will center on the communication aspects of the family system. We will look at the family from a communication perspective, seeing it as "an organized, naturally occurring relational interaction system, usually occupying a common living space over an extended time period and possessing a confluence of interpersonal images which evolve through the exchange of messages over time" (Bochner, 1976, 382). More specifically, we will use the following framework for examining family communication:

> *We view the family as a system in which communication regulates cohesion and adaptability by a flow of message patterns through a defined network of evolving interdependent relationships.*

We view the family as a system—

We see the family as a set of people and the relationship between them which, together, form a complex whole; changes in one part result in changes in other parts of the system. In short, family members are inextricably tied to each other, and each member and the family as a whole reflect changes in the system.

in which communication regulates cohesion and adaptability—

Communication, the symbolic, transactional process by which meanings are exchanged, is the means by which families develop their capacities for emotional bonding and flexibility. Communication facilitates a family's movement on the cohesion/adaptability axis (see Figure 1–1, page 16). We believe that the way in which people exchange messages influences the form and content of their relationships, and that communication and families have a mutual impact on each other. Communication affects the way family members relate, and family relationships affect the communication that occurs.

by a flow of message patterns through a defined network—

Based on families-of-origin and other environmental sources, each family develops its own set of meanings that become predictable, since family members interact with one another in the same manner over and over again. Such message patterns move through boundaries, which define the relationships along specific networks, which determine who interacts with whom.

of evolving interdependent relationships—

Family life is not static; both predictable, or developmental, changes and unpredictable changes, or crises, force alteration upon the system. Family relationships evolve over time as members join and leave the system and become closer or farther apart from each other. Yet, due to the family's systemic nature, members remain interdependent, or joined, as they deal with relational issues of intimacy, conflict roles, power, and decision making. Figure 1–3 on the next page may help you visualize these relationships.

Throughout the following chapters, we will examine the concepts mentioned in this framework in order to demonstrate the powerful role communication plays in family life.

Figure 1—3 _____
Development of Family Meanings

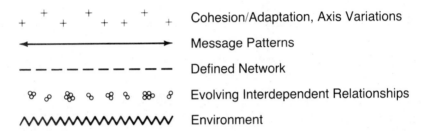

Cohesion/Adaptation, Axis Variations

Message Patterns

Defined Network

Evolving Interdependent Relationships

Environment

Based on their levels of cohesion and adaptability, families develop message patterns that flow through a defined network of evolving interdependent relationships. This occurs within the context of a specific environment.

Finally, let us forecast the types of families we will be discussing in the upcoming chapters. Historically, most literature on family interaction has focused on dysfunctional or pathological families. Early studies examined families with a severely troubled or handicapped member. In recent years, attention has shifted to understanding the workings of the well-functioning, or "normal" family. As you may imagine from our previous description of the status and types of families, there is little agreement on what is "normal." Early writers provided four perspectives from which to view normality: (1) normality as health, (2) normality as utopia, (3) normality as average, and (4) normality as process (Offer and Sabshin, 1984). The fourth later came to be called "transactional systems." Studies of well-functioning families highlight the tremendous diversity of families that appear to be functioning adequately at a particular point in time (Kantor and Lehr, 1976; Lewis et al., 1976; Reiss, 1981; Walsh, 1982; Olson and McCubbin).

In this text, we will focus on communication within the well-functioning family, since this constitutes the major experience for most of us. This book will attempt to dispel two myths: (1) there is one right way to be a family and (2) there is one right way to *communicate* within a family. Throughout the following pages, you will encounter a wide variety of descriptions of family life and communication behavior. Our purpose is to help you gain a better understanding of the dynamics of family communication, not to try to solve specific problems. Hence, we will take a descriptive, rather than a prescriptive, approach.

CONCLUSION

In this chapter, we have defined the term "family," introduced the basic premise of the family as a system, and provided an overview of the state of the family. We briefly described the process of communication and provided our position on communication patterns and family functions, including the primary functions of cohesion and adaptability and the supporting functions of family images, themes, boundaries, and biosocial issues. We concluded with our framework for studying family interaction. We view the family as a system in which communication regulates cohesion and adaptability by a flow of message patterns through a defined network of evolving interdependent relationships.

We hope there is some personal, rather than just academic, gain from reading these pages. Most of you come from families that have their share of pain and trouble as well as joy and intimacy. It is our hope that you will gain a new insight into the people with whom you share your lives. As you go through this text, read with your own family or other families in mind. You may also rely on literary families or families with which you have some passing acquaintance. By the end of the text, you should be able to apply this framework to an unknown family and analyze it as a communication system. We hope you choose to apply what you learn to your own family, although it may be difficult at times.

"Analyzing my own family has not been an easy process. As I began, my entire soul cried out, 'How do I begin to unravel the web of rules, roles, and strategies that make up our system?' I do not claim to have all possible answers; certainly my opinions and attitudes are different from those of the others in my family. I also do not claim to have the answers to all our problems. But I have tried to provide answers to my own confusion and to provide some synthesis to the change and crises that I have experienced. And I have grown from the process."

IN REVIEW

1. How would you describe communication in a well-functioning family?
2. Describe cultural forces that influence interaction patterns in your family-of-origin or in a real or fictional family with which you are familiar.
3. Describe a recurring interaction pattern in a real or fictional family in terms of the predictable verbal and nonverbal messages, including any predictable metacommunication.

4. Using a real or fictional family, give an example of how the family moved from one point on the adaptability-cohesion grid to another point due to changes in their lives.

5. How might the following themes be carried out in family communication patterns?

   —You can always depend on your family.

   —We are survivors.

   —Use your gifts.

   —Take one step at a time.

Chapter 2

The Family as a System

A systems perspective provides the most valuable insight into a family's communication patterns. Because communication is a symbolic, transactional process, focus must be placed on family relationships, not on individual members. In order to understand the communication patterns of a family, the overall communication context, the family *system*, must be examined.

> *"Family life is incredibly subtle and complex. Everything seems tied to everything else, and it's very difficult to sort out what is going on. For example, when our oldest daughter Marcy contracted spinal meningitis, the whole family reflected the strain. My second daughter and I fought more, while my husband tended to withdraw into himself, which brought me closer to my son. In their own ways, the three children became closer while our marriage became more distant. As Marcy's recovery progressed, there were more changes, which affected how we relate now, two years later. That one event highlighted the difficulty of sorting out what is really going on."*

The previous personal statement provides insight into how a family operates systemically and reflects the complexity of the task of examining families from a systems perspective. Everyday systemic patterns are often subtle and implicit with powerful effects. Nonverbal indications of displeasure, avoidance of issues, or ways of expressing affection may dramatically influence how members function. Unless you understand the context, you may not understand the message. In order to understand communication within the family system, this chapter will examine what a system is, how it works, and how it relates to family life.

CHARACTERISTICS OF HUMAN SYSTEMS

Very simply stated, a *system* is a set of objects that interrelate with one another to form a whole. If one component of the system changes, the others will change in response, which in turn affects the initial component. Systems may be closed or open. A *closed system* has no interchange with the environment; this concept applies mainly to physical elements, such as machines, which do not have life-sustaining qualities. An *open system* engages in interchange with the environment and is oriented toward growth; living, or organic, systems such as family systems fit into this category.

A system consists of four elements: objects, attributes, relationships, and an environment (Littlejohn, 1983, 29). The *objects* are the parts of a system; obviously, in the case of a familial system, these are family members themselves. The *attributes* are the qualities, or properties, of the system and its members. Thus, a family or a member has generalized family system attributes, such as goals, energy, health, or ethnic heritage, but each attribute is distinctive to that family or member, such as athletic goals, high energy, ill health, or Polish heritage.

The *relationships* among parts in the family system are the relationships among family members—the major focus of this book. Such relationships are characterized by communication that brings about acceptable levels of cohesion and adaptability at any given point in a family's life. Finally, *environment* is viewed as a system element because systems are affected by their surroundings. Families do not exist in a vacuum—they live within a time period, culture, community, and many other influential factors, such as larger family systems or educational organizations.

A family's environment affects the relationships that develop among its members, who strive to create acceptable levels of cohesion and adaptability within the system.

As you read about the family as a system, you may resist some of the more technical terminology, but you will come to understand the value of a systems approach to family communication and find the terminology helpful rather than cumbersome. Bavelas and Segal (1982) say that when the objects of a system are actually people in relationships with other people, one of the most important attributes of that system is communication behavior (101). In a family systems perspective, one visualizes an image in which the people are in the background and the relationships are in the foreground. A family systems perspective should aid you in analyzing family interaction, predicting future interactions, and creating meaningful changes within the system.

Specifically, we will apply the following systems characteristics to families: interdependence, wholeness, patterns/self-regulation, mutual influence/punctuation, adaptation, openness, equifinality, and hierarchical relationships. (Watzlawick et al., 1967, Littlejohn; Kantor and Lehr, 1976; Kramer, 1980; Bavelas and Segal).

Interdependence

Within any system, the parts are so interrelated as to be dependent upon each other for their proper functioning. Thus, this related dependence, or *interdependence*, is critical in describing a system. For example, the regulatory powers of the human body protect against disease. When infection occurs, white corpuscles multiply and rally to combat the invader and then diminish in number when the infection subsides.

One way to picture the interdependence within your family system is to imagine yourself sneezing in two different locations. If you sneeze while sitting in a bus station, you are likely to get no response from surrounding people, yet if you sneeze while sitting at the kitchen table, you may hear, "God bless you," "Don't get sick before our vacation," or "I hope you're not getting my cold." These comments typify the connectedness characteristic of a human system.

The family is a highly interdependent system because of its powerful and long-lasting effect on its members. Traditionally, this interdependence has been viewed as the means of maintaining a delicate balance among the system's parts, or members. Family therapist Jackson (1975) was one of the first to describe the process of family *homeostasis*, the bringing of a disturbed system back into balance. In Chapter 1, you encountered Satir's image of the family as a mobile in which members respond to changes in each other. As members respond to situations, other members may consciously or unconsciously shift to adjust to the quivering system. Families do not necessarily seek balance; rather, they evolve to, or seek, steady states which are always slightly different from the previous steady state (Dell, 1982; Hoffman, 1980).

You may be able to pinpoint events in your own family that have influenced all members in an identifiable way. Examples in family therapy literature suggest that parents may use, or focus on, an acting-out child to keep them together, or the child may use the parents' overprotectiveness to keep them safely close to home (Hoffman, 54). Thus, interdependence is a powerful element in understanding family functioning. In a family systems perspective, the behavior of each family member is related to and dependent upon the behavior of the others. When changes occur in family relationships, changes also occur in the individuals (Kramer, 45).

Wholeness

A family systems approach focuses on the *whole*; the parts, or members, are seen only in the context of that whole. A nonsystemic approach to families studies the individual members and "sums up" their personalities and attributes to describe the entire family. Littlejohn contrasts the two approaches by suggesting that, in the nonsystemic model, the whole is merely a collection with no unique qualities, "like a box of stones" (30). The systems model reflects an integration of parts. Overall family images and themes reflect this wholistic quality. For example, the Palmers, the McCarthys, or the Boyers have a life that characterizes the family as a whole, above and beyond the life of each family member. The Boyer family may be characterized as humorous, religious, warm, and strong, yet these adjectives do not necessarily apply to each family member. Thus, certain group characteristics may not reflect those of each individual.

In an ongoing human system, the parts, or the people, have importance, but once these parts become interrelated, they take on a life greater than their individual existences. In other words, the whole is greater than the sum of its parts. This phenomenon occurs when two or more people generate energy greater than the sum of their individual efforts. History documents the amazing power of families that accomplished seemingly impossible feats through their members' concerted efforts. For example, certain immigrant families rose to power and fame through the single-minded dedication of their members.

Unique communication patterns between or among family members emerge as a result of this "wholeness." Conflict or affection may become an inherent part of communication between various members. A certain cue may trigger patterns of behavior without members' awareness. Some of these communication patterns will be examined in Chapter 3.

Patterns/Self-Regulation

In your family, what are the appropriate ways to greet other members in the morning? What behaviors are acceptable during a family argument? Which are unacceptable? Human beings learn to coordinate their actions in order to create patterns together that could not be created individually. Although coordination of actions varies dramatically across family systems, each system develops some interactional patterns that make life somewhat predictable and manageable.

Although you may not be aware of it, you have learned to live within a relatively predictable pattern of interaction that characterizes your family system. All systems have repetitive cycles that help maintain their equilibrium and provide clues to their functioning. The importance of the system's patterns lies in their ability to put an act into context. The patterns provide data by which to understand isolated acts that may appear confusing or strange. Interaction patterns provide a means of assessing communication behaviors within a system, because they provide the context for understanding specific or isolated behaviors. For example, taken as an isolated event, it may be hard to interpret such acts as Mike hitting his brother or seven-year-old Sally acting like a baby. Yet, if these acts are viewed as part of a contextual pattern, they may make sense. If parental fighting and Mike's aggressive acts are related, you may discover patterns in which Mike's parents blame each other for his aggression, or you may find that Mike feels guilty for his parents' anger and takes his feelings out on his brother. If every time her mother decides to let Sally do more on her own, Sally acts like a baby, the patterns may indicate Sally's unwillingness to take on more self-responsibility or the mother's pressure to find her own independence. Messages may be discovered through the patterns that the isolated behaviors cannot indicate.

All systems need some regularity and predictability to function. *Rules* are relationship agreements that prescribe and limit a family member's behavior over time. Rules serve as generative mechanisms capable of creating regularity out of chaos (Yerby and Buerkel-Rothfuss, 1982, 2). Family rules govern all areas of life, including communication behavior. We will explore a family's communication rules in Chapter 3.

Traditionally, the function of maintaining stability and predictability has been critical to the continuance of any system; such a function involves calibration. *Calibration* implies checking and rectifying a scale. In the case of a family, it implies checking and rectifying, if necessary, the scale of permissible or acceptable behaviors. Hence, a system engages in what is called *morphostasis*, or an attempt to maintain the status quo. Let us explain this further.

All systems display a need for constancy within a defined range (Watzlawick et al., 147). Thus, a system needs to maintain some type of standard that is reached by noting deviations from the norm and correcting them if they become too significant. The thermostat is the most commonly used example of a calibration instrument. Usually, a home heating mechanism is set for a particular temperature, which allows a defined range of acceptable degrees. If the temperature drops below the lower acceptable level, the heat will kick on and the temperature will rise to within the acceptable range. The entire system may be "recalibrated," or set to a different temperature, if the standard is changed through the use of feedback.

Systems generate negative and positive feedback but, in systems language, the terms are used differently than they are in everyday usage. Negative feedback implies constancy and maintains the standard while minimizing change, whereas positive, or change-promoting, feedback results in recalibration of the system at a different level. No value is implied by the labels. We can visualize this process in the following ways. Figure 2–1a represents a system in which negative, or *maintenance*, feedback prevents change from occurring. For example, this may happen when a man hits his wife for the first time. If she threatens him, "You hit me again and I'll leave you," and he becomes sad or frightened, hitting will not become part of their conflict pattern. In another situation, if one partner indicates a desire for new sexual experimentation but the other refuses, the system will be maintained at the original level of sexual intimacy.

Figure 2–1b represents a system in which positive feedback results in change. For example, if a wife cannot stop her husband's initial attempt at physical abuse, hitting may become part of their long-term conflict pattern.

According to Olson et al. (1979), positive feedback provides the family with "constructive system-enhancing behaviors that enable the system to grow, create, innovate, and change, i.e., system *morphogenesis*. Conversely, negative feedback attempts to maintain the status quo, i.e., system *morphostasis*" (11). In another situation, positive feedback may operate as a father responds to his son's attempts to reach greater physical closeness, as in the next personal quotation.

"As an adult, I became very aware of the limited physical contact I had with my father. Although he would hug my sister, he never touched the boys, with the exception of a handshake. I determined that I wanted a greater physical closeness with him and consciously set out to change our ways of relating to each other. The first time I hugged my father was when I returned from a trip and I walked in and put my arms around him. I was nervous and tentative; he was startled and stiff, but he didn't resist. Over time I continued to greet him with hugs until we reached the point at which both of us could extend our arms to each other. I can now see my brothers developing a greater physical closeness to him also."

When your family's communication rule has been developed over time, your family is calibrated, or "set," to regulate its behavior in conformity to the rule. If your family or an outside force alters the rule, the family is recalibrated in accordance with the new rule. The following example demonstrates this process. An unwritten family rule may be that a sick fourteen-year-old is not allowed to hear

Figure 2—1 _____
Feedback Systems

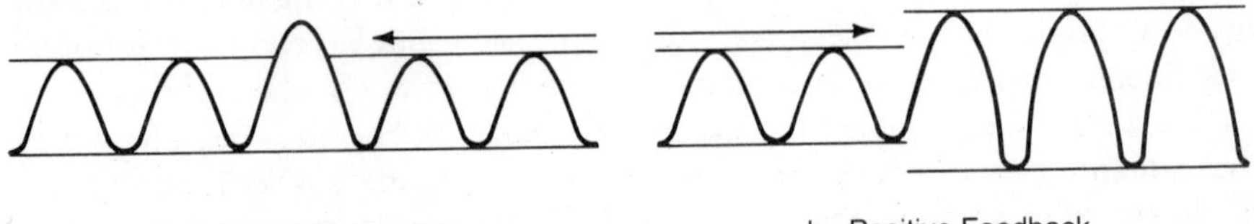

a. Negative Feedback
(no change)

b. Positive Feedback
(change occurs)

the truth regarding his illness. If anyone should suggest that he has a blood disease, negative feedback in the form of a nonverbal sign or a change of subject may keep him relatively uninformed. The family is "set" not to discuss the issue with him. Yet, the rules may be changed and the system recalibrated through a variety of positive feedback mechanisms. If the young man guesses the severity of his illness, he may confront one or more family members and insist on the truth. Once the truth has been told, he cannot return to his previous naive state, and the system will include some discussion of his illness. Another source of positive feedback may be a doctor who suggests that the young man's condition be discussed with him and may require the family to do so. Again, the system would be recalibrated as family members mature and are considered able to handle certain information or experiences.

Mutual Influence/Punctuation

Within a systems perspective, cause and effect are interchangeable. When you function within an ongoing system, each action serves as both a response to a previous action and a stimulus for a future action. The term "mutual influence" implies that once a cycle of behavior starts, each act triggers new behavior as well as responds to previous behaviors. This transactional quality renders pointless any attempts to assign *cause and effect*. Sometimes this process is described as the "nag/withdraw cycle," which is useless to try to explain—"He withdraws because she nags" versus "She nags because he withdraws" (Dell, 26). An example of such a cycle is found in Eugene O'Neill's play *Long Day's Journey into Night*:

> . . . the family members watch the mother closely, which makes her visibly nervous, which makes them watch her closely . . . until the circle winds into a spiral leading to the return of her addiction, which they all fear. The above description could also have begun: the mother is visibly nervous, which makes the family watch her closely. . . . (Bavelas and Segal, 104)

It is pointless to try to identify where a pattern "started," since in most families, patterns of behavior emerge that seem to have lives of their own. Thus, it is fruitless to assign a cause to them, because the behaviors are intertwined. The wholistic, interdependent nature of the system moves behaviors into a cycle.

Punctuation refers to the interruption, or breaking into a sequence, of behavior at intervals in order to give it meaning. Punctuation often suggests that "things started here." Interaction sequences, like word sequences, must be punctuated, or grouped syntactically, to make sense. Behaviors are not just a chain of actions; they may also perform stimulus and reaction functions.

Patterns of behavior may be punctuated in various ways. Breakdowns may occur when people punctuate a communication sequence differently, thereby assigning different meanings to the behaviors. A son may say, "Our trouble started when my mother became depressed," whereas the mother may indicate that the family problems started when her son began staying away from home. Punctuating the cycle according to the son's suggestion would imply a placement of blame on the mother. If the cycle is punctuated according to the mother, the son would be at fault for the family's troubles. The "yes/no" cycle could go on indefinitely. If we work from the idea of circular causality within a system, it seems less important to try to punctuate the system and assign a beginning point than it does to look at the act as a sequence of patterns and try to understand this ongoing process without saying, "It started *here*." In Figure 2–2, you can imagine the different interpretations that could emerge depending on how the cycle is punctuated.

"The best thing we learned in marriage counseling was to stop blaming each other and to start looking for a pattern of behavior that we could control. For example, instead of screaming, 'You started it' if we get into a pattern of one-up, one-down, I have learned to call him on the power play instead of whining, and he has learned to call me on whining and on some heavy-handed moves."

Some families try to explain their difficulties by going back through the past and saying, "It started when he took a job requiring travel" or "Things began to fall apart when my wife went back to work." The actions occurring since those blamed behaviors have so altered the system that a job change in either situation would not necessarily resolve the current issues, because the system has long since readjusted. In addition, specific job situations may be a response to a previous unnamed behavior. Only the current behavior is of value in analyzing the family's life and seeking areas for change. Disagreement about how to punctuate the sequence of events is at the root of many family problems (Watzlawick et al., 56).

Adaptation

As we saw in our earlier discussion of adaptability in Chapter 1, human systems must change and restructure themselves in order to survive. Families constantly restructure themselves to cope with developmental styles and unpredictable crises. Change, or *adaptation*, is a predictable part of the human experience.

Figure 2–2 _____
Circular Causality Within a System

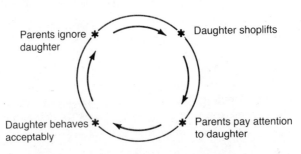

Historically, family theorists viewed the family as a system attempting to maintain stability. Yet, in keeping with a developmental approach, which views families as necessarily capable of adaptation, we stress the relationship between morphostasis and morphogenesis.

In a previous section, we described calibration and feedback within a traditional view of family self-control and response to change. Recent thinking about family systems views the concept of calibration as mechanistic and narrow, since it seems to suggest a static, error-activated process; given a deviation in the system, the mechanism receives negative feedback and brings itself back into line. To view a human process in a totally mechanistic way would be limiting. In her discussion of human systems, Hoffman maintains that human systems are capable of sudden leaps to new integrations, which reflect a new evolutionary stage (54). In other words, families also experience change through leaps—as random and unpredictable forces propel members into new forms and experiences.

At this point, we can put an evolutionary framework around the traditional calibration model, recognizing the attempt at maintaining the current system but also accounting for transformations that change the original system dramatically. This will be further developed throughout this book in terms of the system's adaptive quality.

Openness

An open system permits interchange with the surrounding environment. Whereas closed, mechanical systems do not need outside organisms and will break down if they are encountered, human systems need interchange with other people, ideas, and social systems to sustain themselves physically and psychologically. The family as a social system maintains an almost continuous interchange, not only within the system but across the boundary between its inner and outer environments. Each family operates within the larger *ecosystem*, which includes legal, educational, political, health, banking, agricultural, and economic systems. In our highly interdependent society, a family must function as part of a larger societal structure. As a small child, you may have depended entirely on your family for all your immediate needs, but as you grew older, you needed to interact with nonfamily members in order to function in society. For an entire family to function, such interchange with and adaptation to the environment is critical. Most family members must interact with others for survival and to fulfill physical and psychological needs. Maintaining the bare necessities of life (food, clothing, and shelter) requires a functional relationship with the environment. Education and work provide additional sources of environmental contact, whereas friends, co-workers, and future spouses must be found outside the narrow limits of the immediate family system.

A young family member's encounters with an inspirational teacher, a delinquent companion, a mind-expanding book, or an R-rated movie may influence his or her behavior within the family. In today's society, the media have served as a powerful force in altering family boundaries. Children encounter many ideas or values which may be contrary to parental beliefs, although in most homes, absolute regulation of the media is impractical.

"As a teacher who works with deaf children, I am aware that the feedback I give to a family about their child influences how the family feels about itself. For example, I have been able to demonstrate to parents that their children have the capacity for a full life and that they should not relate to their children primarily in terms of their deafness. I think I have helped some parents feel less guilty or depressed about having a handicapped child. A family that can accept a child's deafness provides a much more supportive atmosphere for the child."

Equifinality

An open, adaptive family system demonstrates *equifinality*—the ability to accomplish a similar final goal or state in many different ways and from many different starting points (Littlejohn, 32). For example, two families may achieve a similarly defined "good life" based on a particular income, education, and relationship level through incredibly diverse means. Both families may have a theme of: "Family members always support each other." Yet, each may work differently toward this goal of predictable mutual support. One family may interpret the theme to mean emotional support, whereas the other may view it as an economic issue. The families may differ in their definition of "need" for support and their demands for repayment. In short, there are as many possible ways of reaching a goal as there are families striving for that goal.

Hierarchical Relationships

Human systems are complex organizations. Many subsystems exist within a hierarchy, each crucial to the functioning of the whole. For example, an extended family may include many smaller family units, which in turn contain subsystems.

The complexity of the family system may be seen through the subsystems that contribute to the family's functioning. Each family system contains interpersonal subsystems and personal or psychobiological subsystems. As we saw in our discussion of "wholeness," knowing the family system does not necessarily mean knowing the specific members or their relationships. Using the family tree in Figure 2–3, we can say that to know the Bennett family is not to know totally Tom Bennett or Rose Bennett, nor is it to know Tom and Rose Bennett's particular interpersonal relationship. Therefore, in addition to a "total group" identity, there is a second level of systemic functioning.

Every family contains a number of small groups, called *interpersonal subsystems*, that are likely to be made up of two or three persons and the relationships

Figure 2–3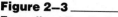
Formalized Family Relationships

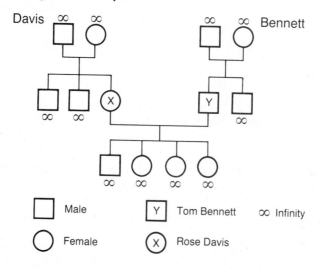

between or among them. Even a three-person system becomes complicated by the interpersonal subsystems within it. A mother, daughter, and grandson triad represents three such subsystems—the mother and daughter, the daughter and her son, and the grandmother and grandson.

Thus, each of the subsystems has to be considered in order to understand the functioning of the whole. Each subsystem has its own rules, boundaries, and unique characteristics. For example, Mom may never tease Janice but easily kid with Doug. Yet, Dad may tease both of them very comfortably and be more affectionate than Mom is able to be. Mom and Doug may spend long hours talking about his future plans, whereas Janice may choose not to discuss this with any immediate family members. Mom, Doug, and Janice may bind together to deal with problems resulting from Dad's poor health.

In most cases, subsystems change membership over time. Yet, certain subsystems may become so strong or tight that particular members feel either overwhelmed or powerless, or feel left out. If the members relate only to specific other members, alliances result.

The easiest pattern to envision occurs when two family members seem joined against the other one. Such triangles are created by the arrival of the first child, but they become problems only if alliances are always formed in the same way, such as if Mom and Doug always ally against Dad, or if Mom and Dad always ally against Janice. Family triangles are characterized by two insiders and one outsider. During periods of stress, the outsider position is desirable; when tensions are low, the outsider may feel isolated. Kerr (1981) suggests that if you understand how triangles function in a family, you will see the absurdity of assigning causes or blame to particular events. The members' interdependence renders such thinking fruitless.

"I saw a dramatic example of a triangle as I grew up in a house where my Dad was an alcoholic. My mother and oldest brother formed a tight relationship against him, and sometimes against everyone else. They agreed on everything, and my brother became my mother's protector. Even when Dad started to get on the wagon, he could not break up that alliance, and I think that was one of the reasons they got a divorce."

Alliances may have positive or negative effects within families. Two or three family members objecting to another's insensitivity may have positive results. An older brother/younger brother alliance could result in the younger one's entering a gang or raising his grades, depending on the model he sees in the older male. Most of us have seen families where two children seem to have a permanent alliance against a third member, resulting in much anger or unhappiness for the "third wheel." As family systems grow larger, the complexity of the interpersonal subsystems develops accordingly. For example, in the Davis-Bennett family, subsystems account for alliances within the formal system (Figure 2–4).

To further complicate the issue, a family system contains a third systemic level in addition to the group and interpersonal levels. Each family member represents his or her own personal or psychobiological system, which is tied to, yet separate from, the family unit. The structure of a family includes the organization of its individual members, or personal subsystems, which possess unique biological and psychobiological characteristics. The experiences encountered by each member differ from those of others in the family and heighten his or her individuality. Hess and Handel (1959) suggest that ". . . in his relationship in the family an individual member strives toward predictability of preferred experience, attempting to discover or create circumstances which fit his image of what the world around him should be—how it should respond to him and provide opportunity for expression of his own preferences" (3). In short, no matter how much three sisters

Figure 2–4 _____
Alliances Within the Formal Family Structure

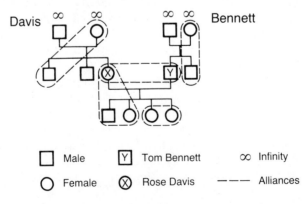

☐ Male	Ⓨ Tom Bennett	∞ Infinity
◯ Female	⊗ Rose Davis	– – – Alliances

may resemble each other, they are psychobiological entities who function partially in an independent manner.

From this perspective, divorce and death do not dissolve family systems; rather, they alter them. These altered systems may become involved in a second marriage, necessitating the interweaving of three or more families into a remarried family system. The organizational complexity of such systems are often staggering as the systems and subsystems interweave to form a new whole. We will discuss this further in Chapter 11.

Information Processing

Every system needs a mechanism by which the parts interrelate. Within open systems, adaptation and change are made possible by sophisticated information processing, or message transmission capabilities. When we talk about human systems such as families, the information processing capacity merges with the communication process so that we are discussing a family's communication function. On the basis of their research in families, Kantor and Lehr assert that "the information processed by the family system is distance-regulation information" (12). Thus, the major information processed by a family system contains the messages that regulate separateness/connectedness, or cohesion. The concept of cohesion was introduced in Chapter 1, and Chapter 3 will further elaborate on messages and meanings.

Communication as a systems attribute establishes and maintains the relationships between people in a family. Processing information, or coordinating meanings, is integral to family functioning.

FAMILIES THAT FUNCTION FROM A SYSTEMS PERSPECTIVE

In the previous pages, we have described major systems characteristics, including interdependence, wholeness, patterns/self-regulation, mutual influence/punctuation, adaptation, openness, equifinality, hierarchical relationships, and information processing. Although this chapter's approach may appear technical, such a perspective may aid you in understanding some of the intricacies of family life. For example, being aware of the process of mutual influence may prevent you from falling into the common trap of "finding the cause" as a way to deal with marital or family problems. Becoming aware of the existence of patterns and rules may allow you to see them where you might not have before. Knowing that families, as human systems, reach similar points in varying ways may encourage you to be comfortable with what appears different.

We will conclude by showing how a systems perspective could affect family functioning if the members themselves were to hold a systems point of view. In identifying optimally functioning families, Beavers concluded that families that consciously operate from a systems orientation function more effectively than those that do not. This does not necessarily mean that family members speak and apply technical systems terminology to their everyday lives; it means that family members hold a flexible position on human behavior. Beavers (1982) describes the four basic assumptions of families that take a systems orientation as follows:

1. An individual needs a group, a human system, for identity and satisfaction.
2. Causes and effects are interchangeable.
3. Any human behavior is the result of many variables rather than one "cause"; therefore, simplistic solutions are questioned.
4. Human beings are limited and finite. No one is absolutely helpless or absolutely powerful in a relationship. (45)

When a family holds the first assumption, members presume that people do not exist in a vacuum and that human needs are met through relationships. Even after children from these families are grown, they seek a sense of human community in new family systems or social networks. The second assumption reflects an understanding of mutual influence. Family members see actions as responses to and stimuli for other actions. For example, anger in one person promotes withdrawal in another and that withdrawal promotes anger.

Persons holding the third assumption recognize that human behavior reflects many influences. Beavers describes this clearly by listing some possible explanations for a three-year-old's spilled milk: (1) accident—no motive, (2) interpersonal meaning—child is upset with mother, (3) child is tired, or (4) glass is too heavy or large for child's hand (145). Whereas a dysfunctional family may always attribute spilled milk to one explanation, an optimally functioning family's responses vary according to each situation. The final assumption implies an awareness that humans are fallible and that self-esteem comes from relative competence. Therefore, total control over one's own life or the lives of others is impossible. Striving for goals in a realistic way is desirable.

Although this chapter has dealt with a systems perspective primarily in an abstract manner, this view may be applied to everyday family functioning in concrete ways. Understanding the family as a system will alter the way you view families, both academically and personally.

CONCLUSION

In this chapter, we have applied a systems perspective to the family. We determined that a family system consists of members, relationships among them, family attributes, members' attributes, and an environment in which the family functions. We examined the following systems characteristics as they apply to family life: interdependence, wholeness, mutual influence/punctuation, patterns/self-regulation, adaptation, openness, equifinality, hierarchical relationships, and information processing.

A systems approach provides a valuable perspective from which to analyze family interaction. When viewed from this perspective, the focus shifts from individual members' behavior to the family as a whole, with its interdependent relationships and patterns, which affect cohesion and adaptability. This perspective allows one to analyze specific behavior patterns in terms of the interpersonal context in which they occur and to understand their meanings in light of the entire family system. A systems perspective has value at an academic level for anyone professionally interested in family interaction. It also has value on a personal level for anyone interested in understanding how families establish and maintain their relationships through communication.

IN REVIEW

1. Using a real or fictional family, describe its calibrated level of conflict in terms of acceptable verbal and nonverbal communication. If applicable, describe attempts to change this calibrated level in terms of positive or negative feedback.
2. Draw a three-generation representation of a real or fictional family (*genogram*), and indicate and explain the alliances among certain family members. See p. 38 for a model.
3. Describe a real or fictional family triangle in which one person regulates interaction between the other two.
4. Using Beaver's four basic assumptions of families who hold a systems perspective, describe some interaction patterns in a real or fictional family that appear to operate from these assumptions.
5. How would holding a family systems perspective affect your work as one of the following: a doctor, teacher, clergy person, school counselor?

Chapter 3

Communication Patterns and the Creation of Family Meanings

Every family creates its own identity. Some families may share the same cultural background, have members of similar ages and abilities, even share values and goals, but they can never give their members the same experiences. The interaction of your family members through greeting, fighting, loving, and teaching creates an overall experience of family life that cannot be recreated by any other group. This uniqueness reflects the family meanings developed through patterned interactions. In the previous chapter, we examined the family as a system. Now we will examine the way in which a family develops its view of reality. We will look at the formation of family meanings through communication patterns and at the way those meanings are influenced by families-of-origin, rules, and networks.

> "My mother and her sisters lived in a very strict home. Before any girl could leave the house, she had to tell my great-grandfather the password, 'Dresses down, panties up.' If she went out with girls, all of them had to say it individually, and if a boy was taking her out, she had to make sure he heard it. We were not brought up that strictly, but very often we will use that expression in kidding around, and dates or visitors never know how to react. Our family has all kinds of secret messages that other people can never figure out."

MEANINGS IN RELATIONSHIPS

Communication, the symbolic, transactional process of sharing meanings, undergirds and illuminates the structure of kinship relationships. The form and content of family messages combine to create a family's view of itself and the world. Family members, through their interdependence and mutual influence, create meanings based on their interaction patterns. Yerby and Buerkel-Rothfuss (1982) maintain that "meaning in the family is achieved—behavior is interpreted and evaluated—as members coordinate their activities through communication" (2).

This coordination may be voluntary or involuntary, but interdependence requires that members function within the system's overall structure.

Communication is not only a simple transmission between people; it also shapes and alters the structure of the family system and the individuals in it. As a family system evolves, the communication among members affects the continuously adapting form of the structure.

More specifically, communication regulates cohesion among family members, and this distance regulation interacts with the family's adaptive processes. Over a period of time, family members come to have certain meanings for one another. According to Hess and Handel (1959):

> On the basis of the meanings which the members have for one another, particular interpersonal ties evolve. The closeness between any two members, for example, or the distance between a group of three closely joined members and a fourth who is apart, derives from the interlocking meanings which obtain among them.   (18–19)

The Creation of Meanings

Each of us learns to interpret and evaluate behaviors within our family system and create a set of meanings which may not be understood by an outsider. In order to see this more closely, let us look at the behaviors of a couple as they begin to form a family system, since the adult partners are the architects of most systems. Family therapist Minuchin (1974) suggests that each young couple must undergo a process of mutual accommodation through which the couple "develops a set of patterned transactions—ways in which each spouse triggers and monitors the behavior of the other and is, in turn, influenced by the previous behavioral sequence. These transactional patterns form an invisible web of complementary demands that regulate many family situations" (17). In order to form a marital system, a couple must negotiate a set of common meanings through mutual accommodation so that, eventually, the meanings for one are linked through conjoint action with the meanings of the other. The negotiation process is both subtle and complex. Some couples never accomplish this task.

A couple must make an accommodation that allows them to use mutually meaningful language. General similarities in their physical and social processes assure some generalized common meanings. However, the intent of some behaviors, if not discussed, may be misinterpreted; yet, these behaviors and their interpretations will become part of the couple's meaning pattern. Usually, the more similar their backgrounds, the less negotiation is needed. With the entire realm of verbal and nonverbal behavior available, they have to negotiate a set of common meanings which reflect their physical, social, and especially their individual processes for viewing the world.

When behaviors are interpreted in the same way or interpretations are discussed and clarified, similar meanings emerge, and communication becomes clear.

If a newly married husband becomes very quiet around his successful, verbal father-in-law, his wife may interpret that behavior as boredom or dislike. On the basis of that interpretation, she may spend time convincing her husband of her father's virtues. If her interpretation is correct, this response may be appropriate. If, on the other hand, her husband's silence actually reflects his intimidation by his father-in-law's status or intelligence, the young wife has misinterpreted the behavior. If these assumptions go unchecked, the result may be a distance between the two generations based on misinterpreted, rather than shared, meanings.

In an attempt to distinguish between distressed and nondistressed couples, Gottman et al. (1977) concluded that nonverbal behavior was an important key. They found that distressed couples were more likely to "express their feelings about a problem, to mind read, and to disagree, all with negative nonverbal behavior" (467–68). Thus, the use of verbal and nonverbal messages and their eventual patterns plays a significant role in a family's existence. Yet, you will always find an exception to the norm—due to a system's equifinality, or ability to reach the same point differently, there will always be examples of the unique happily married couple that breaks all the rules.

Coordinated meanings do not emerge early or quickly within relationships. Partners may struggle for years to gain similarity in interpreting and responding to each other's behaviors. Parents and children may live with serious misunderstandings and mistaken assumptions throughout most of their shared lives.

Meanings in Highly Developed Relationships

As a way of examining how a couple functions when they experience a generally coordinated sharing of meanings, we can examine the characteristics that appear in committed and close relationships (Altman and Taylor, 1973). Among the characteristics of these developed relationship patterns are richness, efficiency, uniqueness, substitutability, pacing, openness, spontaneity, and evaluation (129). The following description of the way in which each of these characteristics relates to communication helps us to see how relationships function when meanings are shared effectively.

Richness refers to the ability of people in close relationships to convey the same message accurately in a variety of ways. Siblings and spouses have many ways of sharing displeasure, delight, or other feelings. Affection may be shared in words, either in a teasing or serious manner, or through looks, hugs, or kisses. "I always thought it was neat that my mother would sit on my father's lap in front of us kids." A relationship without richness remains in a very predictable and limited pattern of "the same old thing."

Efficiency in a relationship refers to accuracy, speed, and sensitivity in the transmission and receipt of communication. "In well-established interpersonal relationships, intended messages are transmitted and understood rapidly, accurately, and with great sensitivity" (131). Family shorthand abounds in which the meaningful raised eyebrow conveys more than words. The comment, "I don't want another Thanksgiving scene" may conjure up similar images in everyone's head of late arrivals, a charred bird, and angry words. Only members of the family group can code and decode the messages' meanings with such efficiency.

Highly developed relationships are characterized by *uniqueness,* or the generation of idiosyncratic message systems. Verbal expressions may take on new meanings; words may be created or used in unusual ways. Certain vocal tones, facial expressions, or body movements may have special meanings understood only by members of the system. If a family member claims a need for "puddling time," other members may willingly withdraw, whereas a neighbor would not associate a pool of rainwater with time to relax alone. In their study of the world of intimate talk and communication uniqueness, Hopper et al. (1981) reported interviewing 112 cohabitating couples about their personal idioms. The results included eight types of idioms: teasing insults, confrontations, expressions of affection, sexual invitation, sexual references and euphemisms, requests and routines, partner nicknames, and names for other persons (28).

Substitutability refers to the ability to convey the same message in alternative fashions when necessary. For example, one need not wait for the last guest to leave the party to convey anger through a yelling match, because nonverbal signs such as a glance, "meaningful" silence, or a specific movement of the mouth will alert one spouse to the fact that the other is extremely angry. Members of a close relationship understand the meaning of the substituted behavior just as easily as they would the usual expression.

Altman and Taylor suggest that these four characteristics of richness, efficiency, uniqueness, and substitutability probably overlap. However, together they reflect the idea that the dynamics of a close relationship involve multiple levels of functioning, including rich, complex communication patterns and a better understanding of the meaning of transactions (132).

Pacing, or synchronization, refers to the coordination and meshing of interpersonal actions as people work into mutual roles and behave in complementary ways. A common metaphor for this coordination is of a free and fluid dance (Rogers, 1984, 7). There is a sense of apparently effortless teamwork demonstrated by the members of the relationship.

"My mother and father have been married for twenty-seven years, and it's amazing to watch them function. One always seems to know what the other is doing and thinking, and they work together beautifully, in the kitchen, in dealing with the children, and in general conversation. I would compare their relationship to a well-oiled machine, but that sounds too cold. It's just that they appear in total harmony with one another."

The *openness* of a highly developed relationship implies verbal and nonverbal accessibility to each other. On one level, openness occurs when personal private information is expressed or received (Montgomery, 1981). Yet, it is not just more intimate interactions that characterize openness, but also the individuals' ability to move in and out of private areas in a quick and facile way.

As relationships deepen, *spontaneity* grows. The informality and comfort of strong relationships allow one to break their patterns. Quick or unexpected love-making, surprise trips, unpredictable comments, and changed plans all have their places as a couple develops a life together.

Finally, such close relationships involve *evaluation,* or the sharing of negative and positive judgments about one another. With the security that the relationship will not end if negative feelings are discussed, family members can express their true feelings in hopes of finding resolution. Alternately, praise need not be threatening or viewed as "moving too fast." Thus, positive feelings are aired that might otherwise be unspoken.

As a group, these eight characteristics provide the backdrop for communication patterns that emerge within particular family systems. Adaptability and cohesion are central to the development of such committed relationships; adaptation is a core feature of efficiency, substitutability, pacing, and spontaneity, while cohesion underlies the development of uniqueness, richness, openness, and evaluation. The security of relationships characterized by these factors allows the widest range of interpersonal behaviors to occur and fosters the continued growth of the individuals and their relationship. Thus, each family develops particular message behaviors that are understood by other members of the system.

When one enters an unfamiliar home as a guest, he or she has to try to adapt to the message systems within that environment. The baby may walk around carrying her "doe," which serves as a blanket and psychological comforter; Grandpa

Couples in highly developed relationships share meanings that promote security and continued growth.

may continually refer to four-year-old Neal as the "heir to the throne"; and the hall closet may be known as the "pit." A visitor must make decisions about the emotions behind the parent's tone of voice that first calls "Matthew" and later "Matthew Noel Wilkinson." Although the father's manner may not appear to change, the visitor learns to respect the whispers of the other family members to "leave him alone right now—he's got that look on his face," since they are reading something unavailable to the untrained eye. "In" jokes and past references abound. Family members may scream and shout in ways that make the visitor most uncomfortable, but no one else appears bothered. On the other hand, the visitor may be hugged and kissed every time he or she arrives and leaves, which could be pleasant or very disconcerting. Over time, these behaviors form patterns that become predictable within each family.

COMMUNICATION PATTERNS THAT INFLUENCE FAMILY MEANINGS

Meanings emerge through the continuous interpretation of and response to messages. Over time, these interactions become predictable and form patterns. A pattern may be viewed as a complex set of "moves," which have been established through repetition and have become so automatic as to continue without conscious awareness. A communication pattern is distinguished by seven characteristics:

a. it is verbal and nonverbal;
b. it is specific to the relationship within the system;
c. it is recurring and predictable;
d. it is reciprocal and interactive;
e. it is relationship defining;
f. it is emergent; and
g. it may be changed by forces within the ecosystem or it may influence changes in that system.   (Yerby and Buerkel-Rothfuss, 7)

This list demonstrates how communication patterns create meanings in relationships rather than just reflect them. We will examine these characteristics in our discussion of the patterns that influence meaning. As we explore the development of family meanings, we will focus on three factors which contribute to the development of family meanings: (1) family-of-origin influences, (2) family communication rules, and (3) communication networks.

Family-of-Origin Influences

"My son's a Kaplan, all right. He'll walk up and talk to anyone without a trace of shyness." "We always fought by yelling at each other and then forgetting about it. My wife doesn't understand this." These typical sayings reflect our perceptions of intergenerational influence. They highlight the potential family-of-origin influence in communication patterns that form as new systems are created.

Family-of-origin refers to the family or families in which a person is raised. Thus, the family in which you grew up is your family-of-origin. Many of you still function primarily within your family-of-origin system. Others have already formed new family systems.

The term "family-of-origin influences" refers to the specific experiences one encounters while growing up, which reflect both a unique combination of personalities and the ethnic/cultural heritages represented by the individuals within the family-of-origin. Although the mutual accommodation and development of common meanings within a marital relationship depend on the physical, social, and individual filters of each person, the family-of-origin background that each spouse brings to a relationship is also a significant social influence. Although many of us may desire a family life different from the one in which we grew up, we find ourselves recreating the familiar in our new relationships. "People often work out marriages similar to their own parents' not because of heredity; they are simply following a family pattern" (Satir, 1972, 127). Reiss (1981) and associates have found historical reconstruction studies to be "in striking agreement on the remarkable persistence of certain fundamental themes and orientations in family life" (224).

Families-of-origin may provide blueprints for the communication of future generations. Initially, communication is learned in the home, and throughout life, the family setting provides a major testing ground for communication behavior. Each young person who leaves the family-of-origin to form a new system takes with him or her a set of conscious and unconscious ways of relating to people. For example, the idiosyncrasies and culturally based communication patterns of the O'Briens may be passed on to generations of children in combination with the patterns gained from in-laws' families-of-origin.

"My mother said my grandmother referred to ice cream as 'I-box' when she was little. My mother called it that for me, and I have taught it to my son. I hadn't thought about it for years, but it just came back when Steven was old enough to ask for it."

Just as simple language terms travel across the generations, more significant attitudes and rule-bound behaviors move from a family-of-origin to a newly emerging family system. For example, in their examination of male and female expressiveness, Balswick and Averett (1977) tested the following hypothesis: Persons whose parents were expressive to them will be more expressive. The authors reported, "Our evidence suggests the expressive children come from expressive parents, or at the very least, from parents who are perceived as expressive" (126).

An emphasis on keeping things "in the family," the acceptability of discussing certain subjects, or the way in which such subjects are discussed may pass from generation to generation reflecting individual and cultural influences. For example, an examination of communication patterns through three generations of an extended Irish-American family revealed great similarities across generations in terms of culturally predictable communication patterns (Galvin, 1982). Respondents from each generation reported their variations on the theme of privacy stated in expressions such as: "What you see and hear in this house goes no further," "Don't advertise your business. Handle it on the q.t." "This information doesn't leave this table."

These general understandings of what to say or how to say it may be accompanied by an understanding of how information should travel, directly or indirectly, through others, as when a mother filters bad news for a father. Sometimes, the transition of such behavior is smooth, because the other spouse has a similar background or does not resist that behavior. On the other hand, wide differences in family-of-origin behaviors can lead to communication breakdowns in the couple's system. In the following example, a young wife describes the differences in nonverbal communication in her family-of-origin from that of her husband.

"It was not until I became closely involved with a second family that I became conscious of the fact that the amount and type of contact can differ greatly. Rarely, in Rob's home, will another person reach for someone else's hand, walk arm in arm, or kiss for no special reason; hugs are reserved for comfort. When people filter into the den to watch television, one person will sit on the couch, the next on the floor, a third on a chair, and finally the last person is forced to sit on the couch. And always at the opposite end!

Touching, in my home, was a natural, everyday occurrence. Usually, the family breakfast began with 'good morning' hugs and kisses. After meals, we often would sit on our parents' laps rocking, talking, and just relaxing. While watching television, we usually congregated on and around someone else as we sat facing the set. Even as adults, no one ever hesitated to cuddle up next to someone else, run their hands through another person's hair, or start tickling whoever happens to be in reaching distance."

The previous example illustrates the extent to which each member of the couple was raised differently and how that can affect the communication behavior in the new system. When you consider your parents' marriage, or your own, you can find instances of this situation in which the rules or networks affect how and what communication occurs. For instance, if you have lived in a stepfamily, you may have witnessed the stress of negotiation involved in integrating your stepparent's family-of-origin influences into a system with communication patterns that already reflected two families-of-origin.

As we saw in Chapter 2, changes in a system depend on the nature of feedback within the system. Negative, or constancy, feedback that reinforces the status quo prevents change or adjustment: "If I don't say anything, he'll grow out of it" or "That's just the way she is, so I'll go along." Positive, or change-promoting, feedback forces the issue into the open in a risk-taking move in the hope that the situation can be changed: "I really need more affection from you" or "Let's cuddle." Since each of us has limited opportunities to really see how other families live, we presume that "our way" is typical. Unless we choose to work with positive feedback, we are likely to perpetuate old, and sometimes unproductive, patterns.

The role of ethnicity may be taken for granted, yet its influence can be powerful. In their examination of Italian families, Rotunno and McGoldrick (1982) highlight the families' cultural enjoyment of celebrating, loving, and fighting and their orientation toward social skills, including cleverness, charm, and graciousness. These behaviors exist within an orientation to values that places heavy emphasis on how actions affect the family, especially its honor. In addition, families function within a network of significant other relatives, *gumbares* (old friends), and godparents from whom mutual support is expected. This orientation stresses parental role distinction, with the father as the undisputed head of the family and mother as the heart, or the family's emotional sustenance (348–47). This generalization about the Italian heritage comes into sharp contrast with descriptions of Norwegian family patterns, which generally stress the importance of emotional control and the avoidance of open confrontation (Midelfort and Midelfort, 1982). Within the Norwegian family, words are likely to be used sparingly; inner weaknesses are kept secret; aggression is channeled into teasing, ignoring, or silence. In terms of male/female roles the man serves as head of the family and exacts discipline, while the woman is the communication center establishing the social network among kin (438–43). The marriage of persons reflecting these two ethnic backgrounds has the potential for misunderstanding unless differences are addressed. Strong conflicts may develop as each plays out behaviors appropriate to his or her family-of-origin. Such differences may never be resolved because of the strength of the family pattern, or compromises may be necessary as the whole family is influenced by social forces.

"Unfortunately, one of the biggest problems in our marriage comes from something that is very hard to change; my husband and I are from very different cultural backgrounds. He is from rural Central America and I grew up in Kansas City. I married him when I was eighteen and he was twenty-six because I was pregnant. He has always treated me as a child even though we now have three children. When I say I would like to get a job or I would like to have more freedom, he gets upset. I want to be part of making decisions and I want to make more American friends. He gets angry because a 'good wife' would not want that."

Although families-of-origin are a primary force in influencing the development of a new system, other sources such as the media, educational and religious institutions, and significant others affect young people's ideas of how family life should be. Print and nonprint media are devoting much attention to the changing roles of men and women, facing many readers and viewers with alternative life-style possibilities. Next-door neighbors, extended family members, and family friends may provide models of various family forms.

When you look at your current interpersonal behaviors, you may see reflections of your family-of-origin. If you have formed a new system, you probably have adjusted to behaviors that reflect your partner's family-of-origin. You will adapt to that family's network and follow some (or all) of its rules. Family-of-origin issues influence all aspects of family communication and account for many of the communication patterns, rules, and networks you bring to a new relationship.

The importance of a family-of-origin is summarized well by Kramer (1985) in her description of its influence on a child's view of the world:

> He observes the environment he inhabits, partakes of its ambiance. He forms values and beliefs; develops assumptions about how marriages and families are and should be; learns about the life cycle, including how to handle the changes of maturation and of aging and death. He learns about power and control and about the consequences of emotions, both his own and others. He is schooled in patterns of communication: what role to take in triangles; how to handle secrets; how to respond to pressure.   (9)

Family Communication Rules

To truly understand a family, you need to become aware of its rules, particularly those regarding interaction. As you learned in Chapter 2, rules are relationship agreements that prescribe and limit a family's behavior over time. A family acts as a rule-governed system: family members interact with each other in an organized, redundant fashion, creating patterns that direct family life. Rules serve as generative mechanisms capable of creating regularity where none exists. In most cases, rules reflect patterns that have become "oughts" or "shoulds." Cronen et al. (1979) suggest that rules exist in social situations because social behavior has regularities, even though individuals may act in unpredictable ways and persons judge each other and hold each other accountable for their actions. Because of their regularities, rules serve a powerful function in coordinating meanings between people.

Although there are individual rules such as "I always bring a gift to a hostess" and standardized usage rules such as "Everyone stops at a red light," we are concerned with the *interpersonal generative function* of rules. This term refers to our tendency to "develop rules unique to a specific interaction situation and to repeat them until they become reflected in patterns of behavior" (Yerby and Buerkel-Rothfuss, 3).

Rules vary on a continuum of awareness. They range from very direct, explicit, conscious relationship agreements which may have been negotiated to the implicit, unspoken, unconscious rules emerging from repeated interactions. Whereas the former are rather straightforward, the latter are extremely complex and convoluted. Because of this complexity, much of our discussion will center on rules that can be recognized, even if they are not named or negotiated.

Development of Rules.   Since birth we have learned to adjust to social and personal regulation, and we have expected others to do the same in a predictable way. We were raised in a world of rules, particularly communication rules, but how did we learn them? We learned some through conscious discussion, but we learned most through redundancy—repeated interactions.

Family rules may be viewed on a continuum of development ranging from conscious direct negotiation between members to invisible, unspoken repetition. In some families, particular rules are negotiated directly, such as "We will never go to bed without kissing goodnight" or "When we have children, I will do X and you will do Y." But most rules develop as a result of multiple interactions. One person's behavior becomes a powerful force capable of evoking a predictable response from the other person. In most cases, these rules are both influential and invisible. They are so much a part of the family's way of life that they are not recognized or named.

"As I look back on my family-of-origin, I can recognize some patterns and rules that I never understood when I lived there. For example, although there was a spoken rule about saying what's on your mind, there was also an unspoken rule: 'Don't criticize your father.' When my brother Jamie mouthed off to my father or blamed him for something, the house would go crazy. My mother would start trying to feed people, and one of the kids would usually take Dad's side and tell Jamie he was wrong."

Many rules reflect the couple's families-of-origin rules which, if not questioned, pass on from generation to generation. If spouses come from families with dissimilar rules, greater struggle will take place before the new system can reach a relatively stable state.

Persons who form a system must be sensitive to the relational consequences of their acts. Consider the difficulties if two people bring to their marriage the following individual rules for behavior during a family argument:

Person 1: If one person discloses a very negative emotion, the other should leave the room to consider it carefully and refrain from spontaneous response.

Person 2: If one person discloses a very negative emotion, the other should respond with emotional supportiveness. To leave the room would indicate total rejection.

You can imagine the process of rule negotiation that would have to occur in order for these two people to achieve a communication pattern with which both of them feel comfortable.

Analysis of any rule-bound system requires an understanding of the mutual influence patterns within which the rules function. Due to the transactional nature of communication within a system, the mutual influence process will result in new relational patterns. This process has been described as follows:

No matter how well one knows the rules of communicator A, one cannot predict the logic of his/her communication with B without knowing B's rules and how they will mesh. The responsibility for good and bad communication is thus transactive with neither A or B alone deserving praise or blame.   (Cronen et al., 36)

Once rules are established, changing them may be complicated and time-consuming unless the family has a flexible adaptation process and can recognize the rule for what it is. When a family rule has been developed over time and members are accustomed to certain "acceptable" behaviors, the family is calibrated, or "set," to regulate its behavior in accordance with the rule limits. Rules function in terms of both positive and negative feedback, although they are more likely to be thought of as negative feedback (limits) rather than positive feedback (growth). These limits can be recalibrated unconsciously or consciously. For example, rules may be renegotiated as family members pass through certain developmental stages. A child of twelve may not be allowed to disagree with his parents' decisions, but when he reaches seventeen, his parents may begin to listen to his arguments. This recalibration may not be a totally conscious process but one that evolves as the child matures toward adulthood. On the other hand, rules may be openly negotiated or changed as the result of various factors, such as member dissatisfaction or feedback from parent-teacher conferences about what is acceptable. "Provide Michaela with more limits." "Encourage Patrick to state his own opinions."

Most family rules exist within a hierarchy. The Parsons and the Coopers may each abide by the rule that troubles are shared with the family first. In the Parson family, it may be a primary concern, whereas, with the Coopers it is not at the top of the hierarchy. Once you learn the family rules, you then have to figure out the importance placed on each of them.

As implied by the word, rules involve *prescriptions*. You may have lived with certain rules for so long without discussing them that the rules are implicit but adhered to as closely as if they were printed on your kitchen wall. Yet, sometimes a member of a family system operates according to rules unknown to the others. A major source of couple conflict centers around the breaking of rules that one member of the pair may not even know exist. "You should know enough not to open my mail or listen to my phone calls." The more conscious the prescriptions, the greater the possibility of their renegotiation at appropriate times.

Imagine trying to function in your family without a large number of rules. You would probably live in total chaos. Rules provide predictability and stability in interactions and serve a *socialization*, or teaching, function for younger members. If every time a "hot" topic such as death or sex arose, a family had to renegotiate each member's response to the subject, the uncertainty would hamper any important interaction. Predictable communication patterns allow a family to carry on its functional day-to-day interactions smoothly. Members know whom to approach about what under which circumstances. There is security in such knowledge.

Function of Rules.   Rules set the limits of cohesion and adaptability within a family. In some families, one may learn that everything is to be kept within the family, intimate physical and verbal behavior is expected, and friends are to be kept at a distance. In others, one may encounter a lack of concern for protecting the privacy of family issues, suggestions that problems be taken elsewhere, and injunctions against changing one's position on a controversial point. Clearly, one's original family serves as the initial source of communication rules, which are eventually brought to a new family system, consciously or unconsciously, and interrelated with a partner's rules. Most children are socialized into these rules by verbal and nonverbal cues. Let's explore this further by using three guidelines: what can be talked about, how it can be talked about, and to whom it can be talked about (Satir, 98–99).

The first set of rules relates to *what* one is allowed to talk about. Can death, sex, salaries, drugs, and serious health problems be talked about in the family? Are there family skeletons or current relatives who are never mentioned? Most families have topics that are taboo either all the time or under certain circumstances. Sometimes family members may openly agree not to raise a particular topic, but usually, they realize it is inappropriate because of the verbal or nonverbal feedback they receive if they mention it.

"My wife and I were childhood sweethearts, and our families had been friends for years. When we married, I never thought to talk about some of our differences. For example, I grew up learning that you never talk about your personal finances outside the immediate family, and I would get really angry when my wife would talk about salaries or mortgages with our friends. I really exploded one day and she was shocked. It never occurred to her that we should not talk about money. Since that time, we've talked about many different 'rules' and resolved some of the difficulties."

Although topics may not be restricted, many families restrict the feelings that can be shared within the system—especially negative feelings that may be totally denied. Emotions such as anger, sadness, or rage may be avoided at all costs and not shared with other family members.

Decision making often provides a fertile field for family rules. Does the system allow children to question parental decisions, or are they "the law" which cannot be challenged? In some families, the inability to question decisions appears very clear, whereas in other cases, the same message is sent with subtlety.

In some families, children may hear such words as, "We're moving and that's final. I don't want to hear another word about it." Other families have rules that allow joint decision making through discussions, persuasion, or honest voting. In such cases, all members are allowed to question the decision.

Once the issue of "what one is allowed to talk about" has been considered, the next issue is *how* one can talk about it. Within your family, can you talk about things directly, really level about feelings on a particular issue, or must you hedge the topic or sneak in another idea? For example, in some families with an alcoholic member, the other family members may say, "Mom's under the weather," but no one says, "Mom is an alcoholic." There is a tacit agreement never to deal with the real issue. In dealing with death, the children may learn that "Grandpa's gone to a better world," but the reality of death is not discussed. Many couples have never drawn up a will, because they cannot find a way to talk directly to each other about the death of one of them. Some parents have prevented the treatment of their handicapped children by referring to them as "different" and ignoring the reality of their disability. Thus, the "how" may involve allusions to the topic or euphemisms for certain subjects.

Most families have rules that lead to strategies for communication—for breaking bad news, asking for money, or expressing anger. Such strategies may involve a change in both verbal and nonverbal communication behavior. A competent woman may suddenly lisp in a childish tone to express disapproval acceptably. Her husband may respond with corresponding parental behavior.

Strategy may involve the timing of conversations, such as "Don't bother your father with that while he's eating," or the timing of discussion on a particular issue, such as "We won't tell Bobby that he's adopted until he's seven years old."

"How" also involves location for communication. Many married couples have agreed not to fight in the bedroom to prevent the room from becoming associated with anger and conflict. Some families have a certain place, such as a table in the kitchen, where the "real" talking gets done. For some young people, the car serves as the place for really good conversations. In a family's communication system, the verbal and nonverbal strategies, including the issues of time and place, indicate how members may talk about things.

The final issue is *to whom* are you allowed to talk? This may be exemplified by the following: "Don't tell Grandma; she'll have a stroke if she hears about it." "Do you think Jenny is old enough to understand about custody?" In some families, the rules for "who" are related to the age of the family members. For example, while children are small, they may not hear much about family finances, but as they grow older, they are brought into the discussion of how money is spent.

You have probably experienced changes in rules as members of your family grew older and the family adapted to developmental or situational events. Sometimes, unforeseen circumstances, such as death or the breakup of a family, move a child into a conversation circle that would have been denied otherwise. A fourteen-year-old in a single-parent family may discuss things with the parent that only the other parent typically would have heard. A widow may discuss previously undisclosed financial matters with close relatives. Family myths dictate the directions of many conversations. The message of "Don't tell so and so—she can't take it" sets up myths which may prevail for years. No one ever attempts to see if Grandma will be outraged or Cousin Alice will be angry—it is assumed, and communication proceeds accordingly.

"When I was growing up, the family myth was that we could never talk about my uncle, who died when I was eight, in front of my grandmother. We were told that 'she just falls apart if you mention his name.' Last Christmas, I stopped over to see my grandmother, and we started to talk about things that happened when I was

little. Somehow, I accidentally mentioned my uncle. This led into a discussion of him, and not only did my grandmother remain very composed, but she was glad to know that I remembered him so well. Obviously, no one checked out the myth that arose around her initial mourning behavior."

In order to fully appreciate the "what," "how," and "who" of a family's communication rules, it is necessary to analyze the system to see which rules are enforced under what circumstances. The following set of communication rules developed within one young woman's family indicate the interpersonal nature of rules:

- Don't talk back to Dad unless he's in a very silly mood.
- When mother is hassled, don't discuss school problems.
- Tell the truth at all times unless it involves a happy surprise.
- Do not fight except with Mom about your appearance.
- Don't talk about the family's money with anyone except a parent.
- Do not discuss politics or religion.
- Do not discuss sex, but act as if it were an acceptable topic for discussion.
- Don't mention Sally's boyfriend except in a very noncommital way.
- Kiss Mom when coming and going. Kiss Dad at night. Don't kiss sisters.
- Family deaths are discussed only in terms of future in heaven.
- Grandpa's cancer is not discussed.
- Mother's pregnancy at marriage is not admitted.

The author of these rules concluded that she had learned to differentiate well among people and circumstances but had not experienced very direct open communication in her family. The factors of what, how, and who provided her with a way for looking at such basic issues within her family's communication rules.

Rules are affected by cultural or ethnic backgrounds. In discussing problems in doing therapy with multi-generational Irish families, McGoldrick and Pearce (1981) suggest that interviews with family members may be frustrated by "clamming up," because there are particularly strong rules about sharing personal information with those of the opposite sex or different generations. Each ethnic or cultural group may have its own rules.

Metarules.   In addition to ordinary rules, there are rules about rules, or *metarules.* As Laing (1972) aptly states, "There are rules against seeing the rules, and hence against seeing all the issues that arise from complying with or breaking them" (106). When a couple does not make a will because of the difficulty of dealing with death, there may also be a rule that they do not talk about their rules about ignoring death. Each pretends they are too busy or too poor to bother. The following thoughtful analysis of the rules in the previous young woman's family indicates this meta level of rule-bound behavior.

"Sex may be a topic that is never mentioned and so, becomes one of those topics you should forget. In order to forget it, you must make the rule saying you can't mention the rule that forbids the discussion of sex. In this way, you can pretend it isn't forbidden and that deep levels of communication actually exist. We may laugh at a guest's dirty joke or my mother will set a very strict curfew for my younger sister, but no one ever directly discusses sex. Yet, we pretend we can."

Perceiving the metarules of your own system is very difficult, because we are not used to thinking about the basic rules, much less the metarules. We live within powerful patterns, giving limited attention to most of them. Yet, they give meaning to our relationships.

Breaking the rules may result in the creation of a new set as the system recalibrates itself to accept a wider variety of behavior. Old patterns may shift. For example, "I have broken the rule about not discussing sex by openly discussing my living arrangement with my mother. She is now completely vulnerable, because she can no longer use the familiar pattern of communication." Although a period of chaos may precede the emergence of a new set of rules, the new system may be more open and flexible as a result.

The process of forming new systems through marriage or remarriage provides fertile ground for renegotiating existing rules and requires adaptation skills. For example, the rules become even more complicated in blended families, where people come together having learned sets of communication rules in other systems. When widowed or divorced persons remarry, they may involve each of their immediate families in a large recalibration process as the new family system is formed. Although rules serve the practical function of getting us from day to day without renegotiating every interaction, they can stifle interaction unless we remain aware of their function and become flexible to change.

Family Communication Networks

Family members use communication to organize themselves into a group that can share messages in a predictable fashion. By establishing certain channels for information, a family shares its meanings through both the interaction and its prescribed flow. We refer to the patterned channels of information flow as *family networks*.

By definition, a network determines the two-way flow of messages from one family member to one or more other members or significant others outside the family. Family members regulate the direction of message flow up, down, or across the lines of the network. The direction of this flow may be horizontal, as when one sister wants to find out something and asks another sister, who in turn may ask another brother, or when parents and children sit down and work out problems together. In such cases, all persons have an equal say, and status or role differences are minimized. The communication is vertical when real or imagined power differences are reflected in the interaction. For example, although the Turner children may share in many family decisions, they know that certain things are not negotiable. Mrs. Turner sets curfew and limits on the car, which means she hands down information on these topics in a vertical manner.

Over time, families develop communication networks to deal with the general issue of cohesion and specific issues, such as carrying out instructions, organizing activities, regulating time and space, and sharing resources. Family adaptability may be seen through the degree of flexibility in forming and reforming networks. Families with high adaptability and flexible rules may use a wide variety of network arrangements; families with low adaptability and rigid rules may consistently use the same networks for all concerns.

These networks are a vital part of the decision-making process and relate to the power dynamics operating within the family. Certain networks facilitate dominance, while others promote more shared communication. Networks also play an integral part in maintaining the roles and rules operating within the family system. Thus, networks and rules have mutual influence—rules may dictate the use of certain networks; networks create certain rule patterns.

Types of Networks. To become aware of networks, observe the usual flow of verbal exchanges between members of a family. Who talks to whom about what? This processing of communication may be horizontal or vertical and take one of several forms: a chain, Y, wheel, or all-channel. Message paths indicate much about family relationships.

"There are four girls in our family, and we have a very set pattern for requesting things from our mother or father. Gina tells Angela, who tells Celeste; Celeste tells me, and I talk to Mom. Usually, things stop there, because she makes most of the decisions. If it is something really important, she will discuss it with Dad and tell me their decision. Then I relay the message down the line."

The previous example demonstrates the *chain network*. It has a hierarchy built into it in that messages proceed up through the links or down from an authority source. Quite often, a father or mother controls the chain network and passes out orders to children. For example, in male-dominated families, the father may control the flow of messages on vital family issues. As in all of these networks, there

Figure 3–1 _____
Chain Network

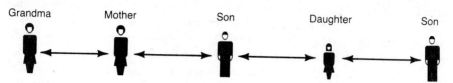

Grandma   Mother   Son   Daughter   Son

are times when the chain has definite advantages. All busy families tend to rely on a chain network when certain members cannot spend much time together.

Sometimes, chains keep certain family members separated. If Annemarie always avoids dealing with her stepfather by communicating all her desires or concerns through her mother, she will remain very distant from him. People may obey the rules about who you cannot talk to directly about a subject by using a chain network. In this type of network, there can be a two-way exchange of information between all except the end members, who have only one member with whom to communicate (see Figure 3–1).

In the _Y network,_ messages are channeled through one person to one or more other family members. In blended families with a new stepparent, the biological parent may consciously or unconsciously set up a Y network, separating the stepparent from the children (see Figure 3–2). For example, such families may have rules that only the biological parent can discipline the children.

The _wheel network_ depends upon one family member to channel all messages to other members. It can be quite autocratic if the control figure in the network operates that way. He or she can filter and adapt messages positively or negatively or enforce the rule about how things are said as they pass through the network. He or she can balance tensions in the family system effectively or ineffectively. The central individual's function may result in dominance or exhaustion. Since only

Figure 3–2 _____
Y Network

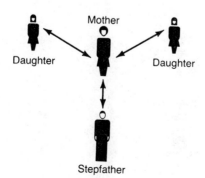

Mother

Daughter   Daughter

Stepfather

one person communicates with all the others, this person becomes critical to the ongoing family functioning. When the communication load is heavy and concentrated, as it can be when all family members want to get off to work or school, the talents and patience of the family member in the wheel network can be severely taxed (see Figure 3–3). In some families, the central member of the wheel network can be quite nurturing and effective in holding a family together.

> "My mother was the hub of the wheel in our family. When we were children, we expected her to settle our problems with other family members. She always knew what everyone was doing and how they felt. When we left home, each of us always let Mom know what we were doing and continued to use her for a sounding board. We felt almost compelled to write or telephone once a week. Mom digested the family news and told my brothers and sisters what each of us was doing. For several years after her death, we children had little contact except occasionally with our father. Now, seven years later, we have formed a new subsystem in which four of us stay in contact with each other. One sister, Mary Alice, is the new hub."

Messages in chain, Y, and wheel networks are filtered and so, can become distorted as they pass from one person to another. A family member can selectively change parts of a message he or she dislikes. This may help to defuse some family conflicts, but misinformation could escalate others.

The *all-channel network* provides two-way exchange between or among all family members. Communication flows in all directions, effective decisions can be made because all members have an equal chance to discuss family issues and respond to them. This network provides for the maximum use of feedback. All interaction can be direct and transactional. No family member serves as a "go-between," and each participates freely in the process of sharing information or deciding issues (see Figure 3–4). Yet, if the rules say that certain subjects should not be raised, access will have little effect. Although this network allows equal participation, it can be the most disorganized and chaotic, since messages flow in

Figure 3—3
Wheel Network

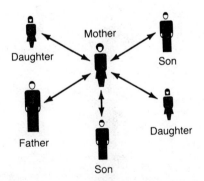

all directions. Each family member may compete for "air time" to ventilate his or her views.

Network Variations. Other networks are possible in families, including combinations under certain circumstances. The ends of the chain may link forming a circle; chains may lead toward the central figure in the wheel. Most families use a variety of networks as they progress through daily life. Special issues arise that may cause a family to change the usual network patterns and adopt new ones to solve the issue. In daily life for example, a family may operate essentially in the chain and wheel networks, but when vacations are planned, the network used is all-channel.

The definition of networks includes the possibility that significant others outside the immediate family may have an influence upon the communication patterns within it if the boundaries are permeable. A *significant other* is a person who has an intimate relationship with one or more of the family members. This may be a grandparent, aunt or uncle, close family friend, lover, or fiancé of one of the children. In some cultures, godparents or old family friends are included in the network. The family member who has ties to a significant other outside the family may very well make decisions within the network that were determined by this relationship. When children leave home and form their own family networks, a parent may remain a significant other and influence the operation of the new network. Problems with in-laws arise often because the networks are intertwined and boundaries are not established.

Family networks tend to change over time. As children grow up and increasingly take over the direction of their own lives, adaptive families often move from the chain or wheel network to the all-channel. The wheel and chain networks facilitate order and discipline but may no longer be needed when children become autonomous and capable of directing their own decision making. Parents may signal their recognition of these changes by permitting more issues to be discussed via an all-channel network. The loss of a member can send the system into chaos. When a key member dies or leaves, entire systems may fragment. After a divorce,

Figure 3—4 _____
All-Channel Network

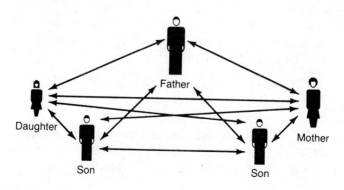

family members must establish new networks, often involving additional members, in order to maintain certain types of contact.

As we saw in Chapter 2, subgroups and alliances may emerge within families—such connections interact with the family networks. The two people on one end of the chain may become very close and support each other in all situations. The key person in the Y formation may ally with another member and keep certain information from the others, or control certain information. Some family members may never relate directly as the parts of the network form small groups that support or relate to each other.

Because each family functions within the larger ecosystem, it must involve itself with a wide variety of social system networks, both informal and formal. For many families, the informal networks created by the community or friends provide support and comfort in crises. For example, families experiencing divorce or remarriage report a high need for community and friend support. Such informal networks also provide valuable information and feedback to a family. In addition, family members become involved in formal networks created by educational, religious, and health institutions. Members must exchange information with representatives of these institutions in order to survive in our interdependent society.

Thus, networks serve a very important function within families. They determine who talks to whom, who is included or excluded, who gets full or partial information, and who controls certain information. Yet, the rules for what, how, and to whom to communicate exist within each style of network.

CONCLUSION

In this chapter, we explored how a family creates its own identity. We examined the importance of coordinated meanings between family members and how those meanings are developed through repeated interpretation and evaluation. We described how meaning functions within close relationships using the categories of richness, uniqueness, efficiency, substitutability, pacing, openness, spontaneity, and evaluation.

We also examined the patterns that family systems need to provide order and predictability for their members, focusing specifically on family-of-origin influences, communication rules, and family networks. We discussed how each contributes to unique family meanings and how each factor influences the others.

As we will see throughout the book, patterns serve as the skeletal structure for family life, reflecting and determining relationships.

IN REVIEW

1. Analyze a two-person family relationship giving examples of verbal and nonverbal communication, which are representative of Altman and Taylor's characteristics of developed relationships (p. 44).

2. Take a position and discuss: To what extent does the family-of-origin influence the communication patterns of future generations?
3. What cultural or unique communication patterns have been passed down from your family-of-origin?
4. Describe three incidents in a real or fictional family's development that demonstrate specific communication rules by which the members live.
5. Using a real or fictional family, describe how the most frequently used communication networks have changed over time due to developmental change or family crisis.

Chapter 4

Communication of Intimacy Within Families

What keeps one husband and wife attracted to each other for years? How do young people move from being "the kids" to being sharing adults with their parents? Why do members of one family drift apart, while members of another remain close and caring throughout a lifetime? Part of the answer rests with the family's level of intimacy.

Every family must engage in the kinds of communication that keep the home running, children fed, clothes washed, car gassed, and bills paid. Life revolves around the patterns and routines that get us from day to day, and communication must support such task-oriented interactions. Yet, all families have the opportunity to provide their members with different kinds of communication experiences—including those that nurture the relationships involved. Such communication contributes to intimacy among family members.

In this chapter, we will focus on how communication influences the development of intimacy among family members. We assume that such intimacy requires effort and risk-taking behaviors but that it provides rewards for the persons who choose to develop such closeness in their relationships. In order to explore how intimacy is communicated within families, we will look at: (1) the development of intimacy, (2) communication strategies that promote intimacy, and (3) barriers to intimacy.

DEVELOPMENT OF INTIMACY

Intimate relationships may be characterized by mutual devotion and committed love involving our intellectual, emotional, and physical capacities (Spooner, 1982; Ramey, 1976). Feldman (1979) suggests that marital intimacy involves the following characteristics: (1) a close, familiar, and usually affectionate or loving personal relationship; (2) a detailed and deep knowledge and understanding arising from close personal connection or familiar experience; and (3) sexual relations (70). With the exception of sexual relations, this definition may be applied to all family relationships. Family intimacy involves mutual devotion and intellectual, emotional, and physical dimensions demonstrated by (1) shared knowledge and understanding and (2) close loving relationships. Such a concept of intimacy is translated into reality differently in every family system and subsystem.

Acceptable levels of family intimacy are calibrated through the interaction of family members. The level established for a particular relationship reflects a meshing of the members' past intimate experiences, need for intimacy, and need for predictability within a relationship. From his work with marital couples, Feldman has hypothesized that some couples experience a nonproductive intimacy-conflict cycle. He suggests that when one member of a couple feels that the intimacy is becoming too great, he or she will initiate some type of conflictual behavior to decrease the amount of interpersonal intimacy.

The same concept may be applied to other family relationships. Each two-person subsystem sets its limits for acceptable intimacy. A small son and his mother may cuddle, tickle, kiss, and hug. A teenager and mother may share important events and exchange kisses on occasion. A husband and wife develop limits for acceptable and unacceptable sexual intimacy as well as for sharing feelings and showing affection. These acceptable limits of intimacy reflect certain ways of showing affection and certain stages in relationship development.

Relational Currencies

As we discussed in Chapter 3, family members develop a set of behaviors that have meaning within their relationships. Thus, a wife may cook beef stew to please her husband or a grandfather may rock a grandchild for an hour while telling him stories of years gone by. Each of these instances represents an attempt to share affection, but the meaning depends on a shared perception. The husband may devour the stew and understand the affection, or he may wish his wife had made lasagna; the grandchild may "snuggle in" or long for escape.

Communication behaviors that carry meaning about the affection or caring dimension of human relationships can be viewed as *relational currency*. This concept is based on the premise that all relationships involve: (1) an investment of time and/or money, (2) a trading of currencies, and (3) a degree of risk-taking. The currencies that are exchanged may be intimate or economic (Villard and Whipple, 1976).

Intimate currencies are personal verbal and nonverbal ways of sending relationship messages. For example, one can smile, hug, engage in intercourse, and exchange secrets as ways of sharing affection. Thus, physical or psychological identity is shared with another. Intimate currencies make a direct statement. The act is the message—a hug means "I'm glad to see you," or "I'm sorry you are leaving." Usually, the sender's intent is clear and easily interpreted. Economic currencies may involve loaning money or possessions, doing favors, giving gifts, or sharing things or time with one another. Economic currencies permit a greater range of interpretation. Exactly what is the message contained within the act of sending a bouquet of flowers? After a family quarrel, does the arrival of flowers mean "I'm sorry," "Let's keep the peace," or "I still love you even if we don't agree on one issue"? The message of such a relational currency may not be as direct as the message sent through a smile, hug, or words of endearment. There are many possible relational currencies; Table 4–1 lists some of the behaviors that family members commonly use to share affection.

Although relational currencies may be exchanged with the best intentions, accurate interpretation occurs only when both parties agree upon the meaning of the act. Misunderstandings may be more frequent when two family systems attempt to blend into a new one. For example, in the man's family, gifts may be given often for no special occasion as ways of saying, "I care." If the woman comes from a family where this was not practiced, she may be delighted to start a new tradition and give and receive gifts at nonspecial occasions, or she may have difficulty adapting to this type of relational message. She might think it is a waste of money to buy non-holiday gifts, or she may never think to reciprocate on ordinary days, leaving her husband to feel unappreciated. Thus, if mutually shared norms for exchanging affection do not exist, family members need to negotiate about this type of communication if relational messages are to be received as they were intended.

Relational currencies that are repeated regularly may come to be taken for granted. The service of an early riser who puts on coffee although she drinks tea may be a service that becomes expected. An empathic listener may be barraged by words from speakers who do not value the listener's investment. Even greetings with hugs and kisses can become routine and lose their meaning in the hassles of everyday life.

Without common meanings for relational currencies, family members may feel hurt or rejected. For example, one spouse may consider sex to be the ultimate currency in married life and place a high value on sexual relations. This may include the expectations that sexual relations will be exclusive to the dyad and that sex will be engaged in only when both people are satisfied in the relationship and desire to have sex. If the other partner holds similar views, the sexual currency will be appropriately exchanged. Yet, if the other partner does not place the same value on the sexual act, finding it acceptable to have sexual relations outside the marriage or expecting to have sexual relations at any time whether or not things are going well for the couple, these two people will have difficulty with the communication of affection through this currency.

Table 4–1
Sample Relational Currencies

Positive verbal statements	Gifts
Self-disclosure	Money
Listening	Food
Facial Expressions	Favors
Touch	Service
Sexuality	Time together
Aggression	Access rights

The term "aggression" connotes actions usually thought to be incompatible with affection. Yet, aggressive actions may serve as the primary emotional connection between members of certain families. Persons who are frightened to express intimacy directly but who wish to feel connected may use verbal or physical aggression as a sign of caring. When adults do not know how to express intimacy in positive ways, children may experience hitting, sarcasm, or belittling as the only means of parental contact. Some conflictual couples may maintain their contact through screaming and hitting, which have become relational currencies within that family system. Such relationships contain limited rewards. Children raised in households in which aggression is a primary relational currency may have difficulty developing strong friendships and marital relationships using such currencies as self-disclosure and positive verbal statements.

The values of currencies often reflect family-of-origin patterns for sharing affection. A man who resists touching and cuddling but does favors for all his friends may reflect a family-of-origin in which males do not hug or cuddle.

"My father never used touch or positive statements as a way of saying, 'I love you.' He always gave big gifts to indicate caring during holidays and birthdays. As a child, it was hard for me to feel loved, since my father did not demonstrate affection. As an adult, I have come to understand the gift giving as my father's way of making contact. He came from a family that was not affectionate, and he was unable to display any of the behaviors that came so easily to my mother. Although I still value touching, positive statements, and self-disclosure as the most important signs of affection, I can make room for my father's way of expressing affection, and I no longer get angry about what he is unable to do."

What happens if family members wish to share affection but seem unable to exchange the currencies desired by others? After interviewing married couples, Villard concluded that spouses with more similar affection exchange behaviors were more likely to report (a) high levels of perceived equity and (b) higher levels of relationship satisfaction, thus greater relationship reward. Interestingly, accuracy in predicting (i.e., understanding) how the other spouse used currencies did not raise equity or satisfaction levels. Just knowing that your husband sends love messages through flowers does not mean that you will be more positive toward this currency if you prefer intimate currencies. People who were very accurate at predicting how their spouses would respond to certain items still reported "low equity and low marital satisfaction if the couple was dissimilar in their affection behaviors" (Millar et al., 1978, 15). Unfortunately, this finding, coupled with the finding that wives are more likely to use intimate currencies, suggests that "many marriages may be predisposed to unhappiness, unfulfillment, conflict and/or divorce because of socialized differences between men and women in how they share 'who they are' and how they manifest 'affection'" (15).

A family's levels of cohesion and adaptability interact with its communication of affection. Highly cohesive families may demand large amounts of affection displayed with regularity, whereas low-cohesion families may not provide enough affection for certain members. Systems near the chaotic end of the adaptability continuum may change the type of currencies used and valued frequently, while more rigid systems may require the consistent and exclusive use of a particular currency. Family themes may dictate the amount or type of currencies used. "The Hatfields will stick by each other through thick and thin" may set the expectation that family caring will be supported by providing money for hard-pressed members. Boundaries may establish which members or outsiders may receive more personal types of affection.

Because the family system evolves constantly, personal meanings placed on intimate or economic currencies change over time. As relationships mature, members may change their ways of sharing affection because of new experiences, pressures, or expectations. For example, certain biosocial beliefs about sex roles may hinder a man from displaying affection at first, but as he becomes comfortable as a father and husband, he may be open to using more intimate currencies. Economic conditions also affect how certain currencies are exchanged. A lost job may result in fewer gifts but more sharing and favors within a family. Such changes may affect the levels of relationships attained by family members. For example, if an unemployed executive is able to share his feelings and frustrations, the self-disclosure may deepen his relationship with his wife. Once employed, he may not have the time or inclination to continue their sharing sessions, and the relationship may return to its previous level of intimacy.

The process of exchanging relational currencies significantly affects the level of intimacy attained by the family members. In the next sections, we will discuss how the depth of a relationship is influenced by the exchange of currencies, and we will expand our discussion of selected currencies.

Relationship Development and Intimacy

Carl Sandburg once said, "Life is like an onion. You peel off one layer at a time and sometimes you weep." People in relationships share their layers, smiling or weeping in parts of the process. Interpersonal ties and, therefore, intimacy develop incrementally as we discover other people or share layers of ourselves through communication. This interpersonal exchange gradually progresses from superficial nonintimate areas to deeper layers of the self. Although we will look at family development in Chapter 9, we will briefly examine relationship development as it affects family intimacy. We exclude small children from this process because relationship development models assume direct and conscious effort on the part of the persons involved.

Social Penetration Model. There are many ways of looking at the relationship development process. Wilmot (1980) talks broadly about relationship initiation, stabilization, and dissolution. In keeping with this overall framework, we can briefly examine the work of Altman and Taylor (1973) and Knapp (1984). Altman and Taylor propose a model of *social penetration*. They hypothesize that interpersonal exchange gradually progresses from superficial, nonintimate areas to more intimate, deeper layers of the self; people assess interpersonal costs and rewards gained from interaction. The future development of a relationship depends on the quality and quantity of these rewards and costs (6). These psychologists propose a model of four stages, movement through which is related to the eight characteristics of a developed relationship discussed in Chapter 3. As you recall, these include: richness, uniqueness, efficiency, substitutability, pacing, openness, spontaneity, and evaluation (Altman and Taylor, 129). The extent to which these dimensions exist in a relationship is reflected by the communication that occurs between the persons involved; each dimension becomes more apparent as the relationship moves through the stages toward the highest point. Movement through the stages also depends on the perceived cost and rewards as estimated by each person in the relationship.

The model is best understood by picturing a continuum (Figure 4–1) with guidelines for movement through the stages. The levels represent where the relationship is at a given time, even if one or the other persons involved wishes it were different. Although we talk about relationship is within a system, each relationship reflects the connectedness or distance between two system members. For example, three sisters would not move through the stages as one relationship. These would be three separate dyadic relationships that might be very similar and overlap, but each relationship belongs to a dyad.

The *orientation stage* represents the first meetings between people. People tend to follow traditional social rules, try to make a good first impression, and attempt to avoid conflict. In short, they try to reduce uncertainty about the other person and increase their ability to predict future interactions. Except for situations that involve babies or very small children, all family relationships start at this point, although some previous information may have been known about the "other." Future spouses may have been coworkers or classmates who met at the watercooler or in geology class. Future stepfathers and stepchildren may have skirted around countless topics as they tried to be polite "for Mom's sake."

The second stage, *exploratory affective exchange*, is characterized by the relationship between casual acquaintances or friendly neighbors. By this point, the

Figure 4—1
Stages of Relationship Development

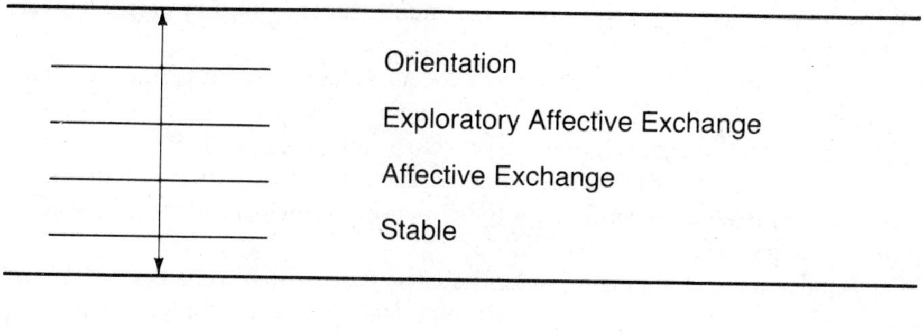

Orientation

Exploratory Affective Exchange

Affective Exchange

Stable

relationship contains some honest sharing of opinions or feelings that are not too personal, but no real sense of commitment exists. Most relationships do not go beyond this second casual exploratory stage.

Countless family relationships remain at this stage. Uncle Ned may be delightful, but you do not seek him out beyond the annual Christmas get-together. Siblings may find friends with whom they have stronger bonds than with one another. Although their relationships may be pleasant, no strong sibling ties exist. Some parent-child or husband-wife relationships function at a level of acquaintances with little sense of commitment or deep involvement.

The third stage, *affective exchange,* is characterized by close friendships or courtship relationships in which people know each other well, reflecting a fairly extensive history of association based on reciprocity. This association may be built over a long period of time or through intense short meetings. Communication includes sharing positive and negative messages, including evaluations. By this stage, members of the relationship enjoy richness and uniqueness. There are private references, shared in-jokes, and mutually understood gestures or glances. Communication sensitivity increases. People outside the relationship may be able to recognize close friends by displays of open affection from touching to teasing. Although very intimate areas of personality may still remain closed, high levels of self-disclosure occur and a strong trust develops. By the time a relationship reaches the affective exchange level, a real commitment exists and the relationship itself is likely to be a subject of conversation.

"My relationship with my daughter in college has developed into a friendship. Karen and I went through some rough times when she was in high school, but in the past two years we have developed a closeness I never thought possible. We can sit down and share some very personal thoughts. I am learning to let her be an adult and have stopped trying to impose my way of life on her. I think because of that she is willing to tell me more about her life. There are certain parts of my life I may never be able to tell my daughter about, but it is such a pleasure to have an adult female friend who is also my child."

Some family relationships may exist at this level for long periods of time, while others remain at lower areas of the continuum. As children grow old enough to try to develop or maintain relationships, they can participate more fully in the transactional process needed to reach the affective exchange level. Often, such abilities are a reflection of the type of communication modeled by older members of the system and the intimacy they encourage.

Such relationship levels are likely to occur in families with themes that support close interactions and interpersonal boundaries that permit extensive sharing. This stage is the highest relational level that many people will ever experience. Many marriages exist at the affective exchange level, and partners remain either satisfied or frustrated, depending on their spouses. Many people find this level of intimacy sufficient.

Finally, some relationships enter the *stable stage,* which is characterized most often by committed, intimate friendships or familial relationships. Openness, richness, and spontaneity abound. In a relationship at this level, you are likely to experience your highest levels of self-disclosure. Both negative and positive aspects of personality are shared and accepted. At the stable level, communication is efficient, verbal and nonverbal cues are easily interchanged, and predictions are made with accuracy. In addition to verbal sharing, there is a freedom of access to each other's personal belongings that may not have been available before.

Yet, even these unique relationships require extensive effort if they are to be maintained. Partners who share a stable relationship are very aware of each other's needs and the ways in which each is changing. They are willing to engage in intense risk-taking behavior to maintain their relationship.

"After twenty-six years of marriage my parents seem to have an incredibly close relationship that I haven't seen in other people. They often hold hands. They share a great deal of common interest in music and will play together. They just can't get enough of each other. Life hasn't been all that easy for them, either. But they have coped with these things together and I think it has increased their love. After all these years of living together, they almost sound alike. They finish each other's sentences and seem to have a shorthand by which they understand each other. I'm very grateful to them for what they have taught me about loving another person."

Such relationships usually require a high investment of time, energy, and sensitivity, but participants find great rewards from their interactions. Again, family themes, images, and boundaries influence the ability of a relationship to move to, or remain at, such an intense level of sharing. The participants have to reach mutually acceptable levels of adaptation and cohesion.

We are not suggesting that a relationship may actually follow the four stages easily and simply. Some relationships may speed through certain stages; others may remain at one stage for years. Other relationships may move through the levels as the partners' lives change. Relationships that proceed too quickly to core areas may have to retrace steps through beginning stages.

Altman and Taylor suggest that the process can be reversed when considering the dissolution of a relationship. For example, a couple may have moved toward the stable stage before the birth of their children, but attending to the children may have taken so much time and energy that the couple's relationship moves to the lower level of affective exchange. We will explore this issue further in Chapter 11.

Model of Interaction Stages.   In his extension of Altman and Taylor's work, Knapp has proposed a model of interaction stages in relationships that details five coming-together and five coming-apart stages (Table 4–2). This model appears more heavily oriented toward male-female romantic relationships.

Knapp suggests that stages overlap each other and therefore defines stages by the greatest proportion of certain activity. A brief review of the coming-together stages will demonstrate their connection to intimacy.

The initiating stage consists of the brief opening period when one first encounters another person. It involves scanning the person according to one's own

Table 4–2
A Model of Interaction Stages

Process	Stage	Representative Dialogue
	Initiating	"Hi, how ya doin'?" "Fine. You?"
	Experimenting	"Oh, so you like to ski . . . so do I." "You do?! Great. Where do you go?"
Coming Together	Intensifying	"I . . . think I love you." "I love you too."
	Integrating	"I feel so much a part of you." "Yeah, we are like one person. What happens to you happens to me."
	Bonding	"I want to be with you always." "Let's get married."
	Differentiating	"I just don't like big social gatherings." "Sometimes I don't understand you. This is one area where I'm certainly not like you at all."
	Circumscribing	"Did you have a good time on your trip?" "What time will dinner be ready?"
Coming Apart	Stagnating	"What's there to talk about?" "Right. I know what you're going to say and you know what I'm going to say."
	Avoiding	"I'm so busy, I just don't know when I'll be able to see you." "If I'm not around when you try, you'll understand."
	Terminating	"I'm leaving you . . . and don't bother trying to contact me." "Don't worry."

perceptions and initiating an interaction. Once communication is initiated, the participants enter the experimenting stage, trying to discover the unknown through rather predictable small-talk exchanges. At this stage, commitments are limited and relationships appear casual, overtly uncritical, and pleasant.

When people becomes "close friends," their relationship reaches the intensifying stage, characterized by active participation and greater awareness of self. This stage involves increased intimacy through personal self-disclosure and verbal changes, such as "we" statements, private symbols and shorthand, and direct expressions of commitment such as "We really have a good thing going." Nonverbal comfort and flexibility increase. Knapp's integrating stage is that of a merging experience when the two personalities seem to fuse, or coalesce. This may be seen in (1) increased attitude similarity, (2) merging social roles, (3) exchange of "intimacy trophies," such as pins or rings, (4) similarity in manner, dress, or verbal behavior, (5) full physical intimacy, (6) established common property, (7) high empathy, (8) synchronized routines, and (9) shared affection for a third person or object (38). This does not mean complete loss of individuality, but does represent high intimacy.

The final stage, bonding, is a public ritual that announces to the world that commitments have been formally contracted (39). In essence, bonding institutionalizes the relationship. Traditionally, this involves going steady, engagement, and/or marriage. Knapp sees bonding as a way of gaining social or institutional support for the relationship. Whereas rituals such as baptism, circumcision, or legal adoption could be viewed as examples of family bonding, it is more difficult to imagine traditionally accepted bonding experiences for homosexual pairs, stepchildren and stepparents, or long-term foster families.

Both Altman and Taylor's and Knapp's models address issues of voluntary relationships. There has been little careful study of nonvoluntary relationships, such as those experienced within some stepfamilies. Such relationships may begin with stages characteristic of deteriorating relationships, such as low self-disclosure and spontaneity (Cooper, 1984).

You should be able to see how some of the previously described stages relate to your own life. Perhaps you developed a deep relationship with an older brother or sister as you grew into a young adult. Perhaps you watched parental or other relationships suffer and move down the stages. Such movement affects not only the participants in the specific relationship but all members of the systems to which they are connected.

In his discussion of relationships in the future, Toffler (1971) raises the issue of expected relationship turnover and suggests that family relationships are expected to last longer than what he considers "medium duration relationships" (relationships with friends, neighbors, job associates, and co-members of voluntary organizations). He suggests that "we expect ties with immediate family and to a lesser extent with other kin, to extend throughout the lifetime of the people involved" (100). However, people involved in long-term relationships cannot remain at a peak level of communication. They cannot center all their time and energy on the relationship. Many relationships will never reach the affective exchange or stable level and those that do can expect to move downward at specific periods with the potential of developing more strongly in the future.

Setting Limits on Intimacy. Although all humans seem to have intimacy needs—to be loved, held, touched, and nurtured—there may also be a fear of intimacy: a fear of being controlled by another, loved and left by another, or possessed by another, all of which keep relationships from reaching high stages of involvement. Thus, the needs and fears, rewards and costs, become calibrated as the balance of the intimacy scale is set, at least for a certain period of time.

Each family system is influenced by its overall themes, images, and boundaries, which indicate some acceptable intimacy limits for family members. Family themes that stress verbal sharing, such as "There are no secrets in this family," may promote honest disclosure if a sense of community and support exists. Otherwise, such themes may promote painful secrets. Risks may be taken with someone you perceive to be a warm caregiver rather than with another you view as an unfeeling "computer." Family boundaries influence how much intimacy is shared among family subsystems and how much intimacy may be developed with those outside the immediate family. Biosocial beliefs may support or restrict the capacity of members in certain roles or power positions to develop certain levels of intimacy. The belief that a father has to remain slightly aloof from his children to be respected in a "head of the household" position limits the level of intimacy he will reach with his children as long as that belief is maintained.

Knowledge about another family member is not sufficient to develop intimacy. Relational growth depends on communication of and about that knowledge (Duck, et al., 1984, 295). In the following pages, we will examine certain communication behaviors that encourage the development of intimacy within marital and family systems. We will focus specifically on confirmation and response, self-disclosure, and sexual behavior.

COMMUNICATION STRATEGIES THAT PROMOTE INTIMACY

The basis for all relationships lies in the members' abilities to share meanings. We previously discussed relational currencies—communication behaviors that carry meaning about affection or caring dimensions of human relationships. At this point, we will examine the use of these currencies to proceed beyond pure functional family interaction. We will explore the ways certain communication strategies foster intimacy between partners and among all family members.

Confirmation

Confirming behaviors communicate acceptance of another human being—thus giving value to the other's existence. Such behaviors are likely to be perceived as rewarding by the receiver. If you remember the distinction between the content and relationship levels in a message, you will remember that the relationship level comments on the bond between people. In other words, ". . . on the relationship level people do not communicate about facts outside their relationship, but offer each other definitions of that relationship and, by implication, of themselves" (Watzlawick et al., 1967, 83–84).

Confirming responses indicate acceptance of self and the relationship definition offered by the other person in that relationship (Montgomery, 1981). Sieburg (1973) provides four criteria for confirming messages. A confirming message: (1) recognizes the other person's existence, (2) acknowledges the other's communication by responding relevantly to it, (3) reflects and accepts the other's self-experience, and (4) suggests a willingness to become involved with the other.

Confirming responses may be contrasted with two alternative responses, rejecting and disconfirming. Whereas confirming responses imply an acceptance of the other person, rejecting responses imply that the other is wrong or unacceptable; disconfirming responses imply that the other is nonexistent. Rejecting messages might include such statements as "You don't know anything," "That's really dumb," "You're a real pain," and "Don't act like a two-year-old." Disconfirming responses occur when a person is ignored, talked about as if he or she is not there, or excluded from a conversation.

"When my sister remarried, she and her new husband tried to pretend they did not have her twelve-year-old son living with them, because her new husband did not really want him. They would eat meals and forget to call him, plan trips and drop him with us at the last minute, and never check on his work in school. The kid was a nonentity in that house. Finally, his father took him, and Derrick seems much happier now."

In order to understand how confirming messages work, let us look at some underlying principles. In their summary of Sieburg's work on confirming behavior, Barbour and Goldberg (1974) developed four descriptive principles (31), which we will examine individually.

1. It is more confirming to be recognized as existing than to be treated as nonexisting.

Sometimes certain family members get the feeling they aren't there. People talk about them in front of them, ignore or interrupt them, misinterpret most of their actions, or refrain from affectionate physical contact with them.

Acknowledgment serves as a critical confirming skill in involving relevant, direct feedback responses. How often have requests for aid or statements about feelings been met with no response? People who care about each other acknowledge that they are listening and give feedback, brief or otherwise, to indicate that they heard the messages. This keeps a spouse, parent, or child from saying "I feel like I'm talking to a wall—nothing comes back."

Verbally, one may confirm others by using their names, arguing with or supporting their ideas, or acknowledging their presence. Comments such as "I missed you, I'm glad to see you" serve to confirm another verbally, particularly when accompanied by congruent nonverbal messages. In their work on communication skills related to marital satisfaction, Boyd and Roach (1977) suggest that a spouse's comments such as "I listen and attend when my spouse expresses a point of view" or "I make statements that tell my spouse that she (he) really counts with me" is characteristic of desirable behavior (541).

Nonverbal confirmation has more subtle but equal importance in signifying recognition. From earliest infancy, recognition serves as the basis for relationships. A child develops his or her earliest sense of recognition through touch. Montagu (1978) describes the importance of human tactile stimulation for the development of healthy emotional or affectional relationships. Direct eye contact and gestures may also serve to confirm another person. The bottom line is that intimacy is impossible without basic mutual recognition by the persons involved.

2. Dialogue is more confirming than monologue.

When family members say things in front of each other "without actually responding in an honest and spontaneous way to each other's ideas and feelings,

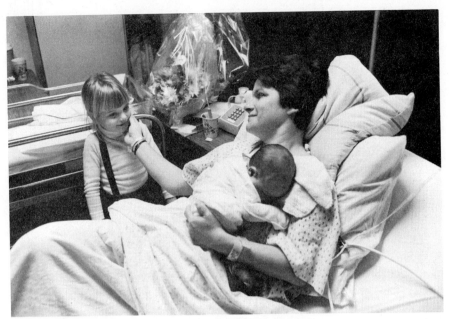

Nonverbal confirmation signifies recognition of family members.

their interaction might be described as a series of monologues rather than a dialogue" (Barbour and Goldberg, 31). Dialogue implies an interactive involvement
between two people. Husbands and wives, siblings, and parents and children must
be able to share attitudes, beliefs, opinions, and feelings and work at resolving
their differences. Comments such as "Because I said so" and "You'll do it my way
or not at all" do not reflect a dialogical attitude, whereas "What do you think?" or
"How can we solve this?" or "I'm upset—can we talk about it?" open the door to
dialogue and rewarding interactions. Boyd and Roach found comments such as "I
'check out' or ask for clarification so that I will understand my spouse's feelings and
thoughts" and "I ask honest direct questions without hidden messages" to be associated with marital satisfaction (541).

Nonverbal dialogue occurs in families where hugs, kisses, and affect displays
are mutually shared and enjoyed and where hugs of consolation or sorrow are
exchanged. Later in this chapter, we will refer to monological or dialogical
approaches to sexuality—or sexual involvement for one's own pleasure versus that
of mutual satisfaction. From our perspective, mutual concern provides confirmation within a relationship.

3. Acceptance is more confirming than interpretation.

We show acceptance when ". . . we respond to the statements of another
person by genuinely trying to understand the thought and feeling he or she has
expressed, and by reflecting that understanding in our responses" (Barbour and
Goldberg, 31). This may involve allowing ourselves to hear things we really do not
want to hear and acknowledging that we understand. Although a mother may find

it painful to hear that her son is leaving college because he has failing grades, she should not insist on an alternative explanation such as "I understand. You just need some time to find yourself."

Nonverbal messages such as a wink, smile, and barely perceptible nod that says "I agree" or "Keep up the good work" reinforce and confirm another family member. Comments or looks that tell a third party "She doesn't mean that" or "What he really means is. . . ." undermine a partner or loved one.

4. It is more confirming to be treated personally than impersonally.

How often have you revealed something to another person and had your feelings ignored? If you say, "I'm really worried about having a healthy baby," a confirming response would reflect the feeling, whereas a more impersonal response would note the statistics on having healthy babies and how you should not worry. When people label you when you are with them, you feel impersonally treated. Remarks such as "The wife likes country music, too" appear strange when both members of the couple are present. Boyd and Roach include "I allow her (him) to speak for herself (himself)" as indicative of communication leading toward marital satisfaction (541).

Impersonal responses are much more formal, contain fewer personal pronouns, and are more indirect than personal responses. When someone close to you seems to treat you exactly the way he or she treats most other people, you may not feel confirmed as special.

Confirming behaviors often reflect the specific roles and cultural backgrounds of one's family-of-origin. Persons who grew up in a family who did not express feelings may have trouble satisfying the reassurance/recognition needs of a spouse. Cultural differences in the use of eye contact or touch may create disconfirming feelings for one partner.

The role confirmation plays in developing intimate relationships cannot be overestimated. If such behaviors are viewed as rewarding and responded to with equivalent acts, a mutually rewarding relationship will result. For family members to move toward intimacy with each other, each person must feel accepted and cared for by the others. Children learn such behaviors by watching other family members and by experiencing the confirmation and affection directed at them. We can carry Montagu's comments a bit further: if "one learns to love by being loved," then one learns to confirm by being confirmed.

Self-Disclosure

People in intimate relationships need to experience openness in their communication in addition to feeling recognized and accepted. Openness (1) allows a person to be perceived by others accurately and (2) reflects the capacity of a person to perceive others as they perceive themselves (Montgomery, 22). This means that persons in intimate relationships engage in the sharing and receiving of mutual self-disclosure.

"I'm always fascinated by all the letters to the advice columnists about 'Should I tell my spouse about . . . ?' and then they mention some secret. I will be married in eight months and, although my fiancé and I have a very special relationship, there are some things he does not know about me and, I imagine, he has some secrets, too. I wonder about the value of total honesty, especially when it could hurt the other person. There are some things I don't think I'd want to hear from him."

There has been much definitional dispute about the term "self-disclosure." When we use this term, we mean "when one person voluntarily tells another things about himself which the other is unlikely to discover from other sources" (Pearce and Sharp, 1973, 414). Thus, it involves a willingness to risk private information or feelings. It also implies a willingness to accept such information or feelings from another. Self-disclosure allows a person to reduce uncertainty about the discloser, predict how rewarding or costly future interactions will be, and evaluate the discloser's personality in terms of similarity, competence, and believability (Berger and Bradac, 1982, 93).

As we discussed earlier, when people move from the orientation stage to higher levels of a relationship, the process usually involves extensive mutual self-disclosure. We make predictions about how others will deal with our disclosures and usually attempt to build up a series of positive experiences before engaging in strong negative self-disclosure.

In her examination of family self-disclosure, Gilbert (1976a) links self-disclosure to intimacy by defining intimacy as "the depth of exchange, both verbally and/or nonverbally, between two persons and which implies a deep form of acceptance of the other as well as a commitment to the relationship" (221). Thus, high mutual self-disclosure is usually associated with voluntary relationships which have reached the affective exchange or stable exchange level and which are characterized by confirmation and affection. Yet, high levels of negative self-disclosure may occur in nonvoluntary relationships characterized by conflict and anger.

Traditionally, self-disclosure has been considered desirable for fostering intimate communication within family systems. Jourard (1971) describes the optimum marriage relationship as one "where each partner discloses himself without reserve" (46). Many current marriage enrichment programs support self-disclosing behavior (Galvin, 1985), as do popular texts on the subject of marital or parent-child interaction. Premarital counseling often focuses on revealing areas of feelings or information not yet shared by the couple.

Yet, as we shall see in the next section, some cautions about unrestrained self-disclosure also need consideration. In order to understand the importance of exchanging in self-disclosure within the family system, we have to review some relevant research and examine the applicability of self-disclosure to developing family intimacy.

Much of the work in self-disclosure has been done through questionnaires and self-report forms rather than examining the actual behavior. Most of this has focused on the self-disclosing behavior of individuals and not on transactional processes. Unfortunately, the questionnaire/self-report data gained from family members, usually couples, has not been linked to clinical material provided by family theorists and therapists. What family material exists focuses on marital couples or parent-child interactions; entire family systems have not received attention. Yet, with these concerns expressed, we can look at some of the findings and draw implications for family relationships.

Research on Self-Disclosure.

Some generalizations can be made about self-disclosure in family relationships, but much of the original research in the area is under review due to more sophisticated follow-up studies. Littlejohn (1983) has summarized the findings of research in self-disclosure as follows:

(1) Disclosure increases with increased relational intimacy. (2) Disclosure increases when rewarded. (3) Disclosure increases with the need to reduce uncertainty in a relationship. (4) Disclosure tends to be reciprocal (dyadic effect). (5) Women tend to be higher disclosers than men. (6) Women disclose more with individuals they like, whereas men disclose more with people they trust. (7) Disclosure is regulated by norms of appropriateness. (8) Attraction is related to positive disclosure but not to negative disclosure. (9) Positive disclosure is more likely in nonintimate or moderately intimate relationships. (10) Negative disclosure occurs with greater frequency in highly intimate settings than in less intimate ones. (11) Satisfaction and disclosure have a curvilinear relationship; that is, relational satisfaction is greatest at moderate levels of disclosure.   (198)

Family-of-origin issues, socioeconomic background, and expectations may influence self-disclosing behavior. Hurvitz and Komarovsky (1977) report a comparison of marital studies done with middle-class high-school graduates in the Los Angeles area and a working-class urban community called Glenton, where most couples did not complete high school. The middle-class respondents were more likely to view spouses as companions to each other with expectations of sharing activities, leisure time, and thoughts. Marriage, as seen by members of the Glenton community, was more likely to include sexual union, complementary duties, and mutual devotion, but not friendship.

In the Glenton study, Komarovsky found that two thirds of the wives had at least one person apart from their husbands in whom they confided deeply personal experiences. In 35 percent of the cases, the wife not only enjoyed such intimate friendships but shared a significant segment of her life more fully with her confidante than with her husband. In most cases, the confidantes were female and almost two thirds were mothers or sisters of the wives. Thus, in this community, marital boundaries did not restrict the communication of private information to others, particularly among women in extended families.

Ethnic heritage may influence the amount and type of disclosure. For example, the Mexican-American society appears to be relatively more open than the Anglo-American society when it comes to discussions of death (Falicov and Karrer, 1980, 423). Whereas Jewish families exhibit verbal skill and a willingness to talk about trouble and feelings, Irish families may find themselves at a loss to describe inner feelings (McGoldrick, 1982).

The effect of age or length of marriage on spouse self-disclosure is unclear, since the content of discussion may vary over time (Waterman, 1979, 226–27). Parent-child disclosure has received some attention, although most of the studies have involved self-report data. From her review of research, Waterman suggests that most mothers receive more self-disclosure than fathers (227). High-school girls tend to remain constant in self-disclosure to parents, whereas boys show an overall decrease (Rivenbark, 1971, 38). Parents perceived as nurturing and supportive elicit more disclosure from children who find those encounters rewarding (Doster and Strickland, 1969, 382). In her study of families with adolescents, Abelman (1975) reports that mutual self-disclosure exists mainly between parents and children of the same sex and adolescent self-disclosure correlates more highly with self-image than with parental self-disclosure (xii). Such a brief review only highlights certain issues but indicates the complexity of a subject that some popular writers tend to treat simplistically as they encourage unrestrained "open" communication in family relationships.

The positive effect of self-disclosure on intimate relationships has been described extensively (Altman and Taylor; Wilmot; Knapp). Clearly shared and accepted personal information or feelings enhance intimacy in a relationship. Yet, such sharing and acceptance is not the norm. In fact, high self-disclosure is not necessarily linked with relational satisfaction.

In exploring the relationship between self-disclosure and marital satisfaction, Levinger and Senn (1967) found satisfied couples disclosed more than unsatisfied couples. However, unsatisfied couples disclosed more unpleasant feelings than satisfied couples. A later study found similar patterns of satisfaction, plus a small correlation between spouses' disclosure levels; both partners tended to be either high or low disclosers (Burke et al., 1976). In your family experiences, you may have discovered that when you were least satisfied with certain relationships, you tended to engage in more negative self-disclosure.

In her work on self-disclosure and communication in families, Gilbert (1976a) raises practical issues, which bear directly on exchanges within family systems. She cites conflicting reports on the effects of self-disclosure on relationships and indicates factors that influence such disclosure, including content (what is said about what topic), valence (whether statements are positive or negative), and honesty. She also suggests that the self-esteem of members may affect self-disclosure in family relationships. Finally, she hypothesizes that medium amounts of disclosure would be associated with higher family satisfaction than either high or low self-disclosure. In order to understand her hypotheses, we need to set some background.

The valence, or positive or negative position toward a particular issue, relates directly to how comments will be received. Most of us appreciate receiving positive self-disclosure, although such positive self-disclosure represents one of the most "neglected areas of communication between partners" (O'Neill and O'Neill, 1972, 11). More frequently, we think of self-disclosure as involving the "dirty laundry," the misdeeds or negative feelings that are likely to cause pain for the listener. Some of the studies cited earlier report that higher self-disclosure levels are more characteristic of happily married couples, but that unhappily married couples are higher in disclosure of a negative valence. Families characterized by pleasant self-disclosure content can experience intimacy at higher levels more easily than those trying to discuss painful, negative-laden issues. For example, talking about a desire for continued sexual experimentation within a generally satisfactory relationship has much greater possibilities of leading to further intimacy than a revelation of severe sexual dissatisfaction.

Although our communication patterns are usually built on the assumption that we are sharing "the truth" with another person, some people are dishonest or inaccurate in their disclosures (Berger and Bradac, 87). These inauthentic disclosures may be difficult to detect but, once discovered, may interfere with future believability and mutual self-disclosure. In marriage, partners may be caught between desires for openness and protectiveness. A husband may be dismayed by his wife's weight gain but knows that bringing up his feelings would feed her low self-esteem. An adult daughter may wish to share her incest experience with her mother but questions destroying her mother's image of her husband.

Satir (1972) views self-esteem as the basis for all positive communication within families. According to her, integrity, honesty, responsibility, compassion, and love flow easily from persons with high self-esteem because they feel they matter. Such people are willing to take risks whereas persons with low self-esteem constantly feel they have to defend themselves. Satir places the responsibility for building self-esteem on families, which have the almost exclusive responsibility for young children's esteem. Abelman found that the self-disclosures of adolescents to their parents seemed more closely tied to their own self-esteem than to the amount of self-disclosure received from the parents. Gilbert supports the relationships between self-disclosure and esteem, maintaining: "Research literature relating self-disclosure to self-esteem, within the context of interaction in family systems, reveals that often people refrain from expressing their feelings because they are insecure about their marriage" (225). Since self-disclosure requires risk-taking, it appears more likely that persons who feel good about themselves would be more willing to take such risks than would persons who have low self-esteem.

Based on a review of self-disclosure research, Gilbert (1976b) suggests a curvilinear relationship between self-disclosure and satisfaction in relationship maintenance, holding that a moderate degree of disclosure appears to be most conducive to maintaining relationships over time (209). This position contrasts sharply with that of Jourard or Lederer and Jackson, who advocate full self-disclosure within relationships. The following diagrams willl help you visualize the differences (see Figure 4–2). According to diagram (a), as relationships become more disclosing, satisfaction moves from a growth pattern to a decline, whereas according to diagram (b), increased self-disclosure is directly related to increased satisfaction. Let us look further at the underlying claims of each position. The

Figure 4—2
Relationships Between Self-Disclosure and Satisfaction

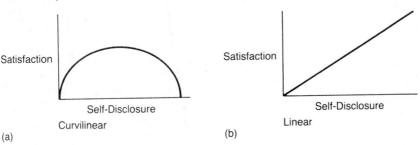

research-based curvilinear view holds ". . . as disclosures accumulate through the history of a relationship and as the nature of the relationship itself changes, then the connection between disclosure and relational satisfaction reverses from a positive to a negative association. . . . this is the way disclosure functions for most relationships" (Gilbert, 211). When you think of many of your friends or relatives, you may realize that you do not share the particularly negative aspects of yourself, or discuss theirs, because this may begin the decline of the relationship. Perhaps you have been in a relationship in which very unpleasant disclosures seemed to diminish or end it. Family members may not have been able to cope with the negative information they received about themselves or other family members.

"As a child, I never fully understood what happened, but there was a big change in the relationships in our house, and there seemed to be a dark secret that no one would talk about. Fifteen years later, I found out from my oldest brother that my father had a short affair with someone at the office, and after it was over he told my mother. I guess she couldn't handle it because she always adored him, and that changed their relationship for many years."

The linear point of view, suggesting that self-disclosure "may and should remain a positive source of relational satisfaction throughout the history of the relationship," clearly describes an "optimum state of affairs" rather than how things usually are (Gilbert, 211). Even Jourard indicates that this is the ideal which is rarely achieved (46).

Yet, the linear relationship and its positive outcomes may occur in special cases when mutual capacity to handle positive and negative deep self-disclosure exists. Such cases, though, are uncommon. Gilbert suggests a threefold process for understanding the potential linear relationship. In linear relationships, the focus has to be placed on the effects that the *response of the other* has on the discloser. She suggests that for such disclosure to exist in intimate relationships, both persons need: (1) healthy selves, including high self-esteem, (2) a willingness to risk a commitment to the relationship and to push it to higher levels of intimacy, and (3) reciprocal confirmation (212). The following diagram (Figure 4–3) presents the possible combinations of approaches to self-disclosure and satisfaction found in the different types of relationships.

This diagram suggests that as relationships move from being nonintimate to intimate, the initial high positive self-disclosure shifts until, at the intimate level, negative self-disclosure gains in importance. In order to handle this and remain satisfied with the relationship, the individuals involved must both be characterized by high self-esteem, a willingness to risk, and high capacities for confirmation and commitment. If these capacities are not present, their satisfaction with the relationship will decline as the negative self-disclosure increases.

Since family life involves long-term involvements, during which people grow and change, it would be ideal if members could handle the negative and positive aspects of each other's development, permitting total honesty within a supportive context. Yet, many negative self-disclosures are necessarily painful for one or both members of the relationship, and each individual's capacity for, and willingness to endure, pain varies. Thus, in many relationships, high levels of self-disclosure result in low levels of satisfaction.

Self-disclosure serves as a powerful tool in relationship development, not just as a by-product of deepening relationships. Researchers are only now carefully investigating why and how persons in a relationship use self-disclosure to reach certain goals (Duck et al., 1984, 299).

The Practice of Self-Disclosure. Now that we have talked about the research and thinking in the area of marital or family self-disclosure, you can think about your own family relationships according to the following general characteristics of self-disclosure:

1. Relatively few communication transactions involve high levels of disclosure.
2. Self-disclosure involves verbal and nonverbal signals.
3. Self-disclosure usually occurs in dyads.

Figure 4–3

Disclosure Processes in Relationship Development: A Linear Versus a Curvilinear Schemata

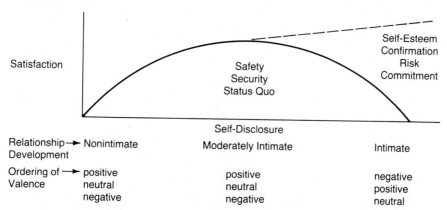

From Shirley Gilbert, "Empirical and Theoretical Extensions of Self-Disclosure," pp. 210, 211–212 in EXPLORATIONS IN INTERPERSONAL COMMUNICATION, edited by Gerald R. Miller. Copyright © 1976 by Sage Publications, Inc. Reprinted by permission of Sage Publications, Inc.

4. Self-disclosure tends to be reciprocal.
5. Self-disclosure increases when rewarded.
6. Self-disclosure occurs in the context of positive, trusting relationships.
7. Self-disclosure usually occurs incrementally with increased intimacy.
(Pearce and Sharp; Littlejohn; Duck et al.)

If you think about family relationships in terms of these characteristics, you can see ways in which family systems tend to encourage or discourage self-disclosure. Considering the time it takes to do the functional things in families, you can understand that little time or energy may be available for the nurturing type of communication that includes self-disclosure. Additionally, with the exception of new couples or newly blended families, there is no need to spend much time revealing past history, since family members have already shared those issues. Hence, risk-taking communication is not likely to occur frequently within family life, but certain developmental or external stresses may trigger extensive amounts.

Although we have emphasized the verbal aspect of self-disclosure messages, a sequence of appropriate nonverbal signals occurring in the context of verbal disclosure also contributes significantly to understanding and the disclosure cycle. For example, nonverbal signals may indicate to a husband that his wife is surprised to find that he has been unaware of her feelings about a given topic (Duck et al., 305). Duck proposes the term "intimation sequences" for these signals in which both partners intimate new levels of evolving awareness within a discussion. Thus, verbal self-disclosure and nonverbal intimation sequences are bound together in face-to-face dyadic interaction.

The issue of self-disclosure in dyads presents us with the intriguing point that many family members never spend one-on-one time with each other. If high levels of disclosure occur mainly in dyads, how often do two-person systems spend time together? How much time does a couple have together after the first child arrives? How often does a parent of four children get time alone with each of them? When do a stepparent and stepchild make time alone for themselves? Such time is important for openness to develop in their relationships. Reciprocity of self-disclosure is critical in dyadic relationships. Many couples report a serious imbalance in openness; traditionally, the female partner discloses more and desires more disclosure, becoming frustrated with the lower male response. In parent-child situations, it is more likely that parents provide the initial impetus and model for self-disclosing behavior. As children grow older, they may begin to share in reciprocal ways with the adults in their lives, depending on what they have experienced, just as the adults depend upon reciprocity to build their own relationships.

Families provide unique opportunities for self-disclosure. Joint living experiences provide needed time and space for such interaction. Yet, this can take place only where positive social relationships, including trust, exist. Parents may find that they have unwittingly halted the development of self-disclosure with a child because they discussed the child's concern with another adult, not recognizing the child's desire for privacy. Unless people indicate how private certain information is to them, another person may accidentally reveal that information to others and destroy the relationship.

"My sister's big mouth almost blew my marriage sky-high because she broke my trust. When Ginny and I had problems in my marriage, I would talk to Margaret, but I trusted that she would not tell anyone. Instead, she told my mother who never liked Ginny much. My mother started asking questions that made Ginny suspicious, and it was finally clear that our problems were becoming a family issue. In order to save my marriage, we dropped out of the family circle for almost two years and even now I am very careful not to talk about anything personal with my sister."

In some nonvoluntary family relationships, especially those involving stepfamilies, the basis for trust may be missing, thereby reducing the likelihood of openness developing in the first two to five years (Cooper). In a family in which the trust level remains high, relatively few moments of high disclosure occur without unhappy repercussions, and, over time, the pattern of sharing develops among members.

In self-disclosure, as in many other areas of life, we are likely to repeat behaviors that are rewarded, or met with positive response. In a family that indicates pleasure at knowing what the members are thinking or feeling, even if the information itself is not necessarily pleasant, the likelihood of continued self-disclosure is great. If self-disclosure is met with rejecting or disconfirming messages, the level of sharing will drop significantly.

Although we have presented self-disclosure as desirable for intimacy development, self-disclosure can also be used to manipulate or control another family member. Partial or dishonest disclosures can undermine trust in a relationship. Therefore, the aims and intentions of disclosure need to be considered when examining its effect on intimacy.

We can hypothesize that self-disclosure bears a direct relationship to family levels of cohesion and adaptation. Extremely cohesive families may reject negative self-disclosure, since it would threaten their connectedness, particularly if the family has a low capacity for adaptation. For example, a highly cohesive family with a theme of "We can only depend on each other" would resist negative disclosures that might threaten their security and cause internal conflict. Such a theme might be accompanied by rigid boundaries which would resist self-disclosures to outsiders.

Families with very low cohesion may tolerate negative self-disclosure but have difficulty with positive self-disclosure, which might lead to greater cohesion. Families with moderate to high adaptation and cohesion capacities may cope relatively well with the effects of high levels of positive or negative self-disclosure. As you have discovered through these pages, self-disclosure is a complicated process that may result in intimacy when two people make the effort to share with each other.

Sexual Relations

How would you describe sexual experience within the marital relationship? As a series of isolated encounters? As an integral part of a growing relationship? Do you see marital sexuality as restricted to "being good in bed"? For most people, sex within a marital relationship involves far more than just physical performance; it involves the partners' sexual identities, their background regarding sexual issues, their mutual perceptions of each others' needs, and the messages contained within sexual expression. All of these issues relate directly to communication—particularly to confirming and disconfirming messages.

Feldman stresses the importance of sexual relations to marital intimacy, yet the quality of the sexual relationship affects, and is affected by, the other characteristics of intimacy—the affectionate/loving relationship and a deep, detailed mutual knowledge of the two partners. In their study of over 6000 couples, Blumstein and Schwartz (1983) report, "Our findings lead to the overwhelming conclusion that a good sex life is central to a good relationship" (201).

In this section, we will view sexual behavior as a form of marital communication as well as a contributing factor in overall marital satisfaction. Scoresby (1977) supports the viewing of sexual behavior as communication and suggests that sexual behavior is a profound source of meaning related to the many facets of the human personality. He maintains:

> . . . sexual expression needs to consist of clear messages that effectively communicate the feelings of both partners. Sexual pleasure that is freely given, in an honest and mutually intimate way, can draw two people together into a loving and passionate bond that is continually strengthened, enhancing the marriage. (45–46)

Socialization and Sexuality. The basis for a mutually intimate sexual relationship reflects the individual development of each of the partners. Clinical psychologist Greene (1970) believes an individual's sexuality remains closely intertwined with his or her intrapersonal, interpersonal, and environmental systems—systems that interlock yet vary in importance according to an individual's age. Greene states:

> The sexual feelings (intrapersonal) and behavior of a person are a reaction to the parental attitudes (interpersonal) in which he was raised. These attitudes, in turn, were handed down by their parents and were largely molded by broad cultural viewpoints specific to their social class (environmental forces). (57)

Most of our sexual conduct is originally learned, coded, and performed on the basis of biosocial beliefs regarding gender identity, learned originally in our families-of-origin. Parents possess a set of gender-specific ideas about males and females that they learned, and they observe "typical" behaviors of girls or boys of similar ages to their children. Based on these and other personal experiences, parents transmit a gender identity from earliest infancy, resulting in children's establishing gender identities at a very young age. This identity is so strong that efforts to alter such socialization patterns must be presented to children before age three or they will have little impact (Gagnon, 1977, 68). Our personal identities include sexual/gender identity as a core component, which influences our later sexual experience. According to Gagnon:

> When we do begin having sex in our society, our beliefs about woman/man strongly influence whom we have sex with, what sexual things we do, where and when we will have sex, the reasons we agree, and the feelings we have.   (59)

Our overall sense of personal identity, with a core sexual identity, is a "prerequisite for intimacy in marriage and sexual relationship" and is also "strengthened and affirmed by experiences of interacting constructively with a person of the complementary sex" (Clinebell and Clinebell, 1970, 138). Sexual experience contains powerful confirming or disconfirming messages.

Many of today's adults grew up in an atmosphere of sexual silence and now live in a world of open sexual discussion (Ryan and Ryan, 1982). Much of what we learn about sexuality takes place within the rule-bound context of each family. If you remember an earlier discussion of communication rules, you recall that most of them are negative directives—"Do not____." Often, communication around sexual issues remains indirect, resulting in confusion, misinformation, or heightened curiosity. Recall how your sexuality was explained to you. You may remember much mystery and confusion as you tried to sort things out. If your genitals were talked about, how were they talked about? What attitudes did you pick up regarding your gender and sexuality?

"I can see my sister trying to deal with having her first son and not being too sure how to deal with his sexuality. Last week Teddy, who is three, went to the bathroom and, after a while, my sister called to him, 'What are you doing?' He yelled back, 'Nothing,' to which she replied, 'Well, cut it out and get out here.' If this is a typical pattern, Teddy may be in for some real confusion about what she is really trying to say.'"

Messages like that in the previous example communicate concern or displeasure, but the issue remains hidden. These veiled messages often continue through adolescence and into adulthood. According to Satir:

> . . . most families employ the rule, "Don't enjoy sex—yours or anyone else's—in any form." The common beginning for this rule is the denial of the genitals except as necessary nasty objects. "Keep them clean and out of sight and touch. Use them only when necessary and sparingly at that."   (105)

In many families, the marital boundary remains so tight around the area of sexuality that children never see their parents as sexual beings—no playful swats, hugging, or tickling occurs in view of the children. Yet, in other families, the marital boundary is so diffuse that children encounter incestuous behaviors as they are co-opted into spousal roles.

The family represents the first but not the only source of sexual information. As children mature, they gain additional information about sexuality from peers, church, school, and the media. When you look back over your childhood and adolescence, what were your major sources of sexual information? What attitudes were communicated to you about your own sexuality? What could have improved the messages you received?

As an individual embarks upon sexual experiences, his or her sexual identity influences the encounters, as does the partner's sexual identity. Open communication becomes critical for both individuals, since a good sexual relationship depends on what is satisfying to each partner. Ryan and Ryan describe the mutuality involved in sexual experience:

> Having sex with someone is a semi-private act. It begins with an invitation, often unspoken by one, and the acceptance, often tacit but clear, by the other. It is semi-private in that the pleasure of sex is one's own, but the quality of the pleasure depends on what the other does. In sex, one is both a giver and receiver of pleasure.   (75)

Yet, some understanding comes only through a combination of self-disclosure and sensitivity as spouses reveal their needs and desires while learning to give pleasure to the other. For some spouses, this involves working on "signal clarification" to minimize miscommunication. From another perspective, we can distinguish between monological and dialogical sex—the former being sexual experiences in which one or both partners "talk to themselves" or attempt to satisfy only personal needs. Dialogical sex is characterized by mutual concern and sharing of pleasure (Wilkinson, 1984).

Yet, often the "rules" of childhood continue to stultify the adult sexual experience, preventing husbands and wives from communicating freely about or through their sexual encounters. The following vividly portrays the euphemistic language characteristic of even long-term marriages:

> Consider the kinds of talk that occur before intercourse in most households. In some the husband or wife may say, "Let's go do it," but such directness is rare. What usually happens is that the husband may say, "I think I will take a shower." What that really says is "I am going to be clean for you." . . . The wife then says, "I will be upstairs in a few minutes." That is a "yes." Or she says, "I am too tired today; I have a headache; I have been to the hairdresser; the kids might wake up." Those are all "no." A man will say, "I am tired; I have got to get up early in the morning; I have some reading I have to do." There is a whole indirect language which people use to say "yes" or "no."   (Gagnon, 208)

Because of their "taboos" regarding a discussion of sexual behavior, many couples rely solely on nonverbal communication to gain mutual satisfaction. For some, this may be acceptable, but for others, unclear messages result in frustration, as partners misinterpret the degree or kind of sexual expression desired by the other. Some partners report a fear of using any affectionate gesture because the other spouse always sees it as an invitation to intercourse; others say that their partners never initiate any sexual activity while the partners report being ignored or rebuffed at such attempts. Mutual satisfaction at any level of sexual involvement depends upon open communication between spouses, yet intercourse, according to Lederer and Jackson is special " in that it requires a higher degree of collaborative communication than any other kind of behavior exchanged between the spouses" (117).

Sexuality and Communication Breakdowns.

Sexuality and Communication Breakdowns. Although sex as a form of communication has the potential for conveying messages of love and affection, many spouses use their sexual encounters to carry messages of anger, domination, disappointment, or self-rejection. Often nonsexual conflicts are played out in the bedroom because one partner believes it is the only way to wage a war. Unexpressed anger may appear as a "headache," great "tiredness," roughness, or violence during a sexual encounter.

Blumstein and Schwartz found that married couples who report fighting a lot about housekeeping, income, expenditures, and whether both should work are less happy with their sexual relationship (202). If partners experience unsatisfying sexual encounters early in their relationship, their " . . . mutual disappointment and embarrassment can easily lead to sensitivity and reluctance to talk about what has been happening to them" (Ryan and Ryan, 80).

As we come to understand more about sexuality through the life cycle, it becomes clear that sexual expectations are altered over time due to developmental changes and unpredictable stresses. Couples interviewed about their sex lives report that they have experienced dramatic changes in sexual interest, depending on other pressures in their lives (Ryan and Ryan, 89). There are indications that sexuality may become more pleasurable in later life when a couple's childrearing burdens cease.

Based on his work in the area of sexual communication, Scoresby developed a chart indicating areas of sexual breakdown. Table 4–3 on page 90 indicates the possible areas of breakdowns related to communication.

Scoresby also describes the advantages of thinking of sex as communication:

1. We become more aware of its complexities and intricacies as opposed to focusing on physical or mechanical procedures.
2. We conclude we'll never utilize all its potential, and this leads us to more fully explore its possibilities. . . .
3. We view the sexual relationship as a continuous process instead of as a series of isolated events.   (46)

Thus, for couples engaged in an intimate relationship, communication about sexuality may deepen the intimacy and provide tremendous pleasure to both spouses.

Table 4—3 _____
Signs of Difficulty in Sexual Communication

Common Symptoms	Possible Solutions
1. Failure to talk openly with each other. 2. Repeated lack of orgasm by female. 3. Tension and lack of relaxation. 4. One demanding the other to perform. 5. Excessive shyness or embarrassment. 6. Hurried and ungentle performance. 7. Absence of frequent touching, embracing, and exchanges of intimacy.	1. Increase each person's ability to self-disclose feelings. 2. Spend increased positive time alone together. 3. Avoid threatening to dissolve the marriage. 4. Check for angry conflict and reduce if possible.

Commitment of Effort

"If you have to work at a relationship, there's something wrong with it. A relationship is either good or it's not." How often have you heard people argue that relationships should not have to take effort and that "working at a relationship is phony"? Relationships need care and attention. It is only through effort and commitment that a love relationship remains a vital part of one's life.

Many factors compete for attention in our lives. Meeting home, work, school, and community responsibilities take tremendous time and effort. The nurturing of a marriage or family often gets the time and energy that is "left over," a minimal amount at best. In most cases, this limited attention spells relational disaster. Unless familial ties receive high priority, relationships will "go on automatic pilot" and eventually deteriorate. The individuals involved will exhibit behaviors representative of those on the lower levels of Altman and Taylor's stages or in the coming-apart stages of Knapp.

Because the family operates within the larger ecosystem including work and school, decisions in family and work arenas impact on each other. There is an interaction between "where people put their emotional energy (home versus work) and their commitment to their relationship" (Blumstein and Schwartz, 173). In this era of dual-career couples and families, commuter marriages, and high technology and subsequent job loss or relocation, family intimacy can be lost. Thus, only conscious efforts to enrich such relationships can preserve or heighten intimacy.

BARRIERS TO INTIMACY

Throughout this chapter, we have focused on communication strategies that foster intimacy. We would be remiss if we did not note the very obvious barriers to such intimacy with which family members must contend. We have suggested that marital or familial intimacy involves confirmation and affection, self-disclosure, and sexual relations for couples; yet, because of the risks and effort involved in intimate communication, such behavior frightens many people. Although most persons would declare a desire for intimacy, many actually experience a strong fear of becoming extremely close to another person. Whitehead and Whitehead (1981) address this directly when they say, "The central threat of any close intimacy encounter . . . is the threat of injury and loss" (223).

There are many reasons for a fear of intimacy, including the following five discussed by Feldman (71–72): (1) People may fear a merger with the loved one resulting in the loss of personal boundaries or identity. This occurs when the "sense of self" is poorly developed or insecure. (2) People may fear interpersonal exposure, since individuals with low self-esteem or low self-acceptance may be threatened by being revealed as weak, inadequate, or undesirable. (3) People may fear attack if their basic sense of trust in themselves and the world remains underdeveloped. (4) People may fear abandonment, the feeling of being overwhelmed and helpless when the love object is gone. For those who have experienced excessive traumatic separations, one way to defend against anxiety is to reduce intimacy. (5) People may fear their own destructive impulses. "When repressive anxiety has not been resolved during the course of childhood development, it becomes a potential stimulus for defensive behavior in adult intimate relationships" (72). Once one has taken the risk to be intimate, rejection can be devastating, resulting in reluctance to be hurt again.

"After our separation, the hardest thing we faced was regaining our sense of intimacy. We had hurt each other so badly that we had to rebuild a whole new sense of trust and sharing. It was an effort to say personal things, to touch each other lovingly, to discuss our feelings. We have been back together for over a year and only now is our sexual life coming around. It had been so important to us before, and we were scared of allowing ourselves to be free, truly free, in that area. Each small risk has been a victory, but it has been a very painful, slow process."

Sometimes intimacy becomes confused with an unhealthy togetherness or extreme cohesion, resulting in a loss of personal boundaries and identity. As you remember, boundaries serve as regulatory factors to help one see differences and similarities within systems and subsystems, providing certain limits and rights.

In families with unclear boundaries, one person's business is everyone's business. A great deal of communication occurs across family subsystem boundaries, and people may feel obligated to engage in high self-disclosure and even seek disclosure inappropriate to the subsystem or role. An adolescent may feel obligated to discuss all of his or her dating behavior with a parent. A mother may discuss marital problems with a teenage son. Yet, the pressuring person requires the other to " . . . be like me; be one with me." He or she suggests, "You are bad if you disagree with me. Reality and your differentness are unimportant" (Satir, 1967, 13), demonstrating the difficulty of negative self-disclosure. Members may require, or sense a demand for, constant confirmation to serve as reassurance that they are cared for. Yet, intimacy becomes smothering if people are fused.

> "When I was still living at home, my mother would often say to me, 'Louise, I'm cold. Go put on a sweater.' A child is more apt to listen to her mother without really thinking about the words, but one day I said, 'Mom, I'm not cold.' This was only a small moment in our relationship, but it typified my struggle to move away from such a tightly bonded relationship that it was hard to tell who was who."

In some families, the parents may be so afraid of sharing both good and bad things with each other that they establish a "united front" for themselves and displace any anger onto a child. Thus, the child serves as a scapegoat while the parents convince themselves that they are experiencing intimacy. Such false togetherness becomes a barrier to true marital intimacy while seriously harming the scapegoated child.

Within disengaged, or very low cohesive, families, individuals do not get through the rigid boundaries to reach each other, and the members may not receive necessary affection or support. Each person is a psychological subsystem with few links to the surrounding family members. Intimacy is undeveloped or at a low intensity level in households where each family member is concerned solely with personal affairs, remains constantly busy, and spends time away from the home. Yet, even if persons spend time together, unless their communication goes beyond the task-oriented type, they may remain generally disengaged. Both types of families set up barriers to true intimacy by smothering or ignoring individual family members.

CONCLUSION

Within this chapter, we have explored the close relationship between intimacy and communication. After describing the relational currencies and stages in relationship development, we examined specific communication behaviors that encourage intimacy within marital and family systems: confirmation, self-disclosure, and sexual communication. Confirming behaviors communicate acceptance of another person. Self-disclosure provides a means for mutual sharing of personal information and feelings. Sexuality serves as a means of communicating affection within a marital relationship. We have suggested that family intimacy cannot be achieved unless members nurture their relationships through care, effort, and risk.

Think about the kinds of interactions you see in the families around you. Is most of their communication strictly functional? Do you see attempts at intimacy through confirmation or self-disclosure? Are these people able to demonstrate an ability to touch each other comfortably? If you think back to Gilbert's model of curvilinear versus linear development of self-disclosure, you can imagine the model applied to all relationships, knowing that only a few are likely to have the mutual acceptance risk-taking capacity and commitment to move toward true intimacy.

All human beings long for intimacy, but it is a rare relationship in which the partners consciously strive for greater sharing over long periods of time. Such mutual commitment provides rewards known only to those in intimate relationships.

FOR REVIEW

1. Trace the development of a real or fictional couple through some of the stages of relationship development, citing representative examples of their communication patterns at each stage.
2. Using a real or fictional family, describe the relational currencies most commonly used. Indicate any family-of-origin influences you see in the current pattern.
3. Describe some disconfirming behaviors that can become patterned into a family's way of life.
4. Take a position and discuss: Under what circumstances, if any, would you recommend withholding complete self-disclosure in a marital and/or family relationship?
5. Take a position and discuss: If you have to work at a relationship there's something wrong with it.

Chapter 5

Communication and Family Roles and Types

One of today's most talked about topics is that of the changing roles in the American family. Many attribute these changes to the fact that 74 percent of divorced women and 55 percent of all married persons with children eighteen years old and younger hold jobs outside the home. (Bureau of Labor Statistics Report, March 1984). Women's roles have changed significantly in the business area, with more opportunities for advancement and less discrimination. Changes in laws providing for equal opportunity have helped. Other changes have occurred in education, with more women returning to college and entering areas of study previously dominated by men; in politics, with women more actively involved in campaigning for social issues and seeking elected offices; in communication, with the media presenting stories of successful women who have combined careers with family life.

> *"I grew up in a very traditional family and held all the beliefs about wives as dependent persons who maintain the home and provide emotional support. By strange fate, I married a man who was raised by a single-parent mother, and he saw women as more independent than I did. Over time, he has influenced me to be more of my own person, to have a career, to be independent in many ways. If I had married a man with the same original conception of husband and wife that I had, my life would have been very different."*

Male roles have changed, but more slowly. Some men, but not a majority, have discovered the joys and challenges of more active parenting, sharing household duties, and nurturing family members. A few have switched from providing the resources for the family to "househusband" status, encouraging their spouses to pursue careers. Rapid changes in society have resulted in some confusion and frustration as family members try to define their roles (Pasley and Gecas, 1984, 401).

In this chapter, we will discuss role development, expectations, performance, McMaster's model, and family types, particularly the role functions necessary to maintain effective communication and how these functions vary over the family life cycle. Role functions differ in a newly married couple, in a family with several children in school, and in a family in which the "empty nest" time has arrived with all children out of the home. Crises such as desertion, divorce, or death can dramatically alter role functioning.

DEFINITION OF ROLES

Role theorists frequently disagree on the definition of family roles (Heiss, 1968; Muchmore, 1974; Linton, 1945). However, we support the view that "family roles are defined as repetitive patterns of behavior by which family members fulfill family functions" (Epstein et al., 1982, 124). Others present a static, or unchanging, image of roles, maintaining that family members hold certain expectations toward the occupant of a given social position, such as "father" or "grandmother." These expectations carry beliefs about how a role can and should be enacted, no matter what the circumstances (Muchmore, 38; Linton, 77).

Rather than take a fixed view of the position of a child or a parent in a family, an *interactive perspective* emphasizes the emerging aspects of roles and the behavioral regularities that develop out of social interaction. Thus, this approach takes into account the transactional nature of the encounters experienced by persons with labels such as "father" or "wife" and reflects the reciprocal nature of roles. According to this interactive philosophy, you cannot be a stepfather without a stepchild, or a wife without a husband; in fact, you cannot be a companionable stepfather to a child who rejects you or be a confrontive wife to a man who avoids conflicts. Yet, roles do not emerge solely through interaction. Part of learning roles occurs by observing and imitating *role models*, persons whose behavior serves as a guide for others (Heiss, 13).

The interactive role reflects: (1) the personality and background of a person who occupies a social position, (2) the relationships in which a person engages, (3) the changes as each family member moves through his or her life cycle, (4) the effects of role performance upon the family system, and (5) the extent to which a person's social psychological identity is defined and enhanced by a particular role. For example, a woman's behavior in the social position of wife may have been very different in her first marriage than in her second, due to her own personal growth and the actions of each husband.

ROLE DEVELOPMENT

Within families, roles are established, grown into, grown through, discussed, negotiated, worked on, and accepted or rejected. As family members mature or outside forces cause change within the family, roles may develop, shift, or disappear. The adjustments may be obvious or subtle, but they do occur as families grow and change.

"Six months ago I married a woman whose husband died one year ago and who has two children. Between us, we now have five children living in the house, and although our own relationship is going well, we are having a hard time fulfilling the role of parent to each other's children. Her two boys treat me like a distant acquaintance. If I try to be affectionate, they pull away. If I give them orders, they will obey me but they certainly cannot put me in the role of father. On the other hand, my kids have been without a mother for seven years and are willing to let Karen get into the mothering act, but she seems afraid to do so. It's like her kids vs. my kids."

British sociologist Bernstein (1970) identifies two primary forms of communication that contrast and typify families, the position-oriented type and the person-oriented type. Position-oriented families are more likely to maintain "sharp boundaries between statuses and social identities along the lines of age, sex, and age-related family roles" (Johnson, 1978, 5). Thus, the behaviors attached to the roles of grandparent, mother, and son become carefully defined and delineated. In a position-oriented family, aunts do X, mothers do Y, and husbands do Z. Person-oriented families center more on the unique individuals occupying each label and have fewer boundaries or exacting rules for appropriate behavior. Johnson describes the communication differences between these two approaches by discussing a hypothetical child—Allison—as she might develop in either family:

If she develops in a position-oriented family, she learns that her role as a child is very communalized; she learns that mother and father can direct and prohibit behavior because they are mother and father and as such need only provide general rule statements as directives of behavior: "You're not to leave the table until you drink your milk," "Apologize to your father," "Be quiet, I'm on the phone." If, on the other hand, Allison develops in a person-oriented family, she will probably be asked to drink her milk, apologize to her father, and be quiet, but these directives are less likely to stand on their own. Allison's parents will provide reasons for the desired behaviors that go beyond mother and father's rights to direct.   (5–6)

Thus, a child raised in a position-oriented family "learns that what can be said and done in relation to others depends on the roles one has relative to others," whereas a child raised in a person-oriented family learns that although role relationships are important, "the desirability or undesirability of certain behaviors depends on reasons that transcend the role relationships and focus on the personal nature of the participants" (6). As we explore the role-related behaviors occurring in families, keep in mind the continuum representing position-oriented and person-oriented approaches to these roles.

Roles are inextricably bound to the communication process. Family roles are developed and maintained through communication. One learns how to assume his or her place within a family from the feedback provided by other family members. "Such a good girl, helping Mommy like that." "I don't think either of us should use four-letter words in front of the children." We talk about what we expect from another as we enter a marital relationship. In-laws may be verbally or nonverbally informed about what is considered appropriate behavior; children are given very direct instructions about being a son or daughter in a particular household. In general, adults tend to use their family-of-origin history as a base from which to negotiate particular mutual roles as they form a family system; children develop their communicative roles through "the interplay of cognitive abilities and the social norms and expectations" (Johnson, 2).

Family roles and communication rules are strongly interrelated, as each contributes to the maintenance or change of the other. Rules may structure certain role relationships, while particular role relationships may foster the development of certain rules. For example, such rules as "Children should not hear about family finances" or "School problems are to be settled with Mother" reinforce a position-oriented role structure; in turn, such a structure contributes to the creation of this type of rule.

In order to more fully understand family roles, we need to examine (1) the sources of role expectations and (2) the determinants of role performance. How many of you remember making such comments as "When I'm a parent, I'll listen to my kids" or "I'd never let my wife go out to work." Each of us has probably spent time planning how we will fulfill a specific future role based on our expectations of how such a role should be performed. Our role expectations for family roles come from a number of sources.

Role Expectations

The society in which we live provides models and norms for how certain family roles should be assumed. Currently, the media are an important societal source of family role expectations. Look at any newsstand and you will see articles on "Being a Successful Single Parent" or "The Changing Grandparent." Television has provided us with many family role models since the time of "Father Knows Best." Advertising reinforces certain stereotypes of how family members should act.

Daily life within a community also serves as a major source of role expectations. As you were growing up, the neighbors and your friends all knew who were the "good" mothers or the "bad" kids on the block or in the community. Ministers, priests, and rabbis presented exhortations for the prescribed "good family life." School personnel could influence adult expectations for what "good" parents would do with their children. Each of us has grown up with hundreds of expectations of how people should function in family roles.

Particular ethnic or cultural groups may hold beliefs about parenting or spouse roles, which are learned by members of the community. For example, in the

Jewish tradition, the role of mother is associated with the transmission of the culture and, as such, carries a particular significance and implies certain expectations.

Role expectations also arise from significant and complementary others. People important to you will set some expectations for how you should act in a future role. Your mother may greatly influence your expectations of motherhood or your father of fatherhood. You may have had a grandmother who taught you caring behaviors that parents should exhibit. A young childless couple may carefully watch another couple with small children to learn to deal with their impending role. *Significant other* can also refer to a lover or someone who cohabits with a family member and influences roles.

Complementary others, those people who fulfill related role positions, have expectations for your role. A husband has expectations for a wife, a parent for a child. During early stages of a relationship, men and women may spend long periods of time discussing their expectations for what being a husband or wife will be like. "I want my wife to be home with the children until they go to school" or "I need a man who will take responsibility for the home and children." As families blend, prospective spouses may talk with their future stepchildren about what they think the relationship should be like. If one partner's expectations are more position-oriented and the other's more person-oriented, they are more likely to clash than if both hold similar orientations.

Additional expectations come from each person's self-understanding in relationship to a future role. A person who expects to fulfill the role of spouse or parent has certain ideas about what such a role entails and how he or she thinks a "fit" between the role and the person can be created. You may find that you relied on a role model or you decided that with your skills or personality you would like to be a certain kind of spouse, parent, or lover.

Although society and others greatly influence our expectations, we put our own special identity into our final expectations of how we will assume a role. Sometimes expectations lead us to a decision not to assume a role. Corder and Stephan (1984) found significant underestimation of the effect of sex-role attitudes on the choices of careers for women, especially the early decisions about combining marriage and family roles and about the way men prefer wives to combine these roles (399).

"*This is probably a reversal of expectations but on the basis of what I know about myself, I decided not to have children. From all I learned and could see, children are a very time-consuming responsibility, and although they bring great joy, they limit certain growth potential for their parents. I knew that career advancement and travel were major goals for me and in order to fulfill those goals, I realized that I could not also have a goal of raising children.*"

Although we have been talking about expectations that occur prior to assuming a role, persons in roles may develop new expectations for that role. For example, a woman may watch her boss take his daughters out to lunch every second Saturday and develop new expectations for her own parenting role.

Role expectations are influenced by an imaginative view of yourself—the way you like to think of yourself being and acting. A mother may imagine going back to work; a father may imagine himself telling his child the "facts of life" comfortably. An integral part of these imaginings is the reaction of other people to one's hypothetical performance. A mother may picture her friends' looks of envy at her ability to juggle a career and home life. A father may imagine his son's eventual gratitude at learning the facts of life from his father. Such imaginings are not just daydreams; they serve as a primary source of plans of action or as a rehearsal for actual performance.

While role expectations represent our notions about how a role could or should be fulfilled, *role performance* is the actual behavior with others, which defines how the role is enacted. Roles are reciprocal, and until they are enacted with others, they are merely expectations.

Role Performance and Accountability

As with role expectations, role performance is influenced by such factors as societal or cultural norms, reactions and role performances of significant and complementary others, and the individual's capacity for enacting the role. Role accountability requires procedures in the family for seeing that role functions are accomplished through family members' development of a sense of responsibility for carrying out their role functions, which include creating monitoring and corrective mechanisms (Epstein et al., 125). Without role accountability, the family system becomes dysfunctional.

Churches may influence whom their members can marry and how parent and child roles are carried out. School and community organizations may give feedback as to how people are doing in their family roles. The extent to which you respond to this feedback determines its influence on you. You may choose to "keep up with the Joneses" or you may decide that the Joneses do not know much about how to live.

The actions of significant or important persons in your life affect role performance. Most of us have experienced the influence of feedback from significant others. Perhaps a friend told you he is not as disrespectful to his mother as you are to yours, and you changed your responses. Or someone might have told you what a good stepparent you are, and you began trying even harder to be a good father to your stepchildren.

Persons in complementary roles have direct bearing on how we assume our roles. Have you ever tried to reason with a parent who sulks, pamper an independent grandparent, or order a willful child? You were probably frustrated in enacting your role. On the other hand, if two complementary persons see things in similar ways, it enhances role performance. A college student who believes that she should no longer have to answer for her evening whereabouts will be reinforced by a mother who no longer asks. Thus, the way others assume their roles and comment on our roles affects how we enact our roles.

Additionally, our background influences our behavior. The range of behaviors allowed by one's background limits what he or she can do. For example, if certain communication behaviors are not part of your background, they cannot appear as if by magic in a particular situation. A father may wish he could talk with his son instead of yelling at him or giving orders, but he may not know how to discuss controversial subjects with his child. Self-confidence in attempting to fulfill a role may affect behavior. A shy stepmother may not be able to express affection for her new stepchildren for many months. Personal needs also get into the picture. If we need to appear helpless, we will not take charge of even simple household situations. The role aspects that we emphasize affect our behavior. If you view the major function of fatherhood as providing for your children, you are probably more likely to take a second job than to take the family on weekend picnics.

Sometimes individual expectations do not match the realities. A woman who had planned to mother many children may find herself uncomfortable with the role of mother to one. A man who had expected to dominate his marriage may find pleasure in relating to an independent wife. On occasion, people discover that they can function well in a role they did not expect or desire.

"I was really furious when my husband quit his sales job to finish his degree. I didn't choose the role of provider and I didn't like being conscripted. But after a while though, I got to feeling very professional and adult. Here I was supporting myself and a husband. I didn't know I had it in me."

As we will explore in more detail in Chapters 9 and 10, predictable and unpredictable life crises affect the roles we assume and how we function in them. Thus, although role behavior functions as a result of expectations and interpersonal interactions, unforeseen circumstances may alter life in such a way that roles change drastically from those first planned or enacted.

In the next section, we will discuss the role functions that adults assume in families. The extent to which each adult assumes certain functions affects both the way roles are enacted and the type of communication that occurs within the family.

SPECIFIC ROLE FUNCTIONS

In order to examine the transactional impact or the mutual influence of family roles, we will use McMaster's model of family functioning. In this model, role functioning is evaluated by discovering how the family allocates responsibilities and handles accountability for them (Epstein et al., 1978, 19–31). In a successful family, allocation of tasks is perceived as fair and reasonable, and accountability is clear. According to this model, five essential family functions serve as a basis for needed family roles: (1) provision of resources such as food, money, housing, and clothing; (2) adult sexual fulfillment; (3) individual development of physical, emotional, educational, and social potentials of each family member; (4) provision of nurturing, support, and counseling; and (5) maintenance and management of the family system (Epstein et al., 1982, 124). These family functions can be categorized as instrumental (providing the resources for the family), affective (support and nurturing, adult sexual needs), and mixed (life-skill development and system upkeep) (120). Within each family system, the existing themes, images, boundaries, and biosocial beliefs affect the way these functions are carried out. As we examine the functions, we will place a greater emphasis on those related to sexual identity, child socialization, therapeutic behavior, and maintenance of the family system, since they have stronger implications for communication.

Virginia Satir's idea that the family resembles a mobile can be adapted to help visualize how various roles function within a family to affect the family system's balance. Figure 5–1 depicts a mobile with the systemic parts balanced by the multiple roles operating within the family, such as provider, housekeeper, and child caregiver. These role functions become attached or superimposed on the family system characteristics because the ways in which the family survives financially or the children behave affect the stress on parts of the system.

Let us next examine each of these five family role functions. Because of the importance of male-female communication and how sex and the biosocial issues involved affect family interaction, we will discuss this function first.

Figure 5–1 _____
Family Role Functions

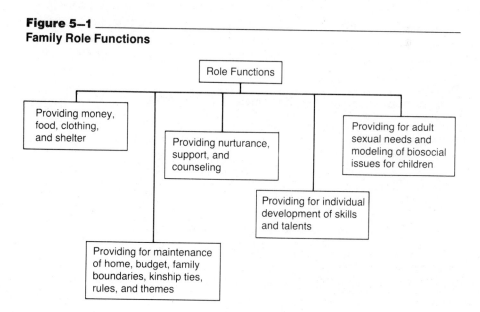

Providing for Sexual and Gender Issues

We will discuss the female and male roles in families, because an important aspect of the adult sexual function is the modeling of biosocial issues for children. We will then develop ideas about sex-role socialization, androgyny, and sexual fulfillment as they relate to family communication.

The ways in which roles evolve in families, such as what "moms" do compared to what "dads" do or how involved or uninvolved aunts, uncles, or grandparents are with the couple and their children have usually been passed on from families-of-origin as beliefs as well as practices or behaviors (Lieberman, 1979, 50). If a couple has diverse backgrounds, role issues are more likely to cause conflicts. Feldman has summarized the numerous research studies on sex roles and found that the prescriptive characteristics listed in Table 5–1 were either expected or allowed in male and female roles (1982, 355).

You may recognize that a discussion of *sex roles*, or what it means to be "male" or "female," overlaps with ideas about marital roles of husband and wife. Societal pressures to perform male or female roles often goes against family roles. An effective mother needs assertiveness, negotiating skills, and group leadership skills to function in her role. Likewise, a husband and father needs compassion, gentleness, and an emotional range of feelings to cope with or understand his spouse and children.

These role characteristics are important because of the ways they can affect family communication. Feldman concluded that the culturally defined characteristics of what was appropriate or inappropriate in sex roles indicate that "men are not supposed to act like women, and women are not supposed to act like men" (355). Further verification of differences between mothers and fathers can be found in a study of full-time employed couples who revealed their perceptions of major parental role responsibilities in raising children. Parents agreed highly on role responsibilities for a male child but significantly less for a female child. More

---

Table 5–1 _____

Psychological Dimensions of the Female and Male Roles

The female role. Women are expected to be (or allowed to be) the following:
1. Home-oriented, child(ren)-oriented.
2. Warm, affectionate, gentle, tender.
3. Aware of feelings of others, considerate, tactful, compassionate.
4. Moody, high-strung, temperamental, excitable, emotional, subjective, illogical.
5. Complaining, nagging.
6. Weak, helpless, fragile, easily emotionally hurt.
7. Submissive, yielding, dependent.

The male role. Men are expected to be (or allowed to be) the following:
1. Ambitious, competitive, enterprising, worldly.
2. Calm, stable, unemotional, realistic, logical.
3. Strong, tough, powerful.
4. Aggressive, forceful, decisive, dominant.
5. Independent, self-reliant.
6. Harsh, severe, stern, cruel.
7. Autocratic, rigid, arrogant.

mothers than fathers indicated similar responsibilities for both male and female children. Fathers placed greater emphasis on girls' acquiring emotional skills and boys' acquiring instrumental skills and attitudes for working in the future. They wanted sons more than daughters taught cognitive development skills, such as reading and writing, assertiveness skills to deal with peer pressure, and questioning skills to evaluate rules and standards (Gilbert et al., 1982, 267). Another study found that daughters were deprived of the training in independence that sons received (Hoffman, 1977, 649). These studies have indicated that many men reinforce stereotypical attitudes about how male and female children should be raised. These attitudes restrict children's development and affect their communication within the family.

Sex-Role Socialization. When you were growing up, what were your family's biosocial beliefs about males and females? Did you hear any of the following? "Boys don't play the piano—girls do." "Girls aren't engineers!" "Boys don't cry." Or perhaps you heard, "Girls can be anything they want to be." "Boys can cry if they're hurt, just as girls do."

This process of learning what it means to be male or female begins at birth. Even as newborns, males and females are handled differently and may be provided with "sex-appropriate" toys. Males and females learn expected behaviors at an early age. Studies of kindergarten children show boys keenly aware of what masculine behaviors are expected of them and restricting their interests and activities to avoid what might be judged feminine. Girls continue to develop feminine expectations gradually over five more years (Hartley, 1974, 7).

Some people believe that separate male and female behaviors are necessary for the continuation of the family as they have known it. Some religious and political groups and certain cultural traditions support strong male-female distinctions, seeing such practices as necessary for continued family existence and development. For example, in the Mormon church, one night a week is set aside as a "family home evening." The father, as "head of the house" has the responsibility to preside, which is in keeping with the church's male-female role distinctions applied to the family. Although you may believe in open and caring communication, you may also believe that men and women should fulfill certain family functions on the basis of sex. For others, such sexually bound distinctions appear repressive. This position is well represented in the following statement: "If men cannot play freely, neither can they freely cry, be gentle, nor show weakness—because these are 'feminine,' not 'masculine.' But a fuller concept of humanity recognizes that all men and women are potentially strong and weak, both active and passive, and that these and other human characteristics are not the province of one sex" (Sawyer, 1970, 6).

Part of the patterning of behaviors the child will imitate comes from the communication rules in the family that pertain to sexual distinctions. Sexually bound rules may determine who can perform or respond to such communication behaviors as crying, swearing, asking for money, hitting, or hugging. The sex-based communication directives you received as a child come into play when you form your own family system. For example, as we noted in Chapter 4, Jourard (1971) suggests that men are thought to disclose less about themselves than women and keep more secrets. Compared to women, men relate more impersonally to others and see themselves as the embodiment of their roles rather than as humans enacting roles. Jourard (1974) believes that men do not express the entire breadth and depth of their inner experience, either to themselves or to others (28). Shimanoff (1983) discovered that men do not trust other men and prefer to express their emotions to women, whom they perceive to be more nurturing (178). Lewis (1978) attributes this behavior to the competition between men, who fear that talking about emotions reduces their competitive edge (120).

Self-disclosure and openness are critical to communication and sharing love within families; if men accept a very restrictive definition of their nurturing communication, they may deprive themselves and their family members of desired intimacy. Women may suffer when female role prescriptions prohibit spontaneous, assertive, or independent communication. Yet, each family member's behavior is constantly modified by the other members with whom he or she interacts.

Androgyny. The concept of androgyny has implications for communication within families (Turner, 1982; Korman, 1983; May, 1980; Adelson, 1980; Murray, 1983). *Androgyny* means "the human capacity for members of both sexes to be masculine and feminine in their behaviors—both dominant and submissive, active and passive, tough and tender" (DeFrain, 1979, 237). Applied to communication, androgyny means the evaluation of all types of issues via communication that

Parents communicate sex-role expectations to their children.

focuses on the merits or demerits of those issues without reference to the sex of the persons involved. Bem (1974) describes the androgynous person as flexible, adaptive, and capable of being both instrumental (assertive, competent, forceful, and independent) and expressive (nurturing, warm, supportive, and compassionate) depending upon the demands of the situation (155).

Androgynous communication happens more in a family system with a person orientation. A position orientation, operating with fixed roles, makes adaptability difficult and maintains gender distinctions (Turner, 7). Korman's comparison of the dating behavior of feminists and nonfeminists revealed that feminists are more likely to share dating expenses and to initiate dates (575). An androgynous gender role orientation was also shown to be an important psychological resource for women in high stress situations (Patterson and McCubbin, 1984, 102).

The goal of an androgynous approach would be not to waste energy creating or maintaining sex stereotypes but to concentrate efforts on communication behaviors that provide options for humans to be themselves. Androgynous married partners have demonstrated more understanding of their spouses. They have perceived emotional messages much more accurately and listened more empathically (Indvik and Fitzpatrick, 1982, 43).

Sexual Activity as Communication. Another aspect of the sexual identity function relates to engaging in sexual activity. Sexual behavior is a form of communication that has a powerful effect on the quality of a marital relationship.

"If there is anything I would wish for my daughter as she enters marriage, it would be the ability to talk to her husband about sex. It was unthinkable to me that men and women could really talk about what gave them pleasure in sexual activity. My husband and I spent years in troubled silence. It took an affair, a separation, and counseling for us to be able to begin to talk about our sexual life."

Even in today's more "open" society, many communication breakdowns stem from an inability of couples to communicate honestly about their sexual relationship. In Carlson's study of the sexual expectations of married couples, 80 percent of both spouses indicated that the husband initiates sexual activity more than the wife, but 45 percent of the husbands felt that both should have equal responsibility. Wives responded differently; only one fourth thought it should be an equal responsibility, and an equal number saw no duty involved (1976, 103). Both spouses in this study disapproved of either refusing sexual relations, but husbands felt more strongly about it. Although most spouses usually granted their partner's request for sex, only 10 percent of the husbands refused or ignored the request compared to 30 percent of the wives. Three fourths of the couples considered sexual activity extremely important to them.[1]

---

[1]From John Carlson, "The Sexual Role," pp. 103, 105 in ROLE STRUCTURE AND ANALYSIS OF THE FAMILY edited by F. Ivan Nye. Copyright©1976 by Sage Publications, Inc. Reprinted by permission of Sage Publications, Inc.

The difference in the responses of wives and husbands indicate potential communication problems. Couples tend to say little to one another about this more intimate part of their relationship. Whether from fear or family rules that inhibit discussion, couples avoid the topic. Feldman observed that a woman's inhibitions against sexual assertiveness prevent her from being active in meeting her needs. This behavior reinforces the man's expectation that she is not interested but goes along with satisfying his needs. This response blocks his empathic understanding of her needs and the circle of poor communication continues (363).

In relationships between couples, unsolved problems in other aspects of their lives can be carried into the sexual relationship. A kind of sexual politics game dominates the relationship and one or the other spouse uses power, excuses, pressure, or ignoring tactics instead of direct communication. Some couples reach a stalemate and miss the potential joys and rewards of intimacy. Others learn to communicate about their sexual behavior.

Providing for Nurture and Support

In a family, members need mutual admiration, support, and reassurance. Marcy needs a hug from her husband Joe when she comes home from a hard day's work. Their children, Jeff, Debbie, and Cheryl, each need to know that their parents enjoy their presence and willingly provide for their needs. In all of these functions, children influence the role satisfaction parents receive. Cheryl's perception of her mother's willingness to listen to her problems affects their communication. Transactionally, family happiness develops when each member meets the needs and expectations of the others. Children are socialized by their parents, peers, and the environment, which, in turn, affect children's capacities to nurture and be supportive.

Developing Nurturing in Children. This function incorporates communication, since it is the chief process used to transmit values of the parents and community to the children. Through verbal and nonverbal permissions, directives, and answers to questions, children learn what parents and society expect of them. The parent who carries out most of the responsibilities of the childcare function has the potential for a greater socializing influence. In one study, although approximately two out of three spouses indicated they shared socialization tasks, observations revealed the wife more involved than the husband. Fathers were more involved with sons than daughters and mothers more with daughters than sons, but overall, mothers did more socializing of both sons and daughters (Gecas, 1976, 39–40). Children experience their fathers as colder, less empathic, and less caring than their "Moms," especially in verbal and nonverbal signs of love (Slevin and Balswick, 1980; Shepard, 1980).

"Somehow it seems easier to raise a girl these days than a boy. Girls can be told they can do anything that was traditionally male or female, but that's not the case

for boys. I finally ended up telling my five-year-old son that he could cry whenever he wanted at home but that he should try not to cry at school. Although I hate to restrict him in this way, I am afraid of how the other children will make fun of him if he 'acts like a girl.' "

Although socialization for nurturing relates directly to moral and cultural values, it can also specify acceptable or unacceptable communication behaviors such as yelling, lying, crying, hugging, directness, and silence. We all experience communication socialization. Our family-of-origin directly affects our childhood and usually our adult communication competence. For example, children who never engage in making decisions, defending a point of view, or negotiating for something will not automatically develop such communication skills when they leave their childhood home.

Yet, in keeping with the interactive nature of roles, children can refuse to accept parts of the socialization process. This frustrates parents, especially those in an extremely rigid family system who cannot be flexible enough to present other options or who may not know other ways to socialize their children.

A father who wants to devote more time and energy to his children and asks to reduce his job commitments runs the risk of being misunderstood by his employers and friends who perceive him as less ambitious or competent. Conversely, a mother who diligently pursues a career and reduces her "home duties" takes the chance of being labeled a "poor mother." Communication between a couple can also become confused if the mother feels threatened when the father demonstrates to relatives and neighbors that he is capable of childcare and insists that the family can live on less money, eliminating the need for his overtime pay. Likewise, the father can feel undermined in his providing role when the wife demonstrates her capabilities in a career and puts pressure on him to take more responsibility for the children (Feldman, 1982, 370).

Providing Support and Empathy. This function, sometimes called the *therapeutic function,* implies a willingness to listen and hear the problems of another. The listening must be empathic in order to give the other the understanding needed or the chance to ventilate pent-up feelings of rage, frustration, or exhaustion. Not only should adults do it for one another, but their children require the same kind of listening.

"My mother has been an incredible support to me. She never made any judgments about my divorce and has always been around to listen to me. She doesn't tell me what to do with my life, but if I'm obviously upset about work or the kids, she will stop whatever she is doing and pay attention to me as if nothing else is going on in her world."

Thus, the supporting function implies empathy, which requires nonjudgmental understanding of another person. In addition to having someone available in times of crisis or to hear about a problem, family members need someone to give them a sense of belonging—a sense of occasional refuge from the realities of the world they want to ignore or gain time to cope with. If the communication channels between family members encourage and permit the expression of open feelings, various individuals in the family can carry out the therapeutic role, which might include offering advice and questioning motives. For example, one brother can serve as sounding board for another.

Parental supporting behaviors provide children with models of such actions. When children receive emotional reassurance and support from parents, they realize they can bring up problems that originate outside the family and get help or understanding. The nurturing function may be carried out by friends or members of the extended family, particularly for single adults or single-parent families where only one adult resides. Severe family breakdowns may occur if boundaries keep members from supportive people. In extremely cohesive families, certain problems may be avoided, since they could threaten the powerful connectedness, while in very low cohesive families, members may not feel that anyone cares enough to listen. Members of such families may need to go elsewhere for emotional support, which leads us to the important role function of providing for the personal development of each family member.

Providing for Individual Development

This role function includes those tasks that each individual must fulfill in order to become self-sufficient. While each family member is part of a system, each must develop his or her own personality in order to take pride in his or her self-concept. The need to be independent and autonomous is as great as the need to be an interdependent member of the family system. A sense of individual achievement in meeting physical, intellectual, emotional, and social demands upon the mind and body is necessary in order to survive meaningfully both in the outside world and within the family. Family members who do not develop this role function can easily become dependent or enmeshed in the system. A "take care of me" attitude on the part of any member diminishes the wholeness and interdependence aspects of the family system. Babies begin life with the need for constant care to survive but must progress toward self-care.

Family members must facilitate for one another opportunities for self-discovery and development of talents. Parents do the majority of this task in their children's formative years, but from an early age, children influence one another's talents. Competition for grades, positions on sports teams or musical groups, and membership in organizations all create options for self-growth.

Providing for Role Maintenance and Management

No family system continues to operate efficiently without members' performing certain tasks. If no one puts money in the bank, checks bounce. If no one disciplines the children, the police may arrive or the school authorities complain of truancy. If no one ever makes dental or medical appointments, the family members' teeth may rot and health fail. This role function necessitates someone taking responsibility for carrying out these tasks.

Children play a vital part in this role function, especially in large families or those in which both parents work. Sometimes they cherish the title "Mommy's helper" or "Daddy's assistant." Older children sometimes spend hundreds of hours baby-sitting, folding clothes, mowing lawns, answering telephones, sweeping floors, and making beds. In any family, the washer and dryer have to be kept in motion and the garbage moved out, or chaos can develop.

One important maintenance function is the maintaining of kinship ties to the extended family network, as well as ties to neighbors and friends. This is a part of management of boundary limits, as is the handling of outside institutions and organizations. We will focus on the kinship function because of its importance to family communication.

Kinship Maintenance.

Kinship involves sharing, participating in, and promoting the family's welfare as contacts are maintained with relatives outside the family home. Parents, children, sisters, brothers, uncles, aunts, cousins, and step-relatives are all involved in maintaining a family network. Whether or not one is included or excluded from family events or hears the latest family gossip signifies one's place within the family system.

While fulfilling the kinship function, family members may operate within their own rules or rituals, and outsiders may not feel welcome or included in the unique family communication patterns. Information about misdeeds of family members (Uncle Mike's divorce, or Brent's involvement with drugs) may be discussed with close relatives, such as the couple's parents or brothers and sisters, but not with cousins, aunts, and uncles.

Holidays are a special communication time in most families. Relatives may travel many miles to share these events. In some families, particularly highly cohesive ones, attendance at get-togethers is mandatory, and only illness or great distance may be acceptable excuses. Exchange through intimate and economic currencies occurs as part of a ritual. In some households, the holidays can cause great pain, since certain "cut-off" members may be excluded, or members of low cohesive families may feel they are missing something.

Women do most of the communicating with relatives. One study found that husbands maintained fewer kinship contacts with their relatives and actually had more contact with their wife's kin. In giving financial aid to kin and settling disputes with relatives, husbands more often made the decisions, suggesting that the husband usually delegates the kinship tasks. Working wives and those with large families gave less attention to kinship tasks. Ninety percent of interaction with kin was concentrated in three areas: visiting, recreation, and communication by letter and telephone (Bahr, 1976).

The single-parent and blended family systems encounter special kinship concerns. For example, in divorced families, there may be special problems in communication with the ex-spouse and his or her new family. One of the ex-partners may refuse to communicate with the other; children may become pawns and resent forced separation from legitimate kinship ties.

Kinship ties can cause communication problems when families-of-origin do not let go of their offspring, even when he or she joins a new system. Frequent contact with the family-of-origin reinforce previous role expectancies. According to Longini (1979), an individual still "maintains the part that has been assigned to him by his family. Clan pressure is a hard thing to resist" (9).

Since a family consists of persons who consider themselves to be a family, kinship ties often include extended family members bound together by caring. Such groups engage in kinship behaviors similar to those previously mentioned. Alternative life-style couples experience additional systemic pressures because of societal biases that make communication more difficult, even with their families-of-origin.

"Since my immediate family is dead and any other relatives on my husband's side or my side live thousands of miles away, we have worked at creating a 'local family.' Over the years we have developed close friends who serve as honorary aunts and uncles for our children. The highlight of our Christmas is our annual dinner when we all get together to decorate the tree and the children get to see Uncle Bernard or Aunt Lois within a family context. I feel closer to these people than I do to many blood family members."

Such activities represent a special way to communicate the message that kinship is important. In this mobile age where families often live great distances from their kin or have few relatives, this idea has merit.

When family members feel safe in sharing their problems, joys, and family celebrations, they reap the benefits of the kinship function. The immediate system experiences the extra security, protection, and warmth of the larger unit of relatives. Ideally, communication can flow from kin outside the immediate family, back and forth with members inside the family, and be enriched and deepened by the support and sharing that occurs. The kinship circle can provide a ring of insulation around the family, with communication serving as the vehicle for support and comfort.

Other role maintenance and management functions include decision making to facilitate the family system's operation; housekeeping and childcare; establishing standards and rules for family members; providing for recreation and health needs; and taking care of family budgets, bills, income taxes and savings/investments. We will reserve our discussions of decision making and conflict for later chapters. Here, we will discuss the housekeeping, childcare, and recreational aspects of family roles, which can occupy enormous amounts of time, especially during a family's formative years.

Housekeeping Management. The *housekeeping function* traditionally has meant that the wife performs the cooking, cleaning, and maintenance of the home, but this is changing. Although one survey showed that 70 percent of the men said housekeeping should be shared, they held that it was more the responsibility of the woman. Interestingly, only 55 percent of the women thought it should be a shared responsibility (Slocum and Nye, 1976, 90). Housekeeping is most likely shared when the wife works full time, serving in a providing function, and when the couple has children. Such families face a time bind and may have to work to find "quality time," or time for nurturing communication to occur.

Most men strongly identify with the providing function and would be reluctant to give it up, but women do not identify that strongly with housekeeping. Women's days as primary housekeeper may be numbered (Slocum and Nye, 99), resulting in extensive renegotiation within families.

Childcare Management. The keeping of the child physically and psychologically safe is also changing. For the child, *management* means being bathed, dressed, fed, housed adequately, and protected from terrifying experiences (Gecas, 33). In our society of smaller families and couples who are childfree by choice, childcare has diminished in importance for some families. Yet, even in small families, the arrival of children requires parents to assume childcare and socialization responsibilities for a long period of time.

"Having a baby was a real shock to our system. Although we wanted a child, we just never understood what a change would occur in our whole way of life. After Andy was born, we had a year in which all we talked about was diapers, formula, baby clothes, and thermometers. When we got some time to ourselves, we were too tired to do more than stare at TV. Our communication revolved around the baby and his needs."

Even when the children leave home, certain aspects of childcare continue. Rossi (1968) sums it up when she declares, "We can have ex-spouses and ex-jobs, but not ex-children" (32). Also, more unwed mothers are opting to raise their children, and more single parents are taking full responsibility for childcare—making it an enormous task in some cases. Parents are under tremendous financial pressure, because it takes thousands of dollars to raise a child. Caring for children involves continual adaptation to their changes, especially as they move through developmental stages, and involves decisions about whether to, and how best to, keep a child physically and psychologically safe.

Recreation Management. *Recreation* means those things you do beyond work for relaxation, entertainment, or personal development (Dumazedier, 1967, 13–14). Families vary as to which parent is responsible for carrying out the recreational function, but research indicates that both spouses consider it important and should be done (Carlson, 137). More husbands than wives plan family recreation activities and feel more strongly about their value. Yet, with the rise of dual-career families and increased opportunities in sports for women, this may change.

Family recreation can be complicated, because individual members have their own interests as well as the desire or obligation to participate in family activities. Extremely cohesive families encourage much group activity, whereas families with low cohesion may not.

Although the recreational function provides opportunities for nurturing communication, in some families, people perform the role in isolation or nonfamilial settings. Stereotypically, men have found a recreational niche in tough, masculine athletic behaviors. Parental behavior telegraphs to children what is expected recreational behavior, and conflicts may result if a child does not measure up. Most of us have seen parents yelling at a Little League umpire or at their eight-year-old batter who has struck out. In some families, recreation, such as bowling or bridge, provides a means to escape from the family. Although some of these times may be important, if all recreation is separate, important shared communication experiences may be missed.

Providing Family Resources

Men are expected to be major providers in families (by a ratio of three to one in most studies) and laws and customs help to carry out these expectations. Studies reveal that both men and women feel that a married women should work only if she wants to do so. If a mother does not have a husband and has day-care services, then a slight majority thinks she should work.

Women have been limited in terms of the providing function, which has traditionally affected their decision making power within the family system. Due to inflation, increasing educational and career opportunities for women, improvements in day care and nursery schools, smaller families, greater numbers of female-headed single-parent families, and automation in the home, increased numbers of women have gone to work; today, women comprise over 55 percent of the work force (Bureau of Labor Statistics Report). Thus, the providing function is being shared or assumed by single heads of families. As more men and women share responsibility for providing resources, greater potential for shared power and decision making results.

Traditionally, married women with a high level of education are more likely to share in providing for the family. Over half of working couples put their income into a joint account from which either member can spend. Another third turns the money over to the wife to manage and disburse (Slocum and Nye, 85–86). This information about how much women provide and how income is managed often brings about conflicts in communication. Such a shift in the providing function has modified the traditional housekeeping function. These changes have a profound effect on everyday communication within the family as well as on male and female familial behavior.

We have examined five functions of adult family roles. Each family combines these functions in unique ways. For example, in the Kondelis family, childrearing and child socialization may no longer be important functions, although recreation may be highly valued and organized by the husband/father. Most housekeeping functions may be provided by a cleaning service, whereas providing may be done by both husband and wife. In the Rosenthal family, the single mother may engage primarily in the providing and therapeutic functions, delegating childcare and socialization functions to the two older children. Recreation may be more individually oriented, while kinship functions may receive limited attention. Research on two-parent black families indicates that there is more role flexibility between black partners and that black fathers play a larger part in housekeeping, childrearing, and nurturing than do white fathers. Additional studies of roles indicate that black women feel freer to initiate sex and find it less a source of tension. (McGoldrick, 1982, 418)

There are other ways of viewing functions that would place greater emphasis on child-related functions, although, as children mature, they participate more actively in many functions. In some single-parent or dual-career families, children may be inappropriately required to engage in a type or amount of activity usually reserved for a spouse. For example, an older child may assume total childcare or housekeeping responsibilities in a busy dual-career household. In a single-parent system, children may be expected to provide therapeutic listening or empathy that might be expected of a spouse in a two-parent household. Members of highly adaptable families may find themselves fulfilling numerous functions on an unpredictable schedule, whereas in highly rigid families, specific functions may be associated with the same individual indefinitely.

THE PERFORMANCE OF ROLE FUNCTIONS

"I have had a great deal of experience with role conflict in my marriage. I spend most of the time with my in-laws wearing the mask of the 'wonderful little woman-wife' who does all the traditional things while they act like guests in my home. I feel such a sense of relief when our visits are over because we each know this is a big fake, but no one will remove the mask."

Our definition of family roles emphasizes the repetitive pattern of behaviors that members use to carry out family functions. Such repetition can cause interpersonal and individual conflicts over role tasks. Repetition can be boring and confining to individuals who find themselves expected to behave in certain role functions in certain ways. Much negotiation occurs as system members attempt to work out their own definitions of the role interchange. We will divide our discussion into (1) interpersonal conflicts over roles, (2) intrapersonal conflicts over roles, and (3) roles and communication competence.

Interpersonal Conflicts Over Roles

While individuals may know what is expected of them in a family, not all members perform the expected behaviors. For example, a husband may relinquish the provider function and decide to write "the great American novel," or he may suffer a fall that prevents him from returning to work. Consequently, his wife may be thrust into providing for the family with resulting potential conflict. When this happens, the organizational structure in the system changes; a new kind of interdependence must evolve. Family messages are punctuated differently; equifinality is achieved by new means. Role changes, especially by parents, upset the balance in the system. Achieving wholeness requires patient communication.

If complementary or significant others have different expectations of the way a person should be performing in a role, conflict may occur. A child may expect far more of a parent in the nurturing function and complain about the lack of emphasis on it. A wife may expect her husband to assume half the provider resonsibility and resent his limited attention to what she considers his duty.

If the priorities or goals of system members are not congruent with each other, role conflict may occur. If money is critical to one spouse and recreation has a high priority for the other, there may be major fights over how much time either spouse or both should devote to moneymaking efforts. For many couples, the addition of the first baby signals a whole set of role changes, which are often accompanied by conflict. One spouse may suddenly devote extensive time to the childcare function, thereby neglecting the therapeutic or kinship functions that the other spouse expects and values highly.

Feelings for the other person may affect the extent to which conflict occurs. A parent may react differently to each child based on the child's behavior. For example, a mother with extensive childcare responsibilities may abuse one child and not another. A child of a single parent may be co-oppted into the therapeutic role and serve as a surrogate spouse to provide emotional support. Usually, such actions lead to later conflict as both parties struggle to maintain roles that are not appropriate to their ages or relationship. Other family members often resent the favored status given to the co-opted brother or sister.

"As the oldest daughter, I ended up with a great deal of responsibility and feel as if I lost part of my own childhood. My mother was an alcoholic and my father and I almost became the 'adult partners' in the house. He expected me to take care of the younger kids and to fix meals when Mom was 'drying out.' I hated all the work I had to do and all the responsibility. He didn't even want me to get married because he didn't know how he would cope."

These behaviors affect all parts of any family system. Although these and other issues lead to interpersonal role conflict, some people experience role conflict within themselves.

Intrapersonal Conflicts Over Roles

Occasionally, people find themselves in roles that do not fit their self-concepts, which leads to internal conflict. Some parents experience difficulty adjusting to childcare responsibilities expected of them. Others find that they did not expect to be breadwinners or do not see themselves as integral members of an extensive kinship network. Such differences between how you see yourself and how you act may lead to intense internal conflicts. In multigenerational systemic terms,

Bradt (1980) suggests that the idea of primacy of the mother developed because fathers and extended family members failed to participate as co-parents, grand-fathers, godfathers, and uncles. He feels that too often the two-parent biological family is isolated, and the economic system operates so that fathers work outside the home, resulting in mother-baby bonds, creating an "omnipotent system" called "Momism" (129).

People sometimes find themselves in roles that they expected to assume com-fortably but which they cannot perform adequately. Although the new "supermom" is pictured as balancing a career, household duties, and childrearing duties with equanimity, many young women have discovered that there are not enough hours in a day to maintain such a schedule, and they cannot fulfill their ideal wife/mother role. This often leads to disappointment and anger at themselves for not fulfilling expectations (Nock and Kingston, 1984; Maret and Finley, 1984; Crother, 1984). Even men who believe in equality experience difficulty in returning the emotional backing and encouragement they receive from their wives. Too many men have not been socialized to assume nurturing roles (Elman and Gilbert, 1984).

Such interpersonal and individual role conflicts necessitate sensitive and extensive communication among members of a family system if it is to be recali-brated to fit the needs of individual members. Roles constitute an important way of regulating family life. Yet, if they are viewed as "set in stone" descriptions of how people in certain family positions should act, they will limit personal and system growth. Thus, roles should be seen as reflections of the individual and his or her interpersonal encounters, a conception which implies a transactional growth process.

COUPLE AND FAMILY TYPOLOGIES

Although role analysis is a very common way of viewing family systems, increasing attention has been given to the use of family and marital typologies for understanding family interaction. A family's behavior and organization can be classified into various *typologies*, or family types, depending upon the patterns of its interactions. When these types emerge, with consistency of behavior under cer-tain recognizable conditions, we can predict members' behavior. Varied approaches have been developed; we will discuss some basic concepts in order to understand their communication implications.

Fitzpatrick's Couple-Oriented Research

One approach to classifying systems may be found in Fitzpatrick's couple-ori-ented research. In her early work, influenced by Kantor and Lehr, Fitzpatrick (1976; 1977) tested a large number of characteristics to find out which made a dif-ference in maintaining couple relationships. She isolated eight significant factors: conflict avoidance, assertiveness, sharing, the ideology of traditionalism, the ide-ology of uncertainty and change, temporal (time) regularity, undifferentiated space, and autonomy. An individual or couple fits a type when their answers indicate they possess a number of characteristics. Fitzpatrick designated relational definitions of traditional, separates, and independents, plus six mixed couple types wherein the husband and wife described their relationship differently. The major mixed type was separate/traditional.

Independent types accept uncertainty and change; they pay limited attention to schedules and traditional values. Independents represent the most autonomous of the types but do considerable sharing and negotiate autonomy. They do not avoid conflict. Independents are more likely to support an androgynous and flexible sex role (Fitzpatrick et al., 1982, 63).

Separates differ from independents in greater conflict avoidance, more differentiated space needs, fairly regular schedules, and less sharing. In relationships, separates maintain a distance from people and problems, even their spouses; they experience little sense of togetherness or autonomy. Separates usually oppose an androgynous sexual orientation and tend to avoid conflict.

Traditionals uphold a fairly conventional belief system and resist change or uncertainty, since it threatens their routines. Physical and psychological sharing characterize the traditional type. This leads to a high degree of interdependence and low autonomy. Few boundaries exist in the couples' use of physical and emotional space. They will engage in conflict but would rather avoid it. Uncertainty and change in values upset them. Traditionals, like separates, demonstrate strong sex-typed roles and oppose an androgynous orientation.

In the 40 percent of the couples whose members were not the same type, most of the husbands labeled themselves as separates and the wives labeled themselves as traditionals. The other mixed types included traditional/separate, independent/separate, separate/independent, traditional/independent, and independent/traditional (64; Indvik and Fitzpatrick, 1982).

Which relational type experiences the greatest satisfaction? Which couples are the most cohesive? In their summary of the research, Fitzpatrick and Best (1979) reported traditional couples significantly higher than the other three types on consensus, cohesion, relational satisfaction, and expressing affection. Independents were lower on consensus, open affection to one another, and dyadic satisfaction; however, their lack of agreement on issues regarding dyadic interactions did not impair their cohesiveness. Separates were the least cohesive but on relational issues appeared high on consensus. Separates demonstrated few expressions of affection toward their spouses and rated lower on dyadic satisfaction. In the separate (husband)/traditional (wife) category, couples had low consensus on a number of relational issues, but they were moderately cohesive. These couples claimed high satisfaction for their relationship and outwardly expressed much affection.

Further findings indicated that couples who agreed on relational definitions agreed with one another on a greater number of issues in their relationship. Those who agreed were also more cohesive. Interestingly, couples who disagreed on typing themselves were as satisfied with their marriages as couples who agreed on their definitions. Enduring relationships were characterized by more variety in the modes of communication used by partners (Fitzpatrick and Best, 167).

Table 5–2 on the following page summarizes the ways in which couple types responded to a variety of relationship measures, including sex roles and gender perceptions. In predicting communication, you might expect that traditional families would demonstrate affection and sharing of the functions discussed earlier in this chapter, with males and females remaining in defined positions. You could expect male dominance in attitudes and values regarding the providing, recreational, housekeeping, sex, and kinship functions, since the traditional type resists change. Since independents are more open to change, they might be more open to dual-career marriages and sharing the providing and housekeeping functions. Because independents value autonomy and avoid interdependence, individual couple members may be freer in their role functions. This self-reliance might better equip independents to handle the unknown and accept the inevitable changes that occur in roles and life.

The potential for problems when communicating about role functions relates especially to the separates who have not resolved the interdependence/autonomy issue in their marriage. Fitzpatrick uses the label "emotionally divorced" for this type, because separates are least likely to express their feelings to their partners. Thus, if a partner is dissatisfied with the role expectations of the other spouse yet cannot freely express these feelings, the relationship suffers.

Kantor and Lehr's Family Types

Relying on intensive study of nineteen families, researchers Kantor and Lehr (1976) developed a descriptive theory of family process. They identified basic component parts of family process and how these parts affected members' behavior (36–65).

As a means of dealing with the basic family issue of separateness and connectedness, or what Kantor and Lehr called "distance regulation," they developed a six-dimensional social space grid on which family communication takes place (70–78, 221). All communication represents efforts by family members to gain access to targets, i.e., things or ideas members want or need, according to these researchers. Specifically, family members use two sets of dimensions. One set reaches targets of affect, power, and meaning through the way they regulate the other—the access dimensions of space, time, and energy. Thus, families regulate the activities of people, objects, and events.

In carrying out the functions in any role, all family members have a target or goal of gaining some degree of affect, power, or meaning. *Affect* means achieving (e.g., in the kinship or socialization functions) some kind of intimacy or connectedness with the members of the family and receiving some reward in the form of nurturing behavior in their verbal and nonverbal communication. *Power* implies a member has the independence to select what he or she wants and the ability to get the money, skills, or goods desired. This freedom to choose what an individual wants gives a family member power and the separateness needed to develop autonomy. The third target is meaning. Each family member in the system seeks some

Table 5-2
Couple Type Differences on Relational Measures

Couple Types	Marital Satisfaction	Cohesion	Consensus	Affectional Expression	Sex Roles	Psychological Gender States (Wives Only)
Traditionals	high	high	high	moderately high	conventional	feminine
Independents	low	moderately high	low	low	nonconventional	sex-typed androgynous
Separates	low	low	moderately high	low	conventional	feminine sex-typed
Separates/ Traditionals	moderately high	moderately high	moderately high	high	conventional	feminine sex-typed
Other Mixed Types	moderately high	low	low	moderately high	depends on mixed type	depends on mixed type

philosophical rationale that offers reasons for what happens to them in the family and outside world. The acquisition of meaning by each member develops stronger self-concepts and provides an explanation of why members live as they do. When family members collectively find meaning in their interactions, cohesion develops.

Kantor and Lehr provide descriptions of the access dimensions (space, time, and energy) from an analogical as well as a physical point of view (66, 78, 90). The spatial dimensions include the way a family handles its physical surroundings (exterior and interior) and the ways in which the members' communication regulates their psychological distance from each other. The time dimension includes a consideration of clock time and calendar time in order to understand a family's basic rhythmic patterns. The energy dimension deals with the storing and expending of physical and psychological energy. Family communication usually involves at least one access dimension and one target dimension. For example, Kathy moves physically closer to Charlie, her husband, in order to gain more affection from him.

Using these six dimensions, the authors have created a typology for viewing families, consisting of open, closed, and random types, acknowledging that actual families may consist of mixtures of types. The ways in which these three family types maintain their boundaries, or regulate distance through access and target dimensions, account for their differences.

Closed families tend to regulate functions predictably with fixed boundaries. Such families interact less with the outside world. They require members to fulfill their needs and spend their time and energies within the family. Usually, there are emphases on authority and the continuation of family values. Events in closed families tend to be tightly scheduled and predictable. Family members often focus on the preservation of the past or plan for the future. Energy is controlled, used to maintain the system, and dispersed at a steady rate. Moderation, rather than excess, prevails (119–125).

In the *open family*, boundaries tend to remain flexible as members are encouraged to seek experiences in the outside space and return to the family with ideas the family may use if group consensus develops. Open families seldom use censorship, force, or coercion because they believe family goals will vary, change, and be subject to negotiation. They carry these characteristics into intimacy and conflict situations. Members are more likely to concern themselves with the present, while energy in this type is quite flexible. Family members do not have total freedom because they cannot use methods of refueling their energy that cause excess harm or discomfort to other family members (126–34). For example, a child cannot play records at the loudest level after ten o'clock at night when other family members wish to sleep.

Unpredictability and "do-your-own-thing" aptly describe the *random family*. The boundaries of space surrounding this family are dispersed. Family members and outsiders join in the living space based on interest or desire, or they voluntarily separate from one another without censure. Social appropriateness holds little importance for such members. Time is spent on an irregular basis. Each individual functions according to his or her own rhythm, resulting in high levels of spontaneity. People may change their minds and their plans at any time. Energy in the random family fluctuates. No one source for refueling has been predetermined by the family. Members may rapidly spend high levels of energy and then need long refueling periods.

> *"I think we must have been a random family during the first ten years of my life. I am next to last of eleven children and by the time I came along, the family was in chaos. The younger kids lived with different relatives off and on until we were almost adolescents. When we did live at home, things were always unpredictable. Every morning my mother would put a big pot of cereal on the stove and people would eat when they wanted. You never knew exactly who was going to be sleeping where each night. When I was about ten, my parents got their own life straightened out and enough older kids were gone so that we could live a more 'normal' life, although I found it hard to suddenly have rules that were enforced and times when I had to be places."*

Table 5–3 summarizes the characteristics that Kantor and Lehr delineated for each of these family types. You may identify more closely with one of the types, or you may find that your family incorporates two of the types. You may also realize how your family has shifted in typology over the years.

> *"As I grew up, my family could be described as a closed family. My parents kept a watchful eye over my three sisters' activities by scrutinizing friends, watching phone calls, keeping strict curfews, chaperoning dates, and generally isolating our family from 'them,' that is, the rest of the South Bronx community. Dad and Mom knew where you were going and whom you were with and told you what time to return. The communication pattern, mostly nonverbal, was also simple: the better you behaved, the more privileges you were allowed.*
> *Then things changed. When my father died, I found myself closer to my mother and vice versa. My sisters also found themselves closer, not only to my mother but to each other. My family has gradually progressed to a more open family. A general rule in our current family is that any requests for either joining or separating are viewed as reasonable and legitimate."*

An interesting comparison can be made between Fitzpatrick's and Kantor and Lehr's research. Olson's model of cohesion and adaptability (see Chapter 1)

Table 5–3

Characteristics of Family Types

Type of Family	Use of Space	Use of Time	Use of Energy
Closed	Fixed	Regular	Steady
Open	Movable	Variable	Flexible
Random	Dispersed	Irregular	Fluctuating

can also be integrated into their thinking. Fitzpatrick's and Olson's early work was greatly influenced by Kantor and Lehr. The terminology each theorist uses can be clarified by remembering that Fitzpatrick's *autonomy/interdependence* means *cohesion* to Olson and *affect* to Kantor and Lehr. *Adaptability* as used by Olson means *power* (measured behaviorally) to Fitzpatrick and to Kantor and Lehr. Fitzpatrick's *ideology* refers to *meaning* in Kantor and Lehr's thinking and does not appear in Olson's work. *Communication* is included in the behavioral data collected by Fitzpatrick. In Olson's model, *communication* appears as an *enabling dimension*, and in Kantor and Lehr as *distance regulation*.

Other Couple Types

Another way to view couples is found in Burgess et al.'s (1963) distinction between two types of marriage: "institutional" and "companionship." In institutional marriages, roles are sex differentiated, meaning males predominantly take charge of the provider, recreation, and sex roles, and wives carry out the childcare, child socialization, housekeeping, therapeutic, and kinship role functions. Husbands are more instrumental and rigid in their roles and wives are more expressive and flexible.

Couples in a companionship marriage place an emphasis upon their personalities' interacting and the affective aspects of their relationship. Love is openly expressed. Sexual enjoyment, companionship, and communication are expected to follow. Burgess believes the family is in transition from an institutional to a companionship type of relationship (Burgess et al., vii).

Using division of family tasks to determine family types, Scanzoni (1980) described three additional distinct types: (1) Head-Complement (meaning the wife does not work), (2) Senior Partner-Junior Partner (meaning the wife is employed but the husband remains the major provider), and (3) Equal Partner (meaning the wife describes herself as a co-provider). He found that wives who are equal partners have "greater labor force commitment, possess higher levels of material resources, participate more fully with their husbands in household task performances . . . than do junior partners" (137).

Roles continue to change, with women experiencing a difficult time adjusting to these changes. Both women and men must be highly dedicated to employment roles to succeed, yet more women than men are also expected to give priority to family roles. One hopeful study has indicated that husbands who agree with interchangeable rather than fixed roles for spousal behavior accept more responsibility for functions identified as childcare, meal preparation, and cleaning, the very tasks that require more time than other functions (Bird et al., 1984, 353). Other studies have proved a strong positive correlation between congruence of role perceptions and satisfaction in those roles. (See Luckey, 1960; Stuckert, 1963; Kotlar, 1965; Taylor, 1967; Baucom and Aiken, 1984; Patterson and McCubbin, 1984).

CONCLUSION

In this chapter, we took a transactional approach to roles, stressing the effect of family interaction on how roles are enacted. We examined the potential effect of position-oriented versus person-oriented role functioning on communication within the family system. After reviewing the various role functions within a family, we presented a typological approach to understanding families and their communication patterns.

A major consideration in examining roles or couple/family types is their dynamic nature, which is viewed in accordance with the personal developments and unpredictable circumstances faced by the people involved. No matter how straightforward each role or type appears, it is assumed and maintained on the basis of personal choice and adaptation to the overall family system.

IN REVIEW

1. Take a position and discuss: A family needs to be more position-oriented than person-oriented in order to function through crises over time.
2. Compare and contrast the communication tasks required in carrying out the role functions involved in providing resources and nurturance for the family. Describe these functions in a family with which you are familiar.
3. Discuss the types of negotiation you believe should occur for a dual-career couple and/or family to operate effectively.
4. Give examples of partners you know that fit Fitzpatrick's couple types.
5. Analyze your family or another real or fictional family and explain why it is an open, closed, or random family type. Cite examples of communication patterns in your answer.

Chapter 6

Power in Families

All families play some sort of power game. Even in the best of families, periodic power struggles occur. The experience of power begins with the birth of a child and continues through each of the developmental stages. We learn power dynamics first in our family-of-origin. The newborn child soon learns how to manipulate Mom or Dad into some kind of interdependence. By the time that child reaches the age of courtship and mate selection, each family member has had vast experience in creating, using, and sometimes enjoying the use of power or being depressed by a lack of it. Understanding how power operates in your family can be quite rewarding, because you have the ability to change the power dynamics, especially as you seek your own autonomy. Your growth can activate a developmental move in another family member, which influences the overall power balance as well as that individual (Terkelsen, 1980, 42).

"In my family-of-origin, my father is the power structure. Nearly all decisions rest with him. My mom does influence the decisions but Dad announces them. Both parents disciplined us as children, but our greatest fear was of our father. He hit us when we needed it. In my present family, my wife and I both share power and responsibility. She doesn't make an issue of authority and neither do I. My wife is very capable of decision making and of future planning, so I go along with her sometimes and she does the same with me."

Remember that successfully carrying out the different role functions requires the use of power. Role functions operate in a power environment that determines the family's decision-making process and the way in which conflict evolves, either constructively or destructively. Remember that some couple types, like traditionals or separates, handle power quite differently than independents. Remember that, in an institutional marriage, the partners view power instrumentally, with the male taking charge of the family finances and resources. In a companionship marriage, the partners are more likely to share power and avoid rigid sex differentiation on household tasks. Remember that some or all of these power dynamics take place in every family system, whether it is an open, closed, or random type. The main power goal in a family is to satisfy the system's needs by doing what must be done (Kantor and Lehr, 1976, 49).

THE CONCEPT OF POWER

Although power may be viewed in many ways, we will examine it within a systems context. Power has been defined as the ability or potential to influence others (Manz and Gioia, 1983, 461). Family researcher Wolfe (1959) stresses that power does not belong to an individual; rather, it is a property of a relationship between two or more persons. Thus, the following definition evolves: "Power, a system property, is the ability (potential or actual) of an individual(s) to change the behavior of other members in a social system" (Cromwell and Olson, 1975, 5). In addition, family power is the ability of individuals to change the behavior of other family members. We must not think of power in a family as static, or fixed. The power dimension in a family system may vary greatly over time, depending upon a host of factors: the age or developmental stage of the children or parents; the amount of predictable and unpredictable stress encountered by the family; and the economic, cultural, or intellectual resources and opportunities of the family. Power operates transactionally in a family, and any power maneuvers within it have a systemwide effect. One member cannot assert independence or dependence on an issue without affecting other members. As one or more members exert power or acquiesce to others' power plays, the whole system may be recalibrated. You may recall from Chapter 2 that a human system has properties of interdependence and wholeness. The transactional nature of power within a family creates interdependence upon one another. Each child or parent has the power to affect the relationships of any other people within the family as long as they allow this to happen. The total potential power in the family system, or wholeness, is greater than the sum of all the individual members' power. The system, through its adaptability mechanisms, reacts to all pressures and maintains balance between the power plays and players.

Power is a family system property, rather than the personal characteristic of any individual member. Power is a dynamic, interactive process that involves one family member who desires something from one or more other members. In turn, these members may affect all other members in the system. Thus, power creates reciprocal causation as family members transactionally interact over an issue. Power has both perceptual and behavioral properties. The way in which one family member perceives the power dynamics helps determine and explain the reasons for that member's actions. Importantly, the same power issue may be perceived differently by every other family member.

Think of family power as a way of examining the process by which group activity is accomplished. The family, collectively as a group, interacts about an end or goal that one or more family member desires. This individual goal sometimes conflicts with group or family goals. For the family member's goal to affect power dimensions, it must imply some form of desired behavior from other family members. Power is the ability of one or more family members to prevail in a family setting of conflicting ends so that he, she, or they achieve their goals (Turk, 1974, 47). Power represents action emerging from the varied talents, interests, and activities that family members are involved in. To understand power, one must identify the pattern of interaction the family goes through to accomplish a goal, which necessitates comprehending the verbal and nonverbal communication among all family members involved.

"It's hard to locate the source of power in my family. My mother appears to have the power because she can be so stubborn and demanding, although my father comes in a close second. Power is enforced merely by the threat of household warfare, which none of us can stand except my mother, who seems to enjoy it. Yet, I can see that my grandmother has great power to change things in our family by influencing my mother, and thus getting to me. She just says a few things that make my mother feel guilty and everyone has to shape up for a week."

Each of us could relate incidents of power plays or describe where we think family power lies, but sometimes we miss a power base or power play because of how we perceive power. In order to understand family power, we will examine: (1) family power domains, (2) development of family power, and (3) the communication of power strategies.

ASPECTS OF POWER IN FAMILY SYSTEMS

McDonald's model of the interrelatedness of units of analysis and dimensions of power (Figure 6–1) helps us visualize power (1980a, 844). The model begins with social power found in our environment. The definition of power includes a multidimensional, ongoing process view in which the family interacts with other systems in the social sphere, such as government, education, and business. Family power is a system property, which divides into marital (husband/wife power, dynamics), parental power (mother/father power), offspring (children/parent interactions), sibling (brother/sister, or combinations of sister/sister and brother/brother), and kinship (grandparent/aunts/uncles/stepfamily members). The power domains explain how power operates in families. To further clarify the concept of power, we will examine three family power domains: (1) power bases, (2) power processes, and (3) power outcomes.

Power Bases

The bases of family power are the resources a family member possesses that increase his or her chances to exert control in a specific situation. No two family members possess exactly the same resources to achieve their ends. You may have

Figure 6–1
Units of Analysis and Dimensions of Power

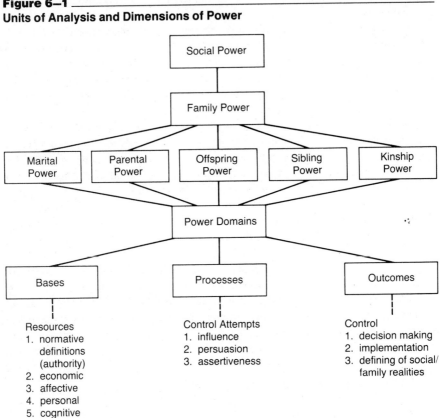

power because of your education or assertiveness. Your sister's power may come from her temper, while your mother may have the power to veto decisions. Yet, unless others respond to these power positions, no power can be exerted. If your brother does not respond to your assertiveness, you are powerless in relation to him. In order to understand the sources of power more completely, let us examine six bases of social power that can affect family systems (French and Raven, 1962; Raven et al., 1975, 218–19). These six are broader in concept than the five in McDonald's model; however, they are close in content.

1. *Punishment*, or coercive power, serves as a power base when you believe someone can punish you for acting or not acting in a certain way. For example, such coercive power may be based on Brian's belief that his wife Margaret can and will punish him for refusal of her requests. A child may hold power by "threatening" to punish his parents by repeated screams. Withholding money, food, or favors are ways of exercising punishment power.

2. *Positive reinforcement*, or reward power, serves as a base when you believe someone can provide you with something you desire. Brian may expect that Mar-

garet will do something nice for him if he cooperates. Messy rooms may be cleaned, dinners cooked, and cars washed for movie money. Rewards can affect your power—if you control the rewards a family member wants or needs.

3. *Expertise,* or knowledge, serves as a power base when you believe another family member knows more about a subject than you do. Expertise derives from Brian's awareness that Margaret has superior knowledge of a given subject or skill to direct him to the best solution. A teenager may instruct his or her mother on car care and maintenance, and she may accept this expertise.

4. *Legitimacy,* or position, serves as a power base when you accept that a particular role carries with it certain legitimate responsibilities. Legitimate power occurs when Brian accepts a certain role in their relationship, believing that Margaret has the authority or right to expect compliance, and he feels obliged to grant it. A daughter may accept her father's curfew because she accepts such regulations as a part of the fathering position.

5. *Identification,* or referent power, serves as a base when you see yourself as similar to another and you accept that position. Identification power occurs when Brian identifies with Margaret, because he feels she possesses attributes he admires, and he gets satisfaction from agreeing with her. A ten-year-old girl may identify with her fifteen-year-old sister and follow her sister's requests in order to feel "grown up."

6. *Persuasion,* or information power, serves as a base when you accept the carefully structured arguments of another. Such informational power develops from Margaret's communication ability to carefully and successfully explain to Brian the reasons for a change. A mother may carefully detail budget problems and persuade her children to keep their winter jackets one more year.

Note that these power terms are defined by the way in which the situation is perceived by others. In a family relationship, no member possesses all six of these power sources equally or uses all of them in a given situation. Some may never be used and others used in combination. It is possible for a husband to use reward and expertise power extensively in his interactions and simultaneously for his wife to use punishment and identification power in her interactions. Children in the same family might use legitimacy and persuasion power, especially if their views are encouraged and respected.

"My husband used to use a great deal of punishment power with the children and now he seems to use legitimacy as a way to get his own way. I have always tried to use a positive reward type of power and have tried to be knowledgeable about a subject before telling others what to do about it. My daughter-in-law tries to use persuasion most of the time. I can just see her planning her arguments. My son tries coercion with the children but seems to rely on legitimacy when he and his wife have differences. The baby runs the whole show sometimes, since he is able to manipulate us all by crying."

Power bases are related to income. According to Blumstein and Schwartz (1983), discovering how money bestows power tells us crucial things about a relationship (53). In their study of American couples, money established the balance of power in all couple types except lesbians. Acceptance of the male as provider gave husbands greater power. Likewise, in male couples, the one who had the larger income dominated. In female couples, this was not true because they attempted to avoid dependence of one woman on the other. In cohabiting heterosexual couples, women used their money to establish equality. Interestingly, the more each cohabitor earned, the more satisfied he or she was with the relationship (53–75). Thus, men and women feel and behave differently about dollars. According to Blumstein and Schwartz, money represents identity and power to men and to women, it represents security and autonomy (76).

Power Processes

The ways in which power operates in a family are revealed by its power processes, or the study of ongoing interaction among family members. These processes affect interactions in family discussions, arguments, problem solving, decision making, and times of crises. McDonald refers to these processes as control attempts through influence, persuasion, and assertiveness.

Researchers have examined the number of times people talk, how long they talk, to whom they address their comments, and how long a talk session lasts. They have also analyzed questioning, interrupting, and silence patterns and concluded that family members who talk most frequently and for the longest periods of time are dominant, and those who receive the most communication are the most powerful (Berger, 1980, 217).

Yet, as you know from your own experience, the longest or loudest talker may not hold the power in each situation. We have to distinguish between the power attempts a person makes and the final outcomes. We can look at assertiveness and control maneuvers that attempt to affect family power. Assertiveness means the number of attempts, for example, that Debra makes to change the behavior of her husband or sister. Control represents the influence or number of effective attempts that Debra made that changed the behavior of her husband or sister (Cromwell and Olson, 6).

In Chapter 3, we examined the complexities of messages and described how impossible it is for a person to avoid offering definitions of his or her relationship with another. All messages in a family are co-defined by the senders and receivers. They contain both report and command factors. Thus, family members may send mixed messages, which are difficult to analyze accurately. When an individual says one thing but means and wants something else, confusion results. Contradiction often appears in the nonverbal aspects of a message. In analyzing power messages, both the content and relationship dimensions must be analyzed carefully to understand family communication. According to Haley (1974), "a person who acts helpless attempts to control the behavior in a relationship just as effectively as another who acts authoritarian and insists on a specific behavior" (371). The following example illustrates how mixed messages with conflicting content and relationship components operate in one family.

"My sisters and I refer to it as the 'Greek Mother Syndrome' since that's our background, but it's the old 'Have a good time and don't worry about your poor old mother' game. My friends think my mother is really neat and flexible because of the things she says in front of them, but only I know what she really means. 'Of course Irene can get her own apartment' or 'Young women need to get off on their own these days' sounds terrific, but I can tell from her tone of voice and her face that she would die if I tried to be that independent."

Power Outcomes

The final area, family power outcomes, focuses upon "issues involving who makes decisions and who wins" (Cromwell and Olson, 6). In this aspect, one or more family members get their way or receive rights or privileges of leadership.

More research has been done on power outcomes, especially on decision making, than on power bases or power processes (Cromwell and Olson, 6). Some of the findings in this area are reported in Chapter 7. Researchers have studied whose ideas are accepted by family groups, who in the family went along with whom, and whose influence counted in which situations. It is easier to measure power outcomes than to measure power processes. Yet, in many cases, predictions made from the processes are not accurate. The loudest, longest talker may not have his ideas accepted. The most persuasive adult may lose to an angry child.

Conflict can function as a necessary condition for power. Through conflict, family members attempt to settle their differences. However, power resources can influence outcomes by suppressing potentially conflictual situations. Power hierarchies in the family system also establish guidelines for power processes that avoid conflicts yet affect power outcomes (McDonald, 843). Family members have orchestration power and implementation power. *Orchestration power* means that a family member usually makes decisions that do not infringe upon his or her time but determine the family life-style and major aspects of the system. The one with orchestration power can delegate unimportant and time-consuming decisions to the spouse or an older child who derives *implementation power* by carrying out these decisions (Safilios-Rothschild, 1976, 339). In the model of power, Figure 6–1, orchestration (related to decision making) and implementation appear under outcomes as controls.

Power bases influence power outcomes. Family members who can provide the greatest rewards may have the greatest power. Often, the balance of power rests with the partner who contributes the greatest resources to the marriage. Resources consist of whatever is rewarding to an individual or a relationship. Thus, a *resource* is anything that one partner makes available to the other to satisfy needs or attain goals (Blood and Wolfe, 1960, 68). Sources of power may be tied to rewards, which affect outcomes. It may be rewarding to avoid punishment, to gain positive reinforcement, to learn from an expert, to live within certain defined constraints, to identify with another person, to be persuaded, or most importantly, to be confirmed by others.

Some family members who give much to others, both emotionally and economically, expect much in return. The family member who suffers from an abuse of power or an injustice caused by one or more members may become upset, and this upsets the family system's balance. A family member who cannot achieve harmony within the system because he or she feels powerless may in extreme circumstances resort to separation, divorce, desertion, suicide, murder, or beatings. The exit act may be an important power play to a family member, but it can create new problems. Children may be trapped and have to wait to exercise their power to reject a defective family system. Family members consciously and unconsciously obtain certain outcomes from the actions they use in a power struggle. In many well-functioning families, members attempt to provide resources for each other in order to maintain a certain level of harmony.

In his review of power in families, Berger suggests that, although Blood and Wolfe found a positive relationship between the income, educational level, and occupation prestige of the husband and the extent of his power, " . . . the *absolute* number of resources a person brings to the marriage does not determine his or her power, but rather the *relative* contribution of resources to the relationship" (210). He maintains that most of the studies he reviewed provide support for the resource theory but found notable exceptions, particularly in studies of other cultures. Berger concludes that resources have been defined narrowly—mainly as economic contributions and social prestige and suggests that family research should include an analysis of resources, such as interpersonal skills, and personality orientations such as dominance, physical attractiveness, and sense of humor (214).

Power in the conjugal dyad involves an examination of the extent to which one spouse loves and needs the other. Safilios-Rothschild (1970), following up on Waller's earlier research on the principle of least interest, suggests that the spouse with the strongest feelings puts himself or herself in a less powerful position, because the person with less interest can more easily control the one more involved (548–49). She also suggests that the existence of an alternative relationship provides power to one or another family member.

"One of the ways I was finally able to live at home with some degree of peace was to make it clear to my father that I could and would go and live with his sister if he kept hitting me. My mother agreed with my position although she didn't like it, and he finally realized I was serious. Once he understood that I had somewhere else to go, he began to treat me better."

In discussing options for couples, Berger states, "The mere existence of alternatives does not ensure increased power for the spouse who has them; in addition, the other spouse must have some degree of commitment to the relationship so that the alternatives of the other spouse represent a real threat" (215). If Pat does not care deeply about Chris anymore, he may not become terribly upset by Chris' affair with another man, and Chris may not be able to use this new interest in a power play to win Pat back. According to systems theory, this change of feelings will affect the mutual influence and punctuation of messages. Remaining in the relationship requires system recalibration if the affair continues.

Couples may enter a relationship with unequal power, but the relationship can balance out over time. One family member may have most of the power in one area and another member in another area, and both may perceive their power as balanced. Also, the sharing of decisions and tasks causes the systemic balancing principle to operate. Many couples may attempt to develop family themes that stress equality of power, and those with children may encourage sharing of power with them. Themes such as "Each person is an individual" or "We respect all opinions" may lead to shared power.

"In the beginning of our relationship, Jack, who is older, tended to dominate. He had had a lover for several years and when that commitment ended, he made up his mind to be more autonomous in any future relationships. I resented his treating me as if I were Bill and assuming that we would conflict in similar situations in the same way. His behavior limited my trust in our relationship. Now that we have been together over five years, and he realizes that the past is not the present, we can make joint decisions, and both of us are much happier. Power flows more equally between us."

Each family uses a variety of power sources relevant to its needs and the personalities involved. In some families, traditional roles, including the biosocial issue of male dominance, are clearly defined, and since no one challenges them, the family operates as if that were the only way to function. In other families, negotiation has resulted in mutually acceptable compromises on power issues. In the following section, we will consider the development of power within marital and family systems.

DEVELOPMENT OF POWER IN FAMILY SYSTEMS

Due to the systemic nature of a family relationship, power occurs in a transactional manner. An alcoholic spouse cannot control the other unless the nonalcoholic spouse permits it. A mother relinquishes her own personal control when she gives a whining child power over her. Only the small child who has limited means of resisting power moves must accept certain power outcomes; for example, an abused toddler has few means of resisting punishment. Women have argued that they also have limited means of resisting power because in our culture, power outcomes have been largely, and sometimes unfairly, managed by men. Society has affected the development of power within families.

Gillespie (1971) claims that as long as the structure of society remains the same, giving men the "right" to make major decisions about moving, careers, investments, and so on, the majority of women have little chance to gain autonomy, regardless of how much good will is on the part of their husbands. Blood and Wolfe disagree with Gillespie, presenting a view that although some husbands have extensive power, they cannot take for granted the authority held by previous generations of men. Today's husband "must prove his right to power, or win power by virtue of his own skills and accomplishments in competition with his wife" (29).

These thoughts about power relationships between men and women relate to family boundaries, themes, and biosocial issues. If a family decides that each member, regardless of sex, should develop his or her potential in order to be self-sufficient, the power process and outcomes will differ from a family that believes men should take care of women. This belief limits the boundaries and possible future power options of female members. In the latter family, the boundaries of female experience more likely would be limited to contacts and training for homemaking and childrearing rather than banking or financial management of a corporation. If, however, the family cultivates a theme of achievement for every member, "The Nicholsens rank at the top of their classes" or "The Jones family will be active in politics and public service," the power dimensions will reflect these goals. Over time, the family system creates patterns of power that reveal to outsiders how these themes operate.

Types of Power Patterns

Spousal authority may be examined by the number and type of areas over which each spouse exercises authority. The spouse with the greater range of authority has the higher relative authority. Spouses may have shared authority, where there are areas of life jointly managed. According to Wolfe (1959), there are four authority types: wife-dominant, husband-dominant, syncratic, and autonomic. In husband- or wife-dominated families, major areas of activity are influenced and controlled by the dominant one. The following statements may sound familiar.

"Mother decides everything and gets her way by using her temper, yelling, screaming, and crying if Dad or any of us strongly object. Father determines when to cut the grass, time for sons to get haircuts, how long my sisters can wear their hair, where to eat or go for entertainment or groceries, and when Mom or any of us kids can leave the house after supper. I wait and wait—until he finally decides he can come home for dinner, get ready to go out, and so on. We never go anywhere on time."

Dominance by one spouse permeates all areas of family power: the use of resources or bases, power processes, and power outcomes. One spouse demonstrates control of power in the system, while the other accepts such control. Thus, one orchestrates power and the other implements it. However, the type of power that families use depends upon the mutual activity or inactivity of all members of the family. Support groups for families of alcoholics or drug addicts recognize how power transactionally affects all members. In these groups, family members learn how to cope with some of the power maneuvers they encounter.

Allen and Straus (1979) found that relationships contain a high amount of violence when the conjugal power structure is either extremely husband-dominant or wife-dominant. A further finding indicated that the lower a husband's economic and prestige resources were relative to his wife's, the more likely he would use physical violence (coercive power) to maintain a dominant male power position (85). Another study revealed that dissatisfaction in marriage relates closely to coercive power on the part of the spouse (Raven et al.).

In couples with more equally divided power, the structure can be described as either syncratic or autonomic (Herbst, 1952, 3–5). A syncratic relationship, characterized by much shared authority and joint decision making, implies that each spouse has a strong say in all important areas.

"When Jim and I married, we agreed never to make big decisions alone, and we've been able to live with that. This way we share the risks and the joys of whatever happens. It just works out best between us if we wait on deciding all important matters until we sound out the other's opinions. Neither of us wants to force the other to accept something disliked. It's when we decide over the little things that I know that each of us respects the rights of the other and wants equal consideration."

In the autonomic power structure, the couple divides authority, i.e., the husband and wife have relatively equal authority but in different areas. Each spouse is completely responsible for specific matters. The division of areas usually coincides closely with role expectations.

Shared power situations reflect specific agreements or role definitions about who controls what situations. The wife might have more power over the budget, vacation plans, and choice of new home and the husband more power over the selection of schools, buying anything with a motor in it, and whether the family moves to another state (Raven et al., 218).

"In our house, I decide long-range programs—repainting the house, remodeling, or landscaping. I also shop for food, liquor, and appliances. My wife selects the nursery schools, arranges for baby-sitters when she's at work, chooses the pediatrician and dentist, and makes the social appointments. Together we make all decisions about housing, summer vacation, spending or reinvesting income from our apartment building, and what movies or sports events we see."

Power and Marital Satisfaction

As you might imagine, certain power arrangements can increase marital satisfaction. High levels of marital satisfaction occur most frequently among *equalitarian* (syncratic or autonomic) couples, followed by husband-dominant couples, and least among wife-dominant couples (Corrales, 1975, 198). In a study of 776 couples in the Los Angeles area, over two thirds of husband-dominant, syncratic, and autonomic couples reported themselves "very satisfied"; however, only 20 percent of wife-dominant couples were "very satisfied" (Raven et al., 274).

Research by Corrales also suggests that women do not seem satisfied when dominating a marriage. In a study in which the wives admitted they dominated, they gave themselves low satisfaction scores. This outcome suggests that wives exercise power by default to compensate for a weak or ignoring husband (211). In this same investigation, one quarter were wife-dominant, but, according to the Blood and Wolfe decision-making scale, these same wives had only 10 percent of the authority regarding final decision making. Corrales explained this discrepancy as follows: "The spouse with little authority may seek less visible ways to make her or his power felt. Interactive control appears to be one such way" (208). One sidelight is that husbands in wife-dominant marriages indicated they were not as dissatisfied as their wives. Kolb and Straus (1974) explain this outcome with their "role incapacity" theory, which posits that when a man relinquishes his traditional leadership role or fails to carry out his part of an equalitarian relationship, the wife becomes dissatisfied, because she feels she married a less competent man (761).

Estimating Spousal Power. In the controversy over who has the most power—male or female—remember that research indicates that men overestimate and women underestimate their power in the family. Self-reports further reveal that individuals underestimate their own power and overestimate their spouse's power. However, outside observers in carefully controlled situations found that both spouses report less power for wives than they actually possess (Olson, 1969, 549). Turk and Bell (1972) substantiated these findings in a later study, which covered power resources, processes, and outcomes and included the couples' children. They observed more equalitarian patterns in the families, but self-report measures indicated that all concerned thought male dominance prevailed (220–22).

As sex-based marital roles continue to change, different uses of power structures may emerge. Women's power should increase. In a study of sex differences in power options, Johnson (1974) demonstrated that men usually use expertise, formal legitimacy, and direct informational power. Women, by comparison, used referent power, helplessness, and indirect information. Ironically, he also found that when women did use sources of power more frequently employed by men, they were labeled as being more masculine and less acceptable. Similar future studies may reflect an emphasis on personal instead of positional roles, resulting in greater equalization of power between sources.

Family-of-Origin Influences.   The type of power processes used by couples can often be traced to their experience in their respective families-of-origin. Growing up in a family in which people were physically controlled may lead a person to adopt the same method, particularly when other alternatives are not immediately available. A son who had a dominant father may find it very difficult to visualize himself in an equal-dominance relationship with his wife.

"My German father and my Irish mother both exercised power over us in different ways. My father used to beat us whenever we got out of line, and that power move was very obvious. On the other hand, my mother never touched us, but she probably exercised greater power through her use of silence. Whenever we did something she did not approve of, she just stopped talking to us—it was as if we did not exist. Most of the time the silent treatment lasted for a few hours, but sometimes it would last for a few days. My brother used to say it was so quiet you 'could hear a mouse pee on a cotton ball.' I hated the silence worse than the beatings."

A family-of-origin serves as the first power base in which a child learns to function. The strategies used there are often repeated later in the child's adult life. Certain types of power moves, such as silence, seem to move from generation to generation, because such control was learned at an early age and often not questioned.

Children and Power

Children have great influence on family power situations. Early studies often ignored them, possibly on the assumption that parents controlled decisions and that children had to follow their directions. Traditionally, parents are expected to control and be responsible for their children's behavior. Couples are expected to raise "nice children" who know their "manners and place." The law also supports the idea of power in the parents' hands. Children must be off the streets by certain hours and attend school. "Probably in no other relationship does a person in our society have such complete power over another," Hoffman (1960) declares, "as do parents over young children" (27). Wieting and McLaren (1975) stress the importance of including children in any study of power and note their impact on making the family system more than the sum of its parts (99). Parents replying to questionnaires indicated that they possessed power, but when trained observers used behavioral methods to measure power, they found that children definitely exercised power in a family (Turk and Bell, 220).

A whole new power scheme emerges when two family members become three, or four, or more. As we saw earlier, alliances can form between and among family members, upsetting the original balance of power. The door is open for a two-against-one power play and all other possible combinations.

> "When I was growing up, I was very close to my father and we usually agreed on things, so my mother began to see it as 'the two of you against me.' I thought it was silly because we enjoyed being together, and we did not mean to be against her, but as I've grown older, I can understand that she felt left out. Now, I often feel outmatched when my son and my husband agree on things and I do not."

Power Interactions. In a study of son-father-mother triads, Strodtbeck (1951) concluded that sons had almost as much power as their mothers in solving problems (471). Other studies proved that children influence the interaction and outcomes of power struggles in families by interruption and other power plays (Turk and Bell; Mishler and Waxler, 1968). Research has shown that adolescents identify with the parent who has the most power over their behaviors; they see the father as holding more outcome-control power (McDonald, 1980b, 291). They seemed to identify more closely with their same-sex parent, making for power alliances. (Acock and Yang, 1984, 487). However, daughters identify with the father when they perceive that he has more legitimate power than the mother. Sons identify with the mother only to the degree that she controls outcomes and has referent power (493).

In many families one spouse consciously or unconsciously co-opts a child into an ally position in order to increase the strength of his or her position. Similarly, children become adept at playing one parent against the other. "Daddy said I could do it" or "If Mom was here she'd let me" has echoed through most homes as new alliances form. Blended families are especially vulnerable as children cite ex-spouse's overruling permissions.

Such alliances often follow a same-sex bias, and boys and girls are expected to be like their respective parents. "My mother and I stick up for each other against the men" represents such a power move.

> "I couldn't believe it when I heard my four-year-old son announce to his mother and two-year-old sister, 'The men will go to the store; the women will stay home.' He then turned and followed me out to the car. When I asked him about it, he replied, 'Men do things together.'"

Power Alliances. Alliances take many forms within a family. Parents may form an alliance against the children, establishing an inflexible boundary that prevents negotiation or discussion. The extended family can become a part of the power bloc to be used in both everyday and crisis situations. In-laws, aunts and uncles, older brothers or sisters, and even friends can become involved in alliances that alter the power in a family. Single-parent families display unique power alliances, due to the presence of one adult. One research team points out a potential advantage for a child in a single-parent family, because the child may negotiate directly with the parent for immediate answers and have direct personal power (Wieting and McLaren, 97). In a single-parent household, a mother cannot say,

"I'll let you know after I talk it over with your father." However, the same child cannot form a parent-child alliance to try to change a decision the way a child can in a two-parent family. Blended families often contend with children's playing one side of the family against the other. "She can't tell me what to do, she's not my real mother" is the kind of communication that may cause years of pain as new roles are negotiated.

Some alliances continue in families over a period of time; others exist only for reaching a decision on a given issue. The results of past alliances can obligate family members to feel they must support another on an issue to repay a debt. For example, "Brad helped me convince Dad to let me buy a new ten-speed bike. Now I ought to help him argue with Dad to get his own car." Wives and husbands can also form alliances with one another or their children and behave in this way. The drawback of alliances and returning favors is that issues never get settled on their own merits. Alliances in some families demand loyalty and "pay-offs," which affect a fair use of power in the family system. It is also another way members of families adapt to the needs and frustrations of living together in the same system. Alliance members are able to pool their individual assets so as to increase their chances of dominance (Turner, 122).

Families that maintain power alliances that do not cross age lines have been shown to function best. This is consistent with systems theory, which recognizes the importance of *hierarchy*, or organizational structure. Parents should not ignore their adult power responsibilities, and no child should feel pressure to assume premature responsibilities (Beavers, 1982, 48).

Power Development. Although young children exercise power (witness the baby who controls a whole family's daily life), they develop more independent power as they grow older. They go from a state of complete dependence in infancy to a state of independence in adulthood when they leave behind most family power constraints.

As children grow and change, they demand and can handle more power within the family structure. Whereas a six-year-old may fight for a later bedtime, a sixteen-year-old fights for independence. A school-age child may begin to have expertise in areas unknown to his or her parents, thereby gaining power. Each of us has seen a small child explain computers, metrics, or a board game to a confused adult. Parents often provide their children with educational opportunities and material advantages that they never had. The resulting knowledge and prestige can give children an additional resource advantage over their parents in power struggles.

Adolescence is a troubled time in certain families as sons and daughters rebel and refuse to accept parental power. Adolescence is also the time when parents can recognize the skills and expertise their children have acquired. In families where power is shared, such changes may be welcome, whereas they may be threatening in a wife- or husband-dominated system. Domineering parents may perceive new skills and knowledge as a threat to their power base. "Oh! You think you are so smart now!" typifies the remarks heard in such families. In a warmer, nurturing family environment, offspring receive positive strokes for their new and expanding talents. A son with expertise in electrical repairs may gain power and importance in the family, because he can do what no other family member can.

> *"By now I'm in charge of all the family cars. I decide what needs to be done when, and I do a lot of the work myself. My mother lets me decide when she gets new tires or a tune-up. I've worked in a gas station since eighth grade, and I'll work there part time even when I start college. I know as much as most of the guys there."*

As families grow and change, the power sources and resources are reflected in changes in the family system. The original power relationship of a couple undergoes enormous modification as the family network increases, fragments, or solidifies. In addition to developmental issues, many other forces affect changes in family power: separation from the family-of-origin or outside influences that affect the family—varying from inflation and environmental factors to changing cultural norms. Parents' competency in relating their needs and desires, first to one another and then to their children, affects power. Spouses' or children's acceptance or rejection of these requests influences power outcomes. The increasing or decreasing independence or interdependence of the couple alters power in the entire family system. If a spouse falls ill or dies, deserts, or divorces, the remaining parent may return to the family-of-origin seeking everything from shelter and funds to advice. This reestablishes ties in the family network that may have been ignored or not needed previously. The single parent left with children must modify family power processes. Power structures are not static. The family power structure changes constantly as members pursue its ends.

THE COMMUNICATION OF POWER STRATEGIES

Throughout this chapter, we have described the communication of power or power messages. Now, we will discuss some communication strategies that affect power.

Confirming, Disconfirming, and Rejecting Behaviors

Confirming, disconfirming, and rejecting behaviors are strategies that affect intimacy development and power. These three strategies can become a part of power messages as family members attempt to separate and connect in one-up, one-down subsystems. In a one-up position, one family member attempts to exercise more power control over one or more other members. The one-down member accepts from the one-up member the control implied in the messages.

Confirming implies acknowledgment or agreement and may be used to gain power as one tries to get another to identify with him or her, or as one tries to give rewards in order to gain power. The careful, nonjudgmental listener may wittingly or unwittingly gain power through the information learned by such behavior. A highly complimentary father may be given power by a child who needs positive support. Such approaches to marital power are found in such books as *Fascinating Womanhood* (Andelin, 1980) or *The Total Woman* (Morgan, 1973) which exhort wives to use positive confirming approaches as a way to gain power in the marital relationship.

The "silent treatment" probably represents the most powerful and most often used disconfirming behavior—a behavior which does not acknowledge the other person's existence. One family member can put another in a one-down power position through the punishment strategy of disconfirmation. "I ignore him; he'll come around" represents such an effort. On the other hand, disconfirming a power message may serve as an effective method of rejecting power. The child who pretends not to hear "clean up your room" messages effectively deflects the parental power, at least for awhile.

Rejecting messages tie directly to punishment messages and are often used as control in family power plays. "I hate you" or "I don't care what you say" may effectively halt control attempts, just as "If you don't behave, you can't go" may serve to pull a reluctant family member into line. The negative conflict behaviors of displacement, denial, disqualification, disengagement, and sexual withholding can also be used as rejecting power moves. We will discuss these behaviors further in Chapter 8.

Self-disclosure serves a major means of gaining intimacy within a relationship, but it can also be used as a power strategy as one attempts to control the other through the "information power" gained by self-disclosure. For example, when a self-disclosure is thrown back at a spouse during a fight, that person loses power. "Well, you had an affair, so how can you talk?" Sprey (1971) describes the human bond as a paradox. He observes that moving closer to another person also necessitates moving apart. The more involved the couple becomes, the greater is the pressure for one or both to possess the other. He believes that intimacy requires "the awareness and acceptance of the stranger in the other" (724).

Self-disclosure may be used as a means of offering power to a loved one in an intimate relationship. The disclosure gives power to the listener in an effort to gain connectedness. Such sharing involves risk and gives the listener "information power," which he or she could use to cause pain or separation in the relationship. In such cases, the more knowledgeable person has the capacity to control the relationship.

"One of the most meaningful times in my life occurred when my teenage daughter and I had an all-night session about love, sex, and growing-up problems. It was the first time I honestly told her about what I went through growing up and how we faced some of the same things. I had always kept those things to myself, but, I suddenly realized that she shouldn't feel like she was different or bad because of her feelings. It's scary to tell your daughter your faults or fears but it certainly resulted in a closer relationship between us."

Power Transacting

The key issue in power is the transactional nature of the relationship. Power must be given as well as taken. This transactional quality may be seen in the research of Rogers-Millar and Millar (1979), in which they examine the distinction between dominance and domineering behavior. They defined *domineering* as the sending of one-up messages, or verbal statements claiming the right to dominate (240). For example, "Be sure and have my supper ready at 6:00 P.M." is the sending of one-up messages that are accepted with one-down messages from the other. Other examples include: "Julie, go to the cleaners and don't forget to get the coat you left behind last week" and "Oh, Janet, I'll do it even if I have to take off work early." Domineeringness comes from an individual's behavior, while *dominance* relates to dyadic relational behavior (Courtright et al., 1979, 181). Courtright and associates' research focused on the area of power processes; they studied the messages exchanged between spouses as they accepted or rejected one another's statements. *Pure dominance* meant the percentage of all one-up remarks made by an individual followed by a one-down response from the other.

Correlating domineering behavior to self-report data, Rogers-Millar and Millar found that " . . . higher rates of wife domineeringness related to lower marital and communication satisfaction for both partners and higher role strain" (244). They found some further important results when they analyzed the *interaction data,* or messages between the spouses. The dominance of one spouse correlated positively to the number of support statements (i.e., agreement, acceptance, approval remarks) and negatively to the number of nonsupport statements made by the other spouse. Nonsupport statements were in the form of rejections, disagreements, or demands. Talk-overs, defined as verbal interruptions or intrusions that succeed in taking over the communication while another is speaking, occurred more frequently in couples who used the domineering style.

Ken: "I want to tell you about this wonderful movie I saw last———"

Kim: "You won't believe who I saw in the bar last night."

Ken: "This movie has such beautiful———"

Kim: "He came over to me, acting as if nothing happened and tried to buy me a beer."

In both wife-domineering and wife-dominant interactions, the discussions were longer. The reverse was true of husbands (245). A second study provided additional conclusions: the more domineering one spouse was, the more domineering the partner became. This indicated a more defensive or combative style of conversation developed from a domineering style (Courtright et al., 183). Frequent question-asking characterized the wife's style of interaction when the husband dominated (Rogers-Millar and Millar, 184). The more domineering the husband, the less accurate were both spouses' predictions about the other's satisfaction with the marriage. The same held true for domineering wives in predicting their mates' satisfaction (187). The researchers suggested that if you did not want to be dominated, you should increase your domineeringness. However, they added that if you do so, be prepared to accept the possibility that both your satisfaction and your partner's will decrease (191).

Other aspects of one-up, one-down communication have been described by Haley as dysfunctional communication strategies for many couples or family members. He suggests that helplessness will influence another person's behavior as much as, if not more than, direct authoritarian demands. One who acts helplessly defines the relationship as one in which he or she is taken care of (371). This kind of behavior in a relationship can be avoided by using qualifications in part of the message that indicate that an individual takes responsibility for his or her decisions. For example, Carlos might say to his brother, "I don't think you should do that, but it's not my duty to tell you so." A husband might say to his wife, "I want your opinion, but I know it's my problem to solve." This approach to communication lessens the likelihood of control by another, thus giving persons possession of their own powers. Thus, the communication strategies used to enhance relationships or to increase intimacy also may be used to gain power.

In order to achieve cohesion, each family has to work out a communication pattern that allows intimacy without overpowering certain members. Corrales states, "The data . . . suggests . . . in this culture, behavior that is more conducive to building self and other esteem seems to be more effectively communicated in an equalitarian interaction structure than in either type of dominant structure" (216). The equalitarian structure includes the syncratic and autonomic types of power sharing. In either of these family types, individuals can deal honestly with their feelings and aspirations. Their more open nature encourages freer communication exchanges than either the husband- or wife-dominant types.

Steinor (1978) distinguishes between "gentle power" and "control power." He describes communication as a form of gentle power: "I can give you what I feel and think. You can understand it and you can compare and decide. This makes people powerful." Ideally, to use communication effectively to counteract the negative aspects of power, there can be no power plays between the persons involved. Steinor suggests that power should not be used to rescue others from solving their own problems. When parents take over their children's problems, they also assume power that is not rightfully theirs. Husbands, wives, or lovers who, through power plays, make decisions for the other, reduce that partner's power potential. An equalitarian family relationship requires that each member have the power to solve the problems they encounter.

CONCLUSION

In this chapter, we have discussed power bases, power processes, and power outcomes as they affect cohesion and adaptability in family systems. The research has indicated that a rigid power structure, characterized by dominance and little

Parents can allow children to assume their own power by letting them make certain decisions on their own.

sharing, restricts family flexibility, reduces cohesion, and adversely affects satisfaction in families. Power in the system constantly changes as a family grows and develops. Although power changes may be more obvious in children as they mature and move from dependence to independence, each parent experiences equal or greater changes. Over time, systemic changes also affect power dynamics in child-free, cohabiting, communal, and homosexual families. All power maneuvers take place within the boundaries the family has established; thus, all communication and activities that take place affect the images, themes, and degree of unity, or cohesion, the family desires. Power operates within a dynamic, growing, interdependent, transactional family system. The sum total of family power is greater than the individual power of each member. Power struggles may develop when an issue becomes important to one or more members. When this happens, and the rational exploration of alternatives ceases, various one-up power maneuvers usually follow. This affects family intimacy, a vital element in meaningful relationships. To resolve differences and avoid becoming the victim of another's power, family members must engage in constructive conflict, since the ability to clearly and comfortably repudiate another is part of the achievement of intimacy.

IN REVIEW

1. How does power affect a family's cohesion and adaptability?
2. Describe how cultural and gender patterns influence the basis of power used in family systems.
3. List ways in which power might be effectively shared in an equalitarian family.
4. Describe the type of power exhibited by a real or literary couple. If it has changed over time, what accounts for the change?
5. What power issues might have to be negotiated as two family systems blend to form a stepfamily?

Chapter 7

Decision Making
in Families

"Can I have the car tonight?" "Should we rent another year or try to buy a house in spite of those mortgage rates?" "Now that the children are out of diapers, could we talk about my returning to work?" "How can we spend more time together?" These types of questions require decisions in order for a family system to operate. One way to measure a family's cohesion involves observing its decision-making process. Cohesion requires an emotional bonding among family members, which does not occur if negative communication behaviors, such as mixed messages, double binds, insults, blaming, and criticism dominate the family's interactions over decisions. Adaptability requires that a family system be able to change. Through effective decision making, a family can balance needed changes with the maintenance of positive themes, rules, role functions, and power dimensions developed in previous decision-making interactions. Think of decision making as a key to facilitating change that achieves adaptability and cohesion in a family. According to Scanzoni and Szinovacz (1980), decision making means getting things done in a family when one or more family members need to agree with others to accomplish something.

> "In the past whenever there has been a major decision to be made, we took a family vote. My father, who assumed the role of the ultimate Decision Maker, devised a rule entitling himself to two votes, as opposed to everyone else's single vote. At times, the females of the family would pool our votes and override his. When this occurred, he would respect our votes unless the issue was crucial to him. In these few cases, his decision was the decision. My mother assumed the role of Advisor of the D.M. She often tried to persuade him about certain issues, and often she won him over."

Although you may not have had an ultimate "Decision Maker" in your family, you probably had some process by which decisions were made, and you had a specific place in the process.

Decision making involves vital communication skills and relates directly to power. Decisions represent a power process. As you might imagine, families are unique decision-making systems, because each family has a history of having resolved or not having resolved past issues effectively. Past successes influence future decisions and affect the processing of current issues. Past failures can bring forth negative skills that impede decision making. Also, any current decision will have future effects, since individuals within the family have to live with or carry out the decision.

Decision making relates to power to the degree that one family member can predict and/or influence the outcome he or she desires. For example, Brent can affect Chris' decision making toward a behavior Brent wants. The degree of power would be the difference between Chris' making a certain choice because of Brent's persuasion and the probability of Chris' doing it anyway. The outcome depends upon the perceptions and intentions of those involved. Thus, determining power involves knowing Brent's intentions and his effect on Chris' decision making (Pollard and Mitchell, 1972, 442).

Your family differs from a small group that comes together merely for the purpose of doing a particular task, because your family has a history of continuous interaction and consists of a combination of interdependent individuals. Even if the decision-making process results in turmoil, your family remains a unit, although sometimes a factional and unhappy one. This is not true of outside groups. If the members cannot reach a decision, they usually disband rather easily. Short of death, divorce, or moving out, families tend to remain together even if members disagree.

Effective problem solving requires that a family be able to resolve its problems with sufficient skills to maintain its cohesion and adaptability. Family decisions can be either instrumental or affective. *Instrumental decisions* require solving rather mechanical issues, such as getting a job to pay the family bills or providing transportation. *Affective decisions* relate to emotions or feelings. Epstein et al. (1982) concluded that ". . . families whose functioning is disrupted by instrumental problems rarely, if ever deal effectively with affective problems. However families whose functioning is disrupted by affective problems may deal adequately with instrumental problems" (119).

"Every Tuesday night is family night, and everyone must be present from 7:00 until 8:30. This is the time when we make certain family decisions that affect all of us. We may make a joint decision about vacations and try to find a compromise that will please everyone. Sometimes Dad will let us decide on a big item to buy with his bonus. Each of the six of us has to finally agree for us to go ahead with the decision."

The location of a family along the cohesion and adaptability continuums affects their decision-making behavior. Highly enmeshed, rigid families may pressure members to reach predictable and low-risk decisions, since change or separation would be threatening. Disengaged systems may have trouble sharing enough information to make reasonable decisions, while families characterized by chaos probably experience few real decisions that stand.

As we examine the family as a decision-making system, we will discuss: (1) a model of decision making, (2) types of family decision making, (3) modes of family governance, (4) steps in decision making, and (5) factors that influence decision making. In this chapter, we will extend our study of power to look in greater detail at decision making as a negotiation process that influences power outcomes. Who influences the decision and how is the influence felt? Who decides what, when, and how certain necessary aspects of family life are resolved? The answers will vary according to how communication is used to maintain the way rules, roles, and power operate within a given family.

The ways in which decisions are made differ greatly within families. Wood and Talmon (1983) present the idea that decisions represent a type of territory that a family develops (347). In this "decision space," the family allows some decisions to be made by individuals, while other decisions require approval from certain subsystems or the whole family. For example, Marissa may ask the whole family's opinion of her Girl Scout project, while her parents' decision to go on a trip without the children may not be submitted to the whole family for approval. Sometimes family members take over another's decision space. For example, a father may offer suggestions and persuasions that are not needed or welcomed yet pressure the person or subsystem making the decision (350). The following model should help clarify the decision-making process.

A MODEL OF DECISION MAKING

This model supports the idea that marital negotiations that lead to decisions can be analyzed in terms of social contexts, processes, and outcomes. In drawing upon earlier work by Strauss (1978), Scanzoni and Polonoko (1980) devised this model to demonstrate the ongoing nature of process and outcome in decision making. They divided family social context dimensions into four areas:

1. *Composition,* meaning ages of spouses, cohabitors or lovers, length of marriage or relationship, whether first or remarriage, ages and number of children, and time available before deadline.
2. *Resources,* including amount of education, salary, job status, amount of work each year, and experience negotiating decisions.
3. *Orientations,* including self-esteem, sex-role attitudes, amount of concern about the outcome, and importance of the issue.
4. *Actor's orientations* refers to each partner's past bargaining experience and how the Actor (spouse) perceives that his or her partner will negotiate. This includes perceptions the couple has about how hard each will bargain, how fairly, and how cooperatively. It also includes how much each can be trusted to follow through on decisions.

Figure 7–1 _____
A Model of Explicit Marital Negotiation

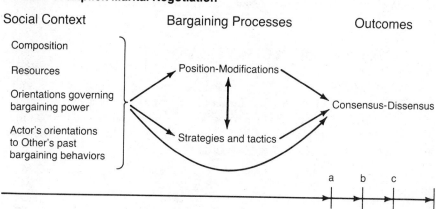

The main part of the diagram indicates how the "one–shot" negotiation works. For example, Kelly and Carmen negotiate a problem, making use of various strategies and tactics and modifying their respective positions as necessary. The vertical arrow represents the interaction that takes place in the course of the bargaining process. The outcome that results is labeled "a" on the time line at the bottom of the model. Once this outcome has been reached, it becomes a part of the social context within which additional decision-making negotiations occur, affecting the future outcome "b." Outcome "b," in turn, provides context for outcome "c," and so on.

This model emphasizes the importance of bargaining as a mediator of power. Scanzoni and Polonko state that this idea "sensitizes us to the notion that power is intrinsically associated with ongoing movement, or process, rather than outcome" (33). This model makes us aware that outcomes often do not end issues. Family members are not always equally satisfied with decisions. The model provides for a repeated series of negotiations occurring over varied periods of time before true consensus happens. Power resides in each partner's or child's shifts or changes in bargaining position (34). The degree of flexibility, or willingness to compromise, enhances the probability of reaching consensus.

Social context variables such as disparity in tangible resources (schooling or salary), differences in intangible variables (self-concept or sex roles), and insights into a family's decision-making history usually have significant impact on process and outcome variables (Hill and Scanzoni, 1982, 935). Research indicates that the greater the education disparity, the larger the amount of disparity will be on three other dimensions: income, self-esteem, and perceptions of past bargaining. Income and self-esteem positively correlate, as do self-esteem and perceptions of past decisions. Other findings show that style of communication has a powerful pervasive effect in determining spouses' responses. A defensive style increases the number of disagreements, as do verbal strategies that are ego centered and evoke memories of past decisions (937–39). Decision making is a multifaceted process.

Understanding the process helps us determine the meaning of an outcome. Other aspects of this model will be discussed later in this chapter.

OUTCOMES OF DECISION MAKING

Each family has its own way of reaching decisions on issues. In his study of family decision-making patterns, Turner (1970) differentiates decision-making outcomes according to the degree of acceptance and commitment of family members. He identifies three kinds of decision making: (1) consensus, (2) accommodation, and (3) de facto decisions (98–100).

Consensus

In consensus decision making, discussion continues until agreement is reached. This may require compromise and flexibility, but the desired goal is a solution acceptable to all involved. Because each family member has a part in the decision and a chance to influence it, they share the responsiblity for carrying it out. In some families, all major purchases are decided on the basis of group consensus. This type of decision making does not occur as frequently as the other two.

Family members share responsibility in consensus decision making.

Accommodation

Accommodation occurs when some family members consent to a decision not because they totally agree but because they believe that further discussion will be unproductive. They may give their consent with a smile or with bitterness. The accommodation decision may represent a great deal of give and take, but no one really achieves what he or she desires. For example, you may want to go to church family camp while someone else wants to play in three ballgames that weekend. Eventually, the family may agree to go on a picnic while the baseball player gets to play one game in the schedule. No one's wants have really been satisfied with the decision; individual wants have been merely placated or postponed to some future time. This kind of decision making tends to leave some or all family members disappointed. When decisions are made this way, factions may emerge, and you may feel obligated to repay people who argued for your goals. This type of decision making may occur in families that pressure for high cohesiveness through their themes and boundaries.

"It's just easier to agree with Dad and let him think his ideas are what we all want than to argue with him. He's bound to win anyway, since he controls the money. Sometimes when we humor his wishes, Mom, my sister, and I can then get our way on what we want to do—sort of a trade-off!"

Sometimes accommodation results from voting as family members line up on one side of an issue and the majority wins. The minority views held by losing family members might have genuine merit, but the losers accept majority rule rather than cause trouble. Anyone who loses consistently finds this to be an unacceptable way to make decisions.

One danger of accommodation is that it encourages dominance behavior. Too often, decisions favor those who dominate, and less aggressive family members develop a pattern of submitting to their wishes. Accommodation may appear to be a decision-making approach that furthers family cohesion and adaptability, but this is not the case. The results are temporary at best, because the communication that goes into accommodative decisions represents compromises made by members out of fear or lack of equal power. Such decisions over time accent separateness and lessen connectedness among family members. Accommodative decision making can also enforce negative family themes and images while implementing stereotyped thinking on biosocial issues, especially in cases of male dominance.

De Facto Decisions

What happens when the family makes no decision or when the discussion reaches an impasse? Usually, one member will go ahead and act in the absence of a clear-cut decision. This is a de facto decision—one made without direct family approval but nevertheless made to keep the family functioning. A fight over which model of TV to buy while they are on sale may be continued until the sale nears an end and Dad finally buys one by himself.

De facto decisions encourage family members to complain about the results, since they played either no part or a passive part in the decision. The family member who acts in a vacuum created by the lack of a clear-cut decision has to endure the harassment or lack of enthusiasm of those who have to accept the decision. Again, dominant family members can easily emerge victorious in too many decisions—their wishes are carried out while those of others are unfairly suppressed (Turner, 99).

"We talked about doing something together as a family last Sunday afternoon. I wanted to bowl. Mom wanted to see a movie. My sister wanted to go to the amusement park. Dad thought a ball game or ride in the country would be OK. No one pulled us together. Finally, it got too late to do anything. Dad took a nap, Mom read, I went over to Chuck's house, and my sister went swimming with a friend."

Although many families, particularly rigid ones, seem to use only one type of decision making, more flexible families vary their styles according to the issues. Critical issues may require consensus, while less important concerns can be resolved by a vote or a de facto decision. As we will see later, the style of decision making experienced in his or her family-of-origin by each member of a couple has a great effect on the decision-making styles they adopt when they form their own system.

STYLES OF GOVERNANCE

All styles of decision making rest on an underlying approach to power. In an interesting approach that combines ideas about family power and decision making, Broderick (1975) has set up three styles of governance based upon Kohlberg's (1964) study of children in different cultures and the universal steps in reasoning that they go through to reach moral maturity. The lowest level of reasoning for decisions was hedonistic self-interest, or zero-sum; the next was based on conventionality and obedience to rules; the third was based on social contract and principles of conscience (118).

Zero-Sum Decisions

Applied to decision making in conflict situations, the first and most primitive way to reach a decision is simply to insist upon your way. Broderick labeled this approach a hedonistic, "zero-sum" power confrontation. This means that in an argument, one person wins and one loses. The sum of their wins (+) and losses (−) is always zero. You have seen this operate between small children who refuse to share. Instead, they shout, "That's mine, you can't have it." Unfortunately, such behavior does not always stop as family members move beyond the toddler stage. In this kind of decision making, each family member insists upon his or her way without compromise. This approach can lead to threats, yelling, browbeating, and slanting of the truth.

Broderick suggests only two circumstances in which families could survive using zero-sum confrontations. For example, if the wife and husband are closely matched, with each getting an equal number of wins and losses, the relationship could continue. Also, if the consistently losing partner feels there are no alternatives and lacks the emotional or financial resources to leave, he or she may remain in the relationship in spite of the heavy psychological cost of lower self-esteem. Children can be victims in this kind of household, because they have no way to escape. Young people caught in this kind of family make such statements as "I can't wait until I graduate and can get out of here" or "I don't like it, but it's not worth fighting over." In time, the losers either leave the family or define their role as second class (119). (See also Turk, 1974, 43.) In zero-sum governance, decisions are static and predictable.

The maintenance of a zero-sum relationship requires coercive power, or punishment, especially the use of fear and threat. Information is of little use, because too much evidence might weaken the position of the hedonist family member who insists upon his or her views. Of even less use is reward power, because the "winner" does not usually sense the need to give anything in return for acceptance of the decision.

"In our house you went along with parental decisions or you were punished—it was as simple as that. I had one brother who was a rebel, and my father would beat him with regularity. My mother usually went along with whatever my father said, because I think she was scared of him, too."

Some family members use force in decision making. In an investigation of how family members intimidate one another, Steinmetz (1977) substantiated that violence as a problem-solving method was learned in a family setting, which reflected society's attitude toward permitting the use of physical force in intimate relationships. The method parents used to solve their problems became the method usually employed to solve parent-and-child and child-to-child problems. Thus, the parental approach to decision making became the model for other family interactions. When verbal aggression and physical force characterized the parents' attempts to make decisions, the same behavior appeared in that of a parent with his or her children or between the children when they disagreed (Steinmetz, 20–21). (See also Raschke and Raschke, 1979; Straus, 1979.) As unfortunate as it seems, many people use fists rather than words to settle family problems (Ford, 1983).

According to our process model of decision making, to be a constant winner requires defensive behaviors and putting up with the loser's submissive behaviors. To lose constantly requires a person to live with low self-esteem and continually try to subvert the more powerful person. The images maintained in zero-sum family relationships foster separateness and reduce the chance for much cohesion. The pattern of adaptability required to maintain zero-sum relationships does too little to develop positive self-esteem for individual members within the family system. In many families, victories are hollow because they curb or destroy ideas and limit decision-making skills in others that might lead to better and more meaningful solutions.

Decisions Based on Rules

A second mode of governance involves the creation and enforcement of rules. A family may live most of its life according to the rules and avoid certain power clashes, as well as certain opportunities for growth. Rules affect decision making because, over a period of time, they become accepted ways to operate when problems arise. Rules evolve from the social contexts of the family members plus repeated family interactions. Broderick distinguished among three types of rules used in family decision making: (1) rules of direct distribution, (2) rules of designated authority, and (3) rules for negotiation (120–21).

"After almost twenty years of working in banking, I decided to return to graduate school to make an eventual career change. My wife worked parttime and we used up much of our savings. As part of the process, we decided ahead of time how much money could be spent for different necessities, and we stuck to it. The children were given a clothing allowance, and they had to live within it or use their baby-sitting money. Although there was some grumbling, most of us stuck to the rules, and we were able to get through a rough period."

Rules of Direct Distribution. Rules of direct distribution imply the dividing of family resources directly among members. This includes the distribution of family income into the amounts available for food, housing, tuition, vacation, and entertainment. Similar distribution can be made of living space—which child gets which room or has to share a bedroom, which shelves belong to each child or parent, and where personal items are to be kept. These rules function to avoid confrontations and reduce power plays in the family through the presolution of possible problems. Rules of this kind require that family members carry around in their heads a whole series of predetermined decisions about matters of family living.

Rules of Designated Authority. Rules of designated authority indicate who has the authority over certain areas. For example, Mother pays the bills and, thus, collects the checks and does the budgeting. Dad does the painting and refinishing and, thus, decides on the materials to use. Lois plays in the band and, thus, does not need to explain her absence for practice after school or help with housework on weekends when the band travels. Sometimes, rules allocating authority contain a series of steps. For example, either Dad or Mom can go out for an evening with friends if the other knows who is going and where. Either can veto such a decision if his or her own job requires overtime work and the children will be home alone. This type of rule, dispersing authority, often relates closely to roles in the family. Whoever controls the kitchen and all of the activities that take place there has the authority to make the decisions in that area.

"As the children grew older, we developed a unique system in our house to deal with responsibilities and chores. Ted and I each had two of the children assigned to us for a month, and those two received orders from one parent and did not have to take orders from the other parent. Each month we switched so the children received supervision from each of us and so they learned to do all kinds of household tasks, not just the outside or the inside type of chore."

Rules of designated authority tend to set clear boundaries for "who may get involved with what." Certain people may have far more decision-making power than others. Yet, children can also have areas of decision making assigned to them. For example, if they do their expected tasks, they can make decisions about their free time. If a son likes to bake and does all of the buying and preparation of baked goods, he may be given the authority over the oven and that part of the kitchen. The autonomic family described in Chapter 6 quite often operates its decision making in accordance with this rule.

Rules for Negotiation.   The third type of rule is based on negotiation. Over time, families can establish rules that govern the process decision making will follow when conflict occurs. Rules of this type imply greater family input in settling differences. It may mean placing a limit on the amount of force or threat one member can use against another. Certain tactics, such as yelling and hitting, can be outlawed and negotiation done only when all involved agree not to interrupt. This approach implies that the decision reached may require compromise or sacrifice on one or more family members' part. Many current marital or family enrichment programs stress how to negotiate differences according to rules that allow all members of the system some input.

As a variation of this approach, Bernhard (1975) stresses that each person has a right to decide what is negotiable and what is nonnegotiable for himself or herself. Others intimately involved have a right to know what is nonnegotiable and can question or evaluate it, but Bernhard believes the final decision should be up to the individual and should be respected. She defines "an area of autonomy as a statement of power in a relationship—subject to mutual acceptance and negotiation—in which each gives to the other the power of final decision making in defined areas of living" (96).

"Ever since the children have grown older, I have declared Saturday as my day to do whatever I desire. It is sacred to me and I only do what I want on that day, even if somebody else will be disappointed. I am wife or mother to four people during six days of the week, and I really need some scheduled time to myself and Saturday's it!"

Thus, the third type of rule involves potential negotiation about what is not negotiable. This approach has the potential to increase family cohesion and provide a method for adaptability. To be successful, family members have to communicate their wishes directly to all other members and take responsibility for their comments. Negotiation implies change and flexibility. If this expectancy of later possible change is recognized by the family, its members realize that negotiation can be another communication skill to use to gain adaptability within their system. It can help keep a system open and flexible.

Decisions Based on Principle

Broderick's third mode involves government by contract or principle. As you might imagine, few families actively operate at this high a level, and those that do usually include older children and adults (121–22). It is based on a belief in the basic human goodness of each family member and their desire to put the family's welfare above their own. Individual family members operate on principles of fairness and concern. For example, if either Dad or Mother works late, they call the other and explain. The operating principle is that neither partner unnecessarily inconveniences the other. Both respect the other's right to make overtime decisions, but fair play motivates each of them to inform the other. This prevents one from preparing food that is not eaten or planning activities that are later cancelled. In this family, there is no rule about hours to come and go but a principle operating that neither will worry or waste the time of the other.

This type of governance works in families with children if the parents have taught them how to use good judgment and value the rights, strengths, and limitations of one another. It requires harmony and cooperation. Disharmony can be handled as a temporary condition that will be resolved by fair decisions that restore balance to a family system. Children realize that they play an integral part in the successful operation of their system. A family might have a contract in which areas of work and play are shared—each member has duties assigned so that time remains for individual and joint family activities. Compromise is a part of this form of governance so that all members' legitimate needs are met.

We have examined both Turner's and Broderick's ways of viewing family decision making. The former relates to the actual behavior, while the latter takes more complex issues into consideration, since it involves a level of moral reasoning reached by the members. Turk (1975) offers another way to combine approaches to decision making when he suggests that choices be divided into either policy-guided or nonpolicy-guided choices (93). If family policy has been established on a given matter, decision making would then be guided by that policy. This would involve the rules established to deal with similar situations. Nonpolicy choices could require either accommodation, consensus, or some form of negotiation to reach decisions. The combination of approaches to family decision making provides a broad background for understanding your own family and those you encounter.

STEPS IN DECISION MAKING

"After my Mom remarried, we had ten kids in the family, so we tried to have a series of family meetings in which certain decisions were made about things like curfew, baby-sitting, household jobs, and use of the cars. Although it didn't always work, we tried to get everyone to say what they wanted. Sometimes we went for hours trying to reach a solution, and sometimes people just went away mad."

As you know, most family decisions are made without a formal decision-making meeting but, on occasion, families decide to reach certain decisions in a relatively formal manner. The issue may be very important, the group may be large, or there may be other factors that influence the decision to follow an agenda.

Let us look briefly at the five problem-solving steps in decision making. It is important to realize that the process may be short-circuited at any point by a family member or alliance that does not agree with certain choices. Or, the family group may reach a decision by skipping some steps.

The first step requires *definition of the problem,* including isolating the parts of it that family members agree need attention. At this stage it is helpful to make sure everyone understands the problem's key terms in the same way. Sometimes, differences in meaning cause part of the problem and delay decision making.

The second step includes an *exploration of the problem* and analysis of the differences. At this stage, all pros and cons should be debated, with every involved family member's having a chance to be heard.

The third step involves setting up *criteria* that any solution or decision should meet. Sample criteria might be: the family can afford the money to do it; there will be enough time available to do it; the decision will be equitable and not take advantage of any member; and the advantages will outweigh possible disadvantages. This important step tends to be overlooked, yet it can help clarify the family's goals and lead to better decisions. It is a listing of what is needed to be fair and just in making a decision that will solve a problem.

The fourth step focuses on *listing possible solutions* that might solve the problem. In this phase of decision making, alternative ways to solve a problem are brought out. If democracy prevails in the discussion, this step gives submissive family members a chance to express their ideas. All participants should be encouraged to contribute suggestions. In this way, if they have a part in the process and are later outvoted, they can feel their ideas were at least considered.

The last step requires *selecting the best solution* for this family at this point in time. The decision mode should represent its best combined thinking and meet the criteria agreed upon in the third step.

Finally, a plan of action for implementing the decision needs to be agreed upon—a plan that will strengthen and enhance the operation of the family system, because a problem that had reduced the efficiency of the system has been solved. Note the steps followed by the family in this example:

"My two brothers and I and our wives actually went through a formal decision-making process as we decided how to take care of my elderly mother after she was unable to live alone. We went through all kinds of hassles on terms such as nursing homes, residential facilities, and social security benefits. We had to set a monetary criteria for any solution based on a percentage of our salaries and based on a location that everyone could reach. Mother had to agree to the solution also. We agreed we could not force our solution on her. Each couple investigated different options, specific senior citizen housing options, live-in nurses, nursing homes, and specialized group homes. Then we all sat around and hashed them out. We finally reached two options that we could live with—a particular senior citizen facility or a nursing home that accepted people who were not severely ill. We discussed these with my mother who rejected the nursing home instantly but who agreed to the senior citizen housing facility."

This planned approach to decision making does not just happen in families. In fact, left to their own ways, most families do not solve their problems in an organized way. Many families become bogged down and never get beyond the first or second step (O'Flaherty, 1974). The possibility exists that "if incomplete decision-making persists, decision issues will eventually be determined by factors other than decision processes of the participants" (Thomas, 1977, 117).

No matter how decision making occurs, whatever style or type of governance is used, the actual process involves many factors. Unfortunately, it is not a very predictable and streamlined process. In order to understand the complexity of the process, we need to examine a number of factors that affect family decision making.

FACTORS THAT AFFECT FAMILY DECISION MAKING

Over the years, each family evolves some patterned ways of solving problems. The decision-making process is more than trial-and-error, although that may be a part of it. Family decisions relate to a variety of factors that explain the actions taken. In this section, we will discuss: (1) how children affect decisions, (2) how male and female role definitions modify outcomes, (3) how the individual involvement of family members and resources influence decisions, and (4) how time available and quality of communication skills affect family decision making.

The Role of Children in Decision Making

By now, you are fully aware that your family-of-origin experiences affect all areas of your life; thus, your decision-making experiences as a child partially determine your approach to adult decision-making situations. On the other hand, your children may have some interesting effects on family decision-making processes. As we noted before, the arrival of the first child opens the door for the formation of triangles or alliances in the family and provides the first opportunity for a chain network by which decisions may be relayed.

Children often influence decisions by forming alliances with one or the other parent or by presenting a united front to a certain proposed decision. In some families, permanent alliances seem to exist. For example, "Dad, Cindy, and Tom always form an alliance to stick together on issues, and that often leaves Mom and me on the other side."

"A trite axiom the two of us share is 'together we stand, divided we fall.' My brother and I took tremendous advantage of the concept of joining throughout our college years. My brother and I marshalled up strategies to combat my parents in order to achieve our ends. At times, we add complexity to the tension-filled situations via pairing one parent off against the other. Sometimes it works, but sometimes we end up losing."

In certain circumstances, children share the leadership in making decisions. Russell (1979) found that this happened in a family atmosphere in which a child or spouse felt support from other members. This atmosphere also made it easier for a less assertive member to risk taking charge of a problem and trying to solve it (43). Through observations of family members during problem-solving sessions, Kolb and Straus (1974) found children exercising leadership in directing outcomes, but "high child power" was associated with low marital happiness (764). They thought this result might have been caused by the societal expectation of father leadership and when he was not the leader, they felt deprived of leadership. On the other hand, certain parents consciously plan to allow their children opportunities to lead or influence decision making as a way of preparing them for future responsibilities. Thus, we can see that children do influence family decision-making patterns.

Sex-Based Roles

The ways husbands and wives define their roles and responsibilities directly affect family decision making. In a study of couple allocation of responsibility for eighteen family decisions and thirteen tasks, Douglas and Wind (1978) selected 240 respondents in six metropolitan areas. The husbands and wives grouped decisions and tasks into areas of responsibility in their families. The findings revealed basic spouse agreement with a group of wife-dominated activities, including washing and drying the dishes, laundry chores, and food budgeting and buying. Other decisions were joint decisions, such as places to go on vacations, who is invited to dinner, what movie to see, the amount to spend on appliances, what furniture to buy or replace, and if the wife should work.

Couples differed on other decision areas. Wives made more distinctions than husbands. Certain tasks were perceived as male-dominated: getting the car repaired, choosing the liquor, maintaining the yard. The same held true on family financial decisions, such as how much money to invest or save, which credit cards to secure, where the family banks, the amount of life insurance needed, who pays the bills, and the buying of men's toiletries and clothing for either spouse. Douglas and Wind suggested that wives make these differentiations because of their perceived degree of influence and competence. Wives think of themselves as less qualified to get the car serviced or select liquor. On financial decisions, some wives indicated more competence and joint participation and involvement. On clothing decisions, wives indicated they often acted as influencer or consultant (39).

It is interesting to note that in this study and several earlier ones, the couples had a harder time identifying who made a decision than who performed a task. For example, a husband could not recall who influenced what in their decision to buy a new sofa or whether he or his wife asked friends over for a barbecue, but he knew who did the dishes regularly and who balanced the checkbook. In talking about how they make decisions, Krueger (1983) concluded that "both spouses tend to avoid singular responsibility" (99).

A family's role ideology determines who carries out certain decisions and tasks. Thus, in male-dominant households, the husband will take over the financial decisions and the wife the household operation. Equalitarian couples will make more joint decisions (Heer, 1963). However, Douglas and Wind found little systematic relationship between couples' role attitudes and responsibility patterns (42). In comparing results with the Blood and Wolfe study (1960), which characterized households based on reported role patterns for certain decisions and tasks, they discovered that few areas were husband-dominant, wife-dominant, or joint decisions in all households. In this study, only car and liquor purchases were usual husband duties and household chores usual for wives. Brand-choice decisions were either husband or jointly made decisions, and entertainment decisions were wife or joint decisions. Financial decisions emerged as the area of greatest variation, with the results almost equally divided between husband-doiminant and joint households (43). These findings indicate that responsibility in families for various decision areas and tasks seldom demonstrates a dominant authority pattern.

Another study of student couples by Price-Bonham (1976) found that resources have a different influence on the decisions of husbands and wives. As we saw in Chapter 6, a resource can be anything that one spouse makes available to the other, helping that spouse to satisfy his or her needs or attain his or her goals (Blood and Wolfe, 68). According to this theory, the spouse who contributes the greatest resources to the marriage will have the greater influence and power over decision making. Resources included in this study were age, income, education, number of children (felt to lower the wife's power but not proven in this study), and father's and mother's occupational status and educational level at the time of their marriage. (This combines the social context variables of composition and resources found in the model, Figure 7–1.) Although each individual indicated the degree of importance each decision had, the results showed little relationship to resource variables (Price-Bonham, 629). Also, the greater the wife's resources, the greater the input she had in decisions in areas affecting living arrangements and activities.

Although the results showed variation, Price-Bonham concluded that ". . . some resource variables do have influence on some decisions" (638). Sprey (1975) also concludes that expertise is a major factor in joint decision-making and problem-solving situations, since resources and skills in each partner result in a division of labor (70). Doherty (1982) discovered that newly wed wives attributed events to causes differently than their husband. Wives who attributed other couples' marital problems to negative personality traits and attitudes were more likely to use verbal criticism of their husbands in problem-solving discussions. The same was not true of husbands, suggesting that an attributional style, which requires assigning causes to events, affects men less in marital problem solving (201, 205). This finding relates to an earlier review of 100 bargaining and negotiation studies that concluded that women negotiate in a reactive, nontask-oriented manner that decreases their skills in problem solving. Women had greater difficulty ignoring provocations and frequently overreacted to situations (Rubin and Brown, 1975). Decisions may appear final at one moment and then be reconsidered at a later time. What seemed to be the best decision, may, upon experience, be proven otherwise and necessitate a new search for a better one. In a viable, open family system, this would be a healthy state—all decisions subject to re-evaluation and study whenever new information or changes seem important to any family member.

The role functions carried out in a family affect the decision-making process. These roles vary greatly from family to family, so each family's decision making must be studied to see whether it fits the generalizations from the research presented.

Individual Resources

How many times have you dropped out of or avoided a family decision-making session because you did not care about the result? If you do not see how things affect you, you are not likely to get involved, even though, as a system member, you will be affected. Not all family members care equally about the outcome of decisions. Antonio's desire to go to college away from home may not affect his younger brothers directly. Mom's desire and need for a new refrigerator may not be perceived as important to a teenager. If money or any other shared resource is scarce, decision making can become a competitive process for the limited resources. Turk (1974) reminds us that "the decisions may be irrelevant or differentially relevant to some individuals and families; even if relevant, the decisions may not be points of disagreement" (44).

Communication in making decisions changes greatly as children grow and develop their own sense of self-sufficiency. The same holds true for parents who also go through great changes and growth. Network formations reflect these changes, as do rule adjustments. As parents grow accustomed to problem solving and encounter different situations demanding solutions, they cannot replicate previous decisions, even if they so desired. The real world does not hold constant. Their personal investment in decisions varies over time with the degree of separateness or connectedness within the family system. The dependence-independence of the members fluctuates as children become adults and leave home. Parents learn from their decision successes and failures with older children and, as a result, the communication going into decision making with younger children may be quite different than it was with older children. In a highly cohesive family, all members are more likely to invest time in important decisions that affect the whole family. However, in decisions that do not jeopardize unity, members may invest little interest and trust the others to be fair.

Since the family is never static, individual members can also be involved in several decision-making matters simultaneously, both within and outside the family. Matters requiring decisions, depending upon their importance, affect the members involved and determine their degree of active or passive commitment to new decisions. Time and empathy certainly affect decisions.

Time. Time is one important aspect of composition in the model of negotiation. Each family has only so much time to spend on decisions, and members compete for the available time. It takes far less time to solve some problems by nondemocratic means. In our earlier discussion of communication networks, we noted how the chain pattern or Y pattern could be used to expedite matters but that the all-channel, equal access network required more time for decisions to be made or carried out. Whichever the network or pattern of decision making is followed, the more democratic and equalitarian the communication, the more likely that additional time has been used. It may be well worth the investment to improve communication in the family system, but the many demands upon family members' time often short circuit decisions. One person can think through his or her own problem more quickly than can several family members, but the person is limited to his or her own input and loses the possibly better alternatives other family members could offer. Too often, families in trouble have not taken enough time to make decisions. Hastily made decisions may require dominant behavior and power plays by some family members to maintain the outcome, which would lead to less satisfaction for other individuals in the family.

Empathy. Empathy, an important element in effective communication, relates to power and decision making. Olson (1969) defines empathy operationally as the individual's ability to predict the decision of the other spouse on presenting problems. The greater the empathy regarding a particular decision, the greater the agreement between the measures of predicted and actual power (549).

If one member of a family exerts too much power in the form of coercion, control, or suppression over another, decision making falters. According to Filley (1975), problem solving requires an equalization of power. He writes of the necessity of providing a favorable power balance by employing problem-solving methods that ensure a balance of power (7).

Outside Influences

Since each family is one permeable subsystem among many, all sorts of outside factors affect how a family makes decisions. Mom's salary, BJ's friends, and Mary Frances' teacher may all affect how a decision is resolved. Children's peers exert strong influence on decision making. In an interesting report on decision making by ninth- and twelfth-graders who were asked to select between alternatives approved by parents and by peers, boys in the ninth grade chose the parent-endorsed alternative more than either ninth-grade girls or twelfth-grade boys. Girls' reponses tended to remain stable over the same period (Emmerich, 1978, 178).

Decisions within a family system often represent compromises or adaptations to other societal systems. School, corporate, and government systems impinge upon families and influence decisions. The interface between any other system and the family can make problem solving easier or more difficult. Other systems also have rules, images, and boundaries that require maintenance and a change process that helps them continue as viable systems. For example, think of how a business where one parent works affects decision making. If the mother must travel, work overtime, or take customers out in the evening, the family makes decisions differently than if this were not necessary. The school-home interface requires other adjustments in decision making, particularly if both parents work or a single parent has chief responsibility for providing income and childcare and nurturance. "Latchkey kids" filling time between the end of the school day and the time a parent arrives home make different decisions than children greeted by a parent at the door.

On a larger scale, "government, business, and industry are deeply and permanently involved in policies that impact upon families" (Hawkins, 1979, 270). Hawkins sees policy decisions by government and industry as often nonfamily-oriented, individualistic, and sometimes inhuman and harmful. As evidence of adverse policies, he cites families' lack of adequate health insurance; restrictions on Medicaid and Medicare; extreme dependence upon schools to do what families, churches, and the legal system used to do; factory closings; nonflexible work hours; and businesses' insistence upon moving plants or personnel (267–68). Decisions forced upon a family by outside agencies restrict individual members' choices and require flexibility and adjustments, sometimes for poor reasons, often resulting in more tension in families.

COMMUNICATION IN DECISION MAKING

Remember our discussion of these family decision-making factors as you read the following results of a comparison of communication and decision making between married and unrelated single couples. Note how communication differs in decision making because a couple operates within their own system, while unrelated single individuals do not have those systemic ties to consider before deciding.

Winter et al. (1973) measured seven aspects of communication: spontaneous agreement (the shared values and like preferences that exist prior to the decision-making process); decision time; choice fulfillment (the number of times a positive or negative choice by one agrees with that of the partner); silence (the length of time no one communicates); interruptions; explicit information (a definite statement of a liked or disliked choice); and politeness (overall impression of how couples treat one another—tone of voice, asking questions, listening quietly, and being supportive). The results indicated that married couples had more spontaneous agreement, were less polite, made more interruptions, and exchanged less explicit information (83). A higher degree of spontaneous agreement would be expected, because a married couple has learned the values and wishes of one another, and each has a history of sharing these values. Married and single couples took about the same amount of time to reach decisions and were almost equally effective in reaching mutually satisfying decisions (88). Unrelated stranger couples listened more respectfully to one another than married couples—a sad commentary on marital communication. Also, when married couples interrupted one another, the communication was impaired. The authors explain: "Married dyads may be hurt or offended by an intrusion because of what this implies about their relationship with a spouse who can affect them deeply. Unmarried couples are less emotionally involved, more task-oriented" (92).

In another study, Krueger found that disagreements serve as a functional part of the decision-making process, particularly when each partner uses positive communication strategies to express their differences. She found this was true except when a sequence began with a disagreement followed too rapidly by another disagreement, which signaled the beginning of conflict escalation. She also noted that partners change subjects sometimes as a transition and at other times to avoid conflict. These changes indicate that couples do not focus for long periods of time on a single issue, thus demonstrating a cyclical model of decision making, with the couple taking up a topic and leaving it but later returning to reach a decision (114).

Throughout this chapter, we have seen that communication plays a key role in determining the outcomes of family decision making. The way in which family members use verbal and nonverbal communication determines decision-making outcomes. The sending of mixed messages by one or more members affects decisions and may alter the cohesion and balance of the family system. Thomas listed the following communication difficulties that hinder decision making:

> . . . overtalk, overresponsiveness, quibbling, overgeneralization, presumptive attribution, misrepresentation of fact or evaluation, content avoidance, content shifting, content persistence, poor referent specification, temporal remoteness, opinion surfeit, opinion deficit, excessive agreement, excessive disagreement, too little information, too much information, illogical talk, and negative talk surfeit. There are some others that are potentially less serious, but if extreme, may interfere to some extent, also. These are affective talk, obtrusions, excessive question asking, excessive cueing, and acknowledgement deficit.   (123)

Researchers have argued over whether the dominant authority structure in a family can be determined from the manner in which decision-making responsibilities have been allocated or from studying the decision-outcomes (Douglas and Wind; Cromwell and Olson, 1975; Safilios-Rothschild, 1970; Sprey, 1975). The conclusion is that family authority and decision making operate together as a dynamic, interactive system, requiring give and take among family members. This complex process can be streamlined by experiences of a life of shared communication.

"For fifty years, Lambert and I have always tried to make decisions together. We try to spend our money as we both see fit and discuss what is important to us. We usually shop together: groceries, machinery, cars, and so on. Even on buying our tombstone, we looked them over and decided on one we both liked. We've had our differences, but we always tried to see things from the other point of view and eventually we'd resolve the problem."

CONCLUSION

In this chapter, we discussed, with the help of a model, a process-oriented approach to understanding decision making. We stressed that negotiation determines the power dynamics in solving problems. Through communication interactions, power is used and decisions made. These decisions may occur in families that govern their systems by zero-sum confrontations, by the creation and maintenance of various types of rules, or by guiding principles of fairness based on conscience.

Next we focused on the decision-making steps that families can use to communicate differences yet solve their problems. Although compromise may be required, this problem-solving approach has the potential to strengthen cohesion in the family. The chapter concluded with a variety of factors that affect communication in decision making. As Scanzoni and Polonko (1980) have said, "Bargaining power is simply the capability to bring about modifications in the behavior of Other, while at the same time being able to minimize Other's efforts to bring about modifications in one's own behavior" (42).

IN REVIEW

1. Give specific examples of social context factors that affect decision making in a real or fictional family.
2. Give an example of a decision that was made in a real or fictional family that illustrates the cyclical nature of decision making.
3. Decide and explain what kinds of decisions the family members in a television sitcom usually make under a variety of situations.

4. Why is the process of decision making more enlightening to study than the outcomes or who had the final say in an argument or decision?
5. If you wanted to improve your decision-making skills and live more happily with a significant other person in your life, what communication behaviors would you try to demonstrate? Make a list of do's and don't's based upon your understanding of ideas in this chapter.

Chapter 8

Communication and Family Conflict

The mere absence of conflict does not make a family function well. Both functional and dysfunctional families conflict, but the functional family processes conflict more positively. In the functional family system, members adapt to the stress in arguments and seek ways to overcome conflict. In spite of the best decision-making strategies, individual family members can feel cheated or misunderstood in attempting to meet their needs within the family system. The way in which a family agrees is important, and the more grounds for agreement shared by its members, the less is the likelihood of disastrous conflict. The way in which a family disagrees is equally important. When in agreement, the family continues to function, but, with too much disagreement, effective functioning ceases. All communication interactions in family conflicts have a transactional effect upon each family member involved.

> *"It took me the first year of our marriage to understand why my wife becomes silent when we argue. Her father is a very large, domineering man and she is very petite. After observing them argue at family gatherings, I began to sense the intimidation she must feel. Then I realized how my style of arguing was very much like her father's. Although we argue differently on different issues, I realized that our new system must have reminded her of unhappy conflicts in her family-of-origin."*

In this chapter, we will examine the conflict process, a model of conflict styles, factors related to the conflict process, and strategies for improving inevitable family conflicts so that they respect individual rights as well as maintain a "united family" image.

THE CONFLICTUAL PROCESS

As we explore the conflictual process, we will see that conflict is influenced by many factors and may range on a continuum from constructive to destructive with varying outcomes.

Conflict Defined

Conflict is a process in which two or more members of a family believe that their desires are incompatible with those of the others. It may be a matter of perception, as when José believes that the degree of intimacy expected of him is too threatening or requires more of him than he is willing to deliver. Conflict may also develop over a difference in attitudes or values. Maria does not enjoy cooking and would rather the family went out to eat pizza than expect her to fix dinner. Conflict may also emerge when one person's self-esteem is threatened. If each person can reach his or her own goals, there is no conflict. Conflict occurs when one person's behavior or desire blocks the goals of another, resulting in "a struggle over values, behaviors, powers, and resources in which each opponent seeks to achieve his goals usually at some expense to the other" (Scanzoni, 1980, 31). Wilmot and Wilmot (1978) define conflict from a communication perspective: "Conflict is an expressed struggle between at least two interdependent parties, who perceive incompatible goals, scarce rewards, and interference from the other party in achieving their goals" (9).

The conflictual process is very complex. For example, Dan may have a fight with his boss; because he cannot take out his anger at work, he comes home and explodes about eating dinner late. Midge and Ben may have a fight just when things seem to be working well—when they have really gotten into a pattern of sharing and affection. Some families never experience a real fight—things just seem to go on without much feeling: no fighting and not much loving.

Sociologist Coser (1967) has declared that ". . . conflict may be a result just as much as a source of change" (32). His ideas can be applied to family systems. A new family member; the acquiring of a new job or home; and the trauma of a divorce, death, or loss of income all have a differential impact within the family system. Disturbances in equilibrium lead to conditions in which groups or individuals no longer do willingly what they are expected to do, since ". . . change, no matter what its source breeds strain and conflict" (32). Family systems experience a constant level of friction, since they continually change to survive and cope with conflict, either realistically or unrealistically. Coser defines *realistic conflicts* as those that result from frustration of one family member wanting something from another member who does not see the necessity of granting the request or meeting the need (98). *Nonrealistic conflicts* are those characterized by at least one antagonist's need for tension release. Within family systems, conflict directed toward members for the improvement of conditions and rights are realistic. Nonrealistic conflicts may result from frustrations caused by persons other than those against whom the conflict is waged. Such behavior may result in misdirected anger or scapegoating. For conflict to be realistic, the communication must be between the family members directly involved in the matter.

If a couple or family plans to share experiences and realizes the advantages of family solidarity, conflict will be an inevitable and valuable part of the process. Too often, family conflict evolves into a stalemate or bitter fight, and no members emerge happily. By exploring the process of conflict and how it can develop realistically or nonrealistically, plus becoming aware of better communication practices to use during conflict, you can better understand the development and management of family conflict situations.

Several studies have concluded that conflicts are present in sucessfully functioning marriages as well as in dysfunctional marriages (Yelsma, 1984; Olson, 1969; Vines, 1979). While all relationships have problems, the successful ones have partners who learn how to negotiate conflicts. In addition, conflict outside the home in jobs, social groups, or friendships can cause unrealistic conflicts within the family. Individuals who live together in a close and intimate relationship cannot expect a conflict-free existence. Studies reveal that, in certain stages of courtship for some couples, there is little conflict, but conflicts develop as the relationship progresses.

In his work on measuring intrafamily conflict, Straus (1979) states that conflict is an inevitable part of all human association and keeps social units, such as nations or families, from collapse. "If conflict is suppressed, it can result in stagnation and failure to adapt to changed circumstances and/or erode the bond of group solidarity because of an accumulation of hostility" (75). Most people, especially those in close relationships, fear conflict and seek ways to avoid it. But avoiding conflict can lead to further difficulties, because the underlying problems causing it have not been solved.

Model of Conflict Styles

Every family member has a distinct conflict style. Each conflicts differently with every other member. Your personality in conflict changes from one family member to another. For example, Mom and Dad have a conflict style that is not exactly the same as the way they conflict with you. You also conflict differently with Mom than you do with Dad. In addition, your experiences within your extended family, plus your perceptions of conflict in other societal systems, affect your conflict style. As you grew up, you learned how to survive conflicts, which became part of your conflict style.

Kilmann and Thomas (1975) have developed a model (Figure 8–1) to demonstrate that conflict style consists of two partially competing goals: concern for others and concern for self. Conflicts contain elements of both cooperation and assertiveness, as well as needs for interdependence.

Let us look at each of these styles, beginning with avoidance. If you are nonassertive, and not particularly interested in cooperation, you avoid conflicts. You will not participate. The storm brews but you seek cover. However, remember that while you might behave this way in a dispute with your older sister, you might be more assertive, and hence competitive, with a younger brother on the same issue. This conflict style particularly hampers communication about intimate matters in cases where one partner simply ignores such topics.

At the lower right of the model is accommodation. This style of conflict happens when you are nonassertive but cooperative. It is the opposite of competition, because you meet the demands or needs of the other person but deny your own.

168

Figure 8–1 _____
Conflict Styles

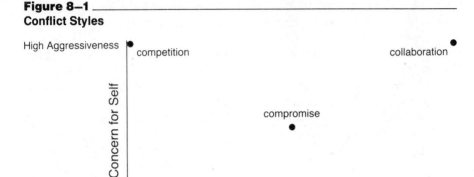

> _"I cannot ever watch Channel 11 [an educational station] when Mom or Willie are home. I don't like to exhibit anger to the degree necessary or use force to change the dial. So to get along, I let it go."_

Competition and collaboration are at the top of the model. Competitiveness requires aggressiveness and going after what you want. Your concern for self is high and, thus, you see conflict as a way to get what you need, regardless of the concerns of others. Competition can be quite selfish if it is your only style of conflict. It can mean "I win; you lose" too often and destroy cohesion within a family. The challenge is to compete to achieve personal goals without taking unfair advantage of other family members. Wilmot and Wilmot changed the term in Kilmann and Thomas' model from high assertiveness to aggressiveness. The latter is more self-seeking and, thus, appropriate to a highly competitive condition. Assertiveness, a more positive term, recognizes the rights of others to disagree (29).

Collaboration occurs when you show concern for those other family members. Collaboration requires that conflicting members seek a solution that enables all parties to feel they have won without compromising issues vital to their needs. Again, remember that your collaboration style varies from member to member. You use your personality differently in conflict, depending upon the family members involved and your closeness to them.

Compromise occupies the middle ground of this model. A compromise represents a solution that partially meets the needs of each member in the conflict. It is an adjustment to the differences that all can accept. In some families, the motto is "Be wise and compromise." Such a family theme recognizes that too much independence detracts from family cohesion and that adaptability via compromise enables more intimacy and tasks accomplished in a family.

This model of conflict style provides a way of sensing how one family member's fights affects another's counter arguments through feedback. This feedback varies between parents and also between parents and each of their children. For example, you are not permanently competitive; it depends upon whom you are fighting. You may carefully watch your conflict style with Dad because of his high blood pressure but not with Mom who enjoys—even encourages—speaking out.

Stages of the Conflictual Process

To better understand this complex phenomenon, let us examine how conflict develops as a positive or negative human process. Conflict develops in stages with a source, beginning, middle, end, and aftermath (Filley, 1975, 7–19; Turner, 1970, 137). These stages characterize conflict as a process:

1. Prior Conditions Stage
2. Frustration and Awareness Stage
3. Active Conflict Stage
4. Solution or Nonsolution Stage
5. Follow-Up Stage
6. Resolution Stage

As these stages are explained, think abut a recent conflict in your family. Did each of these stages emerge as a distinct entity or was it difficult to know when one ended and the next began?

Prior Conditions Stage. Conflict does not occur without a prior reason or relation of the present event to the past experiences in the family. It does not emerge out of a vacuum but has a beginning in the background of the relationship of the people conflicting. The family system or its context establishes a framework out of which conflicts arise. The participants are aware of the family's rules, themes, boundaries, biosocial beliefs, and accepted patterns of communication.

In conflict, at least one member perceives that the rules, themes, boundaries, or beliefs have been violated or that they have been threatened by something inside or outside the family. Prior conditions are present in the absence of conflict but, under pressure, come into play. Prior conditions that may affect a new conflict situation include: ambiguous limits on each family member's responsibilities and role expectations; competition over scarce resources such as money or affection; unhealthy dependency of one person upon another; negative decision-making experiences shared by those involved in the conflict; necessity for consensus and agreement by all on one decision; and the memory of previously unresolved family conflicts (Filley, 8–12). Thus, past experiences set the groundwork for new tension.

Frustration Awareness Stage. The second conflict stage involves one or more family members' becoming frustrated because a person or group is blocking them from satisfying a need or concern. This leads to an awareness of being attacked or threatened by something they have seen or heard, which may be a non-verbal message in the forms of a stern look or avoidance of eye contact. If you closely monitor any developing conflict, usually nonverbal cues of conflict appear before verbal ones. As you become aware of the conflict, you may ask, "What's wrong?" "What's his problem?" "Why am I not being understood?" This frustration depends upon the mutual perceptions of the individuals involved. Such perceptions then determine their judgments of the issues in conflict. Inaccurate perceptions can create conflict where none exists. Perceptions also affect the degree to which the participants feel they will be threatened or lose if the conflict continues. Conflict may end at this stage if one party perceives that the negative consequences outweigh the possible advantages. In families, this happens when one of the members shows signs of power and expects compliance or else. "Backing off" from the issue ends the conflict but does not remove the causes or satisfy the needs that provoked it. This kind of unrealistic conflict may be avoided through self-disclosure. "I'm really just upset about the test tomorrow and I'm taking it out on you" or "You're right—I was selfish and I'm sorry."

Active Conflict Stage. In the third stage, the conflict manifests itself in a series of verbal and nonverbal messages. This symbolic interchange can either be like a battleground or be relatively calm, depending upon the family's rules and style of fighting. In some families, yelling and screaming signal the fight of the decade, whereas others exercise their lungs weekly over minor issues.

Figure 8–2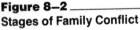
Stages of Family Conflict

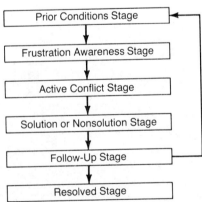

"When my twenty-one-year-old brother Phil leaves the house at noon and comes home at 7:00 A.M. drunk, my Mom and Dad give him the silent 'deep freeze' treatment. Mom won't even fry him an egg or give him a ride to work."

Typically, conflict escalates from initial statements and queries to bargaining or an ultimatum. More will be said later in this chapter about ways to fight fairly and unfairly in families. In the active conflict stage, there is a discernible strategy, or game plan, as one or more family members try to maneuver and convince others of the merits of an issue. The longer the conflict continues, the more the participants' behavior may create new frustrations, reasons for disliking, and continued resistance. During the conflict, sides may be taken as family subsystems and alliances come into action.

Solution or Nonsolution Stage. The active conflict stage evolves into either a solution or nonsolution stage. The solution may be creative, constructive, and satisfactory to all involved, or it may be destructive, nonproductive, and disappointing. The solution may represent a compromise or adjustment of previously held positions. In this stage, how the conflict is managed or solved determines the outcomes and whether positive or negative results follow.

Some conflicts progress into the nonsolution stage. Family members may not have the resources or talents to solve the problem, or after going this far into the conflict process, they may recognize that they do not want the responsibility of carrying out what they demanded. Perhaps they decide they do not want to pay the "trade-off" costs of accepting a change they earlier demanded. This nonsolution brings the conflict to an agreed-upon impasse. Obviously, communication problems can develop if too many conflicts end with nonsolutions. However, every family lives with some unresolved conflicts, because the costs of an acceptable solution outweighed the disadvantages to one or more family members.

"My sister and I are thirteen months apart. We fought like cats through our teens. Jamie would always keep at me until I would reach the breaking point. I would say that my anger was rising. Naturally that was the red flag and we would end up with my crying and her goading me on. It's ridiculous now when I think about how she manipulated me into crying."

Follow-Up Stage. The follow-up stage could also be called the aftermath, because it includes the later reactions that follow the conflict and affect future interactions, such as re-eruptions of the same conflict, avoidance, or conciliation without acceptance. Grudges, hurt feelings, or physical scars may fester until they lead to the beginning stage of another conflict. The outcomes may be positive, such as increased intimacy and self-esteem or honest explorations of family values or concerns. This aftermath stage is linked by a feedback chain to the initial stage, because each conflict in a family is stored in the prior conditions "bank" of the family computer and comes into operation in determining the pattern of future conflicts.

Resolved Stage. This stage occurs when conflicts move out of the family system—they simply no longer affect its balance. For example, a husband and wife may conflict over priorities on bills to be paid. They negotiate and compromise on demands, then stick to their agreement. Time and developmental stages of each family member affect solutions to conflicts. For example, parental conflicts over who will take Steve to school decrease or disappear after he becomes old enough to walk there by himself; the same will be true of parental conflicts over dating rules and curfews when he becomes a young adult. Conflicts over space and territory among six children competing for three bedrooms no longer require solution when all have left home and the "empty nest" remains.

The Conflict Model in Action

To demonstrate the operation of this model of conflict, let us study an example of the Hanrahan family: Dad (45), Mom (45), Frank (21), Louie (19), and Nellie (17). The boys attend the local junior college because the family's funds are limited. At an evening meal in January, Nellie asks her mother if she can apply to a distant four-year college to major in her specialty, marine biology. Mom responds positively, because Nellie has high grades and has been promised financial help on her degree. Frank frowns and stares at his mother, because he assumes that Nellie's request means that he cannot go away to college and silently begins to react. He thinks about other family hassles and recalls other encounters between himself and his sister when Mom took Nellie's side. Frank wonders if Dad or Louie would agree with him that his education was more important than Nellie's. In the past, the men in the family have banded together. All of these prior conditions are important antecedents to the outcome of this conflict.

Communication shifts into the second stage. Louie clears his throat and non-verbally gains his mother's attention by slightly raising his fork and pointing it toward her. He enters the frustration stage, because he too wants to go away to school and fears that planning between Nellie and Mom has gone too far. He thinks there is no way Frank or he can go away to finish their degrees if Nellie insists. Louie announces, "I was going away myself next year." Both his mother and Nellie cease talking and nonverbally check out Louie, their eyes asking the question, "Are you serious?" They discover he is and also that he looks angry enough to fight for the right to go away. They check out Frank, and he looks equally agitated. The sons eye one another for support. The women look at one another as if to say, "Where do we go from here?" This leads to the third stage—active conflict.

"I asked Dad on Wednesday if I could go to the university," Frank declares. The women exchange glances again and then each looks at Dad, who nods in agreement. "Also, I checked with Louie and he didn't disagree." Louie nods to confirm this.

"I never get to do what I want in this family," Nellie says in a defeated voice. "When all of you (looking at each of the men) get through planning, there is nothing left for what I want." Her voice begins to rise as she pushes back her chair and noisily begins to pile up her dishes. "The junior college doesn't even have one course in my field, and I will lose credits when I transfer."

Mom anxiously glances at all the children and then at her husband, who catches her eye and then looks toward Nellie and Frank. His silent message seems to be, "How are we going to solve this?" This scene of conflict could continue in countless ways. The parents could remain silent, and Frank and Nellie could escalate the conflict into a series of harsh remarks, including charges of favoritism or wasting family money, thus repeating unsolved family brawls. The development of the controversy will depend upon what the prior conditions "bank" includes and the family's problem-solving style. What rules does it follow in conflict situations? What rules do the father and mother assume in such disputes? If Mom is the peacemaker, she will smooth things over. If Father is dominant, he will negotiate a settlement—fair or otherwise.

The solution stage of the conflict starts as Dad speaks up: "Wait a minute! Perhaps Mom and I can help this argument." Mom smiles and makes eye contact with Dad to let him know she likes this idea. In this family's conflicts, the parents present a unified position, and the father usually asserts that "he and Mom" will be the arbitrators. Dad asks, "Is there any way Nellie can go another time?" Nellie indicates that will not work by shaking her head. Dad then looks at Frank with an unstated question, inquiring if he has any flexibility and could change his plans. Frank sends back a "no compromise" message. So does Louie. "Well, what can we do?" Dad asks. "Are there any other options?"

This leads to a series of possible solutions. "Couldn't Nellie go to the junior college like we did?" Frank volunteers. "It might take her longer, but by that time Frank and I would be through school and there would be more money for her," Louie suggests.

"Would that work?" Mom asks Nellie. She shrugs, for she does not really prefer that solution. This leads to a discussion of how much money each of the children thinks they will need in the next few years for college expenses. Since education has been a high priority theme in this family, all participants have a vested interest. Both parents want all of their children to have the degrees that they were unable to obtain. Another theme has been to "pay as you go," and, thus, loans have not been considered.

In this family, a compromise solution worked. Mom agreed to accept a full-time position she had been offered and use the income to help pay the increased expenses when Frank and Nellie go away to school. Since this discussion occurred in January, she had nine months before tuition was due.

Dad agreed to increase his credit union savings by 15 percent. Frank and Nellie agreed to secure loans and to work parttime. Louie did not mind staying at the community college, because it has an excellent pre-engineering program, but he received assurances that he could have additional support and not work his first year in the university if he stayed behind another year. The family reached the decision that each child would receive the same amount of money from the parents and that each would have to earn or secure loans for the rest.

The follow-up stage continues the conflict process. The family will store in their "prior conditions" computer the positive aspects of this experience. Louie may feel Nellie owes him a favor, and Nellie may be more willing to agree in a future encounter because Louie accommodated her. They will also store the amount of self-worth and self-confidence each family member has received in this conflict. That is why the feedback link from this follow-up stage back to the first conflict stage is so important. Future conflicts are affected by the positive or negative aspects of current conflict: this family may one day have to renegotiate the allocation of resources for college educations.

If the compromise works effectively, eventually the conflict moves into the resolved stage, a kind of "They lived happily ever after" stage. The family comes to closure with this conflict over resources. However, disagreements or favoritism can lead to the cycle of conflict all over again. The reaching of this resolution stage is a major goal of effective family communication. Otherwise, years later, family bitterness develops as in the next example.

> *"I wanted a degree and my father kept insisting on my being a farmer. When it came time to go to college, no money was ever offered. Yet my brothers received livestock, equipment, and loans to start farming with my Dad. My sisters didn't receive any encouragement or support either for further education. If we wanted to leave, fine, but we couldn't expect any help. I still resent it."*

FACTORS IN FAMILY CONFLICT

You fight with each member of your family in different ways. Over time, most families develop their rules for conflictual situations, and each member stays within the calibrated levels, except for unique situations when he or she may go beyond acceptable fighting levels or reconciling behaviors. A tearful embrace may jolt the family pattern far more than a flying frying pan. A family's systemic nature affects its conflictual patterns, which emerge and maintain themselves. As the system's architects, any type of couple within a family sets the stage for its style of conflict.

Scanzoni (1972) classified couple conflicts into two major types: those that concern the basis of the relationship and those that concern less central issues (73). In the first type, basic values and goals held by one family member are ignored or challenged by another. Conflict over such values as religion, having children, or the need for education can become quite painful or have a dysfunctional effect upon the family system. Unresolved, these conflicts could result in separation or termination of the relationship. The second type occurs when family members seek ways "to change or maintain some part of the distribution of rights and privileges in the relationship" (76). Such conflicts might deal with problems over which bills to pay first or where the family should go for vacation.

Patterns of Family Conflict

In their major study of conflict in early marriage, Raush et al. (1974) found that ". . . whatever the contributions of the specific partners, the marital relationship forms a unit, and the couple can be thought of as a system." Their analysis revealed that the marital unit was the "most powerful source in determining interactive events" (201). Couples developed their own styles of conflict, which were unique to them. Soon after marriage the system had its own fight style.

How does a fight style form so quickly? Do yellers marry yellers, apologizers pair with apologizers? Common sense tells us this is not always the case, yet within a short time, a couple appears to acquire a set of characteristic conflictual behaviors. Raush and his colleagues found similar responses to be one of the major determinants of interaction, i.e., certain conflictual behaviors of one partner were more likely to elicit similar responses from the other (198). The same reciprocal pattern held for negative behaviors, such as coercive tactics or personal attacks. The only exception occurred when one partner rejected the other. Rejection usually met with either coercion or emotional appeals. If each partner rejected the other, communication ended. Family members' use of appeals, whether to fair fighting, justice, promises, or future favors kept the communication process going. Thus, partners were more likely to send similar reciprocal messages than they were to shift to a new message style.

Such reciprocity is a tendency, not an absolute: conflict does not function as a totally predictable ritual with foregone conclusions. Certain partners may have such different approaches to fighting that reciprocity does not emerge. As you saw in the Fitzpatrick typologies discussed in Chapter 5, separates, traditionals, and independents each display particular conflict styles, and it may be more difficult to create reciprocity when different types marry than when similar types marry. Rosenblatt et al. (1979) have found that when one or both partners use disrespect, coercion, and other abrasive factors in their communication, conflicts escalate and couples spend less time togther. Before togetherness, or cohesiveness, can be increased and conflicts settled amicably, couples "must first deal with abrasive aspects of the relationship" (54).

As was noted earlier, Feldman (1979) views a couple's conflictual behavior as part of an intimacy-conflict cycle. Couples move from a state of intimacy as one member became anxious or fearful, which leads to conflict and separation. Eventually, one partner makes an attempt to patch up the differences. The desire for intimacy draws them back together. The human need to be touched, reaffirmed, comforted, and nourished is a powerful conciliatory force in conflicts. At first, one partner might reject attempts to resume more positive communication, but the need for intimacy provides the motivation for repeated efforts to achieve it (69–70). This research relates to our emphasis upon the element of cohesion in all families.

The couple's coming back together does not mean the problem between them has been resolved. Quite often, the issue has not been satisfactorily discussed or even fairly treated in the best interests of one or the other. This means that future communications on the same issue will take up where the old conflict leaves off. Intimacy will again evolve into conflict when one partner feels threatened by the issue or aggressive enough to challenge. Have you heard people fighting and had the feeling you were hearing a rerun or rehearsed battle? Communication reaches the conflict stage because some rules in the relationship have been violated; the system tries to recalibrate itself. The degree and limits of acceptable intimacy and acceptable conflict are important dimensions of a marital system's calibration. When these limits are violated, the intimacy-conflict cycle starts over again. It ends when the couple learns how to listen to one another's problems, needs, and fears and finds answers to these demands so that each can return the support and nurturing the other desires.

Costs and Rewards

Part of a family's systemic function relates to how costs and rewards are negotiated. Conflict may result if a teenager believes the costs of living in a family (rules, obligations, and pressures) outweigh the rewards (emotional and/or economic). Partners stay together as long as the rewards for remaining in a system outweigh the pain or costs of leaving it. Caring for children may be part of a reward and responsibility component in a marriage and hold a family together for a time, but eventually, if serious conflicts continue, one of the partners will leave. To avoid constant conflicts, there must be sufficient rewards in the family system to justify remaining together. Scanzoni states, "If a husband wants certain rewards from his wife then he must provide the rewards that she wants; the same is true for her" (63).

Conflicts may follow when these expectations are not met. When one family member does something special for another, a debt is owed. If the other fails to reciprocate, especially after several requests, conflict will start. Reciprocity becomes, or is a part of, the exchange of costs and rewards in the family. For the family to operate emotionally as a system, this reciprocity does not need to be equal either in amount or kind. Most family members do not keep an inventory up to date, but they know generally who owes them favors. "This reciprocity," according to Scanzoni, "helps to account for marital stability because it sets up a chain of enduring obligations and repayments within a system of roles in which each role contains both rights and duties" (64). To ignore these obligations and repayments creates conflict in families.

Extreme differences in communication backgrounds may present a couple with problems as they try to work out their own style. As couples continue in their relationship, they develop a style ranging from constructive to destructive that characterizes most of their conflictual situations.

"My former husband was a fight phobic like his father. He would do just about anything not to confront me with a problem. According to him, I was perfect. This was to make it look like I was the one who did all the complaining. I found myself

having to gunnysack all my grievances because I could never get them out. Every time I tried to talk with him, he'd avoid the situation by running out, changing the subject, telling me not to yell at him, or making a sexual pass at me which, at the time, I was very vulnerable to. Another one of his famous strategies was to put on a real sorry face and apologize, making some consolatory promise that he most likely had no intention of keeping, since he never did."

The way in which a couple handles secrets also affects conflict styles. Secrets maintain boundaries between a family and its environment, but they can also create boundaries and barriers between members of a couple (Lieberman, 1979, 63).

Roles and Rules in Family Conflict

The way in which conflict is handled in families relates closely to how roles and rules are carried out. Each type of family previously discussed has corresponding roles and rule expectations. Position-oriented parents require their children to ask them for what they want, while person-oriented parents look for consensus among the members and share leadership roles, especially with their children.

As we indicated earlier, conflict may begin when role demands do not coincide with a family member's desires or abilities. He or she may not be prepared to fulfill certain functions. The expectancy that the individual can fulfill the present role causes anxiety and unhappiness (Aldous, 1974). Young husbands raised in households where men never entered the kitchen to help with household chores will find difficulty in doing so, even if they are willing to change. In conflict, family rules determine who can do what, where, when, and how, and for what length of time (Miller et al., 1975, 147).

Stereotyped sex-role conditioning hampers effective decision making and heightens marital conflict. Many men in our society receive training that inhibits emotional feelings and the expression of empathy but permits physical violence as a way to defend oneself. Many women receive countertraining that encourages overexpressiveness of feelings and inhibits constructive assertiveness and negotiation. This lack of expressiveness in husbands during conflicts causes "an emotional overreaction in wives which interferes with their rational problem solving skills and leads to pressuring and coercion" (Feldman, 1982, 356). Other researchers have found that women repress or suppress conscious reactions to threatening, unpleasant messages (Watson and Remer, 1984, 611). In a comparative study, men could identify with confrontation only to a moderate degree, and they had difficulty with empathy and seeing themselves accurately in conflict situations (Remer, 1984, 67).

Family members' closeness to kinship networks also influences conflicts, especially when an urban family moves to the suburbs. Anderson (1982) found that working-class women who moved felt more isolation and experienced more marital conflict than middle-class women who had more role resources in solving transition problems, including staying in contact with kin and friends (431). In addition, research has shown that couples who disagree about a wife's desire to work conflict more. They also argue more about how the children should be raised (Blumstein and Schwartz, 1983, 13).

Communication rules often provide parameters for conflict. The "what," "how," and "who" develop into multitudinous dictates. To what extent can you disagree with your mother? Where, if anywhere, is swearing allowed? What subjects are too painful to talk about? Huber (1984) goes so far as to say that conflicts can only be solved by discovering each spouse's personal rules of living and then modifying those rules found to be dysfunctional. Exaggerated, rigidly held rules of a demanding nature account for much marital conflict (77).

"I get angry when I hear my husband say that our three-year-old stays up all night with her mother. I put her to bed at 8:30 and then she fusses, bangs her head against the bed. He is the one who goes in there and lets her out of bed. He goes to work at 6:00 A.M. and says that he has to have his sleep. I need his cooperation to discipline her, but his temper results in her manipulation of both of us!"

Permissions are always tied to rules and role expectations. Permissions mean the freedom to find out information or to take any action to satisfy a want or need. For example, conflicts develop in families when one member, possibly a parent or older child, refuses permission for another member in the sytem to know or do something meaningful to them. If you want to check in your family to see if a rule exists or test the strength of it, just break the rule and watch what happens. The feedback will quickly make you aware of the rules.

Family and Couple Types and Conflict

Family types and structures can affect their conflict patterns. As a family evolves, the system develops conflictual behaviors, which characterize the group if not the individuals. Using Kantor and Lehr's (1976) types, we can predict how open, closed, or random families will behave in crises or conflict situations. These researchers hypothesized that closed families in conflicts frequently suppress the individual. This type of family operates successfully in conflict if members agree on solutions or accept those handed down to them. However, rebellion results when a member differs, and a permanent schism develops if one or more members refuse to comply with a major decision. Conflict in open families is usually resolved via group consensus in a meeting in which decisions are reviewed and modified. Conflicts are expected and welcomed if they make family living more meaningful. In decision making, every family member can reveal his or her feelings about an issue. This openness means that promises made in family conferences are kept (132). The random family demonstrates no set way to solve conflicts. No one person's views dominate, and ambiguity characterizes the negotiations. Emotional impasses occur when no solutions can be agreed upon. Solutions come spontaneously and creatively. Crises are not taken as seriously as in the other two family types and are viewed more as an interruption of day-to-day events (137).

The Fitzpatrick (1976; 1977) couple types discussed in Chapter 5 also relate to conflict behaviors. Traditional couples seek stability and resist change by confronting rather than avoiding conflict. Independents more readily accept uncertainty and change by confronting societal views on marriage in a much more direct communication style than traditionals. Separates stress autonomy, especially by keeping their own space and distance as a strategy to avoid conflict. They hope to keep conflicts neutral and to a minimum. In conflict situations, independents receive satisfaction from self-disclosure, description, and questioning to receive further disclosure (Sillars et al., 1983, 415).

Family Developmental Stages

Conflict also relates to the developmental stages of the family, which will be detailed in Chapter 9. The issues to be resolved in families vary greatly over the years.

"When I decided to go to New York for a 'cattle call' for a possible movie part, it was the first time I actually argued with both my parents. During most of the argument, my father would not agree that we were in the midst of an argument. 'We're just raising our voices,' he insisted. This was his way of handling the conflict. He didn't want his little boy to grow up and leave. Finally I stopped arguing about New York and argued about how he always denied we were fighting. Finally he admitted we were fighting. Two weeks later I went to New York City."

During the early years of marriage, a couple develops a fight style that may be modified as a family grows. In their analysis of couples who had a child within the first two years of marriage, Raush et al. (1974) identified three stages of development (newlywed, pregnancy, parenthood) that were characterized by varying conflict behaviors, including rejection. They compared these "developmental" couples to couples who did not have a child during those years. During the newlywed stage, the developmental couples generally acted like the other couples in the sample, although certain trends in establishing distance led the researchers to speculate that this group may have had a somewhat more traditional orientation to marriage and male-female relationships (183).

During the later months of the pregnancy stage, husbands increased markedly in conciliatory behavior, a finding consistent with other studies of husband concern. The developmental couples behaved more coercively than the matched couples, which may indicate greater stress due to parenting responsibilities (193).

Finally, during the parenthood stage, four months after the child's birth, both members of the couple appeared to handle conflict less emotionally and more cognitively than their matched counterparts. Yet, the reconciling behavior of the husbands returned to prepregnancy levels. In summarizing their perceptions, the researchers suggested that as marriage progresses through the three stages, ". . . couples tone down the emotional impact of the conflicts by moving from outright rejection of the partner to a more rational argumentative mode" (183).

The early stage of being a "threesome" may lead to difficulties, since roles need to be reworked when a new person begins to compete for affection, often causing one or the other adult to feel left out. Although a joyful time in most families, early parenthood provides great stress that can lead to significant conflicts.

In the early childhood stage, parents often make the decisions and solve conflicts by offering few options. As the child's ability to reason increases with age, the resolution of conflict relates closely to the type of family structure previously outlined. The adolescence period usually presents a greater number of family conflicts. Physical changes in adolescent bodies accompany the search for independence and testing of rules and role expectancies. Intense peer group pressure heightens conflict as family beliefs and practices are questioned. Sibling rivalries increase as older children place more distance between themselves and younger children. Teenagers make space and privacy demands, which may also cause conflict. One study of family conflict and children's self-concepts found no significant differences in self-concept scores of children from intact, single-parent, reconstituted, and other types of families. However, ". . . self-concept scores were significantly lower for children who reported higher levels of family conflict" (Raschke and Raschke, 1979, 367). Broken homes did not yield broken lives, but excessive family conflict was definitely detrimental.

The "empty nest" stage, defined as the period when the youngest child leaves home, presents fewer problems in flexible families than in rigid types. The effects on parents of loneliness, rejection, uncertainty, or worry over capabilities of young adult "children" to care for themselves largely disappear after two years. In fact, this stage has positive effects upon the psychological well-being of some parents, because their child has been successful in making it on his or her own merits. Conflicts develop when the youngest lingers and takes extra years to leave (Harkins, 1975).

Older married couples report significantly less conflict and greater happiness and life satisfaction than do younger couples. Morale increases over time, and older couples evaluate their marriages in a positive manner and describe the quality of their marriages as improving (Lee, 1978, 131).

DESTRUCTIVE CONFLICT

"One member of our family, a stepson twenty years old, enters the house with a barrel full of hostilities and problems. He overwhelms my wife with yelling and screaming and a string of obscenities. My reaction is to tell him to shut up and not to have anything to do with him; certainly not to do anything for him. My wife seethes until she can no longer cope; then she explodes. After a litany of verbal attacks, she retreats behind a closed bedroom door—sealing herself off from the problem."

You have probably been involved in a variety of conflict situations, some of which were difficult but resolved themselves well and others that caused great pain or increased anger. On other occasions, you may have discovered that you were upset but could not put your finger on the exact cause of the problem. Conflict styles may range from the very overt (pots, words, or fists are flying) to the very covert (the burned dinner, late appearance, or cutting joke). Although all overt conflict cannot be labeled constructive, it does let you know where you stand. Covert conflict, on the other hand, places you in a guerrilla warfare situation. "Is she really angry?" "Am I reading things into his behavior?" "Are those mixed messages?" In almost all cases, covert conflict falls into the destructive category.

Covert Destructive Conflict

Covert, or hidden, *conflict* usually relies on one of the following five communication strategies—denial, disqualification, displacement, disengagement, and pseudomutuality. You experience the *denial* strategy most directly when you hear such words as "No problem; I'm not upset," "No, you didn't hurt me," or "That's OK, I'm fine," accompanied by contradictory nonverbal signals. *Disqualification* occurs when a person expresses anger and then discounts, or disqualifies, the angry reaction. "I'm sorry, I was upset about the money and got carried away," or "I wouldn't have gotten so upset except that the baby kept me awake all night." Admittedly, some of these messages are valid in certain settings, but they become a disqualification when the person intends to cover the emotion rather than admit to it.

Everyone has heard a story about the man whose boss yelled at him, but he could not express his anger at the boss. When he arrived home, he yelled at his wife, who grounded the teenager, who hit the fourth-grader, who tripped the baby, who kicked the dog. . . . In some families, this type of incident is not just a story. When you believe you cannot express anger directly, you may find another route through which to vent the strong emotions. Thus, *displacement* occurs. One type of displacement happens when a couple who cannot deal emotionally with their own differences make a child into a scapegoat to receive their pent-up anger. Many families tend to single out one person who appears to be the "acting-out" child but who, in many cases, receives covert negative messages with such regularity that he or she finds it necessary to act out to release the feelings (Ackerman, 1966; Minuchin, 1974; Gurman and Kniskern, 1981). Dogs, kids, in-laws, friends, and spouses all may bear the brunt of displaced anger.

The *disengaged* couple or family lives with the hollow shell of relationships that used to be. Disengaged members avoid each other and express their hostility through their lack of interaction. Instead of dealing with conflict, they keep it from surfacing, but below-the-surface anger seethes and adds immeasurably to the already tense situation.

"My wife and I should have separated ten years before we did because we hardly had any relationship. I was able to arrange my work schedule so that I came home after 11:00 and slept until Norma and the kids had left in the morning. That was

> *the only way I could remain in the relationship. We agreed to stay together until Nick graduated from high school. Now I feel as if we both lost ten years of life and I'm not sure the kids were any better off because we all ate and slept in the same house."*

Pseudomutuality represents the other side of the coin. This style of anger characterizes family members who appear to be perfect and delighted with each other, because no hint of discord is ever allowed to drop the image of perfection. Only when one member of the perfect group develops ulcers, nervous disorders, or acts in a bizarre manner does the crack in the armor begin to show. Anger in this situation remains below the surface to the point that family members lose all ability to deal with it directly. Pretense remains the only possibility.

Finally, we need to note the relationship of sexual behavior to these covert strategies. For many couples, sex is a weapon in the guerrilla warfare. Demands for, or avoidance of, sexual activity may be the most effective way of covertly expressing hostility. Sexual abuse, put-downs, excuses, and direct rejection wound others without the risk of exposing one's own strong anger. Such expressions of covert anger destroy rather than strengthen relationships.

Often, covert behavior is a rejection of family themes that discourage conflict or independence. Themes such as "We can only depend on each other" or "United we stand—divided we fall" encourage covert conflict to occur.

Overt Destructive Conflict

In the first of this pair of quotations, a daughter states her views on the way conflicts are handled in her family. She reveals how her expectations of her mother in the parent role function differs from the mother's actions. In the second quotation, written independently, her well-meaning mother perceives the siblings' conflicts from a different vantage point.

> *"In my family, conflict is settled by the laissez-faire method. My single-parent mother refuses to negotiate conflicts between her four daughters. We fight but with mixed results. I believe this is bad, because it brings out the worst in each of us at times. We never learn from one another—more like survival of the fittest."*

> *"I used to get involved in my daughters' conflicts, especially arguments over borrowing clothes without asking one another's permission. I now try to totally divorce myself from these conflicts when they try to get me to intervene on their behalves. I let them handle it themselves."*

Each of us could list overt forms of destructive conflict that we have participated in or lived through. The following are some commonly used negative behaviors.

Verbal Attack. In all conflicts, the language used by family members has a great impact on the outcome. Word choice reflects the degree of emotion and reveals the amount of respect the conflicting individuals have for one another. Emotional hate terms ("You idiot!" "Creep," "Sneak," or "Liar") quickly escalate conflicts. In some families, swearing is an integral part of venting rage. In others, the rules do not permit swearing, but name-calling replaces it. Each generation has its own slang terms used to put down opponents. Put-downs heighten conflicts and slows the solution process by selecting words that describe and intensify bad feelings. These attacks are usually accompanied by screaming or other negative nonverbal cues. Families handle verbal attacks in special ways, such as gunnysacking and game-playing.

Gunnysacking. A gunnysack is a burlap bag, but according to some family members, a gunnysack is a deadly weapon that implies storing up grievances against someone and then dumping the whole sack of anger on that person when he or she piles on the "last straw." In some conflicting families, members store resentments instead of dealing with them as they occur. Eventually, those members dump out the gunnysack when a spouse, sibling, or parent does that "one more thing." The offender usually responds by attacking back, and the war escalates.

Game-Playing. In many family conflicts, there is a great deal of game-playing. Games are nonproductive ways to solve conflicts. Whether the game is "martyr," "poor me," or "stupid," the interaction leaves the problem unsolved. Bach and Wyden (1966) suggest that most couples would love to stop playing games, since these players never know where they stand. "The more skillful they are, the less they know, because their objective is to cover up motives and try to trick their partners into doing things" (19). Games end when one player refuses to play and be trapped. An essential test of game players is to ask, "How does this solve the conflict on a more permanent basis?"

"I don't remember seeing my parents ever hit one another before they divorced. I do remember arguments. We were hit as children by Dad. Mom rarely spanked us, just threatened that Dad would do it. It seemed as if the longer they were married, the more overadequate Dad became and the more underadequate Mom became. He had a take-charge personality and a hair-trigger temper. She complained to us, seemed like a martyr. She had ways of aggravating Dad. She always covered up for us, did our chores, or they didn't get done until he came roaring home."

Physical Attack. Hitting, screaming, kicking, teasing, grabbing, and throwing objects characterize some family conflicts. In one study of persons between the ages of eighteen and thirty in families with more than one child, physical aggression was used in 70 percent of the families to settle conflicts between parents and their children and by the children to settle disputes among themselves. Thirty percent of the husbands and wives used physical means to resolve their conflicts (Steinmetz, 1977, 19). These conclusions supported two earlier studies using different, larger samples (Steinmetz, 1973; 1974). (See also Steinmetz and Straus,

1974.) Instead of solving conflicts, violence led to more violence. This 1977 study also confirmed previous findings that physical punishment increased rather than decreased aggressive behavior in children. Further evidence has indicated that child abusers are likely to have been abused children (Straus, 1974, 16). Aggressive nonverbal abuse as a way to manage conflicts causes more harm than good.

The overall climate of a family may determine its amount of physical aggression. Too often, the entire setting in which conflict takes place is defensive. As a family member becomes more and more defensive, he or she becomes less able to perceive accurately the motives, values, and emotions of the sender (Gibb, 1961, 141). Such climates are usually characterized by control and blaming, useless behaviors when viewed from a systems perspective that stresses mutual interaction and discourages attempts to assign cause or blame.

A large national study of marital aggression has revealed that teenagers who observe their parents hitting one another are likely to beat their own spouses in later years. This has a greater influence on future behavior than the children's being hit by their parents. Further, seeing the father hit the mother increases the chances that their children will be both victims of such abuse and instigators of it. This means that aggression can be transmitted across generations and is not sex specific (Kalmuss, 1984, 17).

The research on family violence indicates that parent-parent and parent-child abuse becomes a part of role relationships. In physically combative families, such behaviors occur frequently enough for children, husbands, wives, or lovers to become accustomed to it. Kalmuss maintains that ". . . exposure to aggression between specific family members teaches children the appropriateness of such behaviors between the inhabitants of those family roles" (17). Children grow up accepting beatings as part of parents' rights in governing them but not accepting their parents' hitting one another. Children know about other neighbor children receiving physical punishment, but they also know Mom's hitting Dad or vice versa violates a societal norm.

Since abuse in conflicts occurs intermittently, children learn to live with it, because they also see periods of affection and love between conflicts (Burgess and Conger, 1979, 1167). The mixed message of love followed by hate and violence causes children mentally to seek ways to avoid getting hurt themselves. They adopt a "wait and see" attitude and hope the conflicts will not lead to additional violence.

Incest is the most extreme form of family violence. The increasing evidence of this problem has led some researchers to warn that incest occurs in families that are not classified as pathological or perceived as dysfunctional. Incest is related to family stress, and poor management of conflict certainly heightens stress. It is important to note that extreme male dominance of the family, plus weakness in the mother caused by illness, disability, or eventual death, correlate highly with high rates of incest. Further, women who have been abused both in their families-of-origin and by their husbands are more likely to be forced to accept abuse, resulting in submissiveness. This fear toward male assailants increases the likelihood of incest also happening to their children (Breines and Gordon, 1983).

CONSTRUCTIVE CONFLICT

Constructive conflict should be a learning experience for future conflicts. Too often, families repeat nonproductive patterns of conflict and fight in predictable ways. As we said earlier, a couple's manner of dealing with conflict is probably established during the first two years of marriage and remains quite consistent (Raush et al., 204). Therefore, partners may create a fight style in the first twenty-four months of marriage that will characterize the next fifty years. Raush et al. have discovered that harmonious couples consist of two types: "those who manage to avoid conflict and those who deal with conflict constructively" (204). Those who exhibit constructive conflict show "even within the space of a single scene, sequential communication exchange, growth, development, and sometimes even creativity" (203–4). Both types of harmonious couples can avoid escalation.

Elements of Constructive Conflict

Recall the example of conflict over college expenses presented earlier in this chapter as we review the process of constructive conflict.

The following characterize successful conflict management: (1) a sequential communication exchange takes place in which each participant has equal time to express his or her point of view; (2) feelings are brought out and not suppressed; (3) people listen to one another with empathy and without constant interruption; (4) the conflict remains focused on the issue and does not get sidetracked into other previously unsolved conflict; (5) family members respect differences in one another's opinions, values, and wishes; (6) members believe that solutions are possible and that growth and development will take place; (7) some semblance of rules

In the management of constructive conflict, all family members need adequate time in which to express their views.

has evolved from past conflicts; (8) members have experience with problem solving as a process to settle differences; (9) little power or control is exercised by one or more family members over the actions of others. These goals are not achieved in families in which young people fail to learn these communication and problem-solving skills, because their parents either shield them from conflict or typically make the decisions (Hill and Aldous, 1969, 943–44). Effective communication does take place in some families, as in the following example.

> "One of the things that characterize both my parents is their willingness and ability to listen. They may not always agree with us or let us do the things we want but no one feels like they don't care. At least we feel like they heard us, and usually they explain their responses pretty carefully if they don't agree with us. As a teenager, I was always testing my limits. I can remember arguing for hours to go on a co-ed camping trip. Mother really understood what I wanted and why I wanted to go, but she made it clear that she could not permit such a move at that time. Yet, I really felt that she shared my disappointment, although she stuck to her guns."

In a comparative study of the communication patterns of couples who had problems and sought counseling and couples who did not, Gottman et al. (1977) found that in conflict situations, the happier couples began with remarks that told the partner that, although they disagreed on an issue, the other party was a decent human being. They also avoided negative exchanges and ended discussions with some sort of verbal contract to solve the conflict (476).

How do these wonderful harmonious types pull it off? Families seem to be able to manage conflict creatively by recognizing that they have a twofold responsibility—to meet their individual needs and wants and to further enrich the family system. This requires give-and-take, resulting in compromise. The attitude behind this view enhances flexibility and helps avoid conflicts that result from being too rigid and assuming that one family member's views must be followed. A conflict that presents something new to the family system, requiring accommodation or assimilation, tests the strengths and capacities of the system. If the system is flexible and differentiated, family members can more readily accommodate one another, learn new ideas from other members and themselves, and change (Raush et al., 48). Undifferentiated family members become enmeshed in their system and lack the assertiveness or autonomy to handle conflict constructively. In a flexible family, new ideas do not threaten the stability of the relationships, and members can learn from both outside and within the system.

Strategies for Constructive Conflict

Although we will devote most of Chapter 13 to specific methods of improving family communication, we will treat some of those constructive conflict behaviors briefly here.

Listening. A cornerstone to constructive conflict may be found in good listening behavior. Listening is an important communication skill to use to defuse conflict and help clarify and focus on the issues being debated. Empathic listening requires that you listen without judging and try to hear the feelings behind the remarks. This means accurately hearing what the other is saying and responding to those feelings. Remarks like "You're really angry—I hear that" or "I am hearing you say that you have been misunderstood" indicate to a family member that you have listened yet not become trapped within your own emotions or thinking about "How can I best turn off this complaint?" Restating what you have heard a person say can be most helpful in slowing or stopping the escalation of conflict. "Bill, are you saying . . . ?" Asking Bill to repeat his contention is another helpful approach.

Some partners will go so far as to switch roles in a conflict and repeat the scene to check out the accusations. It gives the other person a chance to try out the other person's feelings. Parents may also have their children role play their conflicts.

Gordon (1975), in his Parent Effectiveness Training program, has developed a "no lose" method for solving conflicts that depends on careful listening and involves compromise elements. The Gordon approach asks for those disagreeing to hear each other out, find the areas of agreement, and then zero in on the specific differences. He encourages both sides to seek some reward in the solution of the conflict. "If you let me do X, I'll do Y." The philosophy of caring and pleasing one another is basic to its success. Even on difficult family problems, the method can work because all parties recognize that no one can totally win or totally lose.

Sometimes, flexibility and compromise will not solve conflicts. The consequences outweigh the advantages. An individual's self-worth may be more important than family expectations. Some families permit members to decide what is negotiable and nonnegotiable for them. Stating "This is not negotiable for me at this time" enables one to own his or her position and part of the problem. Being tentative and including the phrase "at this time" leaves the door open for future discussion. Other items may legitimately be nonnegotiable for you on a permanent basis (Bernhard, 1975).

"I used to be terrified to disagree with my father, but within the last ten months or so, because of certain differences that I feel strongly about, I don't back down. We try and talk about my being gay, but when I sense his becoming opinionated and abusive, I say, 'I don't want to argue.' I stick to this rule and he eventually shuts up."

Fair Fighting. Bach and Wyden have developed a process for "fighting fairly." The goal of this process is for the couple to vent or share their feelings but not to take unfair advantage of their partner by using negative communication behaviors that demean one another. When successfully used, fair fighting techniques enable the couple to disagree, even to be assertive, but not to coerce and dominate one another. Bach and Wyden have established nine dimensions on which fair fighting couples are judged during a conflict:

1. Reality—a measure of the authenticity of the fight, based on justifiable, rational factors that feel real and honest.
2. Injury—scored plus or fair (above the belt) if partner can absorb it and minus or dirty (below the belt) if partner is harmed or cannot tolerate the aggression.
3. Degree of involvement of the parties—scored active (+) or reciprocal if characterized by give-and-take and passive (–) if one way or evasive.
4. Assumption of responsibility by the one who began the fight—scored minus when initiator disclaims responsibility or displaces it on others.
5. Humor—plus if it aids tension release and minus if it ends in sarcasm.
6. Expression of aggression—plus if open and leveling, minus if covert and vague.
7. Communication—measure of clarity of both nonverbal and verbal messages. Rated plus if communication is open, transparent, and reciprocal in feedback, minus if characterized by interruptions, poor listening, redundancy, and misunderstanding.
8. Directness that requires a focus on the here and now.
9. Specificity—scored plus if conflicts are limited to specific observable behavior but minus if participants label a specific behavior as part of some larger personality trait.   (162–65)

According to their method, each conflict can be analyzed on an effects-of-fight profile. The effects of conflict evaluated include hurt, new information learned, positional moment (ground has been gained if the conflict ends on a hopeful note), power, fear, trust, revenge, reparation (an apology for wrong or injury done), or reconciliation, centricity (the enhancement of self-worth), autonomy, catharsis (a release of pent-up feelings without acquiring additional guilt or blame), cohesion, and affection (167–69).

The most bitter conflicts in families result from the use of unfair tactics by various members; such behavior can be changed with a commitment to fair fighting. In a fair fight, equal time must be provided for all participants, and name-calling or "below-the-belt" remarks are prohibited. In this system, family members agree upon how they will disagree. The procedures are agreed upon with time and topic limitations. They can be used only with the mutual consent of the parties involved and the assurance that each will listen to the others' messages.

"As a marriage counselor, I have seen many couples fight, and one of the hardest things is to get people to avoid 'red flag' words during a fight. I had one couple where the man would call his wife 'crazy like your sister' referring to his wife's sister who had been in a mental institution, and his wife finally found that calling him a 'faggot' sent him through the roof. It took months to get them to finally agree to drop those words from their vocabularies."

Jim tells his wife, "I'd like to share a gripe with you." "OK," Michaela replies, giving permission for Jim to release his feelings and do so without interruption. "I really felt angry this evening when you told Marissa she didn't have to go to the program with us. You let her run wild."

In this approach, Jim continues to release his anger during the time granted him by his wife. According to the rules of fair fighting, he can only express his anger verbally—no hitting or throwing things. Also, Michaela could have asked to postpone hearing the gripe until she had time to really listen. The idea of asking permission to be heard is essential, because it implies the obligation of the other party to listen.

Michaela can deny the charges Jim makes, which can lead to a careful recounting of what was said and with what intended meanings. This often helps clear the air. She can also ask for a break until later if she becomes angry and cannot listen. She can also admit her error in judgment, if one was made.

Whatever rules or methods couples use in their fighting, the nonverbal aspects of conflict need special attention. Careful monitoring of nonverbal cues often reveals the true nature of conflict. Gestures of threat, harsh glares, and refusals to be touched or to look at others indicate the intensity of the conflict. In a study of marital communication, Beier and Sternberg (1977) found that the subtle nonverbal cues in a couple's messages determine the climate in which either conflict or peace reigns. By observing nonverbal cues, they discovered that couples who reported the least disagreement "sat closer together, looked at each other more frequently and for a longer period of time, touched each other more often, touched themselves less often and held their legs in a more open position than couples who reported the most disagreement" (96). This finding correlates directly with Gottman et al.'s conclusion that ". . . nonverbal behavior thus discriminates distressed from nondistressed couples better than verbal behavior" (469).

Sometimes nonverbal cues contradict verbal statements. A receiver of such mixed messages must decide "Do I believe what I hear or what I see?" On the other hand, supportive nonverbal cues can drastically reduce conflict. For example, a soothing touch or reassuring glance has great healing powers.

Managing the physical environment properly may dampen certain conflicts. Reducing the distance between adversaries may help reduce the noise level. Sitting directly across from someone makes for easy eye contact and less chance for missing important verbal or nonverbal messages. Choosing a quiet and appropriate space lessens distractions or related problems. Thus, conflicting family members need to be aware of all the factors that can escalate a fight.

"One thing I have learned about fighting with my teenage son is never to raise an argumentative issue when he is in his bedroom. Whenever we used to fight I would go up to talk to him about school or about his jobs in the house, and five minutes after we started arguing, I would suddenly get so upset about the state of his messy room that we would fight about that each time also. By now I've learned to ask him to come out or to wait until he is in another part of the house to voice a complaint."

The rewards of better-managed family conflicts are numerous. Better use of positive communication practices stops the cumulative aspect of conflict—a series of minor conflicts left unsolved become a major one and can escalate into separation, divorce, or emotionless relationships Successful resolution of conflict that goes through the five stages of our conflict model (Figure 8–2) leads to emotional reconciliation and affirmation of the participants. It also decreases fear and anxiety within the family. Future joint enterprises become possible for family members. Knowing how to manage conflicts leads to a greater appreciation for the talents of family members and enjoyment of each of them in the "here and now" of living together.

Yelsma's (1984) research emphasizes this conclusion. Couples that had high scores for managing conflict reported the highest degree of marital satisfaction. Also, too high a concern for one's own uniqueness appeared to lessen one's chances for happiness. However, reasonably high self-esteem and high task energy enhanced marital adjustments (60).

UNRESOLVED CONFLICT

What happens in the family if conflict cannot be solved? Usually, a loss occurs, which affects all members as psychological and/or physical estrangement creates and fosters separation among members. Young family members may remain in the home but withdraw from family activities until they go to school or establish a way to support themselves. If circumstances force a continued joint living arrangement, a wall of silence may become part of the family's life-style. Some members may be cut off from all contact with the family; they may be treated as nonexistent.

> *"When I married my husband, I was essentially making a choice between my parents and Joe. Joe is black and my parents said they would never speak to me again if we married. Although I knew they were angry, I thought that they would come around when we had a baby. Melissa is two years old now and my parents have never seen her. My brother and sister have been to see me but I am 'dead' as far as my parents are concerned."*

Many unresolved marital conflicts result in divorce, clearly a rejection strategy. One or both members withdraw, seeing the ending of their formal relationship as the only logical solution. Yet, when children are involved, spouses are divorced from each other and not from the children; not the children from one another. The system alters itself rather than ending. The original family system evolves into new forms, which may include new spouses and children. Legal action does not stop interaction of family members. Unresolved conflicts lead to early dissolution of marriage, with 50 percent of all divorces occurring during the first five years and 33 percent of all separations within two years (Carter and Glick, 1976, 430; Bahr et al., 1983, 801).

Some couples stop their conflicts short of divorce, because the cost of the final step may be too great; yet, the rewards of living together are too few. For these people, destructive conflict characterizes much of their continued shared existence. Such unresolved conflict may add great tension to the entire family sytem, but not always. When an issue is unresolvable, it may be more functional for the family to avoid the issue and direct its communication to areas that bring cohesion (Fitzpatrick et al., 1982, 62).

CONCLUSION

Too many family members have experienced physical abuse when conflicts become destructive. Other families experience intense verbal abuse in the form of swearing, name-calling, and demeaning insults. Still others experience silence or family members' withdrawing into sulking or martyr roles. In some families, a partner or child may well be caught in a survivor role. In this chapter, we have explored the conflict process as a creative activity that can lead to family strength.

Today, there is increasing conflict within families. According to Straus, the swing in the pendulum of family roles, the inevitability of conflict in time of change, and the glorification of aggression and violence provide reasons for greater conflict. The American family lives under many pressures. "Conflict accordingly develops, because the standards of identity support and agreement are unrealistic" (Turner, 159). Yet, families survive. One family realistically faced their problems when they sought outside help—a step that can reward a troubled family system.

"When I asked my wife what she wanted for our 25th wedding anniversary, she said, 'Marriage counseling. The next twenty-five years have to be better than the first.' I knew we had many fights but I never knew she was that unhappy. I agreed to the counseling and we really worked on our differences and ways of resolving them. After a few months, we were able to talk rationally about things we always fought over—money, my schedule, our youngest son. Next month we will celebrate our 28th anniversary, and I can say, 'The last three years were a lot better than the first twenty-five.'"

In this chapter, we have advocated that participants in family conflicts understand the value of conflict and attempt to use constructive or fair fighting techniques within a supportive climate. It is hoped that children in such homes will carry those behaviors into their newly formed systems and perpetuate a constructive familial conflict model.

IN REVIEW

1. Take a position and discuss: Conflict is inevitable and necessary for the development of family relationships.

2. Describe how an individual's conflict style may vary with specific members of the family. Relate to the model of conflict style on page 168.
3. Using the stages of family conflict, describe a recurring conflict in a real or fictional family.
4. The following excerpt from an anonymous author contains some ideas that could relate to conflicts you have had in your family. After reading it, give three examples of conflicts that resulted from poor listening, either from your own family or one that you have observed.

LISTEN

When I ask you to listen to me and you start giving advice, you have not done what I asked. When I ask you to listen to me and you begin to tell me why I shouldn't feel that way, you are trampling on my feelings. When I ask you to listen to me and you feel you have to do something to solve my problems, you have failed me, strange as that may seem. Listen! All I asked, was that you listen. Not talk or do—just hear me. Advice is cheap: 25 cents will get you both Dear Abby and Billy Graham in the same newspaper. . . .

—Anonymous

5. After reading this chapter, list certain insights you have gained that might lead you to change your conflict behavior in your family.

Chapter 9

Family Communication and Developmental Stress

When does a family cycle begin? When does one end and another start? Questions like these will concern us in this chapter about the effects of developmental stress on family communication. We define a *family life cycle* as those important stages of development through which a family passes during its existence.

These stages include separating from one's parents, establishing one's own family, having or not having children, and going from youth to middle age to old age. With the current divorce rate, plus deaths and desertions, some families do not go through this cycle in a predictable pattern. Some families must negotiate divorce, remarriage, or single parenthood during their family life cycle.

Each person in a family follows his or her own *trajectory*, or path, through these developmental stages. The term "trajectory" helps describe the movement a family member makes as he or she progresses through the life-cycle stages (Spanier and Glick, 1980, 98). No two family members go through these stages identically, and the timing varies.

Families evolve and change, requiring their systems to adapt when members leave the original biological family and form a new one, beginning the cycle anew (Duvall, 1977). In fact, one cycle evolves into another like a great family chain with connections from previous generations to the present. The early work of Hill (1970) and the more recent work of McGoldrick and Carter (1982) emphasize the three-generational approach to understanding family life cycles. The many ways and ideas that family members carry from one generation to the next, plus their mutual interdependence, become part of the context for understanding how the family defines life-cycle events.

Family definitions of life-cycle stages alter perceptions of life-cycle events. Think about your own family. When did your parents noticeably begin to treat you as an adult? When did they stop calling you Chuckie or recognize your need for a razor to remove the stubble on your face (or legs)? Some families emphasize *marker events*, or the transition stages in human development, more than others do. Family rules also become a part of a family's definition of life-cycle changes: "You can't go out with boys alone until you are fifteen," "You are not old enough to go downtown alone," or "Until you marry, you will be home by 1:00 A.M."

The way individual family members "organize their experience in their personal stimulus world . . . influences the shared perceptions the family develops of the social world in which they live" (Reiss and Oliveri, 1983, 290). In other words, families view the world differently, which affects their definitions of the kinds of stress that enters their family system. One family perceives the world as consistent, predictable, ordered, and manageable. Another sees the world as chaotic, disorganized, and frequently dangerous.

In this chapter, we will first examine the sources of family stress and then look into the stages of development that can create stress. This chapter focuses upon developmental changes that individual family members undergo, from separation from their family-of-origin into forming their own system and on through the years in a normal life cycle. The next chapter will focus on some of the unpredictable external stresses that occur, such as death, divorce, economic changes, serious illness, or handicaps. To succeed in the developmental process, whether in crises or transitions between stages, all families must negotiate, through communication strategies, the expansion, contraction, and realignment of the relationship to accommodate the entry, exit, and development of family members in a functional way (McGoldrick and Carter, 175).

" 'Jesus, Mary, and Joseph, save my soul!' can be heard from the lips of my mother at least once a day. When you have babies, they eventually grow up. Mom thought three in diapers was bad but since has decided three teens are worse. Presently, we have three teens in driver's ed, three teens tying up the phone, three teens falling in and out of love. Mom threatens to run away once a day. Dad says we drive him crazy and should be locked up until we go away to college. We must be driving our parents nuts."

SOURCES OF FAMILY STRESS: A MODEL

In their work on change in the family life cycle, Carter and McGoldrick (1980) have developed a model of stressors that affect the family system (Figure 9–1). Within the same family, individual members experience and react to these stresses differently. Also, stress varies with the age of each family member and where they are in their life cycle.

The vertical stressors include patterns of relating and functioning that are transmitted down generations involving family attitudes, expectations, labels, and rules. In other words, " . . . these aspects of our lives are like the hand we are dealt . . ."(Carter and McGoldrick, 9). We examined many of these communication-related stressors as we discussed the images, themes, myths, rules, boundaries, and expectations that come from our families-of-origin.

The horizontal stressors include both the predictable, or developmental, issues with which a family has to cope and the unpredictable events that disrupt the life cycle. Pressures from these current life events interact with one another and with the vertical areas of stress to cause disruption in the family system.

Communication differs throughout the developmental changes in family life as the courting relationship moves to marriage or cohabitation and decisions about

Figure 9-1 _____
Sources of Family Stress

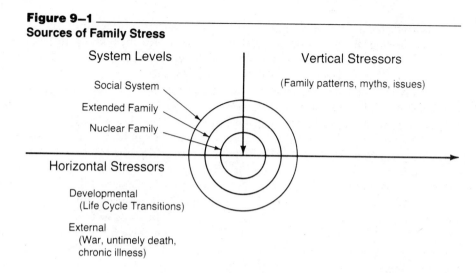

becoming parents or remaining child-free, until eventually the cycle begins to repeat itself. The specific configuration of each family system means that it experiences stages of development slightly differently than other systems, yet, each family passes through certain similar stages within the birth-death cycle.

Many people have spent much of their lives in single-parent, blended, or extended families rather than in a two-parent family. Yet, most people begin life in biological families (mother, father, and children of their union); as the years go by, many of these families evolve into other forms. Other people are born into single families or blended families where one or both parents have children from previous marriages. Some couples do not have children. This chapter focuses more directly on the predictable changes for a two-parent biological family, recognizing that this pattern, lived throughout a lifetime, represents only one family form and is becoming less the norm with each passing year. We will discuss some of the variations of newer family forms in Chapter 11.

GENERAL ADULT DEVELOPMENT ISSUES

Most researchers accept the position that people experience critical periods of change until death. Levinson's (1978) work on the stages of adult male development, described in *Seasons of a Man's Life,* and Sheehy's (1976) popular work, *Passages,* have brought this perspective to the attention of the general public.

Experts differ as to whether or not the developmental focus should be placed on learning theories or on stages. Those who stress learning theories maintain that " . . .learning one task or living through one kind of experience makes one ready for the next, presumably more difficult, task, or open to the next order of experience" (Troll, 1975, 5). Thus, life is viewed as a series of learning experiences that are not tied to a person's age or position in the life cycle. On the other hand, the stage approach emphasizes sequential changes, stressing that all humans experience similar problems or challenges at about the same time in their lives. The stage approach emphasizes sequencing and universality, whereas the learning theory approach de-emphasizes universality, although some experts include sequentiality.

You may be familiar with the work of Jung, Erikson, Havighurst, and Levinson, who have explored developmental crises or turning oints. Jung viewed youth and early adult years as a period when the instincts and vital life forces are in ascendance. The late thirties and forties witness a value reorganization as persons become more cultural, spiritual, and introverted and less impulsive. As a result of this reorganization period, some persons may fall rigidly into old patterns, whereas others experience new growth. Jung also suggested that masculine and feminine features shift into their opposites so that a husband may discover his tender feelings and a wife may find her sharpness of mind (Campbell, 1976, 16).

In his work *Identity, Youth, and Crisis*, Erikson (1968) detailed his eight stages of development through which one must pass successfully in order to master the environment, show a certain unity of personality, and perceive the world and self correctly (92). All of the stages lead toward a sense of integrity, of having lived authentically and meaningfully, so that one can accept old age and death with dignity. Hoffman (1980) describes developmental tasks that must be solved or completed in order to reach life satisfaction within a developmental period. For example, some representative tasks of adolescence include developing a sense of self, acquiring an appropriate sex role, and achieving social maturity. Sample tasks of middle age include relating to one's spouse as a person, adjusting to aging parents, and assisting teenage children to become responsible, happy adults.

After intensively studying the lives of forty men aged thirty-five to forty-five from four occupations, Levinson entitled his book *The Seasons of a Man's Life*, implying that the life course has a certain shape, that it evolves through a series of definable forms. He explains the analogy in the following manner:

> To say that a season is relatively stable, however, does not mean that it is stationary or static. Change goes on within each, and a transition is required for the shift from one season to the next. Every season has its own time; it is important in its own right and needs to be understood in its own terms. . . . It is an organic part of the total cycle, linking past and future and containing both within itself.   (7)

Just as individuals move through the various seasons of their lives, whole family systems also pass through certain seasons, and such passages are reflected in their communication patterns. In the following pages, we will examine some perspectives on family development and change and draw some implications for family communication behavior.

FAMILY STAGES

As you can imagine, we cannot study family change by relying on the different members' stages of development, because the complexity would be overwhelming. Instead, many family researchers have attempted to apply the stage concept to whole families so that the entire system may be thought of as moving through particular stages. Such analysis has difficulties, because families consist of several individuals in different life stages, but it becomes more manageable than trying to account for each person. Such schemes provide simplicity but do not account effectively for families with numerous children or widely spaced children as they go through the middle stages of development. Nor do they focus on adult developmental stages or tasks unrelated to childrearing. More detailed perspectives exist, but their complexity limits their use. No matter which framework we adopt, communication emerges as a critical issue at each stage. Hill highlights the complexity of communication networks and subsystems as a family enlarges and then contracts:

> This intimate small group has a predictable natural history, designated by stages beginning with the simple husband-wife pair and becoming more and more complex as members are added, with the number of interpersonal relations reaching a peak with the birth of the last child, stabilizing for a brief period, to become less and less complex subsequently with the launching of adult children into jobs, and marriage as the group contracts in size once again to the dyadic interaction of the husband-wife pair.   (296)

Based on the findings of many family scholars, we have synthesized the following stages for discussion:

1. Unattached young adults
2. The "engagement" period
3. Beginning marriage
4. Initial parenthood
5. Individuation stages (preschool children, school-age children, adolescents)
6. Families as launching centers (from departure of first to last child)
7. Families in middle years (from time children leave until retirement)
8. Families in older years   (Satir, 1972; Rollins and Feldman, 1973; Hill; Troll; Carter and McGoldrick; McGoldrick and Carter; Nock, 1981)

To further your understanding of the developmental process, imagine the cohesion-adaptability axes (see p. 16) as an overlay for each family system's growth. For example, extremely cohesive families may resist certain changes, such as children leaving home, whereas low-cohesion families may splinter when children start to leave. The capacity for adaptability aids a family in moving through its stages of development. A rigid family may try to avoid necessary growthful change, whereas highly chaotic families may not place enough significance on life changes and rites of passage. Families characterized by low adaptation and high cohesion may fight the passage of time that carries them through developmental stages. Family themes, boundaries, images, and biosocial beliefs further complicate movement through the developmental stages. In order to understand the entire process more clearly, let us focus briefly on each developmental stage.

Unattached Young Adults

Although this stage is not found in other life-cycle lists, McGoldrick and Carter include it as an essential stage that recognizes the young adult coming to terms with his or her family-of-origin and separating to form a new cycle (175). Unless this task is successfully handled, communication problems can develop in the stages that follow. Young people need sufficient autonomy to separate and achieve their goals independently. If they remain enmeshed and overly dependent, this will affect their choices or options throughout their lives. The goal is healthy interdependence, with the parents' letting go and the young adult's establishing a career or completing school, finding close friends and establishing peer networks, defining the "self" as separate yet a part of the family-of-origin. An abrupt cutoff is not the answer. Bowen (1978), a distinguished family therapist, insists that an angry cutoff leaves the young adult emotionally bound to the old system. The ideal would be for the young adult to feel free to achieve his or her own goals and command the respect and encouragement of the parents, even if they might have hoped for other outcomes.

"Last week I met a friend whom I hadn't seen for almost two years. When I asked how her children were, her eyes filled up and she said, 'Larry is in Utah apprenticing as a carpenter, Sam is in South America in the Peace Corps, and Rachel went to England for a year to discover herself before college.' Then she shook her head and continued, 'If I hadn't told them they could be whatever they wanted to be, they'd be home for Thanksgiving.'"

Forming the System: The "Engagement" Period

You have heard the two classic explanations as to why people are attracted to each other—"opposites attract" or "birds of a feather flock together." Some people support the "theory of complementary needs"—that persons tend to select mates whose needs are complementary rather than similar to their own (Winch et al., 1954, 245–48). However, the evidence for this position appears weak (Berscheid and Walster, 1969, 85).

Often, at the beginning of courtship, the members of a couple appear to differ on many issues. Sometimes their very oppositeness is what attracted them to each other, because each sought in a mate someone quite different either from themselves or their parents. However, research indicates that most people select a mate of similar socioeconomic background who shares similar values, interests, and ways of behaving.

Proximity and similarity play a large role in whom one encounters and eventually with whom one develops close relationships. People are more likely to date others who live nearby, attend the same school, or share their social background, which makes it likely that a large proportion of their attitudes and values will be in basic agreement from the start. Once a relationship becomes established, the couple's gradual discovery of just how much agreement exists becomes crucial in determining whether or not they decide to marry (Rubin, 1979, 197).

The choice of mate also depends upon each person's needs and his or her self-perception (Murstein, 1973, 248). Communication will be affected by whether these needs are met or frustrated. Each partner in courtship sets out with some image of the person he or she would be happy marrying. Persons with high self-esteem are more likely to seek partners like themselves and to express greater satisfaction in their marriages. Murstein reports that persons with low self-esteem demand less in their relationships with the opposite sex (248). He also found that disappointment emerges in the verbal and nonverbal messages between the partners when each finds out their intended spouse is not "perfect."

As you probably know, people come together for complex reasons, often unknown to themselves. Yet, if a relationship is to grow and prosper, it must involve intimacy-producing communication. In Chapter 4, we detailed the stages of relationship development. The system formation period, usually involving courtship/engagement, involves a couple's attempt to move from the facades of the orientation, or exploratory affective exchange stage, to deeper levels of communication. Through a variety of communication activities, including self-disclosure, touch, questioning, discussion of family rules and backgrounds, and arguments over values and attitudes, two people discover that they are indeed attracted to one another. This period provides the chance for the couple to share and learn about one another and find ways to communicate effectively. The following diagram partially depicts what happens when two people in courtship communicate.

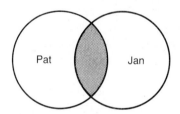

Each circle represents the field of experience of one person. This field includes all his or her family rules, themes, images, experience in roles, hardships or lack of them, success or failure in a previous close relationship, patterns of cohesion and adaptability, and capacities for intimacy and risk taking. The shaded area represents the overlap in the couple's communication. It is the topics, ideas, and feelings that each understands about the other. The couple communicates only when the circles overlap—when one is able to comprehend what the other means by his or her verbal and nonverbal messages. Intimacy increases as they share meanings.

Partners find out through permissions, granted verbally or nonverbally, that there are limits to their communication. Certain topics, feelings, or actions may frighten or offend the other. They create unwritten rules that will govern their communication when they encounter these issues.

As the relationship deepens and marriage appears on the horizon, a series of communication-oriented rituals may occur. The engagement communicates to outsiders the seriousness of the courtship. Quite often, prior to the announcement, verbal and nonverbal signals from the couple indicate a deepening relationship. Significant jewelry may be exchanged; invitations to attend special family events such as weddings, Bar Mitzvahs, or reunions are extended.

"In my family, we always knew when relationships were serious when the annual family reunion time arrived. If you were serious about someone, you were expected to introduce this person to each member of the clan. However, you didn't go through this and take all the teasing that followed unless an engagement followed. Bringing a partner signaled an impending marriage."

Announcing an engagement serves as a type of bonding, a statement to the world that the relationship is formalized. Such an action informs families and friends that a new familial unit will be established. The act of bonding, or institutionalizing the relationship, may change the nature of the relationship. This may be a traumatic period, since some parents, as well as the young adults, have not prepared for this separation. Mothers especially may feel abandoned (Bart, 1971). If the marriage means moving away, the feelings of loss are stronger. Each family faces the issues of cohesion and adaptability as it responds to the questions: How willing are we to allow a member to separate, physically and psychologically, and how willing are we to accept a new member as an in-law? Some families struggle for years with these questions.

The premarital period provides the time for testing, dreaming, and communicating. It is the time when all of the "I love you . . . but(s)" should come out for discussion. It is a time when, through self-disclosure, each partner can let his or her fears and wants be known. It is a time for planning how roles and role functions will be worked out.

The following issues may need discussion: time to be spent with friends, desires for children, sexual needs, career and educational planning, religious participation, money management, home buying, in-laws, and acceptable conflict behaviors. Crucial issues, which all couples face, need to be talked about. Avoiding them sets up the potential for major problems.

The trend today is for shorter engagements; some couples decide to live together during this period. Such an arrangement forces decisions on many issues—sometimes before adequate communication has taken place.

Couples may discover significant differences between them after signing a lease and putting a down payment on the furniture. On the other hand, they may get to know one another apart from families and find out they *can* live together. Because of the high incidence of premarital sexual experience, many couples have engaged in serious communication around sexual issues before their marriage. For many couples, the major issue remains—can each person risk sharing his or her deepest needs or concerns, or is there a fear that such honesty could jeopardize the marriage?

Throughout this period, each person may have to deal with a basic fear of giving up his or her independence. This shift from self to mutuality with another requires time and examination. Persons raised in highly cohesive families may need and demand more mutuality than those raised in families with low cohesion. The issue of separation may be difficult for those who are tightly bound to a family-of-origin. For many couples, the final part of the engagement period becomes hectic with rituals—wedding plans, bridal showers, and apartment hunting. In some families, this serves to involve the parents and to keep the focus off the separation issues until the ceremony is over.

In this discussion, we are focusing on the young unattached person, yet today many individuals involved in remarriage are planning to blend families, so the engagement period becomes fraught with complication as potential stepparents meet potential stepchildren, potential stepsiblings eye each other, and former mates anxiously watch the proceedings.

No matter what form the premarriage period takes, its function remains critical. The adjustments made in the engagement period relate directly to the quality of married life that follows. The nature of a future married relationship is formed "by the way the couple related to one another and how much they knew about each other" prior to the wedding (Rapaport, 1973, 231). In the adjustment period, there needs to be room for changes and flexibility so that the system remains open and does not close out the potential for each spouse's self-actualization through marriage.

Beginning the Marriage

The vows may be repeated before a judge or minister, before 10 or 300 beaming friends and relatives, as two individuals formally create a new family system. The actual ceremony is a communication event—a telegram to the outside world that the ultimate formal bonding has occurred.

For most couples, this stage represents the only period of two-person intimacy for many years to come, since this period usually leads to childbearing. For some couples, the honeymoon serves as an initial transition from the single life to the married state, providing a time for unique physical, sexual, and psychological intimacy, a period to explore their hopes for the future.

> "The period following our marriage, before the children began to arrive, was a critical point. If we had not established a really strong trusting relationship in those first two years, we would have drifted totally apart in the next twenty-three years of childrearing. I didn't realize what a critical period it was until we lost all our time together. If I had it to do over, I would have waited five years before having children, just to give us that building period for sharing who we really were before we tried to deal with who the four new people in our lives were."

Early marriage involves certain predictable tasks for most couples. It is a time of: (1) separating further from the families-of-origin; (2) negotiating roles, rules, and relationships; and (3) investing in a new relationship. We have all heard of the young man or woman who "ran home to mother" every time a conflict arose in the new marriage. Although most couples do not experience this exact scene, most young couples and their respective families have to deal with separation issues as the new system emerges. Some young people find it difficult to separate from their parents, establish an adult identity, *and* assume the role of spouse (Vines, 1979, 8–9). Marriage at this time may continue unresolved conflicts with the parents. The new mate becomes the victim of angry projected feelings he or she did little to deserve. This is a period of unconscious or conscious negotiation between the couple and their families-of-origin regarding how the old and new systems will relate to each other.

"I had known my husband since childhood and we dated since our junior year. Our parents knew each other and we attended the same church—yet we had some real difficulties in the first years of our marriage. I had difficulty in the following areas: (1) learning to live with each other's habits, (2) trying to be a full-time employee and a housewife, (3) deciding which family's house at which to celebrate holidays, (4) telling my husband when I was angry, and (5) dealing with the biggest problem—my husband's mother."

Although not typical of all recently married couples, the previous list of problems appears in the research as quite representative of many issues as people try to negotiate their rules, roles, and relationships. This period is the time for negotiating roles—usually influenced by those brought from families-of-origin. Will the new couple discuss their sexual life openly? Will open fighting be accepted? Who will be told what about their joys and sorrows? Much negotiation relates to previous friends and habits. What will be the role of the "old friends"? How much time will the spouses spend apart? How much togetherness will be demanded?

Equally important, but far more subtle, is the verbal and nonverbal negotiation related to cohesion and adaptability. Each person jockeys for the amount of togetherness he or she wishes as well as for the amount of flexibility that can be tolerated. Such moves are rarely dealt with openly, but the results have long-lasting effects on communication within the system.

As you may well imagine, the images, themes, boundaries, and biosocial beliefs experienced by each partner in his or her family-of-origin affects the new system's development. A woman whose biosocial beliefs and image create a husband who is strong, unemotional, and powerful puts great pressure on her new husband to deal with such expectations. If one partner has experienced themes of open sharing and very loose boundaries and the other partner has experienced the opposite, much negotiation will be required.

As we discussed in Chapter 8, couple conflict patterns tend to establish themselves within the first two years of marriage and demonstrate great stability.

Similarly, the balance of power between a couple is established early in the marriage, based upon how one spouse returns feedback to the other's behavior in decision-making situations (Lasswell and Lasswell, 1973,269). Many couples set lifetime patterns at this point.

In their study of adjustment in newly married couples, Cutler and Dyer (1973) found that communication options varied from open discussion to doing nothing. Husbands, more than wives, adopted a "wait and see" strategy. Wives more often met violation of expectations with open sharing, talking about the problem, or responding negatively. The issues also called forth different behaviors. For example, husbands spoke openly about financial problems but not about their desires for more frequent sex. Wives complained six times more frequently about the amount of time spent at home than husbands. Wives also had more unmet expectations about who was responsible for home care (295).

Many of the previous remarks reflect upon problems that can complicate communication in a new marriage. However, the research indicates that this is a happy stage, and differences are often not taken seriously or allowed to develop into crises.

A couple's ability to invest in their new relationship relates directly to the quality of their communication. The extent to which connectedness and adaptation will characterize their life-style finds its roots in this period. Each person's capacity and desire for intimacy will structure the development of these patterns over the relationship's lifetime. This is a time of investing in the system, risking self-disclosure, building a pattern of sexual communication, confirming, and being confirmed. Time, energy, and risk taking nourish the relationship and establish a range of acceptable intimacy for the system.

For some couples, heterosexual and homosexual, this two-person system will be their permanent form. Partners may not need to add children to their lives or may find it difficult to bear or adopt children. Yet, for most young couples, the two-person system eventually becomes a three-person one, with pregnancy heralding the transition to a new stage.

One of the most important choices any couple makes concerns childbearing. Such a decision should, but does not always, involve intense communication—self-disclosure regarding the needs of each partner and how a child could fit into their lives. Since about one fifth of all children born in the United State were conceived before marriage (Troll, 98), many couples do not experience a lengthy period of intimacy before the child arrives.

Input from all sources affects such a decision. Most women have been conditioned since childhood toward eventual motherhood, although there has been recent counterconditioning toward meaningful careers that may preclude children. The media, parents, friends, and other relatives often pressure the couple to fulfill parent roles and subtly suggest they are being selfish if they do not. Men may perceive children as a way to prove themselves as mature, responsible males. For both spouses, producing a child is partially ego-fulfilling, and they may desire to be the kind of parents they never had.

Initial Parenthood: Birth of the First Child

The first pregnancy signals the many changes to come. Traditionally, pregnancy has followed shortly after marriage. Now, with children often postponed for several years, the first pregnancy forces choices and may cause far more interruptions in the woman's life than marriage did. The intensity of the desire for a child by one spouse or both greatly influences the communication about the parenthood stage from the very beginning.

When a couple desires a child and the pregnancy is uncomplicated, pregnancy can be a happy communicative time with much closeness, if both partners continue openly to share their feelings, fears, and hopes. There is still time to talk and to share without interruptions from outsiders and the third family member. Yet, subtle communication changes occur, as well as changes in conflict patterns. In the last stages of their wives' pregnancy, husbands make greater efforts at nurturing than they do at the newlywed stage. Contrary to popular myth, Rauch et al. found no indication that wives become more emotional in dealing with conflict during pregnancy (204). Three factors influence couples during the transition to parenthood: their views on parental responsibilities and restrictions, on how gratifying childrearing can be for them as a couple, and on their own marital intimacy and stability (Steffensmeier, 1982, 332).

As the wife's body dramatizes the life changes, some couples begin to feel pregnancy has trapped them into a loss of independence. This is a time when the spouses need one another for confirmation of their self-images as individuals and as a couple evolving into parenthood. Women may need extra reassurance as to their continued physical desirability.

As the birth approaches, special communication may take place about naming the child. Naming sessions can be joyful and creative as each suggests names until the couple finds one they both approve. If one spouse dominates and insists upon a certain name, possibly a family "hand-me-down" name, the other may resent it. Yet, names may serve to link family generations.

Additional important communication may center around the role of the father in the birth process. Some husbands or wives are very uncomfortable at the thought of being together in the delivery room, while others express a great desire to share the event. Decisions concerning this issue require careful communication, because years later, one may feel left out or abandoned by the other at this crucial moment.

"I have never felt closer to my wife than at the moment of Ryan's birth. I had helped her breathe, wiped her forehead, and rubbed her back between contractions. I actually felt a part of the birth process. When Ryan was finally delivered, Christie and I cried and laughed and cried again because of the power of the drama we had created. It's indescribable—to share in the birth of your own child."

Many variations of this stage's pattern exist. Although most children are born into two-parent systems, increasing numbers of single women choose to keep their children, so they move directly into the parental stages, either without a male partner or with a male partner who is not a husband.

If you have ever shared a home with a newborn baby, you are well aware how one extremely small person can change an entire household. New parents soon discover that they no longer have the leisure for communication that they once had. You can hear comments like these: "The baby woke up every three hours day and night and we're exhausted. Who can talk when you're half asleep?"

At the point when the dyad becomes a triad, alliances and subsystems can emerge. As was noted earlier, a more complex network begins to develop, and all family members cannot receive undivided attention at the same time. Simply put, all three people cannot relate at one time; they cannot all experience eye contact or direct speech from each other simultaneously. One person becomes the "odd man out," watching the other two relate. This means that when Dad speaks to Mother, their daughter is left out. When Mother replies to their daughter, Dad loses his line to Mother. New potential challenges for communication result. Within this stage, the couple must deal with the following communication-related issues: (1) renegotiating roles, (2) transmitting culture, (3) establishing a community of experiences, and (4) developing the child's communication competence. Families with moderate adaptation capacities are more likely to weather this period comfortably than are relatively rigid systems.

As soon as the child is born, each spouse begins to assume his or her parental role. In some families, parental roles become so powerful that the spouses may lose sight of each other for a period of time. New parents may feel inept caring for their child. Since the mother traditionally has taken the major responsibility for childcare, few fathers have been exposed to much modeling of how to share the caregiving role. Yet, in his summary of research on fathers in childcare roles, Nash (1973) concludes that our society is "mother-centered" and suggests that children with little contact or negative experiences with fathers during the preschool years may develop identification or self-concept problems. The critical period begins early, from the time of weaning to entering school (362). When fathers do become involved in childcare, some evidence demonstrates that they are just as sensitive and responsive to infant cues as are mothers. In fact, fathers of newborns are as competent as mothers in providing attention, stimulation, and necessary care (Sawin and Parke, 1979, 509). Due to cultural and economic changes, many more families are experiencing shared parenting responsibilities. Although men's roles are changing slowly, there are indications that men, especially with working wives, are accepting more family responsibility, particularly if the system is adaptable (Lewis and Pleck, 1979, 429; Patterson and McCubbin, 1984, 100–103).

The father's age may affect how he assumes his role. Very young fathers tend to pay less attention to their wives and children, but fathers over thirty-three are more comfortable in the role. Fathers who have their first child around forty tend to remain involved and concerned longer (Troll, 102). New mothers may have had greater practice or more expectations regarding their parental role than have fathers but the transition is still critical. Older mothers tend to be even more concerned and anxious than are younger ones during the baby's first year. Also, mothers respond differently, depending upon the kind of behavior shown by infants. For example, babies who cry are treated differently than those who do not. Some mothers respond more positively to active babies, others to passive babies, thus underscoring the transactional nature of the parent-child relationship (Troll, 99).

Women may have to deal with the demands of motherhood and with the loss of a job or profession that held high interest or economic value. If they return to work, they must deal with separation from their child. Husband, wife, and infant must communicate to work out their relationships within the context of their roles.

The first child represents a link to posterity and continuation of the family name and heritage—a heavy burden for some children. Thus, parents become involved in transmission of culture and the creation of a community of experiences for their new family. Contact with the extended family increases after the birth of a child. However, the amount of support and quality of help from a couple's parents depends more on their relationships prior to the birth of grandchildren. For example, proximity to grandparents does not necessarily increase emotional or financial support (Belsky and Rovine, 1984, 462). When you think about your own children or of your future children, what parts of your background do you wish to pass on to them? Do you wish they could experience the same type of Passover Seders you did as a child? Do you want them to have a strong African, Italian, or Norwegian identity? Are there family traditions, picnics, celebrations, parties, or Christmas customs you want to continue? What type of sexual identity or religious belief should your children develop? Such are the issues of transmission of culture.

"The birth of our first child revived many issues that we had fought about in our courtship period and that we finally agreed to disagree about. Sean and I were from very different backgrounds, religiously, culturally, and even economically. As a couple, we were able to ignore many of the differences, but once Wendy was born, we each seemed to want certain things for her that we had experienced growing up. And our families got into the act also. We've dealt with most everything except religion and we are due for a showdown on that soon as she is now five and should begin some religious training soon."

For many people, a child represents a link to the past and the future, a sense of life's flow, and a sense of immortality. Hence, children often serve as receptacles for what we consider our best parts, our strengths, and our expectations for the family. Once a couple becomes a triad, certain dormant issues may arise—particularly unresolved ones. A father's unmet personal goals may be transmitted to his son. The couple's differences in values, religious beliefs, traditions, or national/racial/ethnic background may be highlighted by the small member of the next generation. Thus, spousal conflicts may arise over what is to be "passed down." The transmission of both the cultural heritage and the family's own heritage is a demanding, frightening, and exciting task that depends on marital intimacy. Simultaneously, three people are forming a community of experiences, a process begun by the couple but deepened and intensified by the arrival of their offspring. As additional children arrive, the process will be repeated and extended.

"It was amazing for me to watch my sister and her husband with their first child. After almost twenty-five years, my sister could remember so many of the songs that our mother sang to us as little ones. She and Lee took great pleasure in creating new words and expressions from things that Jonathan did. They set certain patterns for birthday parties, established Friday nights as 'family night,' and began to take Jonathan to museums, children's theater, and library storybook programs together. They created their own world, which now incorporated a little boy."

Through communication, new patterns of life are formed and maintained, which reflect the uniqueness of the three-person system. In-jokes, camping trips, burned steaks, sing-a-longs, long walks, or Sunday pizza dinners may all contribute to one family's community of experiences. Young marrieds who have not had extensive contact with their parents may suddenly feel a need to connect their child to grandparents and other relatives. Other couples may find themselves resisting over-eager relatives who wish to envelop the child. Appropriate boundaries usually require careful consideration and negotiation.

Finally, parents are deeply involved in providing their children with a means to deal with interpersonal relationships. Their relationship serves as the first model for the child's development of communication skills. From the earliest weeks of existence, a child learns how much connectedness or separateness is acceptable within the family system and how to attain that level through verbal and nonverbal means.

The first child in a family represents a link between posterity and its continuation into the future.

The moment of birth exposes the child to the world of interpersonal contacts, as a powerful parent-child bonding process begins through physical contact. Montagu (1978) stresses the importance of body contact with the mother. The child makes its first contact with the world through touch, and this becomes an essential source of comfort, security, and warmth (75). Infants explore their world nonverbally through a combination of senses, since they cannot speak or understand verbalizations. Parents can encourage an interpersonal orientation through cuddling and talking with the child, responding to his or her cries, maintaining eye contact, and smiling.

The first few months mark the critical beginning of a child's interpersonal learning. A child's personality is being formed in the earliest interchanges with nurturing parents. By four to five months, a child distinguishes Mother's voice from all others and responds with smiles and sounds. Children begin to respond to words at six to seven months; by nine or ten months, they can understand five or six words and will begin to use language soon thereafter. Children need supportive communication as they go through such cultural processes as weaning and toilet training. Parents set the stage for positive interpersonal development by verbally and nonverbally giving a child the feeling of being loved and cared for.

As more children arrive, much of this process is repeated. And the more children, especially under the age of five at any one time, the greater the demands upon parents to keep the family system balanced. Nevertheless, later births do not cause as many major changes as the first one (Terkelsen, 1980).

Individuation Stages

After the first few years of great dependency, children develop a sense of self and a mastery of skills that allow them to become more independent persons. Such growing independence has a direct bearing on family interaction.

In reviewing the stages of individuation, the periods of child growth and outward movement, we will examine the following three phases. Remember that each family will experience each phase differently, depending on its size and the ages of its members.

1. Family with preschool children (three to six years, possibly younger siblings)
2. Family with school-age children (oldest child six to twelve years, possibly younger siblings)
3. Family with adolescent children (oldest thirteen to nineteen years, possibly younger siblings)

Family with Preschool Children. The preschool family (child three to six years) experiences less pressure than in the previous period. Parents have learned to cope with a growing child. Barring physical or psychological complications, the former baby now walks, talks, goes to the bathroom alone, and can feed and entertain himself or herself for longer periods of time.

Watching a three- or four-year-old, you may be amazed at his or her language skills. A four-year-old may produce well over 2000 different words and probably understands many more (Wood, 1981). Children at this age begin to develop more sophisticated strategies for gaining such ends as later bedtimes or specific foods. They also are likely to express their gender roles nonverbally.

As children become more independent, parents may directly influence their language acquisition skills through enrichment activities. If they take time to communicate with their children and teach them to share ideas and feelings, they improve the child's developing self-concept. The parents' own communication behavior in this stage serves as an important model for the child.

As we noted in our discussion of roles, communication with children will differ depending on whether the family is position-oriented or person-oriented. Whereas a child in a position-oriented family is required to rely on accepted roles as communication guides and is not likely to make communication judgments based on the unique factors in the two-person relationship, the child in a person-oriented family is more likely to provide a range of communicative behaviors and to understand their effectiveness in relation to the specific people with whom he or she communicates.

The difference is essentially one of the degree to which the child is provided with verbalized reasons for performing or not performing certain communicative functions at certain times with certain individuals. Persons growing up in a household where things are done "because I told you to" or "because I am your father" do not gain training in adapting to the unique personal relationships of the individuals involved. Children growing up in a person-oriented family are more likely to receive explanations for performing communication behaviors: "Apologize to your mother because you hurt her feelings" or "I need your cooperation because I don't feel well today."

Children must not only learn to relate to parents or other adults; they may have to incorporate new siblings into their world. During this period, many couples have more children, increasing the complexity of the family's relationship network. The arrival of second and third children moves the triad to a four- or five-person system and places greater demands on the parents. Each additional child limits the amount of time and contact each child has with the parents and the parents with each other. In homes with working parents, children learn to adjust their communication to other caregivers.

Additional children trigger a birth-order effect, which combines with sex roles to affect parent-child interaction. You may have heard characteristics attributed to various people because "She is the middle child" or "He is the baby of the family." There appear to be differences in parent-child communication based on sex and position. Boys may be allowed to ask for more comforting and receive more comforting and praise, particularly if they are firstborn. Mothers tend to become intensely involved with their firstborn children and appear more anxious about their performance in other settings. Whereas mothers are more likely to praise firstborn boys and second-born girls more often, they will generally correct firstborn girls and second-born boys. Finally, mothers are more likely to control their daughters more than their sons (Toman, 1976).

The competition of a second child can threaten the firstborn. Communication about the expected child and sharing the planning with the first child may lessen the concerns.

"Angie was three when Gwen was born, and it was a very hard period for her and, therefore, for us. Angie changed from being a self-sufficient, happy child to a whining clinger who sucked her thumb and started to wet her pants again. Jimmy and I had to work very hard to spend 'special' time with her, to praise her, and to let her 'help' with the baby when she wanted to. Luckily, Gwen was an easy baby, so we could make the time to interact with Angie the way she needed us to."

Parents need direct communication with an older child or children before the next baby's birth or adoption and during the months to come. This may include hospital phone calls or visits and time alone after everyone is home. Even with the best of communication in a family, the first child may have his or her "nose out of joint" a few days after the second arrives home. Siblings three or more years older are more likely to treat the baby with affection and interest, since they are more oriented to children their own age and less threatened by the new arrival. A sibling close in age may engage in aggressive and selfish acts toward the baby (White, 1975, 125).

How parents relate to children affects sibling cooperation. In keeping with the system concept of mutual causality, Bradt (1980) suggests that parents should hold all children in a particular conflict situation accountable for working things out rather than judging one child as "the cause" (133). He also suggests that children may help each other understand relationship issues.

In the three- to six-year stage, children begin to communicate on their own with the outside world. Some attend nursery school, and at five years, most enter kindergarten. Some parents experience difficulty in letting their children go even at this early stage and develop patterns of possessiveness, which eventually result in communication problems in the adolescent and early adult stages.

As children move out of infancy, they become less helpless, and parents gain more control over their own lives, but time alone for the couple remains a problem. Even after they have adjusted to any possible income losses from the new members, husbands and wives are likely to fight over the absence of joint recreation (Troll, 90). Time alone becomes a precious commodity for most couples.

Family with School-Age Children. The school-age family experiences new strains on its communication as the child begins to link further with outside influences. The family system now overlaps on a regular and continuous basis with other systems—school, church, and community. Families with very strong boundaries are forced to deal with new influences. Schools provide an introduction to a wider world of ideas and values. New beliefs may be encountered; old beliefs may be challenged.

At this point, children may spend many hours away from the home environment and influence. The school offers a variety of activities that often extend the school day. Churches provide special religious training and recreational events. Organizations such as the Scouts, YMCA and YWCA, Little League, or 4-H compete for family members' time. Parents communicate rules that set boundaries in space, time, and energy that their children can expend in these new activities. During this period of growth, the child comes under the influence of peer pressures, which may conflict with parents' views. Often, at this age, conflict develops, because the child feels more compelled to please friends rather than parents.

As children continue their emotional and physical growth, their capabilities change. Negotiation and priority setting become important aspects of child-parent communication as extra-familial demands (such as jobs, church, or community responsibilities) conflict with desires to do things together as a family. Family role orientations continue to influence behavior. For example, Bearison and Cassel (1975) found that first-grade children from person-oriented families are more able to accommodate their communication to the perspectives of listeners than are children of the same age who come from position-oriented families. The authors attribute the differences to the more *differentiated* role systems of the children from person-oriented families.

Children at this age prefer peer communication with the same sex and often declare they "hate" the opposite sex. Knowing that this normally characterizes interactions of children between eight and twelve helps parents understand the messages they receive from their children.

During this same period, additional siblings may be added to the family, which greatly complicates its communication network. Triangles and subsystems multiply. "Each time a new person is added, the limited time and other resources of the family have to be divided into smaller portions," Satir (1972) states, "but the mother and father still have only two arms and two ears" (153).

During the school years, the identity of the family as a unit reaches its strongest form. The family can enjoy all kinds of joint activities, which bring a richness to the intimacy of the family relationship (Clinebell and Clinebell, 1970, 120). Due to the intense activity level, some partners neglect their own relationship or use the children as an excuse to avoid dealing with marital problems. Yet, at this point, parents must depend less on satisfaction derived from the child's dependency on them and should be able to gain emotional satisfaction from their spouses. This is not always easy.

"My parents believed strongly in giving undivided individual attention to each child, so as the family grew larger, we developed a pattern of individually talking to our parents about our day. After dinner, each of us seemed to take turns going back into the family room to 'report' on what had happened to us. By the time all five of us were done, it was time for the bedtime rituals. One night, my father came out and stood behind me in the doorway as I waited to go into the dining room, because, he said, 'I want a chance to tell your mother about what happened to me today.' We all thought it was very funny, but suddenly I realized how little time they had to really talk with each other."

This period may be very comfortable for highly cohesive families, since joint activities can be enjoyed, and children still remain an active part of everyday family life. The more parents know about child development in this stage, the more skill they have in creating a supportive environment. In fact, the more parents are aware of the importance of providing play materials and interacting with their children in fun and learning activities, the better will be the language development of their children in these important early stages (Stevens, 1984, 241).

Family with Adolescent Children.   Eventually, school-age children enter adolescence. "Enjoy the little ones while you can; after puberty they won't talk to you for six years." Such comments often greet the person about to embark on parenting an adolescent. During the adolescent period, once described by Anna Freud as a "necessary malaise," parents may see strange behavior, locked doors, dramatic mood swings, and despondency over pimples and members of the opposite sex. All of these behaviors certainly can and do influence communication.

Although a number of recent investigations suggest that the extent of adolescent and parental turmoil during this period has frequently been exaggerated, there is general agreement that adolescence, and particularly early adolescence, has traditionally been a challenging and sometimes trying time for both the young and their parents (Conger, 1977; Herz, 1980).

According to Offer and Sabshin (1984), three major groups of adolescents can be identified. A minority of 21 percent could be characterized as experiencing a tumultuous adolescence; 35 percent moved through the period in spurts emotionally and mentally demonstrating less introspection than other groups, while a third group, representing 21 percent, appeared as models of virtue and confidence. Very few of this final group reported anxiety and depression, but they did report receiving affection and encouragement for independence from their parents. Many experts believe that if one does not experience great upheavals during adolescence, these turmoils will appear later in life (Piers, 1966). The switching of moods in adolescents, varying from helplessness and dependence to defiance and independence two hours later, can be explained in terms of the struggle for *individuation*, the development of a sense of self. In this stage, the adolescent gradually recognizes that his or her parents are not gods and that they can err. The life-cycle task is the mutual weaning of parents and children (Herz, 228).

Teenagers experience internal struggles in coping with sexual changes and individuation. Prior interest in same-sex relationships switches to a growing interest in the opposite sex. "All he does is chase after girls now instead of fly balls." Younger brothers and sisters become "boring" and "tiresome." "Keep Out" signs appear on doors; locks go on diaries; phone calls become private. Young people begin to set their own physical and psychological boundaries, which may limit communication with some or all family members. In girls, the onset of menstruation serves as a marker event that signals approaching adulthood. Interestingly, the English language has a word for this event, *menarche*, but there is no equivalent word for when boys first ejaculate. For boys, this serves as a marker event signaling approaching potential fatherhood.

> *"I grew up in a home where doors were always open, and people knew each other's business. I remember going through a terrible period starting at the end of junior high when I hated sharing a room with my sister. I would spend hours alone sitting on my bed listening to music with the door shut, and if anyone came in, I would have a fit. I even locked my sister out a number of times."*

Adolescence is a time of establishing powerful nonfamilial relationships. Media figures, teachers, or other adults may have been important role models you tried to imitate during your adolescence. Friends, rather than parents, may have been "the first to know," no matter what the news. However, adolescents' values are shaped more by the community in which they live and the adults in their lives than peers. One study found that most teens seek consistent rules in families, schools, and communities (Collins, 1984, 20). The phone calls, peer groups, and new models represent a young person's linking network to the world outside of the family system. They are conduits for bringing new messages into the adolescent's life, which can result in some painful family moments as the young person moves outward.

Erikson maintains that the identity work that a child goes through within the family needs to be similarly repeated with society (128). Kenniston (1979) speaks of the importance of this process "by which the adolescent relinquishes his or her ties to inner representations of good or bad parents, suffers an inner sense of emptiness and loss, and gradually forms new and more adult bonds" (7). Blos (1979) concurs that all youths reach puberty with intrapsychic tensions that require reworking and transcending in adolescence if full adulthood is to follow. From a social-emotional perspective, an adolescent is in the process of slowly moving out of a narcissistic existence, learning to shift from a self-centered to an other-centered position.

During the move toward other-centeredness, a young person begins to develop a true sense of empathy and the ability to take another's perspective (Ritter, 1979, 49). Such capacities eventually allow the growing adult to interact with his or her parents on an adult level. The adolescent period is the one most likely to test the adaptability of the family system. Adolescents overfunction one day and underfunction the next. This changing acceptance of responsibility affects the system (Ackerman, 1980, 150).

The changes between ages thirteen and nineteen coincide with the individuation that occurs when a young person becomes self-reliant and insists upon making up his or her own mind. This leads to independence and confidence in decision making. By asserting his or her developing talents to speak out, work, or perform tasks without constant help and supervision, the adolescent signals to parents that past communication directives no longer fit the situation.

> *"At a time in my life when physical appearance was ranked number one, I was completely distraught over my metal mouth. I knew it was going to be a good two years before the nightmare would end, so I tried not to let it bother me. Sometimes with 'zits' on my face, plus fears of buck teeth, I felt ugly. Getting my braces off didn't make me feel any older, just happier."*

Very strong parent-child bonds may be weakened at least temporarily, and other siblings may react to the adolescent's mood or changes. Adolescents' actions may have repercussions for parents. In her summary of the changes in marital conflict patterns over time, Troll states, "They don't report fighting over their children until the children are old enough to get into deliberate trouble (in adolescence)" (90). During this stage, parents often become aware of such issues as lack of companionship, sexual difficulties, or dominance in their relationship (Ackerman, 1966, 151).

The sexual awakening of their children has a powerful effect on many parents. Opposite-sex parents and children may find a gulf between them as a response to the power of the "incest taboo" in society. Unfortunately, in many families, this results in the end of nonverbal affection, as the next example illustrates.

"I will never forget being hurt as a teenager when my father totally changed the way he acted toward me. We used to have a real 'buddy' relationship—we would spend lots of time together; we would wrestle, fool around, and I adored him. Suddenly, he became really distant and I could not understand what I did, but I did not feel I could talk about it either. Now that I am older, I can see the same pattern happening with the two little girls in the family. Obviously, within his head there is a rule that when your daughter starts to develop breasts, you have to back off—and for him, that means having almost no relationship at all. Now I can understand that it has to hurt him as much as it hurts the girls."

Same-sex parents may face internal conflicts if they perceive a major contrast between their children's budding sexuality and their own sexual identity. Such conflicts are tied to the parents' stages of development and negative self-evaluations. Since facing this issue would be uncomfortable, such perceptions may result in conflict over more "acceptable" issues as friends, money, independence, or responsibility. Adolescents are more likely to accept parental guidelines when they have clear, open lines of communication and feel that their parents respect their values, too (Conger, 207).

Not all adolescents differ radically from their parents on issues. Although some parents may openly conflict with teenagers, many do not. Sixty-three to 85 percent of the youths in a large national study agreed with parental attitudes toward religion, drugs other than alcohol and marijuana, education, and modern goals for women. Fifty-eight percent agreed with their parents about racial issues and conservation of resources (Phillips, 1979, 4). Communication can improve in this period if parents cultivate empathic listening, provide opportunities for adolescents to own their own problems and learn from their mistakes, and love them even when displeased by their actions (McClelland et al., 1978, 49). Communication that encourages the adolescent to be his or her own person without constant criticism can help the individuation process.

The exploring adolescent often challenges family themes, boundaries, and biosocial beliefs. He or she is forever introducing the family system to people or modes of behavior that threaten the family. The adolescent's new input forecasts the eventual departure of the exploring child and forces the family to reevaluate itself (Ackerman, 1980, 150). A relatively flexible family may encounter less difficulty with an acting-out adolescent than a family with rigid rules. You can imagine the difficulties a closed family type has in dealing with adolescents (see Chapter 5). For example, Kantor and Lehr (1976) noticed that stress during the adolescent stage causes the system to change form by developing open strategies. This change produces "a curious hybrid such as a family with closed-system goals and open-system means of attaining these goals" (157).

As adolescents mature, their families may undergo extensive readjustments. Individuation precludes the necessary separation process, which is expected yet painful as young members move toward adult maturity. Communication that supports gradual separation, rather than pushes persons away from one another or holds them rigidly close, eases the transition. Failure to successfully negotiate the adolescent stage, as reflected by an increase in suicides, has caused concern among family experts. In 1985, the National Center for Health Statistics studied Americans ages fifteen to twenty-four and reported a suicide rate of 12.4 per 100,000 adolescents, double the rate of ten years earlier.

Families as Launching Centers

The next stage signals the departure of the oldest children as they are "launched" into the world. It is very difficult to generalize about specific predictable events, since so many different things may be occurring. Most theorists propose some variation of one of the following scenarios: (a) the "empty nest" model, which suggests that at least one of the parents is having difficulty letting the children go, and (b) the curvilinear model, which concentrates on the increased freedom and independence of the parents (McCullough, 1980, 176).

Some young men, and fewer young women, go into the service; many more leave home to go to college, seek employment, or to start a new home. When young people start living on their own, especially if they totally support themselves, they more readily take on the responsibilities of adulthood and caring for themselves and begin the process of becoming emotionally comfortable living apart from their families-of-origin. This is a time of vacating the bedrooms, sending along the extra coffee pot, and letting go of the predictable daily interactions at breakfast or bedtime that tied parents and siblings into a close, interactive system. Tremendous strain may accompany such behaviors if parents attempt to hold on to their emerging adult children.

"In my family, 'launching the young adult' would not be the correct terminology. If you can imagine parents pulling on one end of a rope and the children on the other in a tug-of-war situation, you get a better idea of the type of emancipation that occurred. It was only after my parents lost their end of the rope that they relaxed and accepted the inevitable changes."

If the separation takes place without conflict or parental strings attached, communication usually remains open and flexible. Frequent contact with parents and siblings via phone calls, letters, or visits maintains family links and strengthens the bonds. At this time, communication issues may involve handling debt, negotiating living space, making career decisions, and keeping regular hours.

Some parents force a separation before their children may feel ready for the break.

"Since I've been in college, I call home about once a week and sometimes I sense that my mother is upset about something. If I ask about it, she will say something like 'Oh, don't you worry about it. It's not your problem; you don't live here anymore.' That upsets me, because I still feel I am part of the family."

This often results in hard feelings, conflict, and resentment. Yet, many children resist being "on their own." In some communities or cultures, it is expected; in others, children may remain home indefinitely. For example, many Hispanic, Italian, and Polish families prefer, and sometimes insist, that daughters remain with them until marriage. Getting an apartment would be quickly vetoed for a nineteen-year-old working woman.

Conflicts may occur when young people remain home during their early twenties, since established family rules and regulations tend to be challenged. "You don't need to wait up for me—I'm not seventeen!" "Pay room and board? I can't afford it and make car payments." "I don't have to account for everywhere I go" may typify certain interactions when new adult-adult roles are not negotiated. If young adults remain longer than expected, some families develop adverse effects (Harkins, 1975). Some parents seize their right to time as a couple, and if the children delay leaving, this may create frustrations and negative communication patterns. The failure to leave relates to our earlier discussion in Chapters 1 and 3 of separateness and connectedness. Rather than separate from the family, a young person may remain connected, enjoying the advantages of home and family comforts without working to function as an independent adult.

Major changes occur in the husband-wife relationship as opportunities for increased intimacy present themselves. Troll comments, "Mothers in the launching stage, whose children are getting ready to leave home, are seldom enthusiastic and often bitter about the loss of their husband's affection and companionship. It is only after the children are gone that the second honeymoon occurs—if it is going to" (87). Some men may have psychologically invested more in their relationship than have their wives (Lewis et al., 1979, 517). Further analysis reveals that fathers with fewer children report greater unhappiness over their leaving than do fathers with more children. Also, older fathers react more strongly than younger fathers. This finding further relates to family communication: the most unhappy fathers reported they felt most neglected by their wives, received the least amount of understanding, sensed loneliness most, were least enthusiastic about wives' companionship, and believed their wives least empathic (517). Ironically, Bart's (1971) research with women revealed many of the same complaints about men and the same communication barriers. Although adolescence appears to be a turbulent time, it need not be so. In many families, the postparental period presents few crises and becomes a part of the sequence and rhythms of the life cycle (Schram, 1979, 8). The effects of the empty nest largely disappear two years after the departure of the last child.

Although this period is sometimes tumultuous, it may be followed by increased couple intimacy if the partners can come through the childrearing years together. It is also a time when the middle, or parental, generation has to deal with changing relationships with their own parents and their retirement, disability, dependency, or death (McCullough, 180). In a fascinating study of roles throughout the life cycle, Schafer and Keith (1981) found that equity in the tasks of cooking, homemaking, and providing increase across the stages, with the highest increases in the launching stage and middle years after the children leave home (363).

Families in the Middle, or Postparental, Years

"When the children left, I discovered myself living with essentially a mute man. We hadn't realized that for years we had talked little to one another—that most of our communication was with the children or about them. Since we both worked, always took vacations with the kids, and kept busy chasing after the kids' activities, we never had time for ourselves. Now I've got time to talk and I have to compete with TV—that's the 'other woman' in my house."

In the middle years, after the children have left home until one or both parents retires, communication in the family mainly involves the original dyad. As opposed to earlier days when families were larger and life expectancy was shorter, the empty nest transition now occurs in middle age rather than old age. Many contradictory reports about this period appear in family literature. "Second honeymoons" are counterbalanced by a high divorce rate. Images of decreasing sexuality are matched by reports of this as a period of sexual revitalization (Troll et al., 1979, 40). In short, we are only now discovering what happens as a family reverts to a two-person system. Such factors as health, economics, and social class tend to interact with the couple's development and satisfaction at this stage.

Contrary to some of the stereotypes about older parents' being cut off from the lives of their adult children, contact is usually regular and frequent. Eighty-one percent of the elderly see their children weekly. Between 4 and 5 percent of the aged live in nursing homes (McCubbin and Dahl, 1985, 293). Only one in four elderly persons lives with his or her children, but 80 percent live within one hour of at least one of their children (Walsh, 1980, 198). Such figures raise unanswerable issues. How are such children and parents connected? Are these contacts made out of guilt or need? Do they represent intimate caring relationships? Much adult parent-child interaction appears to be carried out through the female networks rather than through male ones, resulting in a potential distancing of the adult child's father (Troll et al., 103). Mothers tend to remain in even more constant contact with adult daughters, especially those who have children.

The arrival of grandchildren is another opportunity for relationship development. Communication between aging parents and children depends upon the style of grandparenting, partially determined by ethnic ties, personalities, and job status of the grandparents. Neugarten and Weinstein (1964) classified five grandparent styles.

1. Formal—Definite boundaries between parents' and grandparents' roles with grandparents interacting infrequently and doing little babysitting.
2. Fun Seeker—The grandparents take the children on outings or come over to play with them. They need the play as much as the children.
3. Second Parent—Grandmothers often take over while daughter or daughter-in-law works or is incapacitated.
4. Family Sage—Grandparents, especially grandfather, serve as a reservoir of family wisdom and teacher of special skills.
5. Distant Figure—Benevolent but infrequent visitors who appear for family rituals or holidays.   (202–3)

The amount and type of grandparent-grandchild communication reflects the grandparenting style. Formal or distant figures may not attain the same degree of closeness gained by a second parent, but the latter may have to act as disciplinarian, which puts an added strain on the relationship.

Walsh sees grandparenthood as an opportunity for new roles and meaningful interaction, since it usually does not entail the responsibilities, obligations, and conflicts of parenthood. Also, grandparents and grandchildren may have a "common enemy" in the parents (204). Conflicts can result if grandparents are drawn into parental conflicts; on occasion, grandparents act as a refuge for children in a strife-torn family.

In certain cultural groups, grandparents are expected to assume a major role in childrearing; but, in other cultures, if grandparents are coerced into childcare, they are likely to resent it (Troll; Kahana and Kahana, 1970; Lopata, 1973). Such cross-generational contact provides opportunities for extended transmission of culture and for development of a sense of family history. Grandparents serve as one source of a child's sense of identity; children gain access to their roots and have the opportunity to see the functioning of the two families-of-origin that influenced their parents, and hence, themselves.

In spite of the decisions about major changes in midlife, this period can be a happy one for families. Financial worries lessen if money has been managed well over the years. Children become less of an everyday concern and a couple or single parent may have the opportunity to focus on old or new relationships and experiences.

Spouses who had allowed their children to become their main focus for so many years may find themselves back at the lower stages of relationship development. Partners may sense a distance between them and feel unable, or unwilling, to try to reconnect. For many couples, the readjustment to a viable two-person system requires hard work. Divorces occur frequently in this midlife transition period. Vines (1979) states:

> A man has to make new choices to recommit himself on different terms to old ones. He has to accept some responsibility for those aspects of his own motivation and character which keep him from forming more adult relationships with women . . . otherwise he will remain in a stagnant marriage destructive to both partners or he will embark on a new kind of relationship with a wife or lover that repeats old hurtful themes. . . .   (9)

This could also be said of women who become aware of the limitations in their marriages. When crises develop in this period, you hear remarks like these: "I've changed. I'm a different person with different desires." "I either change or I'm stuck forever."

Some women face a particularly difficult transition, because the now empty nest may have been full for so long that an enormous void occurs. Such feelings need to be sorted out and communicated to a spouse so both can understand and support each other's attempts to cope. In this situation, couples must deal with the issue of limited versus expanded roles. Greater freedom from responsibilities may prompt one member of the couple toward expansion and new exploration, while the other spouse attempts to hold on to the marriage and family ties more tightly, resulting in dyadic conflict.

Many families have to negotiate the relationship between parents and grown children, who may now be entering parenthood. Highly cohesive families may attempt to keep inappropriate ties (McCullough, 190). For example, if a child or grandchild is constantly used as a focus for a maturing couple, they are not dealing with their own development.

Older-Member Families

The final stage in the family begins with retirement and ends with the death of one of the couple. The big communication issue of this stage centers around retirement. Some couples experience "reentry" problems when one or both return to the home and remain there twenty-four hours of most days. The increased contact may lead to a deepening of the relationship or result in friction from the forced closeness. The retired person(s) may undergo severe role adjustments and the loss of certain functions (e.g., providing) that served as self-definition. A second issue that affects all communication concerns the health and declining strength of the couple. Ill health creates a need for nurturing communication and taps the couple's physical, mental, and financial resources. Walsh suggests that " . . . a disequilibrium in the marital relationship may ensue with the illness of one spouse" (206).

Yet, this may be a time of rejuvenation. The couple now has time to enjoy one another. A study of couples married over fifty years shows the aging stage as one of the happiest, with more time together for travel and activities, which they previously could not manage (Sporakowski and Houghston, 1978, 325). When postretirement activities continue previously developed needs and hobbies, couples remain happy (McCubbin and Dahl, 1985, 289).

As individuals become older, the family takes on additional importance. Troll et al. summarize this position well:

> Older people sometimes disengage from their roles outside their families, but they rarely disengage from their involvements inside their families. They disengage into rather than from their families. (6)

Interpersonal communication becomes increasingly important at this stage. Many older family members engage in the *elder function,* or the sharing of the accumulated wisdom of their lives with younger people, usually family members. There is a need to feel of use to the coming generations and, for many older persons, such feelings come from revealing information or spinning stories designed to guide the younger listener. Elderly individuals who remain interested and have opportunities for keeping abreast of world and national events enjoy life more and disengage themselves less from the family (Nussbaum, 1983, 317).

Although older Americans see their children with some regularity, many older persons are prevented from maintaining the interpersonal contacts they desire due to concerns of economics, safety, and health. Rising costs of living restrict the travel and entertainment aspects of older persons' budgets, while many urban senior citizens do not feel safe attending evening meetings or social activities.

Such health concerns as decreasing agility or diminishing hearing and eyesight compound the problem of maintaining interpersonal relationships. Frustration and low self-esteem may make individuals reluctant to initiate contact, while listeners may decline, due to their impatience with an older person's infirmities.

Older couples who reach their retirement together may turn inward toward each other and share intensely their remaining years. Loss becomes a part of aging, and this increases when close friends and relatives die. In order to prevent their becoming "the last one out," older couples have to go beyond their age range and establish friendships through communicating with younger adults. This may be difficult if infirmities prevent mobility.

The developmental stages of both middle and older years are important periods for introspection. Intrapersonal communication about the meaning of one's life allows an individual to see his or her life in perspective. This turning to oneself for insights can be painful and lead to despair, because some aging adults sense their faults and shortcomings and recognize that too little has been accomplished, and too little time and energy is left to change. This affects their self-concept and interpersonal communication with other family members. The intrapersonal communication in these last two developmental stages has systemic effects, because the aging individual coming to terms with his or her own sense of wholeness affects other members' sense of wholeness, interdependence, and mutual punctuation. Intrapersonal communication becomes successful in these stages when aging family members integrate their sense of past history with their present status and find contentment in themselves (Streever and Wodarski, 1984, 277).

Reminiscing is an important part of both the intrapersonal and interpersonal communication of the aging adult. After sorting memories, Grandma or Grandpa often want to share their reflections. This oral history can enrich a family, especially its members' sense of their family-of-origin. It gives the elderly a chance to communicate to those they love, helped raise, or even harmed by their actions their need to "set the record straight" or to correct, and express sorrow for, mistakes.

"I'm glad my Dad lived past seventy-five. Only then did we come to terms with one another. Long after he retired, he mellowed and became approachable. He talked about the depression, the war years, and the struggle to pay for the farm. Then I sensed what had made him so tough and noncommunicative."

After the death of one spouse, the other must face the adjustment inherent in becoming a widow or widower. Working through the grief period, an older family member may make great demands on younger members who may be resentful of, or unprepared for, such pressures. This is coupled with the younger members' personal grief at the loss of a parent. The surviving spouse has to renegotiate roles and boundaries as he or she attempts to create or maintain interpersonal contacts. It is important that older family members have a say in their care and be a part of all communication that concerns them as long as possible. They remain happier and healthier in their own homes, living as independently as health permits (Barry, 1983, 268). In fact, a family who shows too much concern can hamper communication by insulting the elderly living on their own (Nussbaum, 240).

Transitions Between Stages

It is important not to underestimate the effects of transitions between each of these developmental stages. Haley, Bowen, and other therapists have observed that dysfunctional families have members who fail to make these transitions at the appropriate times in their lives. These members cause imbalance in their family systems by remaining "stuck" at one developmental stage and not moving on. In these same troubled families, they have observed a piling-up effect, with one or more members stuck at the same stage. Some of these same family members experience external stresses (illness, separation, divorce) simultaneously with developmental changes and become unable to cope. However, functional families take these stages in stride and experience the transitions with temporary, but not permanent, stress.

This does not mean that marital satisfaction does not suffer during the family life cycle with consequent effects upon family communication. In a large study, which followed couples from the childless stage through the years of childbearing, adolescence, and stages beyond, Olson and McCubbin (1984) found a steady decline in satisfaction that did not level off until the children began to individuate and separate from their parents. Then, satisfaction increased in the postparental period when the children left and established their own families (9). Regarding cohesion and adaptability over the stages, they found wives believed their families more cohesive and adaptable than did their husbands. Adolescents consistently reported lower levels of cohesion and adaptability than either of their parents. In fact, cohesion and adaptability declined in the first five stages to the lowest points in the adolescent and launching stages and increased in the last two stages (235). Not only does this show differences in perceptions by family members but differences between stages that affect communication. Interestingly, families coped with these stresses by using the communication strategy of reframing their difficulties in ways they could manage (236). This required the communication skills of negotiation, problem solving, and decision making.

Nock found that functional families experienced transitions as challenging and, at times, unpleasant events, but not as long-lasting negative influences. Transitions into marriage or birth of a child, for example, affected family functioning, but the family progressed through them in a normal maturation process. Transitions out of marriage, such as divorce, desertion, or death, had negative effects and caused higher stress over longer periods of time (709–10). Steffensmeier (1982) studied the transition into parenthood and concluded that whether couples experienced difficulty with the stage depended on their views on parental responsibilities: the amount of gratification they received from the role and the quality of their intimacy and stability prior to and during this developmental stage (331). Thus, transitions are like hurdles set before a functional family. Normally, they are easily taken in stride, but if other factors intervene, the family has more difficulty. Communication is affected accordingly.

CONCLUSION

Throughout this chapter, we have looked at the effects of developmental stresses on communication within families. As families move through the years, each generation faces predictable developmental issues as couples marry, beget children, and live through stages of child development superimposed upon individual adult developmental changes. As children leave home to form new systems, the original couple, if still intact, faces the middle years and adjustment issues. The cohesion-adaptability axes overlay each system's personal growth, while themes, images, boundaries, and biosocial beliefs may be challenged and changed as the years pass.

The entire family developmental process is extremely complex and challenging. Foley (1974) summarizes the adjustments briefly and well:

The fantasy of the engagement period yields to the reality of daily life. The birth of a child changes the dyadic system into a triad, and presents the possibilities of alliances and splits in the family. The departure of the last child for school brings about a definitive drift into middle age for the couple. The marriage of a child brings still another period of adjustment and initiates the process of the return to the dyadic state. All these situations can be described as normal or developmental, and all of them can cause problems in a marriage if one or another cannot make a transition.   (87)

Every stage of the life cycle brings new challenges and opportunities. Meeting these demands leads to changes in each family member's personality, through his or her successes and failures during each stage (Offer and Sabshin, 1984, 422).

IN REVIEW

1. Using your own family or a family you know well, give examples of verbal or nonverbal communication patterns that seemed commonplace at different developmental stages in the family life cycle.
2. Referring to your own family or a family you have observed, describe how a couple has dealt with the communication tasks of incorporating a child into their system and dealing with the following communication related issues: (1) renegotiating roles, (2) transmitting culture, (3) establishing a community of experiences, and (4) developing the child's communication competence.
3. What appears to characterize communication in families during the period when there are one or more adolescents living within the system?
4. How is communication affected by the moving out of young adults in the launching stage in two-parent systems? In single-parent systems?
5. Compare and contrast communication patterns you have observed in the interactions between middle-aged and older family members. To what extent were reminiscing, reflection, and sorting out important to members at these stages?

Chapter 10

Family Communication and Unpredictable Stress

Most of us imagine life will continue in a relatively predictable pattern. We do not really believe we will win the lottery. We do not expect to parent a handicapped child. We think our family members will live together to a ripe old age. Sometimes we are correct; often, we are wrong. Our lives contain different types of stresses. In addition to the developmental, or more predictable, stresses faced by family systems, we must also face unpredictable, or external, stresses. *Unpredictable stresses* are brought about by events or circumstances that disrupt life patterns but that cannot be foreseen from a developmental perspective. Such stresses may be positive, although more frequently they are perceived as negative. These are the "slings and arrows of outrageous fortune," shocks to the system. Such stresses conjure up images of loss such as that involved in untimely death, divorce, economic reversal, or serious injury. Some positive events, such as a large inheritance, a job promotion and transfer, or the rediscovery of long-lost relatives, are also stresses for the system.

Although we are dealing with unpredictable stresses as distinct from the more predictable developmental changes, there may be certain overlaps. Becoming pregnant or having a child may be considered a developmental event, but an unwanted pregnancy or the birth of a severely handicapped child may also be classified as an unpredictable stress. Death is a developmental experience for all persons, but the untimely death of a family member is a severe crisis for the system. Whether the entire family, or only certain members, are initially affected by the event, the family system will eventually reflect the tension of such stresses in its communication behavior.

"There were nine children in our family, and three had muscular dystrophy. I remember how hard it was for Mom to accept their illness. She wouldn't talk about it within the family. Her rule was that it was better not discussed, yet I would find her alone in her room crying. We all learned from Marilyn, Dan, and Virginia. Communication reached a tense stage when Marilyn was the first to die. We knew

the fear and panic in Dan and Virginia. It took time to get them to talk about these fears and finally, near their own deaths, they would joke about who was going next. All of this was strictly with two sisters and myself. Mom, Dad, and the rest couldn't handle any humor on the subject. I feel they would like to have shared these feelings with all of us, but some of the living in our family put great distance between themselves and those who were dying.'

In the previous chapter, we presented a model of family stressors (Figure 9–1, p. 195) and described the developmental stresses a family faces. In this chapter, we will concentrate on the second type of horizontal stressors, the external, unpredictable, stressors. We will examine (1) unpredictable stress and family coping patterns and (2) communication during the process of coping with unpredictable stresses.

UNPREDICTABLE STRESS AND FAMILY COPING PATTERNS

Stress involves a physiological response to *stressors*, events or situations that are viewed as powerful negative or positive forces. Individuals or families under stress reflect these physiological changes through their anxiety and attempts to cope. Let us look at some general family stressors and the ways in which families attempt to respond to pressure.

Family Stressors

In his early work, Hill (1949) studied stress in families and noted four family disruptions that cause crises. These include: (1) the "dismemberment," or coming apart, of the family due to the death of a husband, wife, child, or grandparents; (2) the "accession" or addition of new or returning family members, such as stepparents, an unplanned baby, or a former deserter; (3) the "demoralization," or sense of disgrace, which may result from infidelity, alcoholism, nonsupport, or addiction; and (4) a combination of the above, which could include suicide, imprisonment, homicide, or mental illness (10).

Later work on general life stressors classified forty-three events that cause stress (Holmes and Rahe, 1967, 215). The top twelve stressors would have a strong impact on the families of the individual involved. Holmes and Rahe ranked these crises and placed an impact value on each, as shown in Table 10–1.

Bain (1978) used this rating scale in his research on a family's ability to cope with transitions. He found that a family's capacity to cope depends upon the psychosocial factors involved in a crisis. He noted that differences in the effects of stress on families depends upon the nature of the social relationships within which the changes had to be made (67, 685).

Table 10–1 _____
Life Events that Cause Stress

Rank	Event	Mean Value
1	Death of spouse	100
2	Divorce	73
3	Marital separation	65
4	Jail term	63
5	Death of close family member	63
6	Personal injury or illness	53
7	Marriage	50
8	Fired at work	47
9	Marital reconciliation	45
10	Retirement	45
11	Change in health of family member	44
12	Pregnancy	40

Other works on family stress deal with similar issues while introducing new ones, such as stresses of aging and extreme environmental stress (McCubbin et al., 1983). The latter refers to the families whose lives unfold within a uniquely oppressive environment, including refugee and ghetto situations. The writers emphasize the possible productive outcomes of stress, the role of the community, and the family's adaptive and problem-solving capacity. In order to understand unpredictable crises in a family, we will look at a model for how families cope with this stress.

Model

Each family exhibits unique coping behaviors. _Coping_ implies "the central mechanism through which family stressors, demands and strains are eliminated, managed or adapted to" (McCubbin, 1983, 3). The primary models currently used to understand family crises have evolved from Hill's original model, which proposed that:

> a [the stressor event], interacting with b [the family's crisis-meeting resources], interacting with c [the family's definition of the event] produces x [the crisis]   (McCubbin and Patterson, 1983, 8)

Let us explain this further. The stressor, a, represents a life event or transition that has the potential to change a family's social system. Such events as the loss of a job, untimely death, serious illness, or good luck in the lottery may fall into this category. The b factor represents the resources a family can use to keep an event or change from creating a crisis, such as money, friends, space, or problem-solving skills. This factor ties into a family's levels of cohesion and adaptability in terms of how it has learned to deal with various crises over time.

The c factor represents the importance a family attaches to the stressor (a). For example, in one family, a diagnosis of a member's juvenile diabetes might overwhelm the entire system, whereas another family might cope well with that news, perceiving the diabetes as a manageable disease, one not likely to alter their lives drastically. The definitions of both the family and families-of-origin may come to bear on the perception of crises. For example, a three-generation family that has never experienced a divorce may define a young granddaughter's marital separation as a severe crisis. Together, *a, b,* and *c* contribute to stress that is unique to each family, depending on its background, resources, and interpretation of the event.

The *x* factor represents the amount of disruptiveness that occurs to the system. It is characterized by "the family's inability to restore stability and by the continuous pressure to make changes in the family structure and patterns of interaction" (McCubbin and Patterson, 10).

Other family researchers have developed a Double ABCX model based on Hill's original work but incorporating post-crisis variables (Figure 10–1). Whereas Hill's *abcx* model focused on pre-crisis areas, the Double ABCX model incorporates the family's efforts to recover over time. In this model, the *aA* factor includes not only the immediate stressor (e.g., death) but also the demands or changes that may emerge from individual systems' members, a system as a whole, and the extended system. McCubbin and Patterson suggest that the *aA* factor includes: (1) the initial stressor, (2) normative transitions, (3) prior strains, (4) the consequences of the system's coping attempts, and (5) ambiguity. For example, if a young father dies, the system must deal with the immediate loss as well as economic uncertainty and changes in the mother's role. In addition, the normal growth of children may soon require the family to cope with an adolescent's need for independence. This is compounded by any prior strains, such as in-law problems or mother-daughter conflicts. A consequence of the family's attempts to cope might be the mother's new job, which keeps her from meeting the children's needs for

Figure 10–1
The Double ABCX Model

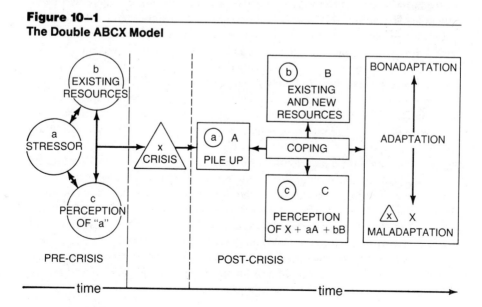

active parenting. Finally, ambiguity might be caused by the confusion of new roles now that Father has left the system. Boundaries shift. Mother might consider remarriage. Changes become expected. Thus, aA is larger than the original conception of a.

The bB factor represents the family's ability to meet its needs. This factor includes family resources from an individual, system, and community point of view. A family may use existing and expanded resources. *Existing resources* are part of a family's background. In the case of death, these may include the ways in which a family coped in the past when Father was gone on business. The expanded family resources emerge from the crisis itself. A widow may create such resources by studying accounting, which leads to increased income, or by sharing in a widows' self-help group. The emerging social support systems are a critical element in the bB factor.

The cC factor is the way in which a family interprets a crisis, including the meaning the family gives to the stressor event and to the added stressors caused by the original crisis, plus its perception of how to bring the family into balance. When a young father dies, a family must cope with that event and its meaning. The members must also interpret the change in finances, changes in the mother's role, and how the entire family is affected. Families who cope well can manage the situation through flexible changes in responsibilities and through support of one another. Families who have difficulty coping cannot see a sense of challenge and find themselves overwhelmed, with little sense of hope or opportunity for growth.

The xX factor is the effect of the family's adaptation on the individual, system, and community levels. Family adaptation is achieved "through reciprocal relationships where the demands of one of these units are met by the capabilities of another so as to achieve a 'balance' interaction" (McCubbin and Patterson, 19). If members' demands are too great for the family's capabilities, there will be an imbalance. There will also be imbalance if the family demands more than the community is capable of providing. For example, the family and work community may create an imbalance by demanding too much of one parent. The positive end of the continuum of outcomes of a crisis, called *bonadaptation*, is characterized by balance between (1) member and family and (2) family and community. The negative end, or *maladaptation*, reflects imbalance or severe losses for the family. In some families, drastic changes allow members to renegotiate their relationships in positive ways. Thus, disruptions may have positive or negative effects on the family system.

In keeping with this orientation toward family coping, Bain supports the importance of: (1) the amount and type of recent stress a family has faced, (2) the type of support from institutions, (3) the support from a family's social network, and (4) the magnitude of the role changes involved. The ways in which a family has established patterns of cohesion and adaptability have great bearing on its ability to cope with external stress. From our perspective, a family with a high capacity for adaptation and above average cohesion is likely to weather stressor events more easily than families who are rigid and fragmented. More adaptable families have the capacity to find alternative ways of relating and can adjust their communication behavior to encompass an event. As shown in the example at the beginning of the chapter, a family that has a rule against discussing debilitating illness has little ability to cope openly with and communicate about the impending death of a member. During a crisis, family members often wish to rely on each other for comfort and support, a behavior that cannot suddenly occur if the family has a history of separateness.

Such issues also interrelate with family functions related to boundaries, themes, images, and biosocial issues. Families with rigid boundaries may be unable to cope adequately when severe external stresses occur. By greatly limiting communication with such institutions as hospitals, courts, and schools, members deprive themselves of necessary information and possible emotional support. Additionally, boundaries that prevent a social network (friends or extended family) from knowing what is happening within the family eliminate potential sources of strength and comfort that might help "carry" a family through a critical period.

"When my father died suddenly, I was almost totally unable to cope with life for many months. Both my mother and I were in shock, and we were unable to help each other with our grief; in fact, we experienced a great deal of conflict with each other. My major support through that period was an older woman friend who would listen as I would rage, or cry, or question. Unfortunately, my mother would not allow herself to use such an 'outside' support system, and she never fully recovered from losing my father."

Families with themes of total self-sufficiency or images of rocklike members may find support from strong members of the family. Members may find that such themes and images prevent them from turning outward when the pain becomes too great for the family to handle functionally, resulting in severe conflict or separation. The number and magnitude of stresses may determine how functional these themes and images can be.

Finally, families with inflexible beliefs related to such biosocial issues as sex roles or authority may find such beliefs aid them through a crisis or may interfere with its resolution. For example, in a family that sets very distinct male-female roles, the father's loss of a good position may leave the family emotionally and financially devastated, since this belief causes the man to feel inadequate and prevents the woman from working to support the family.

Although we think of most crises as caused by negative events, it is possible for seemingly positive events to create great stress. Newspapers contain accounts of the pressure put on lottery winners by the expectations of family and friends and the loss of a settled way of life. A long-wished-for promotion may be accompanied by the loss of a familiar co-worker, pressure to succeed at a new level of responsibility, and the possibility of a stressful family move to a new city or neighborhood. Family members may find it painful to cope with the marriage or the departure for college of a much-loved child. Great joys may be accompanied by great losses.

Since communication affects and is affected by all these behaviors, it plays a central role in the experiencing and eventual resolution of such stresses and contributes specifically to the family's movement through stages of stress reaction. In some families, members use direct verbal messages to explore options, negotiate needs, express feelings, and reduce tension. In other families, the members' stress may be apparent through the nonverbal messages that indicate their anxiety and other feelings. Members constantly interpret others' verbal and nonverbal messages as part of the coping pattern.

Stages of Family Crisis

In any serious crisis situation, a family goes through a definite process in handling the grief or chaos that results. Depending upon the event, the stages may last from a few days to several months or years. These stages may be more pronounced in the case of a death, divorce, or news of an incurable illness, but in any crisis, family members experience a progression of feelings from denial to acceptance. Yet, since no two families accept crisis in the same way, and because family systems are characterized by equifinality (see p. 36), they will reach the final stages of the process in a variety of ways. The following stages approximate the general process of dealing with severe stress. Although the stages usually follow one another, they may overlap, and some may be repeated a number of times.

1. Shock resulting in numbness or disbelief, denial
2. Recoil stage resulting in anger, confusion, blaming, guilt, and bargaining
3. Depression
4. Reorganization resulting in acceptance and recovery
   (Kübler-Ross, 1970; Dunlop, 1978; Parkes, 1972; Feifel, 1977; Mederer and Hill, 1983)

The process of going through such stages after a serious life event usually results in transformation of the system. Persons may find themselves more separated from, or connected to, different members and may find a shift in adaptability patterns. Communication behavior reflects and aids progress through the stages. Understanding the process allows one to analyze others' progress through the stages or to be more understanding of one's own behavior and personal progress.

At the *shock stage*, family members tend to deny the event or its seriousness. Denying comments such as "It can't be true," "It's a mistake," or "It's temporary" are accompanied by nonverbal behavior, such as setting a dead person's place at the table, misplacing attempts at smiles and encouragement with a terminally ill person, or spending money lavishly when the paycheck has been cut off.

Most persons quickly move from this stage and exhibit behaviors that indicate a recognition of reality. Principal family members acknowledge their grief and feel the pain of the loss. Crying or sullen quietness for those who find it hard to cry characterizes communication. The truth of the crisis news begins to take on fuller meanings, such as "Mom will never get well" or "She has left and will never return." This kind of reasoning sends messages to the self that confirms the reality.

Denial is transformed into an intense desire to recapture what has been lost, especially in the case of a family death, desertion, or severe injury. This may lead to attempts to recapture memories, for example, "I keep expecting to see her in the kitchen."

After the initial blow, the family may move into the *recoil stage* of blaming, anger, and bargaining. Blaming often takes place as the grieving family members seek reasons for what has happened. This may include blaming the self ("I was too trusting; I should have watched closer" or "I never should have let her go") or blaming others ("It's his own fault" or "The doctors never told us the truth soon enough"). Such behavior may be interspersed with feelings of "It's not fair," "Why did this happen to us?" and "We don't deserve this." Anger may be directed at the event or person most directly involved or may be displaced onto others, such as family members, friends, or co-workers. Attempts at real or imagined bargains may occur. "If I take a cut in pay, they could hire me back." "If you come back I'll stop gambling forever."

Thoughts of the unfairness of the world, that God has been cruel to let this happen, that potentials of the members involved had never been realized and now never will be, fill the minds of family members and then are released to one another. Again, the pain of the loss comes out through strong feelings.

Usually, family members need to talk about what has happened. In fact, they often retell the crisis news over and over, a normal and healthy response for the family as they feel the intensity of the loss. This is especially necessary for families that will experience a long period of suffering because of death, incurable illness, permanent injuries, a long jail sentence, or mental breakdown. People outside the family often fail to understand the communication that goes on within and may attempt to avoid the people or the subject, not recognizing that support may only be possible from those not as directly affected. Families may allow their boundaries to become more flexible in order to gain this support. Often, family confusion and disorganization may be so great that outsiders tend to take over and guide decision making.

The release of hurt feelings leads into the third stage—depression. At the depths of depression, a family realizes their old status quo or balance will never return. The death, divorce, or injury cannot be undone, and turning back the clock is unrealistic. The loss of a good job, especially one that has been held for many years, may not entail the same emotions as death or divorce, but the adjustments forced upon a family to cut back its standard of living, for example, can also lead to depression. Some people in this stage speak of having a sinking feeling— a sense of helplessness in not knowing or even caring about what to do. Verbally and nonverbally they communicate an overwhelming sadness usually accompanied by a tiredness and slowness of response.

Grief-stricken people normally pass through this stage to what they describe as a "turning point." Usually, a decision on their part marks the event. It may be a decision to take a trip, to sell a failing business, to get rid of mementos that serve as daily reminders, to register with a placement bureau, or to join Alcoholics Anonymous. Nonverbally, this decision signals that the individual has moved into the fourth crisis stage—*acceptance* and *reorganization* of events in his or her life to effect a recovery. This stage is characterized by family members' taking charge of their lives and making the necessary changes forced upon them by the crisis. They may not like the changes required, but they communicate an ability to cope in spite of the loss. Reorganization may require all sorts of adjustments, and the time required varies greatly with the type of crisis and the individuals involved. It may take six weeks for one family to recover from a job loss, and another family suffering a death or divorce a year to eighteen months to achieve a semblance of balance in the system.

If emotions in crises could be charted on a linear scale, the line would descend to the lowest point with depression. The descent begins with the impact of the news and continues the downward spiral with some rises in the recoil stages to descend again as reality returns (see Figure 10–2).

Throughout this process, communication links members in sharing their reactions and links one or more to outside sources of institutional or social support, which can provide acceptance of the emotions which need to be expressed. If a family or member is cut off from support, the process may not be complete—the family may remain stuck at some point, unable to complete the process and reach acceptance. In the next section, we will consider some common types of family crises and the communication issues involved with each.

COMMUNICATION AND SPECIFIC FAMILY CRISES

As we noted earlier, each stage of the coping process carries with it communication tasks, which must be accomplished in order for family members to move ahead in resolving a crisis. In this section, we will briefly examine the specific family crises of untimely death, illness or handicaps, and divorce from a communication perspective.

Communication during these crises is difficult when family members fear talking about the issues involved or if they feel discussion makes matters worse.

Figure 10–2 _____
Linear Scale of Emotions During Crises

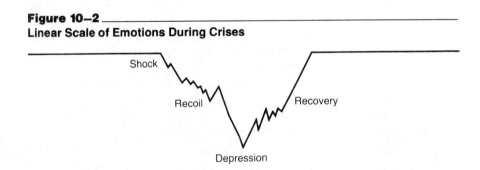

Shock

Recoil

Recovery

Depression

Such silence blocks the natural process that a family must go through to reach recovery. Although we will focus on these three major crises, less dramatic events, such as moving, losing a job, dealing with alcoholism, or receiving a promotion or large inheritance, also disrupt the family system.

Untimely Death

The finality of death closes off relationship options, making it an emotionally overwhelming crisis for most families. Although the death of any family member carries with it a sense of grief, the death of an elderly person who has lived a full life usually does not contain the anger aroused by untimely death, nor does it carry the potential for major role changes among young or middle-aged family members. Hence, we will discuss untimely death as an unpredictable crisis.

A system experiencing the permanent loss of one member must eventually adapt to becoming a system of a different number of people, e.g., a five-person system becomes a four-person system through the death of one member. Bowen (1976) calls death our chief taboo subject. "A high percentage of people die alone, locked into their own thoughts which they cannot communicate to others. People cannot communicate the thoughts they have lest they upset the family or others" (336). Subsystems may form to keep the subject unmentionable. Two people may draw in a third to relieve tension, or they may collude to avoid any discussion of the impending death (Herz, 1980, 235–36).

Persons who are dying and their family members often resort to silence, new rules, and verbal games to maintain a two-sided pretense that "Everything is going to be all right." Family members in their own grief may go into a denial of the information of a terminal illness. They shield the dying from such knowledge and begin a series of new communication rules around the dying person. Some families go so far as to forbid any discussion, even by nurses, of the patient's health with the patient. Everyone is to keep fooling the patient at all costs. This can create monumental stress for a rational, articulate human who has the capacity to cope with news of his or her own death, since the subterfuges necessary to "keep up the front" often become transparent. Often, the dying member knows and then has to play a game of not knowing to protect the rest of the family. Such rules block dealing with all the interpersonal feelings, caring, and relationships, as well as with some of the immediate fears and loneliness.

"I will never forget my uncle's complaining bitterly two days before he died about his family treating him like a helpless child and insisting he would recover whenever he started to talk about dying or his fear of never leaving the hospital. I was only fourteen and did not fully understand what he was trying to tell me at the time, but I never forgot his pain or anger as he tried to explain the feeling of dying without emotional support."

Dunlop declares that " . . . the dying person has his own grieving to do. We should remember too, that the dying person is not just losing himself (which is a considerable loss that other grievers are not having to deal with), but the dying person is also about to lose everything which is important and everyone who is significant to him and whom he loves" (2). Kübler-Ross suggests that we should regard death as an "intrinsic part of life" and discuss it openly like other events in family life (141). The question should change from "Do I tell?" to "How do I share the information?" (28). She discovered that almost all terminally ill patients realized they were dying whether they had been told or not (31). If a family confronts the issue openly, they can, according to Kübler-Ross, go through preparatory grief together, which facilitates the later bereavement process (169). Parkes recognized that the anticipatory grief in communicating about dying can be quite painful, but it has the potential to lead to a kind of tranquility for the family members who share it and leaves more satisfying memories of the dying person for survivors (131, 154).

Reasons vary for not telling a family member that he or she has a terminal illness. Dunlop states, "Perhaps it is done out of the belief that if the dying person were told he was dying, he would become depressed and despondent, however, in time he will be both, and must be both if his dying is to have some psychological comfort to it" (5). In determining whether to tell a patient, Verwoerdt (1967) lists these criteria: (1) the dying member's emotional and intellectual resources to handle the news, (2) what the dying member already knows or has guessed, (3) the personal meaning the disease has for the dying based on his or her knowledge of others who had the same terminal illness, and (4) the degree to which the dying member wants to know his or her fate (10). The answer to the question of whether to tell the dying, in Dunlop's opinion, requires considerable skill in assessing verbal and nonverbal communication from the dying person (121). Dunlop concludes that a dying person who wants to know has that right. He calls it an absurdity to leave the decision to the physician who "may in fact be the least prepared to make one in which the patient's emotional well-being is at stake" (11). Bowen would concur with Dunlop: "Problems occur when the closed communication system of medicine meets the age-old closed system between the patient and family . . ." (337).

Even those persons who choose their own deaths find many of their messages are ignored. In the United States, over 25,000 people commit suicide each year (Lineham et al., 1983). A disproportionate number of older people and young people are found in those numbers. In many cases, their attempts to communicate suicide plans go unrecognized until after the event. Parents of young people are advised to watch for such behaviors as talk of suicide, giving away of possessions, abnormal cheer after depression, and loss of appetite. Those who deal with the elderly are advised to look for depression, withdrawal, isolation, changes in sleep patterns, lower self-image, and bereavement (Wass and Myers, 1982, 133). However, many refuse to see such signs for what they are.

Using Kübler-Ross' five stages, we present one model for the process of dying: (1) denial, (2) anger, (3) bargaining, (4) depression, and (5) acceptance (36). The sequence may vary, but eventually the dying person will progress through all of them if he or she lives long enough and does not become stuck at a particular point, since the length of time one stays in a stage varies according to the individual. Persons may move back and forth through the stages.

Persons preparing for death need to express their denials—to articulate why such cannot be the case, to explore other remedies. They need to vent their anger at themselves, those they love, and possibly at God, science, or other institutions. Bargains must be struck or attempted—silently and openly. Finally, the loneliness, fears, and practical concerns must be unloaded, ranging from "What is really on the Other Side" to "How will they run the house without me?" Crying, praying, philosophizing, swearing, touching, worrying, and some joking contribute to the conversations.

Regardless of the phase, dying persons need an empathic listener who does not insist they will be better if they think about something else. Most dying people welcome an opportunity to talk about their deaths (Parkes, 131). Bowen, who has counseled dying patients for over thirty years, declares, "I have never seen a terminally ill person who was not strengthened by such a talk. This contradicts former beliefs about the ego being too fragile for this in certain situations" (337). Kübler-Ross agrees, "Dying persons will welcome someone who is willing to talk with them about their dying but will allow them to keep their defenses as long as they need them" (37). She further states that those patients who die comfortably have had a chance to rid themelves of guilt and were "encouraged to express their rage, to cry in preparatory grief, and to express their fears and fantasies to someone who can sit quietly and listen" (119). For family members, this means giving a dying person free expression to sort out his or her feelings, even though the other members may be in pain. Family members can create a sense of oneness that facilitates open expression of fears of dying—fears unlike any previously encountered. Although watching a person die can be devastating to the family members, ". . . terminal illness of a family member (unlike sudden death) does allow the family, if the system remains open, to resolve relationship issues, reality issues, and to say the final goodbye before death" (Herz, 228).

After the death of a family member, the other members go through a bereavement process, from numbness to pining to depression to recovery (Parkes, 7). Whereas losing a family member through early or untimely death used to be a pervasive aspect of life even in the early 1900s, now it is a rare event (Uhlenberg, 1980). Hence, the untimely death of a member isolates a family and often forces it to cope without extensive community support. An unexpected death, either by accident or illness, forces a family into an initial state of shock. Eventually, the shock wears off and the bereavement process begins. The event traumatizes family, even in cases where members know of an impending death. The survivors experience anger and depression. There may be many regrets about unspoken issues. "If only I had told him how much I loved him." "If I had only taken more time to listen to her." Survivors, too, need supportive listeners.

It is important to recognize the process nature of grief and realize that people will be upset and irrational and communicate differently. If the death has been caused by a long terminal illness or injury, the bereaved may have been so occupied

The death of a family member forces the family into an initial state of shock, after which bereavement begins.

with the care of the individual and with maintaining a semblance of order in the family system that only the death frees them to get in touch with their feelings.

Much also depends upon the place that the deceased had filled in the family system. The death of a parent of young children leaves many childrearing jobs and family responsibilities to the remaining parent. "The loss of a husband, for instance, may or may not mean the loss of a sexual partner, companion, accountant, gardener, baby-minder, audience, bed warmer, and so on depending upon the particular roles normally performed by this husband" (Parkes, 7). The surviving spouse has additional burdens, because he or she must learn new role functions and do so without the aid of the principal person that had been depended upon. If the household contains young children, the remaining parent has to help them through the crisis without allowing his or her own emotions to create distance from the child (Herz, 229).

The death of a child carries with it parental images and hopes for the future. Such circumstances usually result in great family pain. From her summary of the literature on childhood death, Herz suggests that family disruption is a common aftereffect, with divorce or separation occurring in a large number of the cases (228).

Many families experience a return of sadness or distancing communication on anniversaries of deaths of family members. Such dates serve as markers of loss, forcing memories to surface with great force. Thus, the death of a family member alters the entire family system, requiring the other members to go through a grieving process with as open communication as possible, in order to reintegrate the smaller system at a later point.

Illness or Handicap

A family with a permanently handicapped or seriously ill member goes through an important coping process before coming to terms with the problem. Coping with a child's birth defects or the effects of a debilitating disease or accident requires major adjustments involving physical and emotional energy. The immediate disruption to the family in no way equals the long-term drain on family resources and energies required to help the injured family member deal with what may be a lifelong situation.

In a description of the mourning process that parents of impaired children undergo, Moses (1978) suggests that it parallels the stages of coping with death described by Kübler-Ross. In a similar vein, Fortier and Wanlass (1984) propose a stage model describing the family process that follows the diagnosis of a handicapped child. Each of these stages has a communication component. The stages include: impact, denial, grief, focusing outward, and closure.

At the *impact* stage, the family learns, immediately or gradually, of the child's handicap, e.g., muscular dystrophy. Anxiety and tension characterize this period. Usually, the family responds in a frantic and disorganized manner. Information given to the family about the disability reassures rather than informs or educates. The family can absorb very little information and has very limited responses. Usually, the *denial* state follows the initial impact, carrying with it a sense of disbelief and distorted expectations. Parents may reject the diagnosis, fictionally explain the child's failure to perform normally, and find themselves unable to hear what others are saying about the problem. It is a period of fear and isolation.

Anger and sadness characterize the grief. Parents question why this happened to them or to their child. They may blame each other for the disability, isolate themselves from interacting with usual friends and extended family, and prevent open and supportive communication. These parents experience great sadness, which they may try to keep from each other, yet they need support systems to accept it. Often, sharing in support groups of parents with similarly affected children provides a sense of comfort.

Eventually, parents move toward the *focusing outward* stage, beginning a process of seeking information, discussing options, asking for help, and expressing feelings. Signs of relief are evident at this point as the family moves toward dealing with the issues. The *closure* stage represents a reconciliation with reality and sense of adaptation to the child's needs. The family pulls together and adjusts in ways that allow the members of the altered system to move forward and to communicate directly about their concerns.

A family working through the process experiences each of these stages. Some families may experience one stage very briefly and find themselves stuck in another for a long period of time. Some families block this mourning process by preventing the necessary communication at each stage. This is most likely to occur when individuals or systems operate according to such rules as "Keep a stiff upper lip" or "Solve your own problems." The family must support open communication if the system is to move through the necessary stages.

An older injured patient may also experience similar stages when faced with his or her own disability. The person who loses a limb or a vital capacity mourns the lost leg, eyesight, or strength by responding with denial strategies, expressions of anger, attempts at bargaining, depression, and eventually, if the process is not arrested, acceptance. Communication must be kept open and the injured or ill member given free rein to express his or her feelings.

A serious handicap or disease affects the overall family system. As might be predicted following the onset of a chronic disease, it is typical for a patient to assume a central position in the family. This shift in focus, if continued over a long period of time, affects marital and parent-child relationships. In some families, adolescents may use illness to cross generational boundaries and regulate marital distance or parental conflict (Frey, 1984, 253). Parents who are forced to focus on a demanding child have little time or energy to deal with each other. In a review of literature on illness from a family perspective, McCubbin et al. suggest that communication breakdowns occur between family members and between the family and relatives or neighbors. They attribute this breakdown to a lack of leisure time and less energy for the relationships (360). In a study of the coping patterns of parents with a child with cystic fibrosis, these same authors have found that both parents contribute to the coping process, but the mother's coping behavior focuses more on the interpersonal dimensions of family life—family cohesiveness and expressiveness (367).

In her study of the impact of physical disabilities on the marital relationship, Thompson (1979) reported that the disability puts stress on the marriage, usually in negative ways. For some couples, it limits their ability to have a family. Couples with families have reported their inability to go certain places or do certain things together. In addition, role function burdens placed on the spouse who was not disabled adds to the families' stress. A severe illness or handicap stresses a family system over a period of time. As in the Double ABCX model described earlier, the family marshalls its current resources at the outset of the crisis and then develops new resources to carry them through the crisis. The ability of family members to communicate in a direct and supportive manner directly influences the coping process.

Separation/Divorce/Desertion

Unlike death, which forces a family to adjust to a smaller number of members, the family in a divorce must adapt to a fragmented state, at least temporarily. In most cases, except total desertion, each parent remains somewhat involved with the children, thus continuing the parenting aspects of the original system (Weiss, 1975).

Although divorce alters a family system, it does not end it, except in cases of total desertion or total distancing of partners without children. Where children are concerned, a couple is divorced *to* each other rather than *from* each other. Family members remain linked around the children and must find ways to function as a transformed system.

A systems view of divorce acknowledges that both partners contribute to the dissolution of a marriage. Blame does not lie with one or the other. When you think about the issues of mutual influence and punctuation, it is fruitless to assign blame, since the immediate split may have been preceded by months or even years of ineffective communication. At some time in their relationship, each partner failed to meet the needs of the other and a painful new pattern emerged.

The separation and divorce processes essentially follow the pattern described earlier in this chapter. At some point, the spouses mourn the loss of the relationship, although one or the other may have mourned the "death" of the marriage years before the divorce became a reality. Initially, spouses may deny that anything is really wrong and communicate to children or others that "Our problems aren't all that serious" or "Daddy will be back soon so don't tell anyone he's gone." As the reality takes hold, anger, bargaining, and depression intermingle. There may be attempts at reconciliation. "We had a great thing going once; we can have it again." Failed attempts may be met with such messages as "After all I've done for you" and "What kind of a mother would move out on her children?" which serve to release some of the tension. Painful accusations and negative conflict are often heightened by the adversary positions required in many legal divorce proceedings. Finally, depression reflects the sense of loss and/or rejection often accompanied by great loneliness.

In terms of communication, the couple may experience a descent through the stages of development in the "social penetration model" described in Chapter 4. Thus, they move from whatever stage they had reached, e.g., affective exchange, back down toward the lower stages. Altman and Taylor (1973) suggest that as their relationship falls apart, partners gradually withdraw affect and intimate contact, and are likely to deal with one another to a lesser extent (7).

In other words, as a relationship deteriorates, the high self-disclosure, predictability, uniqueness, openness, and spontaneity that characterize the higher levels of a relationship disintegrate. Little effort is invested in the relationship; risk taking declines.

Eventually, communication moves down the continuum toward orientation level behavior. Personal issues are avoided, nonverbal behaviors are restrained; little uniqueness and spontaneity remain. Many former spouses relate to each other as casual acquaintances or almost strangers except perhaps around highly charged issues such as money and children.

According to Knapp (1984), a relationship that is "coming apart" reflects: (1) a recognition of differences, (2) an experience of constricted interaction,

(3) a sense of stagnation or marking time, (4) a pattern of avoidance, and finally, (5) the immediate or protracted experience of termination (40–44). Partners at these stages create messages that communicate an increasing physical and psychological distance and an increasing disassociation from the other person (189). Levels of cohesion drop to reflect the distancing; little connectedness remains.

Edwards and Saunders (1981) have developed a model of marital dissolution that stresses the importance of (1) marital congruity, or "the degree to which there is concordance in the spouses' perceptions of their relationship," and (2) commitment, or the degree to which the self is identified with the marital relationship. Without high levels of congruity and commitment, reached in most cases by open communication, the prognosis for a relationship is poor.

Studies have shown adverse effects of divorce on children (Hetherington, 1973; Wallerstein and Kelley, 1975, 1980; Westmen, 1972). Some have especially indicated problems in the pre-divorce, transition, and early post-divorce periods, with children acting out their frustrations and rage. After a year to eighteen months, most families adjust to the crisis; children may have accepted and may even like the changes.

"My dad and mother divorced last year. I can spend any weekend with him or stay during the week when I am not in school. I didn't think I would like the arrangement, but it's better than their fighting all the time. Now I have a house in the suburbs with Mom and an apartment in the city with Dad."

As a result of their longitudinal study of divorcing families, Wallerstein and Kelley expressed surprise at the limited communication between parents and children about the divorce, suggesting that the " . . . telling is not a pronouncement but should initiate a gradual process" (40). In many cases, children are informed about the divorce but not encouraged to discuss their concerns. Four fifths of the youngest children in this study were not provided with either an adequate explanation of assurance of continued care (39). Because parents are so anxious about the discussion, many make it impossible for the children to express their feelings. Children may be told "You'll see more of Daddy now" or "You'll be able to get a dog," comments intended to make the child feel positive but which deny the child's distress. The abruptness of communication about the divorce often contributes to the children's inability to explore the issues and to release their feelings directly. Whereas loss through death involves a socially expected mourning period, there is no socially sanctioned mourning period for the loss of the "family that was," a situation that may prevent the use of resources available to a child. Just as there must be support systems available to the child at the time of divorce, there must also be resources available during the post-crisis period.

Usually communication between former spouses becomes less conflictual in the years following a divorce. Hetherington et al. (1976) found that two months after the divorce, 66 percent of the exchanges between partners involved conflicts over finances, support, visitation, childrearing, and relating to others in the system (423). This same study followed families over a two-year period and noted that conflicts and contact with fathers diminished over time. This statement from the study certainly reflects the changing nature of communication in divorced families:

> The divorced mother tries to control the child by being more restrictive and giving more commands which the child ignores or resists. The divorced father wants his contacts with his children to be as happy as possible. He begins by initially being extremely permissive and indulgent and becoming increasingly restrictive over the two-year period, although he is never as restrictive as fathers in intact homes.   (425)

Other researchers believe this study makes an important contribution to understanding post-divorce interaction patterns. It describes the cycle of negative parent-child interaction that occurs in many families as the acceptable levels of anger are increased (Levitin, 1979).

Although it is impossible in a divorce to remove all the negative aspects of stress upon children and their communication, parents can certainly reduce the stress. If neither parent uses the child as a go-between, nor encourages "tattletale" behavior, opportunities for conflict are reduced. If each supports the other's discipline, the child cannot play one against the other.

Throughout any of these crises—death, illness, handicaps, or divorce—the family's capacity for open communication, reflective of its levels of cohesion and adaptation and its images, themes, boundaries, and biosocial beliefs, determines how the system will weather the strain. A family with low cohesion may fragment under pressure, unless such pressure can connect the unconnected members. A family with limited resources for adaptation faces a painful time, since such crises force change upon the system, which must respond with internal changes of its own. A family whose images and themes allow outside involvement in family affairs may use its flexible boundaries to find institutional and social support. A family with rigid biosocial beliefs faces difficult challenges if key family figures are lost or injured and others are not permitted to assume some of the role responsibilities. Throughout this process, communication among family members either facilitates or hinders the revising of the system to meet the demands of the crisis.

Every family undergoes periods of unpredictable stress. Many of these stresses are not as immediately critical as death, illness, or divorce, but they do eat away at members' resources. Negative stresses, such as alcoholism, drug abuse, child abuse, economic reversals, and job transfers, take their toll on a family's resources. Even such seemingly positive experiences as having a gifted/talented child, getting a high-powered position, or receiving a large sum of money can stress the system. In order to understand a family's coping capacity, we must examine a family's immediate and post-crisis resources. Only then can we judge the long-term effects of the crisis as either destructive or growth enhancing for the members involved.

CONCLUSION

In this chapter, we have looked at communication through unpredictable life stresses. Specifically, we focused on (1) the process of dealing with unpredictable stresses and (2) communication during certain major stressful life events, such as death, illness, handicaps and divorce. Over the years, every family system encounters external stress from crisis situations as well as stress from developmental change. The system's ability to cope effectively with stress depends on a number of factors. The Double ABCX model provides an effective explanation of family coping, because it focuses on pre-crisis and post-crisis variables. The magnitude of role change is also a predictive factor in coping. Families that are willing to maintain flexible boundaries, communicate with and accept support from institutional sources (Parents Without Partners, church groups, and medical organizations) and social networks (friends and extended family) are more likely to work through their crises and return to functional communication than are those who block outside support.

Death, illness, and divorce necessarily alter family systems over long periods of time. Communication may facilitate or restrict a family's coping procedures. In most families, sharing of information and feelings can lower the stress level. The family with flexible boundaries has the capacity to accept support and the potential for surviving crises more effectively than families who close themselves off from others.

IN REVIEW

1. Using a real or fictional family, analyze the effects on the family of a severe stress that directly and ostensibly affected only one member (e.g., drug problem, serious car accident, or severe illness).
2. Using the same example of family stress, compare and contrast an analysis of the problem according to the ABCX model and the more recent Double ABCX model.
3. Describe how a "happy event" has brought high levels of stress to a family with which you are familiar.
4. How do different cultural and/or religious attitudes toward death aid or restrict the mourning process for surviving family members?
5. What guidelines for communication would you recommend to spouses who have children and are about to separate?

Chapter 11

Communication Within Various Family Forms

As you listen to everyday conversation, read the newspaper, or watch television, you are confronted with discussions of "the breakdown of the American family." Such terminology is misleading and potentially destructive. Our culture appears to have an idealized view of the family, vividly depicted in holiday television advertising, which involves a middle-class, "natural" family with smiling grandparents. In reality, this two-parent, blood-related system represents only one family form, and only a small percentage of today's American families.

Harevan (1982) suggests that American families have always represented great diversity and that our nostalgia is for a lost family tradition that never really existed. Historically, the American family has fulfilled its members' extensive economic, socialization, education, and emotional needs. Harevan expresses her concern with the idealized two-parent, middle-class family, claiming, "American society has contained within it great diversities in family types and family behavior that were associated with the recurring entrance of new immigrant groups into American society. Ethnic, racial, cultural, and class differences have also resulted in diversity in family behavior" (461). She concludes that Americans experience continuing diversity in family patterns, thus making it unrealistic to talk simply about **the** American family.

In this chapter, we will look at some of the specific communication issues and behaviors related to a variety of family forms. Because there has been limited research on some of these forms, we may hypothesize communication implications that do not appear in the literature. Yet, any overview of family communication would be incomplete without reference to interaction across family forms. The following pages will focus specifically on communication within: (1) single-parent systems, (2) stepfamily systems, (3) homosexual partners and parents and same sex couples, and (4) other variations.

Families created through adoption are one form of "the American family." Whatever its form, a successful family fulfills its members' needs.

COMMUNICATION WITHIN
SINGLE-PARENT SYSTEMS

As we indicated in Chapter 1, a single-parent family consists of one parent and one or more children. This formation may include: an unmarried woman or man and his or her offspring; men and women without partners through death, divorce, or desertion and the children who remain; single parents who have adopted or foster children. We also discussed the increase in American single-parent systems, noting that in 1982, 20 percent of children under eighteen were living with their mother only, while 2 percent were living with their father.

At the beginning of this decade, the number of households maintained by a woman without a husband reached 15 percent. The percentage of families maintained by a man without a wife was 3 percent (Gongla, 1982). Although the majority of these systems are created through divorce, the number of single women who choose to raise a child without a husband is rising. By 1982, 18 percent of American births occurred to unmarried women. Thus, the single-parent system usually results from the loss of a parent figure but may result from the addition of a child through birth or adoption. For many children, the experience in a single-parent system is temporary until the parent remarries. Given the current divorce and remarriage rates, a larger percentage of the American population will spend some time as a member of a single-parent system. In 1979, Raschke and Raschke suggested that, "This means approximately 46 percent of the children have experienced or are experiencing a single-parent home" (367). As one more complicating factor, nearly all fathers work, and three fourths of the mothers with children aged six to seventeen work. More than half have children under age six (Gaylin, 1977). Such reality leads to complicated, pressured lifestyles.

"When I divorced, I only had one eight-year-old child, and dealing with her became so difficult that I can't imagine what families with three or four children do. First, Adrienne had to deal with the tension between her mother and me and the divorce. She had a lot of anger about that, and we spent hours talking about why Mommy and I could not remain together. Then she had to adjust to me as a single parent when she visited me, and we had to work out our rules for living together. Her mother and I had to communicate often about Adrienne's emotional and economic needs."

A major problem for single-parent families is task overload, most evident in the life cycle of single mothers with young children. Compounding this, social isolation, increased anxiety, depression, and loneliness also affect the single parent. Beal (1980) reports that single parents frequently find themselves emotionally cut off from extended family relationships and social networks (257). Divorced persons find themselves separated from their spouse's extended family as the boundaries are tightened against them. Spouses give up couples who were once friends shared with a spouse (Goetting, 1982), a situation that removes some support for childrearing. Unmarried women with children may find more support within their extended families, particularly in matriarchical systems.

Shifting subsystems and networks may be a problem. The two-against-one model of the two-parent home may force children to abide by parental wishes; when one parent leaves the system, some power may be removed from the parental image. Any troubled parent-child relationship cannot be adequately balanced by the other parent. When one parent leaves the system, the other may attempt to place a child in the vacated role to provide emotional support or perform household duties. The child may become the confidant or share decision making. "You're the man of the house now" typifies this lowering of boundaries between parental and child subsystems and often results in communication breakdowns. This new role may place great pressure on the child, alienate the child from other siblings, and eventually interfere with the normal process of separating from the family at the appropriate developmental point.

In a description of his adolescent life in a single-parent home, Goldberg (1983) remembers his worries about support checks, the parental date who might appear at breakfast, and the younger siblings who could not remember a two-parent household. He indicates the difficulty of trying to give advice on dating, give support on childcare, and stay in the middle between warring parents. Such experiences are not rare as parents lower boundaries due to their own needs.

Numerous researchers have debated the problems of the single-parent family, especially its effects upon children. These studies have importance because they relate to family communication. In measuring self-concept, which also includes assessment of social and personal adjustment, Raschke and Raschke found that children were "not adversely affected by living in single parent families but that family conflict and/or parental unhappiness can be detrimental" (373). In this important study that compared intact families with single-parent families, they discovered that in both types, there was a high correlation between perceived parental happiness and children's healthy self-concepts. Their work concurs with Burchinal's (1964) findings that adolescents in broken, unbroken, and reconstituted families did not suffer adverse effects in their adjustment or developmental characteristics (50–51). Herzog and Sudia (1971) examined research on the effects of children living in fatherless homes and concluded there was little evidence to support the assumption that households headed by women had a detrimental effect upon children (Raschke and Raschke, 368). Beal (1980) stresses the importance of distinguishing between life in conflict-laden intact families and life in well-functioning single-parent homes, concluding that the latter leads to better adjustment (257).

Certain economic concerns in the single-parent family have direct bearing on communication patterns. When a single mother's income is low and the father fails to pay for child support, many children become pawns in the battle. Communication with their father may be restricted, or they may become part of a chain network relaying requests for, and responses about, the money. In either situation, the children experience great stress. According to the United States Census Bureau, 54 million women and children get less than half of their court-ordered payment and 28 percent get nothing. This economic pressure escalates stress within the single-parent system.

In her summary of research findings on single-mother homes, Gongla indicates the following major points: (1) children can develop normally in warm and not conflict-ridden families; (2) children gain in responsibility and power by performing some of the volume of tasks, which cannot be performed by one parent; (3) initially, the mother may be restrictive and the children may be aggressive, but this changes over time if supports exist; and (4) interdependence of family members grows (11). The role of the father in the family after divorce, separation, or out-of-marriage birth is important. Researchers suggest that maintaining supportive contact on important child-related matters has beneficial consequences for the mother and children (Gongla, 20). Children who are not forced to choose between parents suffer less stress than those who are discouraged, directly or indirectly, from such contact. Gongla concludes her summary by calling for more research concentrating on the single-parent family *as a family*, from a systems perspective.

The type of communication possible within single-parent homes created through death or divorce reflects the ability of the family to adjust to the new systemic arrangement, whether through the permanent or partial loss of a member. As conflicts diminish, increased cohesion may develop among members. Families with high adaptability can create new and functional communication networks. In almost all cases, boundaries are adjusted to reflect the system's need or desire for outside influence. Themes, images, and biosocial beliefs may also experience adjustment. No matter what, a family with low adaptability will face a more painful time than a family with high adaptability, as evidenced by the following family's inability to adapt to a new identity as a single-parent system.

"My father died a slow death of diabetes when my sister and I were eight and six. He had always been the head of the family, and my mother depended on his leadership in everything. For ten years, we operated as a fractured family. You could say our theme was 'We can't be a family without a man.' We couldn't get any identity of our own, and we hitched ourselves to all kinds of other people and tried to find new families for ourselves. Finally, we got some counseling and learned that three women could create a functional family unit. A single-parent family does not have to be a second-class family."

Any single-parent family, whether formed through the loss of a parent or addition of a child, needs support from its community of extended family and friends. The family may also need economic or counseling support, depending on its specific needs.

For members to share affection and communicate in a nurturing way, some functional stability must exist. If not, all the family energy will be devoted to issues of basic life necessities, a concern that often invokes conflict.

Eventually, many single parents marry and form stepfamilies. At that time, they must alter the single-parent system to create a larger, two-parent system, which includes children from one or both parents. This transition brings new stresses and communication concerns. We will address stepfamily concerns in the next section.

COMMUNICATION WITHIN STEPFAMILY SYSTEMS

The stepfamily has been compared to a challenging and complex chess game, to a delicate and intricate spider's web, and to a chaotic and confusing toddler's birthday party (Einstein, 1980). No matter what the analogy, the stepfamily is a complex, growing, and little-understood segment of American family life. At the start of the 1980s, 35 million adults were stepparents. One child in six was a stepchild (Visher and Visher, 1982). The term "stepfamily" refers to many types of family forms, which can be created as two adults and the children of one or both come together. These systems, although similar to other two-parent forms, have eight characteristics:

1. A history of loss emerges for those who were previously in a two-parent system.
2. Some or all members bring past family history from a relationship that has changed or ended.
3. The couple does not begin as a dyad but rather, parent-child relationships predate the spousal bond.
4. One or two biological parents (living or dead) influence the stepfamily.
5. Children may function as members of two households.

6. The family has a complex extended family network.
7. Strong triangles exist, which involve biological parents/former spouses that influence the stepfamily.
8. No legal relationships exist between the stepparent and stepchildren. (Visher and Visher, 1982; Einstein, 1982; Mills, 1984)

As was noted in Chapter 10, as a stepfamily forms, one marriage does not end and a totally new system begin. Death or divorce do not dissolve a system, rather they alter it. After a death, the remaining family members are faced with the necessity of restructuring themselves into a smaller system—the hold must be closed—the family cannot continue limping indefinitely due to the "missing" member. After a divorce, the members may exist for a long period of time in an altered system of the same size, which still functions around issues of the children or monetary considerations. Eventually, altered systems may expand into stepfamilies.

These stepfamilies continue to be influenced by the original marital system. In their discussion of forming a remarried family, McGoldrick and Carter (1980) suggest that the emotions connected with the breakup of the first marriage can be visualized as a "roller coaster" graph with peaks of intensity at the points of:

1. Decision to separate;
2. Actual separation;
3. Legal divorce;
4. Remarriage of either spouse;
5. Death of either ex-spouse; and
6. Life cycle transitions of children (graduations, marriage, illness, etc.).   (271)

In a divorce that includes children, each of these points causes disruption for original system members and must be handled carefully in order to keep a remarriage stabilized. Many counselors consider that a couple is divorced *to* each other rather than *from* each other, especially when children are involved. Thus, a full reconstituted system is formed. For example, a family system may expand to include a woman, two children, her current husband, and her former husband who has remarried and has a stepson. The following diagram (Figure 11–1) will demonstrate how the original marital system of Peggy and Seth has grown and altered. Although Seth does not live with his children and former wife there are emotional, economic, and practical ties which bind all these people to each other. If Maryanne has difficulty in school, her mother, natural father, and stepparents may all be affected by the problem.

In order to understand the complexity of stepfamily life, particularly in its first years, we can examine a model of a stepfamily, which describes the stages most families experience as they try to blend two systems, at least one of which reflects a previous parent-child relationship.

Papernow (1984) describes seven stages of stepparent development and places these within a developmental framework for stepfamilies, which includes early, middle, and later stages. (See Table 11–1.)

Figure 11—1 _____
Reconstituted Family System

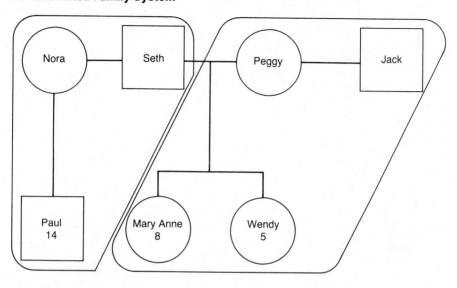

Within the early stages, the stepfamily remains divided primarily along previous system lines in terms of emotional support, agreement of rules or rituals, and general alliances among people. During this early period, stepparents fantasize about what can be created. They may imagine that they will rescue stepchildren from inadequate situations and that they will create a loving, nurturing, devoted new family characterized by emotional sharing. Most new stepparents report a high level of fantasies and hopes for family life, as well as high expectations for gratitude from the stepchildren (Turnbull and Turnbull, 1983). On the other hand, the children are more likely to fantasize the departure of the stepparents and the reunion of their biological family, unless one of the biological parents is dead or has deserted the family.

At the assimilation stage, members become acutely aware of their different rhythms, rules, relational currencies, and everyday behaviors and recognize the difficulty in blending them. Stepchildren experience tremendous clashes of loyalty as they try to sort out how to deal with a stepparent without being disloyal to the same-sex biological parent. Often, this confusion is exhibited through anger or indifference. The biological parent, pleased to have an adult partner, is frightened by that partner's inability to establish satisfactory relationships with his or her children. Most stepfamilies encounter a persisting inequality of the biological parent-child relationship; therefore, truly shared parenting functions seldom become reality (Mills). It becomes clear that something is not working, but due to fear of repeated failure, it is too frightening to address the issue directly.

The confusion of this early stage affects the entire larger system of grandparents, aunts, uncles, and cousins who have to negotiate their relationship with this new family. This extended family might include four sets of grandparents as well as

Table 11–1 _____
Stages in Stepfamily Development

Early Stages:	1.	Fantasy
	2.	Assimilation
	3.	Awareness
Middle Stages:	4.	Mobilization
	5.	Action
Later Stages	6.	Contact
	7.	Resolution

large numbers of relatives who have experienced close connections to certain members of the reconstituted system. These extended members provide feedback to the family on how they are seen, either by emphasizing the differences (giving expensive toys to biological grandchildren and token gifts to a stepgrandchild) or by reinforcing the newly formed system by treating all children equally. During these early stages it is hard for the adults involved to share what is going on within them and to really hear what their spouse is saying. Their dreams and fantasies are hard to forgo. Reality implies pain and conflict.

As the early stages conclude, family members begin to be aware of their situation and start to make sense out of what is happening to them. According to Papernow, "While the pain doesn't go away, the picture of where it comes from and why it hurts so much gets clearer" (358). The biological parent may be feeling great stress as a central figure trying to protect the children and mollify the spouse, finding little gratification in either.

Although some families remain stuck in the early stages for many years, most systems move on to the middle stages and begin the process of mobilizing their resources and airing differences. During this period, spouses are more likely to address their differences directly, expressing feelings, needs, and perceptions about life in the stepfamily. Such directness may lead to many conflicts, but open conflict is important. At the time, some of the issues may appear trivial, but the conflicts represent the underlying issues of changing the family's structure. Such comments as "You're too tired to go to the grocery store but when Jill calls you are awake enough to pick her up from work!" address the alliances and strengths of certain boundaries within the system. A stepfather may claim that he needs time alone with his wife, upsetting her children but strengthening the marital boundary. A stepchild may express concern at the interrogation that follows every visit with her natural mother, demanding privacy in that part of her life. Biological parents may indicate their distress with the expectations of extended members from both original systems.

_____

"One of the hardest things about being part of two stepfamilies is learning how to adapt to each situation. Although I live with my mother and her husband, much of the time I spend vacations with my father, his new wife, and her three children. In my mother's home, we talk about almost anything very freely. People tend to say what is on their minds, argue about their rights, and be up front with problems. I

> *have much more trouble in my father's house, since 'peace at any price' seems to be the ground rule. You learn to avoid painful topics, smile most of the time, and praise the food. Fortunately, I only have to do this on vacations.''*

As the middle stages continue, the family moves into an action mode that marks the beginning of truly working together. This involves sharing the former dreams and expectations while remaining connected enough to engage in active problem solving around past and current issues. Some solutions may reflect former ways of doing things for certain members, while others involve creative attempts to represent the desires of the blended group. For example, a family may decide to adopt certain holiday rituals that one part of the system experienced before, while creating new ones reflecting the new system. Although the time when a stepfamily identity is being built is a perfect time to establish new traditions (Einstein, 1982), many families never discuss expectations; all members assume that old ways will be carried on. Such silence only deepens the pain as members feel misunderstood or disconfirmed.

Because part-time stepparenting can be very stressful for the family and visiting children, family members may agree to change the way they function when noncustodial stepchildren spend time at their house. They may move to low-key sharing of time rather than a frantic period of "entertainment." In other circumstances, spouses may decide to limit a child's access to his biological mother's charge card because it creates inequity among all the children. Most families at these stages renegotiate rules for everyday events and discuss acceptable ways of handling anger and affection within the system. They may begin to create an identity for themselves in a positive light, instead of working from a sense of deficiency. This action period reflects a sense of "we-ness" for stepfamilies who believe they are taking charge of their destinies.

As families enter the later stages, members experience greater intimacy and authenticity. In this stage " . . . the couple relationship, previously polarized by step issues, is now more often felt as an intimate sanctuary in which to share these issues, including painful or difficult feelings (Papernow, 360). The triangles that had consumed the couple's attention and energy have diminished, allowing them to function more adequately in all areas of family life.

Eventually, the question as to how biological parents and stepparents are to be integrated into the children's lives is resolved. Papernow ascribes the quality of the stepparent role in this way:

(a) The role does not usurp or compete with the biological parent of the same sex; (b) The role includes an intergenerational boundary between stepparent and child; (c) The role is sanctioned by the rest of the stepfamily, particularly the spouse; (d) The role incorporates the special qualities this stepparent brings to this family.   (361)

Family members experience a sense of clarity and security, which is even reflected in their language. Confusion about how to refer to family members has passed; discussion of the stepfamily is comfortable. Levels of openness once considered impossible may now exist. The original fantasies have been explored with reality.

The step relationships at the resolution stage not only provide a sense of satisfaction but also feel reliable. Family members have developed dyadic relationships characterized by personal interaction, not just by marital merger. Present situations move into the foreground, while past struggles and issues become part of the background. This does not imply permanent resolution of all issues, because certain concerns reappear indefinitely—the later phases of the "roller coaster" graph described earlier.

The complexity of stepfamily formation is reflected in members' communication concerns and patterns. As a married system forms, partners bring communication patterns from: (1) families-of-origin, (2) the first marriage, and (3) the period between marriages. Children bring patterns from the second and third situations. Forming such a system requires extensive initial adaptation if acceptable cohesion levels are to be reached. Family members are cast instantly into multiple roles. A single man may become husband and stepfather. A woman may become wife, stepmother, or even stepgrandmother with a simple "I do." The results of research on stepparent and children relationships indicate areas where problems in communication can develop.

Each member of a remarried system must participate in the creation of new family themes, images, boundaries, and biosocial beliefs. Disparate backgrounds and negative feelings about the remarriage will result in intense periods of conflict, reflected verbally and nonverbally, as family members jockey for position and power. The former oldest child may fight against the role of middle daughter. A child used to great freedom and autonomy may rebel against themes that push for strong cohesion and similarity among family members. Each new system must negotiate such boundaries issues as:

1. Membership (Who are the "real" members of the family?)
2. Space (What space is mine? Where do I really belong?)
3. Authority (Who is really in charge of discipline, money, or decision making?)
4. Time (Who gets how much of my time and how much do I get of theirs?) (Carter and McGoldrick, 269–70)

Biosocial concerns, such as male-female roles or authority positions, may need extensive or limited negotiation, depending on the family's previous positions on such issues.

Communication networks must expand to encompass new members and possibly to maintain ties with first marriage members, as children and former spouses and extended family members attempt to maintain necessary contacts. Children may be confused by adjusting to the functioning of two separate households. This may be compounded by pressure, negative remarks, or overt conflict between members of former systems. Children may feel "pulled to one side." Each group may establish communication rules to keep information from the other. "Don't tell your mother about my trip to Mexico" or "Don't mention that I'm dating someone." Children may be filled with secrets and resentments, which they cannot divulge. A difficult situation arises as former spouses criticize each other in front of the children. Lutz (1983) found that the area of greatest stress for adolescents was experiencing one natural parent's talking negatively about the other natural parent (374).

If members of the extended family take sides, the children suffer additional pressures. A spouse may unwisely permit relatives or friends in the children's presence to make derogatory remarks about the other spouse. A grandmother may remind the children of the "no-good" qualities of their father and when the children become boisterous, argue, or get into fights, may declare, "You're acting just like your father."

Children need to understand that they did not cause the divorce if they are to be able to communicate openly with both parents. Each parent needs to assure children that it's acceptable to love the other parent and that parent-child love in no way diminishes because of divorce. Nothing positive in communication can be gained by "bad-mouthing" the ex-spouse. Often, one spouse says little, but children sense the nonverbal communication when the other's name is mentioned. Divorced parents need to remember that as children grieve, they may act out their own feelings of loss and alternately blame one parent for the divorce (Luepnitz, 1979, 84), or they may take out their anger on a stepparent.

Eventually, most remarried systems stabilize, and children and parents report satisfaction. Gilford and Bengtson (1979) analyzed data from 1,056 married members of three-generation families. Their data included once-married versus second or third marriages, as well as generation factors, and concluded that, on positive or negative dimensions of marital satisfaction, the trends were uniform on such independent variables as chronological age, duration of marriage, and sex. In all types of marriages, the levels of satisfaction resembled a "U-shaped curve"— highest at the beginning, declining in childraising and middle years, and then increasing in old age (394–96).

Reconstituted systems are becoming a common part of the American way of life, but the issues of living in such a system remain varied and complex. To date, our society's vocabulary has not even developed words to deal with the roles and relationships involved. For example, a child has no names for her stepgrandparents, no way to easily communicate about her relationship to the son of her father's second former wife, no name for the first stepfather who is now divorced from her mother. Such difficulties make contact with outsiders and institutions more difficult and sometimes more painful. As society becomes more comfortable with these new family forms, we will develop more effective ways of communicating about them.

There is still much to be learned about communication within a stepfamily, a form that usually involves nonvoluntary relationships (Cooper, 1984). This growing segment of family life presents challenges that have yet to be fully appreciated from a communication perspective.

HOMOSEXUAL PARTNERS AND PARENTS

In our society, alternative family forms are becoming more commonly recognized, including same-sex couples and families headed by homosexuals (Macklin, 1980). In describing the recognition of various family forms, Harevan suggests that an alternative, such as same-sex couples, is not necessarily a new family form but rather a form that is becoming more visible. Although census figures on female couples and lesbian couples are not available and almost no hard data exist on homosexual parents, there is growing evidence indicating the scope of these family forms. According to DeVito (1979), depending on the data used and the definition of "gay" or "lesbian," statistics range from 4 to 25 percent. Golanty and Harris (1982) estimate that 5 to 10 percent of the population maintains sexual and emotional involvements exclusively with members of the same sex.

In this text, we are concerned with homosexual persons who have formed couple attachments in which they consider each other as family and with those who are functioning as parents. The 1983 study *American Couples* included same sex couples as a significant part of their population. Blumstein and Schwartz (1983) explain the decision, noting that in the late 1960s, the Kinsey Institute found that 71 percent of their sample of gay men between ages thirty-six and forty-five were living with a partner. In the 1970s, Bell and Weinberg (1978) found strong support among lesbians for being in a permanent relationship (45). Blumstein and Schwartz suggest that until the 1970s, gay men and lesbians were a real but fairly invisible part of the American population. Yet, the authors suggest that "couplehood," either as a reality or as an aspiration, is as strong among gay people as it is among heterosexuals (44). In their work on homosexual relationships, Bell and Weinberg identified what they called the "close couple," or the homosexual relationship most similar to heterosexual marriage. In this relationship, partners are sexually exclusive and rely on each other for interpersonal satisfaction. Other studies in the 1970s and 1980s point toward the desire for couple relationships within the gay male and lesbian community (Weinberg and Williams, 1974; McWhirter and Mattison, 1984; Majors, 1984; Johnson, 1984).

Although many similarities exist between heterosexual and homosexual couples, dramatic differences also exist. Some of the differences include areas of relationship development, sources of recognition/support, and ways of dealing with money, sex, and power (Majors; Blumstein and Schwartz; De Vito).

In describing gay male relationships, Majors maintains, "Sound research has indicated that significant differences between male/male couples and male/female couples do indeed exist and drastically alter the nature of all aspects of relationship formation and development" (1). In Chapter 5, we discussed the influence of role expectation on role performance. Yet, in most cases, young homosexuals are denied role models and positive images of long-term same-sex relationships. Such a lack of role models forces a more pressured trial and error discovery in relationship development and maintenance. Majors suggests that this is particularly difficult for males, because men in general are "less likely to develop the interpersonal skills that make for easy and comfortable dealing with feelings, sharing of inner concerns, empathy and listening skills" (6). The lack of role models exacerbates the situation.

The lack of interpersonal and institutional support creates great pressure for homosexual partners and parents. Many individuals cannot tell even their own families about their life-style. Others feel comfortable sharing their relationship with only very few friends or family members. In certain urban areas, the large rec-ognized gay community has provided support for couples or families, but in other areas, persons live in secretive isolation.

Even when partners are recognized as a couple, the interpersonal support remains different. For example, De Vito suggests that two men who have been together for twenty years are not related to as husband and wife, yet we have no appropriate term. "In gay parlance they are 'lovers' but as popularly used and understood the term is too general and does not include the years of commitment, the permanency of the relationship, and a host of other dimensions that are included in both the denotative and connotative meanings of the term marriage" (8). Some homosexual couples live together openly after going through marriage ceremonies similar to heterosexual rites (Stinnett et al., 1984), but such com-munity celebrations are rare. Most couples are forced to rely more on each other to meet interpersonal needs than are their heterosexual counterparts.

"One of the most difficult parts of our life-style is the intense dependence we have to have on each other because we cannot discuss our relationship or certain other serious aspects of our lives with many other people. We experience an isolation as we function among friends who live a heterosexual life-style and can be more open about the good and bad parts of their lives. I value the closeness of our relationship, but I recognize the strains caused by the need to depend so totally on each other."

Coupled with limited interpersonal support, homosexual partners and par-ents receive almost no societal support. Whereas spouses in heterosexual partner-ships become immediately eligible for health insurance, tuition rebates, or organizational benefits, long-term homosexual unions entitle a partner to nothing. The child of a partner cannot receive tuition rebates or other medical benefits. Most religious or educational institutions give little or no support to homosexual partners or parents. These few examples highlight the kinds of pressures placed on long-term same-sex relationships that heterosexual couples do not experience.

In their massive study of couples from the perspectives of money, work, and sex, Blumstein and Schwartz uncovered many differences between heterosexual and same-sex couples and also between gay male and lesbian couples. We will highlight just a few. The authors report that money establishes the balance of power in relationships, except among lesbians. Whereas in heterosexual couples the greater the amount of money the wife earns the freer she is to spend the money as she sees fit, in lesbian couples the balance of power is not related to income. "They make a conscious effort to keep their relationships free of any form of dom-ination, especially if it derives from something as impersonal as money" (55). In gay male couples, income is an extremely important force in determining which partner is dominant. When partners are disappointed with the amount of money the couple has, they find their entire relationship less satisfying, except among lesbians. Schrag (1984) reports that money and property seem to be the most emotional and practical issues a gay couple deals with as they negotiate a long-term partnership.

In their examination of work issues, Blumstein and Schwartz found that same-sex couples primarily face the issue of how to keep the relationship together in the face of career demands. This contrasts with the heterosexual concern of who has the right to work. The majority of same-sex couples believe that both should work, although lesbians are more likely to feel obligated to support a partner than are gay males. Same-sex couples, due to a lack of traditional marital role models, tend to negotiate each conflict rather than rely on societal expectations or previous gender role models for their answers. In dealing with the issue of "work vs. the relationship," the researchers found same-sex couples to be relationship-oriented. Lesbians of all ages cannot seem to find enough time to share together. Gay men appear more satisfied with the time they have available to them. Blumstein and Schwartz speculate that one reason same-sex couples are so relationship-centered may be their capacity to spend their leisure time together, having been socialized to enjoy many of the same activities and interests.

"There's a comfort just being in the same room together. We can sit and be quiet and feel very comfortable for hours. We often find ourselves doing the same things, buying the same cards, planning the same meals, starting to say the same things. Although we grew up in different areas, we are very much alike and share almost the same interests. We can leave a great deal unsaid and still understand each other."

Blumstein and Schwartz report that sexual frequency varies among the couple types. Gay men have sex more often in the early part of their relationship than any other type of couple. But after ten years, they have sex together far less frequently than do married couples. Lesbians have sex less frequently than any other type of couple. The quality of sexuality is important to all couples. In same-sex couples, it is the more emotionally expressive partner who initiates sex most frequently. As a distinction between same-sex couple types, gay men value physical attractiveness of a partner more highly than do lesbians.

In their summary of findings, Blumstein and Schwartz highlight the unique situation of lesbian couples:

Lesbians are in a double bind: On the one hand, they want a great deal of attention and communication from a partner. On the other, they do not want a partner who is too relationship-centered that she has no ambition or attachment to work. Lesbians want an intense home life, but they also want a strong, ambitious, and independent partner. They want to give a great deal, but only if their partner gives as much. (328)

In addition to the relational issues faced by same-sex partners, some couples also deal with parenting concerns. There is very little research on gay male or lesbian parents, yet it seems reasonable to assume that communication around this issue would be difficult. A national survey found homosexuality to be the single most difficult subject for parents to discuss with children (Yankelovich et al., 1977). Discussing one's own homosexuality with a child creates enormous concerns. In one of the few studies in this area, Miller (1979) found that gay men feared the revelation of their gayness to their children, because most feared it would lessen the children's respect and affection for their fathers. Of the men who had told their children, all found the children more positive than had been anticipated (548). The children reported that their father's honesty had relieved some family tension and helped to strengthen the parent-child relationship. Children who showed the greatest acceptance of their fathers were those who were gradually introduced to the subject of homosexuality through printed material, discussion, and meeting gay family friends before the full parental disclosure.

Although same-sex couples represent a small percentage of American families, they are included as a family form, due to the growing societal recognition of the existence of long-term committed relationships within the gay community.

OTHER VARIATIONS OF FAMILY FORMS

Although there are many other family forms that could be considered, we will highlight three: cohabitation, communal families, and joint custody/co-parenting. These forms are becoming increasingly common in our society.

Cohabitation

If you live with a boyfriend or girlfriend for three weeks, are you a cohabitor? If you keep two apartments but sleep together in one or the other are you a cohabitor? Definitions of cohabitation abound; as we use the term, *cohabitation* means a couple who have been living together at least four nights a week and for a total of five months in the previous year. It is a year-round arrangement and does not coincide with semester schedules for university students. A commitment to each other and recognition of each other as a "family" is also implied. This definition limits the number of couples within our discussion.

We cannot estimate with any accuracy the population of cohabitors. Unmarried couples living together totalled 1,988,000 in 1984, a figure that has tripled since 1970. Putting these figures in perspective means that 4 percent of all couples, or one couple in twenty-five, is unmarried. Whereas some cohabitors have never been married, others have experienced one or more marriages.

Communication differs in some respects between cohabiting and married couples. Without the legal ties and ceremonial rituals that publicly announce the relationship as a long-term commitment, partners may have difficulty communicating to friends and relatives that their living together, especially in the beginning, represents love more than sexual needs.

Statistical estimates of the number of couples who cohabit and eventually marry vary from one in four to one in eight; thus, the partners themselves may fear that their relationship will not last. This can influence patterns of conflict and decision making. It may be a factor in the findings of a recent study of cohabiting couples who married; in the year after the marriage, wives perceived a significantly lower quality of communication, and both spouses reported significantly lower marital satisfaction (De Maris and Leslie, 1984, 77). In another study, couples who had not cohabited had higher marital adjustment scores one year after marriage than did those who had cohabited (Watson, 1983, 145). The results of the latter study contradicted earlier studies, which had indicated that cohabitation effectively screened out incompatible couples, served as a training/adjustment period for couples and improved mate selection and the chances of avoiding divorce (Macklin, 1972; Ridley et al., 1978; Trost, 1975; Watson). In fact, earlier studies found little evidence that cohabiting couples had more difficulty remaining married than those who had not lived together prior to marriage (Bentler and Newcomb, 1978; Jacques and Chason, 1979). The differences in these studies may be in the ages of the couples or the definition of cohabiting used, or it may be that cohabiting couples who marry expect more from marriage and adapt less readily to role expectations of conventional marriage (De Maris and Leslie, 83).

As we discussed in Chapter 5, role performance may differ greatly from original expectations. Being a wife or husband may bring with it a set of pressures from the spouse or other forces that cause the role to be played out differently than expected. Rogers (1972), in his book *Becoming Partners*, records poignant statements about this process from two young people who married after living together for a lengthy period of time:

Dick: "When Gail and I were living together we were sort of equal partners in making the living, and if we were broke, nobody really took the blame for it; but when we moved back and came into such close proximity with our respective in-laws, all of a sudden it became *my* fault when we weren't making any money, and *I* was the bum who wasn't going out and looking for work."

Gail: "I sort of had expectations like he did, you fall into a role even if you don't want to . . . of a husband is supposed to be this way and a wife is supposed to be this way . . . So it put me into a big conflict because I'm thinking, 'Well, I've *got* to be like this, I'm married and I'm supposed to do this. . . .'" (43)

In this case, both personal expectations and family pressure forced individuals to view their roles differently than they expected. The lack of clear definition of cohabiting roles may increase the partners' sense of individual freedom.

Blumstein and Schwartz found that cohabiting couples regard money, sex, and work differently than do other couples. These varying perceptions influence the ways cohabiting couples negotiate differences and establish patterns and rules affecting their interaction. Cohabiting couples reported a stronger sense than married couples of each partner's contributing his or her share.

Cohabiting women view money as a way to achieve equality in their relationships. Thus, cohabiting women seek independence and want to avoid economic dependence or dominance by the man in their household. The cohabiting men expect this behavior more than do married men. The cohabiting partner with the greater income determines more of the couple's recreational activities, including vacations. Cohabiting couples usually maintain separate checking accounts, and when they do, they fight less about finances than do married couples (53–109).

These same researchers found that cohabitors believe that both partners should work and expect sharing of housework. Yet, women do more of this work than men. Male cohabitors, more than married men, rank the relationship as more important than their job. However, male cohabitors are more competitive with their partners, but the partners' success or lack of it has less effect on the relationship. Cohabitors more frequently spend time on their own, including going places alone or with friends than either married, gay male, or lesbian couples.

Sexual communication also differs, since cohabitors report having sex more frequently than do married couples. Cohabiting women more readily express an interest in sex by initiating it, but in a long-standing relationship, the male cohabitor usually resents it.

Many parents of cohabiting children have difficulty accepting their children's wishes to live together in a trial marriage. Family communication can be difficult at holidays or other times when parents are confronted with visiting cohabitors' requests to share a bedroom, especially when other relatives plan to stay in the same household.

Fear of conflict may motivate cohabitors to lie or mislead others about the nature of their relationship. Frequently, communication in the family network becomes quite complicated, with certain members or subsystems knowing the "secret" and others kept uninformed.

Cohabitation represents a small but growing type of family form with certain unique communication concerns.

Communal Families

Approximately three million people live in communal families (U.S. Census Bureau, 1980). Such families include individuals and/or small families who join together to share living space and economic and emotional support. They live largely in urban areas and consist of young professionals who band together partially for economic reasons and for a shared sense of family life. Some group members want to continue experiencing the closeness and mutual interdependence they knew in their family-of-origin, while others join communal families to experience and help create a supportive environment they missed in their past. Communal families vary greatly in size, from three members to over ten. Most frequently, communal families have consisted of both sexes. Cohabitors are not usually found in communal families, although cohabitation may occur.

Successful communal living necessitates careful communication among the members. Rules and boundaries require negotiation and respect for such decisions. The cost of a large house or apartment, large quantities of food, maintenance, and heating may require that each family member or subsystem contribute money or work in an equitable manner. Communication in this family form depends on amicable equality and sharing. Rules jointly agreed upon have to be maintained over every issue from who can enter the communal family to how one can leave it, either voluntarily or by a vote to exclude. Seniority within the family may become part of the rules governing who heads the household or who gets the larger bedroom when a member leaves (De Mott, 1983, 26). Without careful communication about long-range goals and metacommunication about the group process, a communal family may dissolve.

Interviews of communal family members have indicated that the degree of separateness or connectedness the individuals feel affects the amount of cohesion within the household. Further, the emotional life both within the successful communal family and in the individuals changed toward more openness, cooperation, and consideration for others as the group stayed together (Brandwein et al., 1983).

If the members' ideals are too diverse, communication may be difficult. The communal family must establish some form of governance in order to survive. Power struggle between adults would require compromise, and inequality in individual resources can create problems in decision making. Individuals may leave their communal family when they decide to marry or cohabit. However, successful communes often include couples, some with children. Others include single parents, either fathers or mothers who received custody. These parents find the communal family helpful in sharing childcare. Communal living can be an excellent way for their children to have a relationship with opposite-sex adults who serve as role models, much like an aunt or uncle. The communal family represents a small percentage of American families with very specific communication issues and concerns.

Co-Parenting and Joint Custody

Before closing the issue of various family forms, we must recognize the growing relational style called *co-parenting*, an arrangement whereby divorced parents accept equal responsibility for care and maintenance of their children. Co-parenting can take on a variety of forms, but it means shared or joint custody, with the children living alternately with each of the two parents. Some couples have worked out weekend or every-other-night arrangements, or three or four nights with one parent and then an equal number with the other. Instead of separating the child, more or less permanently, via divorce from one parent, this arrangement enables the child to know and share time with each (Galper, 1978). Some children readily adapt to the two-home situation and, after a short time, prefer it. The following account describes such a working arrangement.

"In the year following the divorce, we continued to fight constantly over raising Mike. At school, Mike was constantly in trouble. As a father, I wasn't satisfied with an overnight visit on the weekend, and I kept running over to the house to see Mike before his mother returned from work. We worked out an every-other-night agreement, but this seemed to be too much moving back and forth for Mike. We switched to changing every three days and this suited everyone fine. Every other weekend I am free to date or entertain. Mike has his own room, clothes, and toys at each home, including a dog at mine and a cat at his mother's. Now Mike does well in school—when we settled down, he did, too."

Co-parenting requires cooperation and a commitment to the idea. It necessitates both parents' living close to one another, although some couples who have moved to different cities alternate school years. Both parents experience the joy and share the tribulations of childraising (Nehls and Morgenbessner, 1980, 117). Both parents assume active responsibility for the children.

Co-parenting requires a special skill in communicating between the parents, plus their new partners. They have to separate early their marital troubles from their parental roles in order for it to work. If the former spouse's communication remains conflictual, a child will be constantly in the middle of a war. Yet, if the parents can maintain open and supportive communication with each other, the child may experience two supportive environments. Nevertheless, the children must have the capacity to adapt to the functions of two different households. In remarried systems, stepparents must become heavily involved in the process if it is to succeed.

Joint custody has to be part of co-parenting, but many more families choose joint custody without the co-parenting dimensions. Co-parenting, by definition, includes shared physical custody, while joint custody may mean only shared legal custody, with each parent having an equal say in medical, religious, or educational concerns. Some partners fear that joint custody will open up old arguments and continue the dominance of one ex-spouse over the other or prevent them from moving or making decisions that best serve their interests and needs in the future.

Twenty-seven states now have joint custody laws. One study revealed that parents who share custody return to court less than half as often as couples in which one partner receives complete custody (Clausen et al., 1983, 44). Joint custody especially appeals to fathers who want to remain in close contact with their children and have more decision-making rights about their children's lives. Grote and Weinstein (1977) believe that joint custody is "an ideal solution and viable alternative that cries out for acceptance. Joint custody is viable and practical because it maintains the much needed familial structure in our society" (43). Joint custody works best when parents accept their past differences and decide that "the best interest of the children" is a goal worth cooperating to achieve (Scheiner et al., 1982, 105).

Successful co-parenting or joint custody requires the parents to work out an interactive "divorced relationship." Communication must be frequent and constructive, involving joint decision making and mutual support. Clearly, this involves effort and patience, but for many parents, it represents the best alternative for their children and, therefore, is worth the effort.

Due to the more limited range of role models for some of these forms, the successful development of families discussed in this chapter require extensive effort and mutual understanding on the part of the members involved. Without the ability to share information and feelings and to negotiate constructively, the stresses may lead to dissolution. Maintenance of the system depends on the actions of its members.

CONCLUSION

In this chapter, we developed a position stated earlier in this text—there is no one right way to be a family. Within these pages, we examined the concerns of the single-parent system, which may experience destructive pressure without appropriate economic, emotional, and social supports. We discussed the development of stepfamilies, the process of blending two systems, and the communication tasks inherent in this process. We presented an overview of the homosexual family, discussing the strengths and difficulties of this relationship and the communication skills needed by the members. Finally, we highlighted the areas of cohabitation, communal families, and co-parenting/joint custody and discussed their special communication concerns. Each of these family forms requires the conscious effort of members to communicate their needs and feelings during the development and maintenance of the family. In short, we are reminded of the effort it takes to create a family, of any form, that works.

IN REVIEW

1. How can society better handle the language concerns of various family forms?
2. What do you see as some communication-related differences between a single-parent system with three children and a two-parent system with three children?
3. Apply Papernow's model of stepfamily development to a real or fictional stepfamily, indicating: (1) experiences similar to or different from the model and (2) communication patterns indicative of certain stages.
4. Take a position and discuss: When children are involved, ex-spouses are divorced "to" each other rather than "from" each other.
5. What criterion would you establish for considering unrelated persons as a family?

Chapter 12

Family Ecology: Spatial and Temporal Dimensions of Communication

All families function in an environmental context of space and time, an aspect of family life that is frequently ignored. Yet, to fully understand familial interaction, we need to explore family relationships through the dual lenses of space and time. A discussion of the nonhuman aspects of the environment as they interface with the lives of family members will deepen our understanding of family communication.

> "Everyone in our family must be home between 6:00 and 7:30. Dinner is never until 7:00, and no one goes out before 8:00. The time before dinner is spent between the family room and the kitchen. This is the social hour. We usually discuss what has gone on during the day and what will go on that evening. We talk in groups of twos and threes. Mom is usually in the kitchen, Dad is in his chair, and the rest of us flow between the rooms. We all speak to each other at dinner. We have a big table with Dad and Mom at either end and the four of us in our specific seats. This conversation continues throughout the time it takes us to clean the kitchen. It is not unusual for us to sit in the kitchen and talk late into the evening. It is a special time, the time that we're all home, and the kitchen seems to be the best place for sharing to take place among all of us."

The following questions may stimulate your initial thinking about family relationships as they are affected by space and time:

1. Where did you go to talk to your parents about personal problems when you were younger? What time of day was best for this type of discussion? Were there rules about places for serious conversation?
2. How was dinner organized in your home? Did you all eat at the same time while sitting in specific places, or did you eat when you felt like it while sitting anywhere you chose? Were there certain rituals connected with particular meals?
3. Could you shut the door to your room to be alone? How long would you be alone before someone tried to get you back with the rest of the group?

If doors were closed, did you knock first or did you just open them and walk in? Did family members have special spaces which were theirs?

4. How were holidays celebrated in your home? Who was included? How did the house reflect the event?

5. As a small child, what were the safety boundaries around your home that you could not cross? A neighbor's yard? The apartment hallway? A road? How did this change?

6. What "family activities" existed in your home? What happened during these times? What percentage occurred inside the house? Outside the house?

These are some of the issues we will explore further as we view family interactions through spatial and temporal lenses and investigate the interaction between these nonhuman environmental factors and the interpersonal relationships within a family. We will see how cohesion and adaptability are affected by and affect these environmental forces. We will also explore how the environment contributes to a sense of family identity.

Advances in environmental psychology have led architects, designers, and social scientists to focus more directly on the nonhuman environment as a context for, and type of, communication. Just as the human environment creates verbal and nonverbal messages, the nonhuman environment constitutes a system of communication that is learned, socially read, and structured like language (DeLong, 1974). As you will see in the following discussion, we learn to react appropriately within particular dimensions of space and time because of the messages we receive from them.

Psychologist Scheflen (1971) suggests that hierarchical levels of social relationships, including parent/child and family relationships, provide and demand certain traditional patterns of task performance, spacing, speech, and body language, and each of these traditions dictates how we are to think and feel about every kind of situation. He maintains that these systems of behavior are organized spatially and temporally (429–30).

From our perspective, the environmental issues of space and time provide part of the boundaries that limit and define a family's experience and, hence, communication behavior. If you analyze the structures within which you relate to people, you will begin to understand how the structural design, arrangement of furniture and objects within the structure, and time of day or year within the structure can influence: (1) who interacts with whom, (2) where, (3) when, (4) for how long, and (5) the kinds of things about which they can communicate. In more concrete terms, certain family members are more likely to have greater interactions because they share a room, play basketball in the backyard, or sit up together for an evening cup of coffee. Whereas basketball games do not foster intense, deep conversations but provide shared positive experiences, talking in your room or at the kitchen table with one other person may lead to special and deep conversations and greater cohesion; it may encourage the airing of strong conflicts that result in greater distance, or possibly, greater closeness. Thus, the environment and the people in it combine to form a communication system.

Duncan (1964) stresses the interdependence of a way of life and its setting. Failure to respect this intrinsic wholeness is done "at the peril of overlooking the interrelations on which depend the stability of the system as a whole" (69).

Reiss et al. (1981) refer to space and time as two fundamental resources a family requires for conducting its day-to-day life. They propose that families are "strikingly different in their management of these two resources," and that these differences are crucial in how a family defines itself (233).

Communication occurs within a context, which influences what kinds of interaction can and will occur. Places, as well as people, form the context for communication events, and, although physical home or time patterns do not **determine** the kinds of family interactions that take place, they do **influence** interactions that occur both within and outside the home. Thus, we assume a family ecology viewpoint, which recognizes that the total environment has a strong impact on family development. The family and the environment interact and develop a mutual influence pattern; no family remains untouched by its surroundings.

ENVIRONMENTAL FACTORS

In this chapter, we will examine the environmental factors of space and time and then demonstrate how these interrelate with each other and affect communication within family systems.

Space

Anthropologist Hall (1966) conceptualized the ways in which we use space, including fixed feature space, semi-fixed feature space, and informal space (103–12). *Fixed feature space* refers to that physical space organized by unmoving boundaries, such as walls in a room or the unmarked line dividing space that is understood by those who use it. The latter may be called a nonphysical or psychological boundary. Each type serves as a recognizable boundary to which inhabitants must adapt. The actual wall between the kitchen and dining room may keep the cook out of the conversation. Such boundaries are obvious. Yet, if you shared a room with a brother or sister, you may remember the times that your side of the room and his or her side became separate territories, and you did not cross the line, drop things on the other bed, or sit in the other chair.

Semi-fixed feature space refers to flexible space created by the arrangement of furniture and/or other movable objects over which the inhabitants have control. You probably remember rearranging your room according to your moods or having to help rearrange the living room when one of your parents decided to foster conversations or to encourage interaction at a party.

Informal space deals with the way people handle their bodies or the spatial needs they carry with them that vary according to situations. Hall has divided the distances at which a person relates into four major levels: intimate space, ranging from zero to eighteen inches; personal space, ranging from eighteen inches to four feet; social space, including four to twelve feet; and public space, which encompasses interactions at distances over twelve feet.

Whereas "intimate space" encourages the nonverbal expression of such emotions and behaviors as hugging, kissing, tickling, lovemaking, wrestling, hitting, and whispering, "personal space" supports interpersonal discussions, decision making, and the sharing of emotions with some physical contact. Within "social space," small groups may engage in social or business conversations. "Public space" encourages short discussions or waves and greetings from a distance. Touch is not possible, but unique communication signs, such as a wink or a disapproving look, may travel between persons who know each other well.

Extensions of Hall's work in *proxemics,* the study of distance as a function of communication, have yielded some interesting variations. Lomrantz (1976) has demonstrated that proxemic rules vary with culture, while Tennis and Dobbs (1975) examined the effects of age and sex on interpersonal distance and found that distance increases with age, is greater in males, and increases more in males than in females as they age. Scott (1984) raises issues about the choice of location and comfort, and topic and distance, indicating the role of discomfort and the ways in which initial topics may set spatial distances for continued topics.

Territory. To understand the use of space, we must look at the related factors of territory and privacy. A basic concept in the study of animal behavior, *territoriality* involves "behavior by which an organism characteristically lays claim to an area and defends it against members of his own species" (Hall, 7). It provides a framework for doing things: places to learn, places to play, safe places to hide. Hall relates territory to the concepts of fixed feature space when he suggests, "The boundaries of the territories remain reasonably constant, the territory is in every sense of the word an extension of the organism which is marked by visual, vocal, and olfactory signs and, therefore, it is relatively 'fixed'" (9). For our purposes, family territory may be understood as an area that a member of a close-knit group in joint tenancy claims and will "defend." In other words, one stakes out real or imagined space and lays personal claim to it.

Scheflen maintains that those who own a territory or others who recognize it behave in particular ways as they approach the boundary, even if it is not marked by fences, walls, or other barriers. He suggests that small territories may be marked by postural behavior, such as an arm that defends a space or by the placement of possessions. Even unmarked boundaries can be noted by the behavior of people who cross them and "lower their heads, exchange at least a token kinesic greeting, and change their walking posture" (431). People defend their territory through verbal and nonverbal communication strategies, such as aggression or dominance.

Territory in a home may be as real as "my parents' room," or as nonphysical as "Mike's part of the yard." Places may be recognized as belonging to someone by decrees ("This is my chair"), by tenure ("I always sat there"), by markers ("We left our books here because we were coming back"), or by agreement ("After I've had the hammock for fifteen minutes, it's your turn"). If you think about your own home, you should be able to identify numerous territorial behaviors by which members declare their spatial demands. Some of these behaviors may also indicate a desire for privacy within certain space. Yet, without mutual agreement among those who believe the territory is "theirs" and other potential users, the concept of limited use may eventually disappear or conflicts about the use will arise.

Privacy. Privacy may be viewed as the "claims of individuals, groups, or institutions to determine for themselves when, how, and to what extent information about them is communicated to others" (Westin, 1967, 10). Privacy maintains an individual's need for personal autonomy, through which he or she can control the environment, including the ability to be alone or to have private communication with another. Some homes encourage such privacy while others cannot or do not. If you share a home with seven others and a bedroom with two others, privacy may be a luxury attained only outside the home. Yet, in certain households with ample physical space, privacy is restricted by family rules. Privacy and territory interrelate to provide the means of protective communication, such as the sharing of confidence, problems, and affection.

"My mother was fanatical about closed doors. If my door was closed, she would open it and say, 'We have no secrets in this house,' It drove me crazy. I couldn't even read a book or talk to a friend without leaving the door open. Now I encourage my kids to have a private place where they can be alone without someone else's bothering them."

As with space, territory and privacy are relative within and between cultures. In certain types of homes, personal places and possessions are held in high regard, whereas in others, total sharing is the norm. One gains privacy in some cultures by isolation, whereas in other cultures, psychological withdrawal permits privacy while among many people. In his study of urban families, Scheflen asked women, "What do you do when you want to be alone?" and discovered that one half of the Puerto Rican wives "did not comprehend the implication of the question in American middle-class terms. They said they never wanted to be alone . . . the other half said they went home to the family" (437). These women thought the researcher was asking about wanting to be away from neighbors and people in the street.

The interaction of the factors of space, territory, and privacy may be viewed through a discussion of the spatial model provided in *Inside the Family*. Family researchers Kantor and Lehr (1976) discuss certain spatial dimensions as a part of a family's mechanism for maintaining an ongoing system. Although their discussion covers physical space and the analogous regulation of ideas and events, we will concentrate only on their physical dimensions. They suggest that a family engages in bounding, linking, and centering as they live within a spatial dimension.

Through *bounding*, a family regulates physical traffic across its borders. A family demarcates a perimeter and defends its territory. It says, "This is ours, we are safe here" (68). It may defend these territorial borders through the use of devices to regulate entrance to the home. Buzzers, doormen, peepholes, bushes,

Private space encourages the development of personal autonomy.

and double locks all provide some privacy and daily control over the domain. Children may experience a designated territory, which is permitted for safe exploration. In housing projects, there may be no safety beyond the front door, so the boundary may be synonymous with the apartment. In other areas, a neighbor's yard or the road in front may be the limits.

Linking relates to the regulation of distance within the house. A large dining room table may encourage people to come together and may set up some interaction networks. Or, because an apartment is so small that everyone needs to eat and interact in the living room, members may retreat to their rooms to study or to "regain a sunny disposition." At a family party, teenagers may be channeled to the yard and basement while adults maintain their own conversations away from younger ears, everyone may interact together, or a variety of patterns may develop.

Centering relates to a family's ability to regulate space according to its values and beliefs. Thus, space reflects the family's view of itself and supports the values held by the members. There are family rules for how space is used (when one may go outside, who may be allowed in). There also may be specific ways of using things to keep the family in touch with each other. Blackboards, memo boards, and notes can keep a family in touch. Objects that remind a family of its identity and values, such as crucifixes, travel posters, or trophies, serve a centering function. Highly cohesive families may have stronger rules about family togetherness and how to achieve it within the home than families characterized by low cohesion.

Time

The way in which a family lives in time interacts with where it lives in space. Although we all function in the present, we may experience an orientation toward the past or future, which supersedes our lives in the present. Each person orients himself or herself to the past, present, or future. We all have met people who live in the "good old days" and whose communication reflects a respect for, or delight in, yesterday. A present orientation reflects a concern for the "here and now." Current relationships are valued and current joys and sorrows take top priority. In a present-oriented family, less time is spent reminiscing or planning than is spent on daily issues. A future orientation emphasizes what is to come. Planning, dreaming, or scheming characterize such a mind set and have typified many American families on their way to "the good life." Such orientations may be reflected in household furnishings, contacts with kin, patterns of friendship, attitudes toward money, and career planning (Reiss et al.). Time is a commodity, the use of which indicates much about a family's view of the world.

While orienting refers to an overall temporal perspective, *clocking* refers to the daily use of time. It regulates the order, frequency, length, and pace of immediate events. Certain family rules, such as who talks first in certain situations or who gets the last word, may be part of a subtle sequencing pattern. On a more obvious level, some families must establish functional rituals for moving into a day.

> *"In our attempt to maintain a two-career family with two small children, we have become very organized. We have very specific morning patterns so we can get out of the house on time and in a good frame of mind. I get up and start to make breakfast. My wife then gets out of bed, dresses, and starts to wake our daughters. When they come into the kitchen, I dress while Helen fixes the rest of breakfast. During the week, no one eats breakfast until he or she is dressed and ready to go. This way we can have a semi-peaceful morning, talk a little, and minimize the conflict."*

Families clock how often and for how long things may be done. Growing up, you may have experienced limits on how often you saw certain friends or how long you were allowed to argue with them before someone yelled, "That's enough." All families need some built-in repetition and guidelines to keep their lives functional. Clocking also refers to the speed with which a day is lived. Do you do fifty-two things and call it a "good day," or do you like to take things easy and maintain a slower pace? A family's pace may be related to Hall's characterizations of people according to their use of time: monochronic and polychronic. *Monochronic* people compartmentalize time. They schedule one thing at a time and become disoriented if they have to deal with too many things at once. *Polychronic* people tend to keep several activities going at once, perhaps because they are so involved with one another. Hence, one group comfortably separates activities, while the other tends to collect them (173). Although these characteristics are more likely to be related to an overall culture, certain points on the continuum between the extremes may characterize specific family members. Also, pacing varies with age, health, and mental state. Large variations in pacing often lead to conflict among family members.

An additional aspect of time involves *synchronization*, or the process of maintaining a program for regulating the overall and day-to-day life of a family. Often, this is done through discussions or assessments of how things are going and a setting or reaffirming of plans or priorities. Family members must integrate their individual schedules into an overall way of spending time. A spouse may turn down a position that requires a great deal of travel because it would keep him or her away from the family for too long. Another couple may agree to a long-term separation because a current commuter marriage would set the groundwork for a desirable lifestyle or professional growth in five years. Family discontent may lead to a reorganization of original priorities. Some families may establish respect for individual "clocks," whereas others may dictate a "family clock" to which everyone must adhere. Just as other factors are culture bound, the use of time varies according to culture. For example, American families may stress punctuality, whereas Latin-American families may not recognize this as a value.

Space and time are synchronized to some degree in families as members go about the patterned routines of their lives (Reiss et al.). There may be appropriate times for being alone and times when it is not permitted. Children may be allowed to play in adult spaces until an adult indicates that the space is taken. Holidays may require the presence of all family members in a particular space for a specified time, particularly if their themes stress such togetherness and if the images held by most are of a close-knit group that plays together. Biosocial beliefs interact with the ways in which time may be spent "legitimately" by males or females. The degree of synchronization may distinguish well-functioning families from those experiencing conflict and/or change. For example, collective activities cannot be planned because of disagreement about the plans, the values of approaches, and the commitment to the outcome. Thus, space and time are important dimensions of a family's communication context. In order to fully understand the interrelationships of these factors, we need to examine the family dwelling as a specific communication context.

THE HOME WORLD: OUTSIDE AND INSIDE

In our society, we sometimes use the terms "home" and "house" (or apartment) synonymously, although the terms may carry different meanings. Not all houses or apartments qualify as "homes." Many environmental scholars believe that a "person's concept of home is better understood as a *relationship* to such an environment, rather than the environment itself" (Horwitz and Tognoli, 1982, 335). Yet, we view the physical dwelling as an important factor in the development of a sense of home, which must be examined in conjunction with related environmental factors, such as the way in which time is used within it. Thus, we will examine the home environment to understand how it influences the family.

The house influences the interactions that occur within it, since its structure and design affect the development of relationships between and among family members. In his work on environment and interaction, psychologist Osmond (1970) has distinguished between sociofugal and sociopetal space. *Sociofugal space* discourages human interaction; *sociopetal space* supports it. ". . . Sociopetality is that quality which encourages, fosters, and even enforces the development of stable interpersonal relationships and which may be found in small face-to-face groups, in homes or circular wards" (576). Both the exterior and interior of a house and the way time is used within it can contribute to the creation of a sociopetal experience for the family.

Exterior Arrangement

A dwelling's exterior may affect the types of interactions family members have with the community at large and specifically with neighbors. Some studies of homogeneous populations indicate that housing planned for easy social interaction (such as doors opening on a common court or homes built around a cul-de-sac) promote neighborliness (Chilman, 1978, 108). A family with flexible boundaries in a safe territory that desires interaction with the community may choose to use the openings of a house to invite in the outside world. Neighborhood children may run through unlocked doors or friends may shout at the window or through the screened door. In some urban communities, the house may overflow to a porch, steps, or the street below where folding chairs extend the living room to the sidewalk. A less-scheduled, flexible family can make time for these distractions more easily than a family that runs on a tight clock or has little adaptability. In some cases, visitors may be welcome from dawn through dusk.

Housing Placement. Housing placement influences with whom you interact and therefore, to some extent, with whom you develop friendships. In a famous study, researchers Festinger, Schachter, and Beck (1950) examined the development of friendships in a new housing project for married students. This development consisted of apartment structures arranged in U-shaped courts with the two end structures facing the street. They were able to demonstrate the two major factors that affect friendship development: (1) distance between apartments and (2) the direction in which an apartment faced. Friendships developed more frequently between next-door neighbors and less frequently between persons who lived in apartments separated by more than four or five other apartments (156). The researchers also discovered that those who lived near the mailboxes, stairways, entrances, and exits tended to make more friends in the building, because they saw more residents regularly. If your front or back door leads into a heavily trafficked area, you have a greater chance of developing neighborhood relationships and becoming a central part of the communication network than if you live off the beaten track.

The Neighborhood. The surrounding territory may partially dictate a family's way of relating to the outside world. A planned community may expect certain social responses from its individual households; those who choose to live another life-style may find themselves ostracized. Dwellers in a particular community may have expectations for coffee klatches in each others' homes or participation in creating a float for the Fourth of July parade—activities that require space and time commitments. As families move from one home to another, a new community can partially influence their interactions.

We are witnessing a growth in planned communities, ranging from such highly structured communities as Reston, Virginia, to more informal communities that may result from a builder's conception of how a particular ten acres might be developed. Even some high-rise buildings attempt to foster a sense of community through the integration of stores, athletic facilities, and movie theaters into their overall construction plans.

Certain communities may prevent attempts at socialization or communication because the territory is "unsafe." Scheflen conducted a classic study of 1200 primarily black, Puerto Rican, and Eastern European families living in the East Tremont urban ghetto in upper Manhattan. He reported that within this area:

> A black teenager can often go out for the evening. But the Puerto Rican child may not even be allowed to go out of the apartment let alone the street or to a neighbor's house. The mother may consider any area outside the apartment to be dangerous, and often she is right.　　(437).

In St. Louis, Missouri, urban high-rise buildings in the Pruitt Igoe housing project were razed because of the dangerous conditions created by this type of housing. Life in "unsafe" territory is accompanied by many rules about whom not to talk to. Yet, even if you get to the street in such a territory, you may find that surrounding territories, a gang "turf," or a different ethnic ghetto can limit movement.

Certain territories encourage or permit particular behaviors. For example, a single family home may not encourage romantic behavior in teenagers due to the presence of other family members, but the car or a secluded hallway may provide the environment for such behavior.

"I observed a difference in the socialization process in my housing complex and the project building. My peers in the project stayed out much later and had more freedom to go places than those in the housing complex. They began to have sexual intercourse and children at an earlier age. I observed intimate behavior when I visited my friends, while on the elevator or walking up the stairs. The parents knew what their kids were doing and acknowledged the fact by trying to get them to use some type of birth control. They had boyfriends before my friends from the housing complex and I did and they began kissing early in grammar school."

An increasing architectural concern is the development of appropriate housing for the aged. A growing awareness exists of the need for elder housing that

(1) encourages social interaction and (2) stimulates participation in new activities (Jordan, 1984). Thus, buildings designed for senior citizens may have carefully designed eating or recreation areas and programs ranging from drama and exercise classes to intergenerational day-care experiences.

Creating Privacy. If a family values privacy, its dwelling, no matter what kind or size, may reflect this desire. Shrubs, doorbells, peepholes, locks, shades, and signs discourage casual approach. Architects have offered guidelines for maximizing privacy in order to encourage concentration, contemplation, and self-reliance. Some suggest achieving this through "careful organization of the plan of the dwelling, placement of windows to avoid surveillance, and the provision of a buffer zone or 'locks' at the entrance to private spaces" (Lennard and Lennard, 1977, 51). A family can create similar buffer zones or boundaries by turning off the phone, establishing rules or hours for visiting, and appearing not to have the time for interaction. Lack of availability sends a temporal message about the desire for limited interaction.

As a variation on the senior citizens' community, builders are examining an Australian concept of "granny flats," or elder cottages. These small, self-contained, mobile structures are designed for elderly people who want to "maintain their independence but . . . live next door to family or friends who can provide practical and emotional support" (Guion, 1984, 9). Such houses give privacy plus contact when desired.

Interior Arrangement

House interiors are organized spatially and temporally. Inside the house, the fixed and semi-fixed feature spaces stand as supports for or as barriers to communication. The interior design influences how much privacy can be attained and how easily members can come together. One way to view a house spatially is to start with the floor plan and determine the possible relationships that may or may not occur based on how space is arranged.

Rooms and Floor Plan. In his classic work on house design and interaction, architect Kennedy (1953) concerned himself with the "livability" of a house. He attempted to explain the types of living activities in relation to the public and private zones of a home. The more public zones provide great possibilities for social interaction, whereas the more private zones exclude persons from some or all interpersonal contact. Different areas of the home may be associated with specific family functions and hence, to the system and subsystem boundaries. Various levels and types of interaction are acceptable in different spaces, reflected in the range of highly interpersonal to highly private spaces. As you move through a home, the spaces may become more highly private to members, while persons outside the system or subsystem may be excluded from certain spaces. In many homes, there are spaces for interpersonal interaction with guests, close friends, and other family members. For example, in one family, visitors may have access to living, dining, and kitchen areas but may not enter the bedrooms under usual circumstances. In another family, there may be a formal living room for socializing or communicating with guests and a family room for relaxing and talking with members of the family. Some families establish clear spatial boundaries for nonmembers; others do not.

Member boundaries may vary also. Some families set rigid standards for privacy. In such cases, bathrooms and bedrooms are locked, and special possessions are concealed (Reiss et al.). On the other hand, you may come from a family where one person may be showering, the next brushing his teeth, and another urinating in the same small bathroom. Such variables as age, sex, culture, and family size all interact with the spatial dimension.

The actual floor plan can dictate which persons will have the greatest contact and, potentially, the greatest communication. If you share adjoining territories with your sister, you are more likely to communicate with her than with some other family members. If Mother spends large amounts of time in a particular territory (kitchen, study, studio), the people who use that or adjoining territories have greater access to her. If she spends more time in a central place, such as the kitchen, she is more likely to serve as a network hub.

"When my mother remarried, she married a widower with eight children, which meant that our family suddenly had twelve children, ten of whom lived at home. This led Mom and Grant to remodel the attic, where they created bedrooms on the second floor. This really determined the way relationships developed in the family. I didn't see much of the boys who stayed upstairs or who were out playing sports. Because we were on the same floor and always were in and out of each others' rooms, all the girls became really close, and some of us would sit up until 2:00 in the morning talking about people and things."

The size of a dwelling affects the distances between the people in it. Small apartments force greater contact than do large houses. Yet, even when space is held constant, families differ in their use of informal space. In his study of distance between interacting family members, Steinglass (1979) found average distance ranging from four to nine feet.

Space in some houses may discourage communication among family members. Although in previous generations children shared beds and rooms, many children today have separate rooms equipped for autonomous living. This may lead to a loss of experience in certain types of interpersonal encounters. While one room per child does give everyone privacy and a sense of self, the linkages between them may not occur. If each child has his or her own room and toys or even a television set and stereo, sharing and problem solving are avoided also. Thus, two children do not have to decide together, for example, which television show to watch, rather "You watch your show, I'll watch mine." Similarly, if a child and parent are at odds and the child has a nice setup in his own room, he can easily say, "I'm leaving. I'm going to my own room." That room then becomes an escape hatch when personal relationships falter (Kahn in Eshbach, 1976, 3). In certain large homes, no one may know if the others are home or what they are doing.

Yet, in many cases, small, cramped quarters result in difficulties or pressure. For example, a study of 200 families suggests that there is a marked difference in stress levels between families with one bathroom and families with a small half-bath in addition to the bathroom (Guenther, 1984). A new set of stresses befall a divorced parent when children visit, and the space adequate for one or two adults does not comfortably hold four or five. Families experiencing the "refilling nest" syndrome report stress as adult children return to live in a home which had been adapted in their absence. Many of today's families are attempting to integrate home and occupational spheres. Just as multiple simultaneous roles have been thought to be stress-producing for farm wives (Berkowitz and Perkins, 1984), the new rise of cottage industries and part-time work at home adds stress to family interaction.

Countless ethnic families have experienced stress due to crowding. Many Asian immigrants choose to sacrifice short-term needs for adequate shelter in hopes of providing professional career education for their children. Yet, the self-sacrifices can be great. The loss of familiar environmental and social support networks makes the family's functioning more difficult (Shon and Davis, 1983). Large families in Scheflen's East Tremont study lived in small apartments, and most of the time, everyone functioned in the living room. In the Puerto Rican families, all members remained in the living room either bundled together or divided between the TV area and conversational area. Few secrets or personal conversations occurred within these systems. Black women attempted to keep the living room as a parlor, although children usually had to be allowed access to it. If company arrived, the children were likely to be sent to play in a bedroom. Conversations were more likely to be separated for "appropriate ears." Often, an overlapping of space occurred in these cramped quarters so that space was scheduled to be used according to the time of day.

> In one Puerto Rican family breakfast occurred at a fixed time every day. Then father went to work, the children settled down to watch television, and Mother began a highly regular schedule of chores. In the afternoon a single visitor came, sat in a particular chair and talked with the mother. At noon each day the older children were allowed to go out for an hour. (These observations were made in the summer when school was not in session.) Then at a fixed time the mother cooked dinner, and the children ate in the living room. An hour later the father came home from work, sat at a small table in an alcove and had his supper served to him. Then Mother cleaned up and the family settled down for an evening in the living room before the television set. In this case the same sites were used by the same people each day, according to a regular schedule of household activities. (444)

In many homes, individuals or subsystems may have to plan for time and space to be alone. Sometimes it may be very structured, or sometimes it seems to occur naturally, as noted in the following contrasting situations:

"Growing up, there was a rule in our house that no one bothered our parents before 11:00 A.M. on Saturday. Their bedroom door was locked, and it was understood they were not to be disturbed."

"My parents still manage to have some privacy, although I don't know how, because their bedroom door has always been open to us day and night, and many times it serves as a place to go if you cannot sleep."

In each family, rules evolve for locking doors, opening drawers, reading mail, or using another's things. Sometimes status or liking can be understood by watching the access patterns within a household. Parents may have the right to invade privacy; babies may have access to places that are off limits to teenagers or vice-versa; or a favorite sibling may be able to borrow clothes, records, and money or use special space. Furniture arrangement may encourage or discourage particular types of interaction. Themes, images, and biosocial beliefs interact with spatial and temporal environments.

For many families, mealtime has specific rituals and is a communication event that takes place in a very specific spatial and temporal setting. A study of dinner time in middle-class families with small children revealed that dinner occurred in a dining room, dining area, or kitchen at a dinner table that was almost always rectangular. The formal eating territories were distinct.

> Within families the members sat in the same places at the table every evening. Among families, the only invariable positioning of family members at the dinner table was that the father occupied one side (the head of the table by himself). Mother's position could be either opposite him, or on his right or left. In about half of the families observed, the mother and father sat opposite each other at the table. . . . In over two thirds of our families the mother sat next to the youngest child in the family.   (Dreyer and Dreyer, 1973, 294–95)

Yet, in a different social/economic setting, things are done differently. Scheflen found that the average ghetto kitchen measured nine by twelve feet and held cabinets, closets, sink, stove, and refrigerator. If a table existed, it was small with two or three chairs pushed against the wall. Because there were no dining rooms, all the members of large families could not physically eat together, resulting in two major adapting patterns. Some members carried their plates to the living room and ate off their laps; some of the children were fed from a small children's table in the kitchen. In the middle-class family, mothers welcomed others into their domain, but in cramped quarters, a mother usually staked out the kitchen as her territory and would not welcome "intruders."

Furnishings and Decor.   Aside from layout, the furnishings and use of a home also influence communication. If you think about some homes in which you have lived or visited, you may remember the qualities that made them supportive of interpersonal interaction. There may have been arrangements of chairs or couches in the family room conducive to relaxed conversations. The kitchen or den may have been designed in such a way that you felt comfortable and relaxed enough to really talk. Perhaps you and your best friend were allowed the privacy and time to talk alone for hours in your bedroom. On the other hand, you have probably visited in homes with a cavernous living room with plastic furniture covers and you realized that the environment was working against meaningful communication. Scott has examined choice of living room seats for specific discussion topics with specific people. He found that ". . . both the topic and the indicated relationships of the person in the other chair were significantly related to distance between the chosen chairs" (35). Distance may not determine, but it does affect, communication.

Additionally, the quality of communication in a home may be enhanced by a decor that either stimulates conversation or represents an integral part of the family, which allows you to understand the inhabitants and talk about appropriate topics. Intriguing pieces of art, rock collections, matchbooks, family pictures, hunting rifles, or plants may provide the stimulus for good interaction. Certain items may lead you to the "core" of the family. Symbols of religion, ethnic heritage, hobbies, and family life may indicate what is important. The lack of such display may also make a statement. One home designer indicates, "People have begun to reexamine the role of possessions in their lives—the energies they take to maintain, the ways they may restrict one's freedom and out of this there's been a certain paring down, rather than a building up" (Murphy, 1984, 98D).

The aesthetic design of a room, lighting, and acoustics play their part in influencing communication. In the often-replicated beautiful-ugly room study by Maslow and Mintz, experimenters asked subjects to rate photographs of faces as they sat in a variety of rooms (beautiful, average, ugly) which were alike except for decor. The experimenters and subjects engaged in various escape behaviors to avoid the ugly room. The ugly room was variously described as producing "monotony, fatigue, headaches, discomfort, sleep, irritability, and hostility." In contrast, the beautiful room produced feelings of "pleasure, comfort, enjoyment, importance, energy and desire to continue the activity" (Knapp, 1972, 31). This correlates with Mehrabian's finding (1971) that people tend to be more pleasant in pleasant settings rather than in unpleasant settings (75–76). We do not mean to imply that you must grow up in beautiful and expensive surroundings in order to have good communication within the family. Pleasant surroundings can enhance relationships if they help people become comfortable and relaxed, but so many other factors intervene that environment cannot be seen as the single influencing factor. Some researchers go so far as to say that the quality of relationships is not really affected by the quality of habitat, except in extremely adverse conditions but that ". . . high satisfaction with home and community may ameliorate high dissatisfaction with mate or parent-child relationships" (Chilman, 1978, 106).

Family Fit and Environment

Probably one of the more interesting analyses of relationships between people and their home environments is the Lennard and Lennard delineation of the "fit" between the style of family interaction and the home environment: the isomorphic fit, complementary fit, and "non-"fit (58).

Isomorphic fit implies congruence between the family and its environment. It occurs when aspects of the environment are clear expressions of the family's identity, of the way the members relate, and of the way they see the outside world. Let us use the Cameron family as an example. The Camerons could be characterized as a generally cohesive and highly adaptable family with few intrafamily boundaries, who live by such themes as "We work hard and play hard" and "We stick together in the hard times." The Camerons (mother, father, four boys, and one girl) have bought a large, old farmhouse and have torn out some of the walls on the first floor to create more open space. The Camerons engage in outdoor activities together, and exhibit a rough-and-tumble style of interpersonal interaction. The farmhouse contains a large "mudroom" for skis and assorted sporting equipment. The large kitchen provides a place where the family can congregate when someone is cooking, or a number of people can be involved in a cooking operation at once. The family room is a place that invites informality and occasional wrestling matches. The house does not have a formal living room. The bedrooms are small, but since no one seems to spend time alone, it does not matter. The Camerons and their home fit well.

A *complementary fit* implies a balance of opposites among two or more aspects of a family's interaction and home environment. This kind of fit can reflect the complementary elements that exist within the family, or it can be consciously selected by a family in order to balance or counteract a special feature of family life. For example, the Muellers are a blended family with four teenagers (two from each former system) who tried their best to avoid one another when they first began their new life together. At that point in their development, interaction was difficult. The family was characterized by low cohesion and limited adaptability. Themes at this period reflected the lack of connectedness, such as "We don't get too involved." In the former family homes, each child had a large, well-equipped room to which he or she retreated whenever any discomfort arose. When the families merged, the parents purposefully invested in a townhouse with fewer, smaller bedrooms. This forced the two boys to room together and all four young people to spend time in common areas, such as the attractively furnished family room. The parents consciously selected a home-style that was complementary to the life-style that had evolved in their former homes.

The *"non"-fit* category includes those homes that are unsuited to the family's interaction pattern. Obviously, most lower-income housing falls into this category, since many families are trying to fit large numbers of people into a few tiny rooms that cannot hold them comfortably. Yet, this style need not apply just to families economically unable to afford larger housing. When the Morris' married, they decided not to have children. During their early thirties, they built their "dream house," a wood and glass structure with such features as cathedral ceilings, an open walkway across the top of the living room, open stairways, and a small kitchen with a breakfast bar for all their meals. Their life was characterized by a belief that "We are complete as a couple," and their energies were directed toward cultural and educational pursuits. As they approached forty, they rethought their decision regarding children, and at age thirty-nine, Sharon Morris brought home a baby girl to the "dream house." During the next few years, the Morris family and the house entered a non-fit stage. The unrailed walkway across the living room became a dangerous bridge, and their daughter could not be left alone on the second floor. She fell off the stairs many times. The lack of a regular dining area became a problem. The dream house now has gates, railings, plexiglass panels, and other odd additions.

The concept of fit also applies to how families use time. An isomorphic fit characterizes a family that functions according to a particular orientation and clocking pattern, which reflects that family's values. The Breznehan family consists of a father and three school-age children. Their world involves, among other things, swimming, baseball, and soccer, along with orthodontist visits and newspaper routes. This is a present- and future-oriented group of people who can adapt to tight schedules and fast pacing. Gus Breznehan's schedule is flexible, and he can adjust it relatively easily. Since family priorities include getting ahead and self-improvement, this life-style is consistent with group goals.

Grant and Jean Foster are a couple whose jobs take them to exciting places, and whose pace of life never slows down. They place great priority on their marriage and value a connected interpersonal relationship, believing that "Together we can cope with whatever life deals us." Yet, they became afraid that this hectic, work-oriented life-style could destroy their relationship unless they created a retreat for being together. Scorning a fashionable high-rise condominium, they bought a large, old farmhouse in a growing suburban area and dedicated themselves to redoing the home in precise historic fashion and to cultivating large flower and vegetable gardens. Except when Jean travels, they spend most of their personal time at a slower pace and in a past orientation to consciously counteract the hectic, present-oriented pace of their daily lives. They have created a complementary style of living with time for their personal hours.

A small baby has thrown the McConnell family into a temporary non-fit situation. As a two-career, sociable couple with good positions, they had planned a life-style in which each person would take equal responsibility for the baby, whom they expected to take to many social functions. Five months into parenthood, they became totally frustrated trying to share responsibilities, because Tim's job requires that he stay late for meetings and Myra's real-estate position requires her to drop everything and run when a potential buyer wants to talk. Although Melissa is a healthy baby, she gets fussy and seldom sleeps through the night. She cannot be taken easily into adult social situations. Thus, each parent needs more ability to live in the present and according to the baby's schedule. Each also needs time to do more around the house.

You can see the need for an integration of the spatial and temporal needs of a family with each other and how some people can integrate these with their levels of cohesion and adaptability for a comfortable fit, while others have real difficulty.

A past-oriented family may take great pleasure in remodeling a large, old home. Such people may enjoy investing the effort in order to live in a home that represents a previous era. Another family who loves to participate in sports may choose an apartment that does not require much maintenance or care, thus freeing the family to engage in their activities. At other times, people have to make some drastic changes in order to alter their spatial and temporal milieus. Thus, we may find fits that indicate certain aspects of our lives are well integrated, or we may find ourselves in fits that we wish to change.

CONCLUSION

In this chapter, we have examined the family environment, which creates its own communication modality. Each family uses space and time as major pattern regulators affecting who interacts with whom, where, when, for how long, and about what. A consideration of family ecology leads us to conclude that a relationship exists between family members' communication and the spatial/temporal world in which the family functions.

Yet, other factors also influence every communication act. A big, new house may lessen but not solve all a family's conflictual problems unless new negotiating behaviors also accompany the move to larger quarters. Slowing down the pace by eliminating activities may have a limited effect on relationships unless the new lifestyle includes positive interpersonal messages and activities for people to share within the more or less frantic world. Large families in small apartments have the capacity to develop strong nurturing relationships, just as a co-parenting situation does not mean that the quality of a mother-daughter relationship needs to be cut in half. Unlimited time together has the potential to enhance a relationship, but the quality of the interactions will finally determine the nature of the relationship. Lennard and Lennard explain this issue as one of control: "To the extent that the interrelationships between a family and its environment are made explicit, the family's area of freedom and control is enlarged" (49–50). Awareness of these factors can help you begin to alter or modify your spatial/temporal environment to enhance your relationships. Spatial and temporal factors can only create an atmosphere conducive to nurturing family communication. It is up to the people involved to carry through.

IN REVIEW

1. Take a position and discuss: How significantly does the physical environment affect family interaction patterns?
2. Describe how the cultural dimensions of space and/or time has affected the communication patterns in a real or fictional family.

3. Using the floor plan of a home found in a magazine or newspaper ad, predict how this floor plan might affect the interaction patterns of a family who lived there.
4. Using a real or fictional family, describe the spatial and temporal "fit" between the family and its environment. If possible, cite implications for the family's communication patterns.
5. Take a position and discuss: To what extent should communities support the development of restrictive housing, i.e., housing excluding children or for senior citizens only?

Chapter 13

Improving Family Communication

What do you do if you are not satisfied with the way your family functions? To what extent can family members create new patterns, develop different ways of loving, fighting, or making decisions? Up to this point, we have discussed a primarily descriptive view of issues related to family interaction, while stressing the importance of communication in building family relationships. We will now examine the process of conscious family change.

Since families are human systems, they have the potential to grow and change in desired directions, although such growth may require great effort, pain, and risk. The systems perspective implies that whenever change is attempted by some members, it will be resisted by the other members who wish to keep their system in balance. It is difficult, although not impossible, for an individual to initiate change in the system. Change is more easily accomplished when most or all members are committed to the desired alternative way of relating.

There is no "one right way" for all families to behave—the members of each family have to discover what works well for their system. Communication may be considered the cornerstone for changing family systems. Hopefully, families develop flexible communication patterns that support the growth of the system and its members.

The communication behaviors learned within a family-of-origin will greatly influence a person's future relationships, particularly his or her family and friend relationships. These communication patterns tend to pass from generation to generation unless they are consciously changed.

Finally, we recognize that our own biases prevent us from being purely descriptive in our discussion of family interaction. Our personal and professional beliefs have been reflected in the previous pages and will be even more obvious in this chapter on change. One of our most firmly held beliefs is that families have the potential to change and improve their interaction patterns.

"In my own marriage, my wife and I have been using two mechanisms to serve as a kind of check-up on our marital relations. First, we have learned to communicate

both the negative and the positive feelings we have. Periodically, we sit down together with no outside distractions and, while maintaining eye contact, express our innermost feelings. Another check we use is the presence of a third party (who is a close friend) in a dispute when we are unable to settle it ourselves. This third party has been able to point out to us behavior of which we were unaware.''

Throughout the book, we have focused on healthy, or functional, families rather than dysfunctional, or severely troubled, families, recognizing that every functional family has its low as well as its high periods. Yet, we must be careful not to dichotomize functional/dysfunctional or healthy/unhealthy in an either-or manner. We must think of families on a continuum, even though our language refers to them in ways that sound less flexible. In this chapter, we will examine (1) some of the factors that characterize functional families and (2) approaches for developing and maintaining desirable communication within families. These will include personal, educational, and therapeutic approaches.

THE FUNCTIONAL FAMILY

As we noted earlier in this text, equifinality implies no one definition or description of a functional family; instead, functional families take on various styles with certain similarities. As you have participated in and observed families over the years, you have probably found some that appeared to work well. People in them seemed to "have it all together." Yet, each of these functional families probably had differences as well as similarities in the way members related to each other.

General Views

In this section, we will highlight the thinking of a number of family experts on the well-functioning family. Each expert reflects his or her own professional and personal orientation to family life, as evidenced by the emphasis given to different topics.

One way of interpreting successful family functioning is to understand its position on the circumplex model, which assesses the family's cohesion and adaptability (Figure 1–1, p. 16). These researchers have indicated that families at different stages of development seem to function better in different areas of the model (Olson and McCubbin, 1983). For example, young couples without babies function best in either the upper right- or lower left-hand quadrants. Adolescents function best in the central, or balanced, area; older couples relate best in the lower right-hand quadrant (237). This means that young couples without babies would be found at the high end of the cohesion/adaptability scale or in the lower opposite side with lower cohesion and adaptability. It may seem contradictory, but young couples seem to be either highly cohesive and enmeshed or rather disengaged and low in cohesion and adaptability, with possibly numerous ties to their old friends and families-of-origin at this point in their new marriages. Adolescents function best when they have average cohesion, being neither enmeshed with parents or disengaged, and when their adaptability is midway between rigidity and chaos. Obviously, these results indicate adolescents' needs for a family system without threats or rigid rules. Older couples function best when cohesion is high but adaptability is low—more rigid. Older family members need the closeness of family ties and so, give up their adaptability, accepting and adopting more rigid boundaries on their lives.

Although results may differ for families from particular backgrounds or ethnic origins, these findings help us maintain a flexible attitude toward well-family functioning.

Satir (1972) maintains that untroubled and nurturing families demonstrate the following patterns: " . . . self-worth is high; communication is direct, clear, specific, and honest; rules are flexible, human, appropriate, and subject to change; and the linking to society is open and hopeful" (4). In other words, she sees that untroubled families contain people who feel good about themselves, level with each other, function within a flexible system of rules, and whose boundaries are flexible enough to permit extensive contact with new people and ideas.

In addition to understanding Satir's values, including leveling, or direct, open communication, it is important to recall our discussion of the curvilinear self-disclosure model (Figure 4–3, p. 83), which suggests that totally honest communication can be handled in the unique cases where mutual high self-esteem, risk, commitment, and confirmation exist. Such communication may not be possible or desirable for every family.

In his description of functional vs. dysfunctional families, therapist Stachowiak (1975) identified four factors of family effectiveness: (1) family productivity or efficiency, (2) leadership patterns, (3) expression of conflict, and (4) clarity of communication (70). Stachowiak also emphasized the importance of family adaptability. In his study of families performing small-group tasks, he found that adaptive families reached many more group decisions in the allotted time period than did maladaptive families. Members of adaptive families "tend to emit many short speeches over a given period of time, while members of maladaptive families tended to emit fewer but longer speeches . . ." (70). Negotiation was more difficult in the latter group.

Painful conflict patterns characterized maladaptive families, whereas functional families tended to have the resources to deal with and resolve issues. Finally, Stachowiak found that maladaptive families were likely to perform behavior that avoids direct communication (turning away or avoiding eye contact), and maladaptive families had more "general speeches" (conversation not directed at any family member) than did adaptive ones. Thus, the patterns described by Satir appear reinforced by this indication that functional families are more likely to be characterized by flexibility and clarity of communication.

Yet, there are other ways of characterizing the functional family. In his comprehensive review of concepts of healthy family functioning, Barnhill (1979) isolates eight dimensions of family mental health that can be grouped according to four major areas. You will see some direct similarities between his conclusions and those of Satir and Stachowiak. Barnhill's eight dimensions of healthy family functioning can be grouped into the basic family themes:

I. Identity Processes
  1. Individuation vs. isolation
  2. Mutuality vs. isolation
II. Change
  3. Flexibility vs. rigidity
  4. Stability vs. disorganization
III. Information Processing
  5. Clear vs. unclear or distorted perception
  6. Clear vs. unclear or distorted communication
IV. Role Structuring
  7. Role reciprocity vs. unclear roles or role conflict
  8. Clear vs. diffuse or breached generational boundaries   (96)

Barnhill stresses the importance of gaining a sense of self through individuation and mutuality. For him, *individuation* refers to "independence of thought, feeling, and judgment of individual family members" which involves "a firm sense of autonomy, personal responsibility, identity and boundaries of the self" (95). In a family where members have a sense of their own competence and believe they can make their own decisions, people are more likely to allow others the freedom to be themselves. Self-worth tends to be high when family members feel they can express their individuality within the system.

Mutuality involves a sense of intimacy or emotional closeness that occurs between two individuals with clearly defined identities. If members become enmeshed, they cannot be separate enough to experience being close, because the fusion is too powerful. Likewise, if two people are isolated from each other, they will remain disengaged. A daughter drawn into a parent-child conflict to the extent that she feels the conflict as if she were her mother experiences extreme enmeshment. A child totally isolated from her parent's interactions may experience a sense of great disengagement. Think about the difficulties you have seen in families where everyone is expected to be part of everyone else's business; it is hard to grow up in such a system. Likewise, in families where members are ignored or abandoned, healthy individual growth is painful. Thus, these criteria relate to a family's capacity for adaptation.

Healthy family members can accept and deal with the inevitability of change yet maintain consistencies that provide security and responsibility. Barnhill suggests that flexibility and stability succeed where rigid responses deny the need for change (95).

"My grandmother has always sworn that my sister looked just like her daughter, Lorraine, who died at sixteen. She has tried to replace her daughter with her first granddaughter in the hopes of reviving a communication pattern that once existed but now is gone. Yet, my sister Lori has had to fight this distorted perception all her life, and her communication with Grandma is very confused."

Such communication may be reflected in members' inability to check out their perceptions and to metacommunicate, that is, to talk about their communication. Clearer perceptions and communication permit them to deal with conflict and intimacy openly and honestly.

People in healthy families tend to make conscious or unconscious agreements about their role relationships. Those in complementary roles appear comfortable with those role definitions that emerge through interaction. Additionally, appropriate generational boundaries are respected. Children are not co-opted into parent roles; in-laws are not enmeshed with the marital couple. Clarity of generational boundaries contributes to appropriate role development.

When you look at Barnhill's dimensions, you can see that each of these eight factors are interrelated. For example, clear communication facilitates role reciprocity; individuation facilitates clear generational boundaries. According to Barnhill, Satir, and Stachowiak, communication is a central factor in healthy family functioning. These therapist-scholars stress the need for clear, flexible, and open communication among family members.

In his systemic research on family competence, Beavers (1976) views families on a continuum of functioning, ranging from severely disturbed, to midrange, to healthy. He details each of these continuum locations in terms of five major areas: power structure, degree of individuation, acceptance of separation and loss, perception of reality, and affect. His data suggest that families with adaptive, well-functioning offspring have a structure of shared power, great appreciation and encouragement of individuation, and ability to accept separation and loss realistically. Additionally, they have a "family mythology consistent with the reality as seen by outside observers, a strong sense of the passage of time and the inevitability of change, and a warm and expressive feeling tone" (80). Beavers describes healthy families as "skillful interpersonally" and with members who can participate in and enjoy negotiation; respect views of others; share openly about themselves; see anger as symptomatic of necessary changes; view sexual interest as positive; establish meaningful encounters outside the family system. He found that the most effective families use humor, tenderness, warmth, and hopefulness to relate. Family members make negative feelings known but do so with a keen awareness of whom or what they dislike. Also, they are supportive while doing so. Effective families more readily recognize their conflicts, deal with them promptly, and find solutions quickly (79).

In his later work, Beavers (1982) holds that well-functioning families consciously operate from a systems orientation, characterized by a flexible position on human behavior. We discussed this concept in detail in Chapter 2 (page 27).

In a survey of professionals in family-related areas, Curran (1983) found "the ability to communicate and listen" selected most frequently as an indicator of family health. She lists these hallmarks of a family who communicates well:

1. Parents demonstrate a close relationship;
2. Parents have control over TV;

3. All family members can listen and respond;
4. Family recognizes and values nonverbal messages;
5. Family respects individual feelings and independent thinking;
6. Family avoids turn-off and put-down phrases;
7. Family members interrupt, but equally;
8. Family processes disputes into reconciliations.   (55)

We will summarize this academic look at healthy families with a conclusion drawn by Gantman (1980). She contends that the well-functioning family:

> . . . demonstrates high levels of efficiency in behavior and decision making. Healthy family members are supportive, expressive, and communicate in noisy, discontinuous speech patterns. The power structure of the family is well defined with father as the most frequent leader. The generational boundaries are clear. Members demonstrate respect for each other's uniqueness. There is an adaptive mechanism to cope with disequilibrium without requiring a rigid hierarchy or return to a status quo.   (118)

Before leaving this area, we will examine the perceptions of a different type of family analyst. In her book, *Families*, journalist Howard (1978) presents another conception of functioning families. The author has traveled across the country, interviewing the members of various types of family systems (two-parent biological, blended, single-parent, and extended, including social, racial, and sexual variations) in an attempt to understand what makes them work well. In her conclusion, she lists the general characteristics of what she calls "good" families (241–45):

1. Good families have a chief, heroine, or founder—someone around whom others cluster. Such a person may appear in different generations, but somehow this figure or figures set an achievement level that inspires others.

"I grew up in an extended family with my grandparents and great-grandparents. Although there was no one living in the base household while I was growing up, many of the family members had lived with the dominant figures at one time or another. My great-grandmother was very special. Everyone in the family loved and respected her and we would sit for hours listening to how she and our great-grandfather started their lives together with nothing in a strange city. She has always been someone I looked up to."

---

2. Good families have a switchboard operator—someone who keeps track of what the others are up to. This person also may be the archivist who keeps scrapbooks or albums that document the family's continuity.

3. Good families are much to all of their members but everything to none. Links to the outside are strong, and boundaries are not so tight that people cannot become passionately involved in nonfamily activities.

4. Good families are hospitable—there are surrounding rings of relatives and friends who are cared about and supported, just as they serve as the family's support system and as extended family members in many cases.

5. Good families deal directly with problems. Problems and pains are not avoided in hopes they will disappear. Communication is open. Countless rules do not exist to restrict touchy or painful topics of conversation; people level with each other directly.

6. Good families prize their rituals. These may be the formal traditions of Passover, Christmas, birthdays, funerals, or the informal ones unique to the individual family or clan—the annual Fourth of July picnic or St. Patrick's Day party that becomes a unifying ritual to the people involved.

7. Good families are affectionate and willing to demonstrate and share that affection with other family members. Children learn this pattern of affection from their first moments.

8. Good families have a sense of place—a sense of belonging that may be tied to a specific geographic location or to the mementos that make a house a home for specific individuals—the old dining room table, the Hummel figures, or the photographs that declare "This is home." You may find comfort in being a Bostonian or Iowan, or you may carry with you important pieces of your life that symbolize roots and family connectedness.

9. Good families find a way to connect to posterity. For many, this involves having children; for others, it means becoming involved in a sense of the generation—connecting to the children in some way.

"My husband and I decided that we did not want to have children of our own, but we realized that we would miss out on a very important area of life through the decision. So, we decided to consciously put children in our lives in other capacities. Although our sisters are many states away, we have become 'aunt' and 'uncle' to some of our friends' children and enjoy the pleasures of spending a good amount of time with them and participate in the usual childhood rituals—birthday parties, confirmation, etc. These children have become a very important part of our lives."

---

10. Good families honor their elders. The wider the age range, the stronger the clan. This may involve biological or "adopted" grandparents and vice versa, but strong families have a sense of generations.

Many mobile two-parent biological families have attempted to gain contact with the older people through intergenerational church or community groups which encourage the building of three- and four-generational communities of caring people.

As you read these descriptive and prescriptive views on well-family functioning, what is your personal reaction? Are these views too idealistic or too culture specific? What characteristics would you defend as critical to well-family functioning? In the next section, we will discuss your authors' personal reactions to these issues.

Author Views

We will close this section by presenting some of our beliefs about the healthy family, based on our concern for communication within such a system. In order to do this, we return to the issues introduced in earlier chapters. A healthy family recognizes the interdependence of all members of the system and attempts to provide for growth of the system as a whole, as well as the individual members involved. Such families develop a capacity for adaptation and cohesion that avoids the extremes of the continuum but changes over time, reflecting the course of external and developmental life events.

Members of functional families are joined to the system yet able to differentiate themselves from their families; changes are incorporated into the system's life. These basically flexible and cohesive families have themes, images, boundaries, and biosocial beliefs consistent with their position on the adaptability/cohesion axes. Such families also work to uncover and understand their themes, images, boundaries, and biosocial beliefs (although they may not use those terms for such characteristics) so as to consciously accept or modify them. Such families value open, clear, and caring communication; understand that they can change their system's communication patterns; and consciously strive to improve their communication so as to promote acceptable levels of intimacy and to modify unhealthy conflict. Such families are willing to take risks in order to grow.

We have been influenced by the experience of counseling families. We repeatedly see families who lack the necessary communication skills to negotiate their difficulties. Recurring themes, boundaries, and rules from couples' families-of-origin interfere with their present relationships. Often, our task involves helping family members sort out both the values and weaknesses of past experiences and learn how they can use these in combination with the resources in their own family.

Family systems need constant and consistent nurturing. In most families, day-to-day routines overwhelm members' lives, resulting in primarily functional rather than nurturing communication patterns. Families can profit from taking time to ask, "How are we doing as a family?" and "How could we improve our communication?" In the following section, we will examine several approaches for doing just that.

APPROACHES FOR IMPROVING FAMILY COMMUNICATION

"My husband and I are team leaders for the Jewish Marriage Encounter, and we keep trying to tell our friends that every marriage should have an 'annual checkup.' People spend thousands of dollars on 'preventative maintenance' for their cars, teeth, bodies, and homes, but how much do we spend either in dollars, effort, or time to have a marital examination? Too often in attempting to get couples to attend

> *an Encounter weekend, I am told, 'Our marriage is OK' or 'We don't need to go on any weekend, as we have no problems.' I am both angry and sad at such blindness, stupidity, and fear. There is not a marriage existing that does not have some problems, and if they are not attended to, they will get bigger."*

If you believed that communication in your family could be improved, what would you do about it? Or, if this has already occurred, what did you do? Would you be willing to talk about the difficulties with other family members or to participate in a structured improvement program? As we saw in the last two chapters, a family goes through predictable developmental stresses and unpredictable external stresses, which affect the system's well-being, but often, members do not know how to help themselves deal with the difficulties.

Concern for family issues appears widespread in all areas of society, resulting in the growth of preventive approaches designed to aid family members before things really fall apart. A walk through a local bookstore reveals many books and magazine articles on improving your marital or family life. There are checklists, rules, and prescriptions for family meetings, intimate vacations, and constructive conflict. Most of these prescriptions contain some directives about improving communication among family members. Many appear as a panacea, a pill which, once taken, will miraculously transform the withering relationship into a happy, healthy, and functional one. Seen in this light, they are doomed to fail. Yet, many Americans have found relational growth and change through certain marital or family enrichment approaches, which are carefully designed and involve motivation and effort on the parts of the participants.

During the course of your lifetime, you may have participated in family meetings, marriage enrichment programs, or family therapy sessions. These activities represent the varieties of approaches available to family members who wish to improve communication within the system. We will now examine a continuum of approaches, ranging from the more personal to the instructional, and finally, to the therapeutic for families experiencing dysfunctional communication. Most of the individual and instructional approaches are designed for functional couples or families who wish to enrich their relationships.

Personal Approaches

> *"When my own marriage was falling apart, I found the most necessary ingredients in turning things around were desire and work—on both our parts. I clearly remember the night I made two decisions. First, I really wanted to keep our marriage, and second, I was willing to do anything to make it work. My wife had seen more value in the marriage all along, so when I shared these feelings with her, we both committed ourselves to creating a new relationship. The intense part of this struggle took over two years, and without this deep desire and belief that we could make it, I never would have been able to continue working over such a long period that was such a painful part of my life."*

Do you believe that a couple or family can deal with their communication problems on their own? Many individuals have consciously set out to change their communication with other family members. Many couples or whole family systems have tried to change old, dysfunctional communication patterns. Many of these endeavors reflect a personal approach in which system members embark on the process without significant active outside support.

In some homes, husbands and wives attempt to identify recurring, potentially upsetting "trouble spots" in their relationship and to plan how to avoid them. They may come to recognize points in their lives when intimacy or conflict is too threatening; this knowledge helps them reconcile their differences.

Other couples practice their own rules for fair fighting, perhaps constructed through an agreement never to hurt each other badly. They may agree to avoid gunnysacking and physical abuse. They may struggle to restate the other's position or to find areas of compromise. They may be willing to return to an issue later when some of the emotion has worn off. Parents may force themselves to develop new vocabulary when dealing with children, reflected in the use of "I" statements rather than blaming "you" messages, or to share their feelings when objective analysis would be more comfortable but less effective.

In-laws may restrain themselves from asking questions that could be considered meddling, while children may refrain from "answering back," even though the temptation is very great. Family members may seek quality time together to eat, sing, ride bikes, or just talk. A couple may attempt a second honeymoon. Father and son may find a mutual hobby or discussion area of joint interest.

You may wonder "How do these things start?" In some systems, one or more members have a nagging feeling or definite belief that things could be different. They may compare themselves to other families and see something lacking. They may encounter new ideas or models for relationships through the media, friends, or religious and educational figures. Then, they take the risk of trying out new behaviors and evaluate their effectiveness. If only one member attempts to change the system, he or she is likely to meet with strong resistance.

In the next few pages, we will describe some examples of personal approaches taken by couples or families who attempt to change their system on their own.

Couple-Oriented Approaches. The "checkup" stands as an important concept in relational enrichment. In their well-known work, *Mirages of Marriage*, Lederer and Jackson (1968) call for marital checkups, saying, "It seems to us that marriages deserve the same care and attention given our bodies, or our automobiles" (358–59). Such preventive work can keep couples from destructive relationship patterns and keep spouses in close communication with each other. The authors suggest that checkups can be done by individual appraisal (least desirable), joint evaluation, or through work with a caring third party (nonprofessional). Checkups may also be accomplished with a professional counselor.

Lederer and Jackson provide another major concept that may be used in conjunction with the checkup—the *quid pro quo.* "*Quid pro quo* literally means 'something for something.' In the marriage process it means that if you do so-and-so, then I automatically will respond with such-and-such" (178). It implies reciprocal behavior, which may be unconscious. *Quid pro quo* recognizes the efforts of both partners to be peers and provides a technique enabling both parties to communicate and maintain their self-esteem. Most couples have an unspoken *quid pro quo*, which becomes a set of ground rules but which, when broken, results in marital conflict. Couples need to recognize their *quid pro quo* and to consciously bargain with each other for fulfillment of individual needs. Ideally, spouses reach a level of negotiation whereby " . . . each has those things which are most important to him and at the same time tries to nourish the well-being of the other to the maximum extent" (286). In short, rewards are gained by both.

The *quid pro quo* approach suggests that couples set aside weekly sessions of an hour each devoted solely to the specific bargaining process. These sessions are designed to help each spouse really hear what the other is saying. Spouses learn to listen, to take directions, to develop effective questioning skills, and finally, to bargain constructively with each other. Eventually, a couple reaches the point of exchanging "viewpoints about what each feels is necessary to determine the extent to which these aims are compatible, and to decide what can be done about them" (301).

Such approaches as the "checkup" and the *quid pro quo* represent only two of many methods for working on a marriage. Self-help books provide hundreds of experiential communication approaches for couples to use as they attempt to improve their relationships. Some couples will set aside one time each week or each month to "check in" on how they are doing. They may stay home, go out for coffee, or meet for lunch—but the topic discussed is their relationship. Other couples form or join informal growth groups focused on marital or family issues.

"We have belonged to a couples group within our church for four years now and have found it has brought us closer to each other. The group of five couples functions as a support system for the individuals. People are free to bring up their problems in parenting, or in relating to spouses or to our own parents. By listening to other people's problems and hearing how they deal with situations, we are learning to relate to each other more effectively."

Family-Oriented Approaches. In addition to couple-oriented self-help methods, approaches exist for whole families, the most common of which is the family meeting, or family council. Growing up, you may have participated in some variation of this approach. A family council may be defined as "a meeting together, as a group, to attempt to solve democratically problems which affect one or more members, or which affect the group as a whole" (Weaver and Mayhew, 1959, 72–73).

In their early study of family councils, Weaver and Mayhew found that most families did not meet regularly; half held meetings at the request of the children, and half indicated they required attendance. Ninety percent of the parents indicated that they "sometimes" followed through on the decisions made in council; only 8 percent said they always did. Although almost all used democratic procedures and two thirds attempted to teach democratic procedures by direct instruction, only a few were willing to be bound by the decision made in the council (73). The families reported the council most useful for issues of household duties, allowances, purchases, and vacations. Although many family meetings are rather informal affairs, there have been attempts to establish much more structured family gatherings.

Rudolf Dreikurs (1964) is known for his work in *family councils*—meetings of all members of the family in which problems are discussed and solutions sought. He recommends that councils be established formally as an ongoing part of family life. A definite hour on a definite day of the week should be set aside for this purpose; it should become part of family routine. Every member is expected to be present. According to Dreikurs, should one member not wish to come, that person must still abide by the decision of the group. Therefore, it pays for him or her to be present to voice an opinion. The principles of family councils include:

> Each member has the right to bring up a problem. Each one has the right to be heard. Together, all seek for a solution to the problem, and the majority opinion is upheld. In the Family Council, the parents' voices are no higher or stronger than that of each child. The decision made at a given meeting holds for a week. After the meeting, the course of action decided upon takes place and *no further discussion* is permitted until the following meeting. If at that time it is discovered that the solution of last week did not work out so well, a new solution is sought, always with the question "What are we going to do about it?" And again, it's up to the whole group to decide! (301–2)

Such experiences provide children with practice in discussion and decision making, which may prove extremely valuable in later family life. Obviously, many families attempt to join together for more than solving problems.

The Mormons' Family Home Evening is probably the most well-known family meeting program. Established in the late 1950s, the program requests Mormons to set aside Monday evenings for family group meetings or activities centered around the annual guidebook *Family Home Evening,* which contains weekly lessons. One evening in the program might resemble the following:

> The father takes charge of the meeting in what the Mormons call his priesthood role—a role that makes him responsible for instruction in the faith and leadership of the family. All sessions open with a prayer, followed by a hymn, and then discussion of the lesson. . . . the instruction ends with members sharing ideas on how they can apply the lesson to their daily life in the family. The meeting concludes with another prayer. Refreshments follow. . . .   (Brommel, 1978, 6–7)

Although its emphasis is on religious instruction, *Family Home Evening* materials often contain ideas appropriate for improving interpersonal communication. Discussion of such topics as "learning to love each other" and "organizing yourself" requires self-disclosure, risk taking, and sharing. Listening skills are frequently taught. Many of the ideas suggested for sharing require the family to use positive modes of communication. Recently, other churches have developed similar programs, such as The Christian Life Home Curriculum of the Christian church (Disciples of Christ) and the Family Life Program of the Christian Family Movement (Roman Catholic). Countless variations of family evenings are being developed by religious and community groups.

One such approach is known as the Family Cluster, best described as a "group of four or five complete family units which contract to meet together periodically over an extended period of time for shared educational experiences related to being in relationship with their families" (Sawin, 1979, 27). Through Family Cluster, families gain mutual support and help in developing skills that enhance family relationships. A Family Cluster may consist of two-parent biological families, single-parent families, childless couples, single persons, or one or more persons who live together. The designer suggests, ". . . when starting a new family cluster, it is usually helpful to begin with a unit of communication . . . communication is a vital force for group building, as well as a crucial element in the family system" (47).

"As a single person, I have found it very rewarding to belong to a Family Cluster because it provides me with a support system of caring people, and it allows me to be of service to some of them in return. I truly enjoy interacting with the children in our Cluster, and I'm known as the 'game lady' because I usually spend part of my time playing games with the children. I enjoy interacting with young people, and their parents are pleased."

Some programs for family enrichment have stressed the importance of parents' educating their children to seek peace and justice both in the political and personal arenas. Such writers as Kathleen and James McGinnis and Michael True suggest that parents develop a consistent set of humanistic values and then struggle to live by them and teach them to their children. They present goals and values for families to achieve and ways for parents to communicate these to their children and communities (McGinnis, 1981, 2, 91; True, 1982, 182, 123). Such programs emphasize conflict management, listening, problem solving, and building self-esteem.

The previously discussed approaches are only a few of the many ways of involving individuals, families, and groups of families in enriching their relationships. Where do you see yourself in relation to such approaches? Would you be willing to make the effort required to participate fully in a *quid pro quo* bargaining session or in a structured Family Council meeting?

In addition to personal approaches, couples or individuals may attempt to improve family communication through direct instruction.

Instructional Approaches

If a member of your family suggested that you all go on a communication enrichment weekend, how would you react? Would you be willing to attend some sessions on improving parent-child communication with your children or your parents? The past two decades witnessed a tremendous growth in educational, marital, and family enrichment programs designed for individuals and for whole family systems. Their purposes are educational, not therapeutic; they are oriented toward enrichment, not counseling.

"Both my wife and I had been previously married before we met each other. We were scared that if we got married, some of the old patterns would repeat themselves for both of us. Therefore, before we got married, we attended a Couple Communication program in our town. Although we communicated relatively well, this program made it easier for us to be honest and to hear what the other person was really saying. We took it seriously and did the exercises at home. I believe it really helped us in our first year of marriage when things got tense."

Most persons who attend enrichment programs are self-referred and self-screened. Potential participants receive the message "If your marriage or family life is in serious trouble, our program is not for you. We are designed to help good relationships become better." If identified before the program, couples contemplating divorce or families experiencing chaos are referred to therapeutic means of dealing with their problem or to enrichment programs that use trained counselor-facilitators (Hof and Miller, 1981, 41).

Marital Enrichment Programs. These programs are designed to enhance couple growth. Family growth may result in an extension of change in the marital pair. Most programs insist that the couple attend together in order to affect the system.

Communication skills appear as the core of most of these marital enrichment programs. According to Wackman (1978), the communication emphasis may be attributed to three factors. First, research on marriage has shown a consistent, though modest, relationship between "good" communication by members of a married couple and marital satisfaction and happiness, while research with "healthy" families indicates the same moderately positive correlation between "good" communication and satisfaction of family members. Second, theoretical developments in thinking about the family system focused on the crucial role of communication in both marriage and the family. Third, communication training seems to be an easy, safe, and nonthreatening way to bring about enrichment, since communication skills and principles can be taught fairly readily (3–4).

Although there are numerous systems-oriented marital and family enrichment programs that stress communication, we will examine only a few representative ones. The most well-known and frequently attended marital enrichment programs include the religion-based Marriage Enrichment, Marriage Encounter, and Marriage Communication Lab programs and the privately developed Couples Communication Program (Otto, 1975; Koch and Koch, 1976; Hof and Miller; Garland, 1983). Each places a heavy emphasis on communication. We will briefly describe how each program functions with the understanding that there may be some variations depending on sponsoring groups and specific leaders.

One of the Marriage Enrichment programs sponsored by the Methodist church is a small-group experience conducted by a leader or leader-couple who works with four other couples through a structured weekend. After having been prepared by leader modeling, reflecting, and role playing, each couple engages in a series of interactions within the small group framework. Couples prepare for this through guided rehearsal sessions with nonspouses. Group members also give feedback to each couple. Some of the weekend experiences include: sharing the qualities one admires in his or her spouse, sharing the behaviors that make one feel loved when performed by the spouse, and discussing wished-for behaviors from the spouse. Thus, intimacy receives great focus. The actual sharing and discussion behavior is constantly monitored and corrected by the team leader, who is trying to teach communication skills. The small group functions as a powerful support system for trying new behaviors.

Marriage Encounter is a weekend program conducted by three couples and a religious leader. The format follows a simple pattern. Each husband and wife "give" each other the Encounter, with the team members merely providing the information and modeling to facilitate each couple's private dialogue. Through a series of nine talks, team members reveal personal and intimate information to encourage participants to do the same when alone. After the talks, each husband and wife separate and write individual responses to the issues raised in each talk. Specific questions to be considered may be provided, or the individual may write his or her feelings about the topic. The couple then comes together for private dialogue using each other's written responses as a starting point. The Marriage Encounter process involves exposition, reflection, encounter, and mutual understanding. Dialogue topics include understanding of the self; relationship with the partner; and the couple's relationship with God, their children, and the world. Although the program began within the Catholic church, the past years have witnessed the growth of Jewish and Protestant Marriage Encounters.

The Marriage Communication Lab of the United Methodist Church consists of a couple-led small group weekend experience. The lab experience includes sessions on group building and sharing expectations, communication skills, conflict management, sexuality, trust and values, roles, expectations, and goal setting. Couples perform most of the work within the small group framework, using a learning pattern of "do/reflect/draw conclusions" (Hopkins and Hopkins, 1976, 229). Time may be taken to allow a couple to work through a real issue, one they are dealing with, in front of the other couples, in order to receive feedback.

The Couples Communication program involves a small group experience for five to seven couples meeting one night a week for four consecutive weeks with an instructor. The "couples" may be spouses, friends, or work teams. This program serves as an educational experience in which couples identify, practice, and experiment with communication skills around topics of their choice. Each couple receives feedback on their skills from the leader and other couples. No attempt is made to deal with the content of an interaction; the focus remains solely on skills accomplishment. Practice sessions are held with nonpartners, but the final demonstration of skills occurs with one's partner. The approach in Couples Communication is to have the couple do exercises so they can experience new ideas and approaches to relating to one another, not just learn about them (Garland, 21).

Sometimes, variations of weekend programs are done over eight to fifteen weeks in two- to four-hour sessions. The advantages include spaced learning and the opportunity to do homework and practice new skills, but such disadvantages as fights, irregular attendance, and the routines of daily life weaken the communication focus (Hof and Miller, 82, 83).

As you read the descriptions of these marital enrichment programs, it becomes clear that communication assumes a major place within each. Desirable interpersonal behavior may be taught differently through modeling, role playing, lecture, guided feedback, and readings, but it is incorporated into each program. The unique feature of such programs is the learning context—you learn and practice communication skills with people with whom you have a relationship. In her summary of the communication instruction contained within these four marital enrichment programs, Galvin concludes:

> All programs give attention to the five skills of empathic communication, recognizing and owning feelings, descriptiveness, self-disclosure, and behavioral flexibility, with descriptiveness receiving the least attention except in Marriage Enrichment. The skills of self-disclosure and recognizing and owning feelings command extensive attention as each program devotes a large proportion of its time to the area of feelings. Marriage Enrichment provides the most predictable structure and uses the most direct approach to teach these skills. Marriage Encounter relies heavily on modeling and direction to teach communication skills. (26–27)

These programs represent some of the more established approaches. Many others exist. For example, in his IDEALS program (Institute for the Development of Emotional Life Skills), Bernard Guerney combines behavior modification with techniques from Carl Rogers' client-centered therapy in an attempt to teach empathy to married couples. IDEALS sets forth rules of talking and listening—knowing when to talk and when to listen. Groups of three or four couples work for six months with a trained leader, learning and practicing these rules until they become automatic. Many other churches and private organizations run unique marital communication programs for their own congregations or constituents.

Appraisal of Marital Enrichment Programs. Although these programs may sound very exciting, we need to note some cautions in considering their effectiveness. There may be difficulties in attempting to teach communication principles and skills without a shared desire on the part of both partners. If such mutual commitment does not exist, the results may be contrary to the expected outcomes.

Additionally, the skills must be combined with a desire or spirit of good will to motivate partners to use them appropriately (Miller et al., 1975, 150; Davis et al., 1982; Stevens, 1984).

The research on these programs does not attribute undisputed success to their efforts. Gurman and Kniskern (1977) summarized twenty-nine studies that purported to examine the impact of marriage enrichment programs. Although positive results were found in a majority of the measures, most studies used self-report measures in which the questionnaires or interviews were administered immediately after the program. Thus, few changes in behavior or long-range effects could be documented. Although the programs are designed to help couples with satisfactory marriages, Powell and Wampler (1982) found that this was not always the case. Many couples entered such workshops because they felt a need for help. They suggested more stringent controls and measures to determine each partner's commitment to the enrichment experience and also examinations of the makeup of the control groups (392).

In their admittedly critical appraisal of the Marriage Encounter, Doherty et al. (1978) suggest that the program can create illusions through emotional "highs," deny the importance of differences between people, lead to a kind of ritual dependency and guilt if the couple does not engage in the follow-up, and other possible difficulties. Yet, these authors also point out the strengths of such a program. In her follow-up study of Marriage Enrichment couples, Ellis (1982) reported that participants talk more freely about their feelings to spouses and to other persons than they had before their involvement. Former participants are able to express negative feelings more constructively. Yet, some participants reported that although they were emotionally expressive during the weekend, they could not sustain this later (205–06). Additional critiques of programs note positive and negative effects (L'Abate, 1981; De Young, 1979; Wampler and Sprenkle, 1979).

Even the structure of the program may affect the outcome. In a study comparing psychological changes in couples who attended a weekend program with couples who were involved in a five-week program, the latter group gained more improvement in their marital adjustment scores. In both groups, wives changed in more positive ways than did their husbands (Davis et al., 89).

Research on the long term effectiveness of marital enrichment programs is too limited to draw conclusions. We need more information in order to answer Wackman's important questions about the impact of such programs:

1. Do the programs result in changes in communication that last for a reasonable period of time? And if so, do the changes in communication skills result in positive changes in the relationships so that marriages are truly enriched?
2. Do the marriage programs result in changes that generalize to other relationships, particularly with children, thereby enriching family life?
3. What are the major factors in these programs that create the impacts that occur—specific skills taught? format (group vs. individual couple)? degree of structure?   (6–7)

Family Enrichment Programs. Although programs for families have developed more slowly, many marital programs are creating familial counterparts, encouraging entire families to examine and improve their relationships. The Marriage Encounter Program now offers the Family Weekend Experience. As in Marriage Encounter, the family members "give" each other the weekend. Parents and their children of school age spend their waking weekend hours in a local facility engaging in activities, listening to short talks, seeing films, and holding family discussions. Families are encouraged to examine their everyday lives, to discuss nine "blocks" to a family relationship, such as fighting, criticism, or indifference, and the means to overcoming such blocks, including listening, acceptance, and respect. Family members experience personal reconciliation with each other and plan ways to maintain the feelings of closeness they have achieved. The Marriage Enrichment weekend has spawned a family-oriented weekend, and Guerney and his colleagues have developed filial programs for skill training in interpersonal competency between children and parents and adolescents and parents. Numerous other groups have developed educational types of family growth groups focusing on communication (Sawin, 61–68).

One of the most widely accepted family-oriented programs has been PET, Parent Effectiveness Training, through which couples, without their children, attempt to learn more effective parenting skills, relying heavily on communication strategies. Designed by psychologist Gordon, this program requires parents in PET groups to follow a carefully prescribed eight-week, three-hours-per-session, series of lessons. In these twenty-four hours of instruction, parents learn specific ways to handle a variety of family problems. For homework, parents fill out exercises in the PET *Workbook* and read assigned chapters in Gordon's (1975) book, *Parent Effectiveness Training.* This program encourages parents to examine their own self-concepts, to re-evaluate their verbal and nonverbal messages, and to find new approaches to deal with old problems, primarily through communication.

Using lectures, questions and answers, small group discussion, and role playing, PET stresses effective communication. Listening skills receive the greatest attention within the course. Two of the eight lessons deal totally with developing listening skills, and all others incorporate ideas based upon an understanding of what Gordon calls the "active listening method." This method requires learning how to accept whatever the child shares without intervening or judging. Parents are taught to restate to the child what they heard to check on whether their listening was accurate and to do this without anger or judgment.

PET also focuses on sending parental "I-messages" and deciding who owns the problem—the child or the parent. This program describes twelve "blocks," or obstacles, to effective communication and finally, after intermediate lessons on parental power and conflict of values, presents a "no-lose" method of problem solving. In short, PET serves as a parental communication program.

The "Understanding Us" program relies on the circumplex model of family systems as its conceptual base (Carnes, 1981). Referring to the model as a "family map," the program attempts to help family members understand themselves from a systems perspective during a four-session course. After examining themselves in light of the topics: (1) adapting, (2) caring, (3) growing, and (4) changing, family members are expected to achieve a deeper understanding of their system and options for change.

As a final instructional example, we turn to the Baha'i faith and its approach to family life. In his analysis of the influence of Baha'i faith beliefs on family communication, Ward (1980) describes the communication-related behaviors taught within the faith. Members learn a consultation process, which includes identifying the problem, agreeing on the facts and relevant principles, discussing the alternatives fully and frankly, and agreeing on a decision to be put into action (5). Families are expected to use these steps for dealing with any decision they must face. Additionally, the faith emphasizes the need to teach children the process of asking questions and to encourage them in such behavior. Stress is placed on "verbal-factual" accord to the extent that "Children are not to be given answers which later have to be denied, but rather, can be elaborated on" (6). Families are encouraged to engage in frequent family study-discussions as a means of teaching the faith and exploring values and personal issues and to seek means of discipline that do not include "striking or vilifying" the child. In addition, all members of the faith know that any difficult problem may be brought to the local Assembly for counseling. These teachings interrelate to form a communication pattern by which the family lives.

Finally, there are many self-help groups oriented toward specific topics that also provide formal or informal instruction in family communication for their members. Such groups include: Alcoholics Anonymous, Al-Anon, Parents Anonymous, Families Anonymous, Parents Without Partners, Parents of Gays, Families Who Have Adopted Children of Every Skin, Compassionate Friends, and Candlelighters.

In the next section, we will introduce the therapeutic approaches to improving family communication. Because this text is concerned with communication issues of functional families, we will treat therapeutic approaches only in order to extend the continuum of options for improving relationships. There is a vast body of literature that explores these approaches in detail, so we will only highlight some relevant issues.

Therapeutic Approaches

For those families who live with dysfunctional communication or experience temporary crises, therapeutic interventions may be warranted. Individual therapy has long been an established approach to dealing with personal problems or illnesses. Many people finding difficulties within themselves and their relationships have been assisted through a one-to-one therapeutic relationship in some type of counseling setting. This counselor-client situation represents the traditional therapeutic approach.

Yet, in the 1950s, some therapists began to find success working jointly with a parent and child or a husband and wife. Eventually, some therapists asked to see whole families for a session. These sessions proved so valuable that certain therapists elected to work with husbands and wives, parents and children, or whole family systems on a regular basis, thus forming the basis of systems therapy.

"Two years ago, my family went into therapy because my younger brother was an alcoholic, and his treatment center required the entire family to become involved in the treatment program. Over about a year we were able to understand the patterns of family interaction that 'fed' Chris' drinking problem. The therapist kept stressing that Chris' drinking was a family problem, not just Chris' problem. The therapy forced my mother and stepfather to deal with some problems in their marriage that they had been ignoring and allowed us to make enough changes that Chris could return to the house and to high school and control his drinking."

Napier and Whitaker (1978) describe the process by which therapists decided to look at whole systems.

Some therapists discovered the family system by being bruised by it . . . working with an individual and being totally defeated by the family's power over the patient; or seeing the client "recover," only to witness all the progress undermined by the family; or treating the scapegoat child "successfully," only to find another child in the family dragged into the role; or working with an individual patient and feeling the fury of the family's sudden explosion just as the patient improved.   (52–53)

In many cases, once therapists examined a whole family system, they realized that there would not be a "problem" member, a symptom bearer, if it were not for the rest of the system's dynamics. Thus, events in families must be examined in the context in which they happen and attention given to how communication among family members affects connections and relationships (Papp, 1983, 7).

Family therapy looks at the family unit as the client to be treated; the focus shifts from the individuals to the entire unit and the relationships among people. Ackerman (1966) describes family therapy as " . . . the therapy of a natural living unit; the sphere of the therapeutic intervention is not a single individual but the whole family unit" (209). Thus, the attempt is made to change the system, not just the "problem" person or identified patient, since this person may be thought of as acting out the system's problems (Satir, 1967; Gurman and Kniskern, 1981; Haley, 1981; Framo, 1982).

The primary goal of family therapy is to "effect changes in the interpersonal relationships among members of the family system" (Kramer, 1980, 101). Presently, there are many schools of thought regarding the most effective ways to alter family systems. Therapeutic approaches reflect psychodynamic, communication, structural, and behavioral theories (Goldenberg and Goldenberg, 1980). Therapists may work with individuals, couples, families, or entire social networks. Whereas one therapist may value an examination of family history to uncover transgenerational patterns, another may focus exclusively on the "here-and-now" interaction patterns.

Family therapy from a systems perspective emphasizes the interdependence of members. The analysis of communication patterns and familial relationships can result in positive change.

For many families, the systemic orientation of family therapy has provided the basis for their eventual change. The emphasis on patterns, rather than individual blame, has permitted all members to accept some responsibility for their current state and has given them keys to future change.

As you change the current communication patterns within your family system, many options are open to you, ranging from individual efforts on the part of family members, to participation in organized programs, to seeking counseling for the system. From our perspective, the most exciting aspect is the possibility of change. Communication can be improved; families can grow together. We do not deny the effort, time, or pain that might be involved; yet, a nurturing family is worth it.

CONCLUSION

In the beginning of this chapter, we focused upon the characteristics of functional families. Then, we went on to describe personal, instructional, and therapeutic approaches for developing and maintaining desirable family communication. These programs can be helpful and, by taking the participants away from the daily routines of family life, provide a chance to objectify family system experiences. Our thinking and working with families has convinced us that a family system unexamined by its members usually has more communication problems than one that seeks to understand its interactions. The approaches discussed here provide opportunities for such examination.

We have grown from the process of writing this book and hope that you have developed new insights about families in general, and your family in particular. We close with our belief, shared with Beavers (1976), that a healthy family may be viewed as a "phoenix." It grows in an atmosphere of flexibility and intimacy. It accepts conflicts, change, and loss. It declines—to rise again in another healthy generation, which, in turn, produces healthy family members.

IN REVIEW

1. What goals and criteria would you establish for a successful marriage or family enrichment program with a communication focus?
2. Take a position: To what extent should couples be required by religious or civic institutions to take pre-marital workshops or counseling?
3. Analyze the prescriptions for marital or parent-child communication found in a popular book or magazine article and evaluate their effectiveness based on your understanding of family systems and communication patterns.
4. In what ways would you predict family therapy would differ from individual therapy?
5. How would you describe communication in a well-functioning family?

Bibliography

Abelman, Adrienne. "The Relationship Between Family Self-Disclosure, Adolescent Adjustment, Family Satisfaction, and Family Congruence." Unpublished dissertation. Northwestern University, 1975.

Abelsohn, David. "Dealing with the Abdiction Dynamic in the Post Divorce Family: A Context for Adolescent Crisis." *Family Process* 22 (1983): 359–84.

Ackerman, N. J. "The Family with Adolescents." *The Family Life Cycle: A Framework for Family Therapy.* E. Carter and M. McGoldrick, eds. New York: Gardner Press, Inc., 1980, 147–70.

Ackerman, Nathan. "Family Therapy." *American Handbook of Psychiatry.* Silvano Arieti, ed. New York: Basic Books, 1966.

A. C. Nielsen Company. *'84 Nielsen Report on Television.* Northbrook, IL: A. C. Nielsen Co., 1984.

Acock, Alan C., and Wen Shan Yang. "Parental Power and Adolescents' Parental Identification." *Journal of Marriage and the Family* 46 (1984): 487–94.

Aldous, Joan. "The Making of Family Roles and Family Change." *The Family Coordinator* 23 (1974): 231–35.

Alexander, J. F. "Defensive and Supportive Communications in Family Systems." *Journal of Marriage and the Family* 35 (1973): 613–17.

Alexander, Sharon. "Improving Sex Education Programs for Young Adolescents: Parents' Views." *Family Relations* 33 (1984): 251–57.

Allen, Craig M., and Murray A. Straus. "Resources, Power, and Husband-Wife Violence." *The Social Causes of Husband-Wife Violence.* Murray A. Straus and Gerald T. Hotaling, eds. Minneapolis: University of Minnesota Press, 1979. Also reference to article in *Journal of Marriage and the Family* 41 (1979): 85.

Altman, Irwin, and Dalmas Taylor. *Social Penetration.* New York: Holt, Rinehart & Winston, 1973.

Alvy, Kerby T., and Howard Stanley Rubin. "Parent Training and the Training of Parents." *Journal of Community Psychology* 9 (1981): 53–66.

Amomons, Paul, and Nick Stimett. "The Vital Marriage: A Closer Look." *Family Relations* 30 (1980): 37–42.

Anderson, Carol. "The Community Connection: The Impact of Social Networks on Family and Individual Functioning." *Normal Family Processes.* Froma Walsh, ed. New York: Guilford Press, 1982, 425–55.

Anderson, Stephen A., Candyce Russell, and Walter R. Schumm. "Perceived Marital Quality and Family Life-Cycle: A Further Analysis." *Journal of Marriage and the Family* 45 (1983): 126–35.

Anderson, Trudy B. "Widowhood as a Life Transition: Its Impact on Kinship Ties." *Journal of Marriage and the Family* 46 (1984): 105–14.

Aneshensel, Carol S., and Ralph R. Frerichs. "Stress, Support, and Depression: A Longitudinal Causal Model." *Journal of Community Counseling* 10 (1982): 363–76.

Bach, George R., and Peter Wyden. *The Intimate Enemy.* New York: William Morrow & Co., 1966.

Baden-Marotz, Ramona, et al. "Family Form or Family Process: Reconsidering the Deficit Family Model Approach." *The Family Coordinator* 28 (1979): 5–14.

Baer, Diane, and Christopher H. Spicer. "Communication and the Dual-Career Couple: A Literature Assessment." Convention Paper, SCA, 1983, Washington, D.C.

Bahr, Stephen J., C. Bradford Chappell, and Geoffrey K. Leigh. "Age at Marriage, Role Enactment, Role Consensus, and Marital Satisfaction." *Journal of Marriage and the Family* 45 (1983): 795–803.

Bain, Alastair. "The Capacity of Families to Cope with Transitions: A Theoretical Essay." *Human Relations* 31 (1978): 675–88.

Ballering, Laurie, and Alberta Koch. "Family Relations when a Child Is Gifted." *Gifted Child Quarterly* 28 (1984): 140–43.

Balswick, Jack, and Christine Averett. "Differences in Expressiveness: Gender, Interpersonal Orientation, and Perceived Parental Expressiveness as Contributing Factors." *Journal of Marriage and the Family* 39 (1977): 121–27.

Bandler, Richard, and John Grinder. *The Structure of Magic.* Palo Alto, CA: Science and Behavior Books, 1975.

Bankoff, Elizabeth A. "Social Support and Adaptation to Widowhood." *Journal of Marriage and the Family* 45 (1983): 827–39.

Baranowski, T., et al. "Family Self-Help: Promoting Changes in Health Behavior." *Journal of Communication* 32 (1982): 161–70.

Barborin, Oscar A. "Coping with Ecological Transitions by Black Families: A Psychosocial Model." *Journal of Community Psychology* 11 (1983): 308–22.

—. "Families and Households: An Analysis of Emergent Needs and Service Innovation." *Journal of Community Psychology* 10 (1982): 74–81.

Barbour, Alton, and Alvin Goldberg. *Interpersonal Communication: Teaching Strategies and Resources.* ERIC/RCS. Speech Communication Association, 1974.

Barnhill, Laurence R. "Healthy Family Systems." *The Family Coordinator* 28 (1979): 94–100.

Barry, John R. "Alternative Living Arrangements for Older Persons." *The Personnel and Guidance Journal* 61 (1983): 267–68.

Bassoff, Evelyn Silten. "Relationships of Sex-Role Characteristics and Psychological Adjustment in New Mothers." *Journal of Marriage and the Family* 46 (1984): 449–54.

Bate, Barbara, and Lois S. Self. "The Rhetoric of Career Success Books for Women." *Journal of Communication* 33 (1983): 149–65.

Bateson, G., and J. Ruesch. *Communication: The Social Matrix of Psychiatry.* New York: Norton, 1951.

Bateson, Gregory. "Breaking Out of the Double Bond." *Psychology Today* 12 (1978): 43–49.

Baucom, Donald H., and Pamela A. Aiken. "Sex Role Identity, Marital Satisfaction, and Response to Behavioral Marital Therapy." *Journal of Consulting and Clinical Psychology* 52 (1984): 438–44.

Bavelas, Janet, and Lynn Segal. "Family Systems Theory: Background and Implications." *Journal of Communication* 32 (1982): 99–107.

Baxter, Leslie A., and William W. Wilmot. "Communication Characteristics of Relationships with Differential Growth Rates." *Communication Monographs* 50 (1983): 264–72.

Beal, Edward W., M.D. "Separation, Divorce, and Single-Parent Families." *The Family Life Cycle: A Framework for Family Therapy.* Elizabeth A. Carter and Monica McGoldrick, eds. New York: Gardner Press, Inc., 1980, 241–64.

Beavers, W. Robert. "A Theoretical Basis for Family Evaluation." In *No Single Thread: Psychological Health in Family Systems.* New York: Brunner-Mazel, 1976.

—. "Family Variables Related to the Development of a Self." Timberlawn Foundation Report No. 68. Dallas, TX, 1972.

—. "Healthy, Midrange, and Severely Dysfunctional Families." *Normal Family Processes.* Froma Walsh, ed. New York: Guilford Press, 1982.

Beavers, W. Robert, and Mark N. Voeller. "Comparing and Contrasting the Olson Circumplex Model with the Beavers Systems Model." *Family Process* 22 (1983): 85–98.

Beck, Scott H., and Rubye W. Beck. "The Formation of Extended Households During Middle Age." *Journal of Marriage and The Family* 46 (1984): 277–87.

Beier, Ernst G., and Daniel P. Sternberg. "Marital Communication: Subtle Cues Between Newlyweds." *Journal of Communication* 27 (1977): 92–103.

Bell, A. P., and M. S. Weinberg. *Homosexualites: A Study of Diversity Among Men and Women.* New York: Simon and Schuster, 1978.

Belsky, Jay, and Michael Rovine. "Social-Network Contact, Family Support, and the Transition to Parenthood." *Journal of Marriage and the Family* 46 (1984):455–62.

Bem, S. L. "The Measurement of Psychological Androgyny." *Journal of Consulting and Clinical Psychology* 47 (1974):155–62.

Bentler, P. M., and M. D. Newcomb. "Longitudinal Study of Marital Success and Failure." *Journal of Consulting and Clinical Psychology* 46 (1978): 1053–70.

Berger, Charles R. "Power and the Family." *Persuasion: New Direction in Theory and Research.* Michael Roloff and Gerald Miller, eds. Beverly Hills: Sage Publications, 1980, 197–224.

Bergquist, Beatrice. "The Remarried Family: An Annotated Bibliography, 1979–1982." *Family Process* 23 (1984): 107–19.

Berkowitz, Alan, and H. Wesley Perkivs. "Stress Among Farm Women: Work and Family as Interacting Systems." *Journal of Marriage and the Family* 46 (1984): 161–66.

Bernard, M. L., and J. L. Bernard. "Violent Intimacy: The Family as a Model for Lover Relationships." *Family Relations* 32 (1983): 283–86.

Bernstein, Basil. "A Sociolinguistic Approach to Socialization: With Some Reference to Educability." *Language and Poverty.* F. Williams, ed. Chicago: Markham, 1970.

Bettelheim, Bruno. "How Do You Help a Child Who Has a Physical Handicap?" *Ladies Home Journal* 89 (1972): 34–35.

Bienvenu, Millard. "A Measurement of Premarital Communication." *The Family Coordinator* 24 (1975): 65–68.

Bilge, Barbara, and Gladis Kaufman. "Children of Divorce and One-Parent Families: Cross-Cultural Perspectives." *Family Relations* 32 (1983): 59–72.

Bird, Gloria W., and Gerald A. Bird. "Determinants of Family Task Sharing: A Study of Husbands and Wives." *Journal of Marriage and the Family* 46 (1984):345–55.

Black, Elizabeth. "The Newest Profession." *Reader.* January 21, 1983, 8–9, 32–38.

Blau, Peter. *Exchange and Power in Social Life.* New York: John Wiley and Sons, 1964.

Bloch, Donald. "Family Systems Medicine." Speech presented at the Chicago Family Therapy Conference at Northwestern University, 1984.

Blood, Robert O., and Donald M. Wolfe. *Husbands and Wives: The Dynamics of Married Living.* New York: The Free Press, 1960.

Blos, Peter. *The Adolescent Passage.* New York: International Universities Press, 1979.

Blumstein, Phillip, and Pepper Schwartz. *American Couples.* New York: William Morrow and Co., 1983.

Bochner, A. P. "Conceptual Frontiers in the Study of Communication in Families." *Human Communication Research* 2 (1976): 381–97.

Bochner, A. P., D. L. Krueger, and T. L. Chmielewski. "Interpersonal Perceptions and Marital Adjustments." *Journal of Communication* 32 (1982): 135–47.

Bodin, Arthur M. "The Interactional View: Family Therapy Approaches of the Mental Research Institute." *Handbook of Family Therapy.* Alan S. Gurman and David P. Kniskern, eds. New York: Brunner-Mazel, Inc., 1981.

Bogdan, Jeffrey. "Paradoxical Communication as Interpersonal Influence." *Family Process* 21 (1982):443–52.

Book, Cassandra, ed. *Human Communication.* New York: St. Martin's Press, 1980.

Booth, Alan, David B. Brinkerhoff, and Lynn K. White. "The Impact of Parental Divorce on Courtship." *Journal of Marriage and the Family* 46 (1984): 85–94.

Booth, Alan, David Johnson, and John N. Edwards. "Measuring Marital Instability." *Journal of Marriage and the Family* 45 (1983): 387–94.

Boulding, Elise. "Family Faber: The Family as Maker of the Future." *Journal of Marriage and the Family* 45 (1983): 257–66.

Bowen, Murray. "Family Reaction to Death." *Family Therapy: Theory & Practice.* Phillip J. Guerin, ed. New York: Halsted Press, 1976, 335–49.

—. *Family Therapy in Clinical Practice.* New York: Aronson, 1978.

—. "Toward the Differentiation of a Self in One's Own Family." *Family Interaction.* J. L. Framo, ed. New York: Springer Co., 1972, 190–99.

Boyd, Lenore, and Arthur Roach. "Interpersonal Communication Skills Differentiating More Satisfying from Less Satisfying Marital Relationships." *Journal of Counseling Psychology* 24 (1977): 540–42.

Brackett, Cathryn, and Alicia S. Cook. "Mothers' Perception of Their Competence in Managing Selected Parenting Tasks." *Family Relations* 31 (1982): 489–94.

Bradt, Jack O. "The Family with Young Children." *The Family Life Cycle: A Framework for Family Therapy.* Elizabeth A. Carter and Monica McGoldrick, eds. New York: Gardner Press, Inc., 1980, 121–46.

Brandwein, Nancy, Jill MacNeice, and Peter Spiers. *The Group Handbook.* New York: Acropolis Books, 1983.

Branowski, T., et al. "Family Self-Help: Promoting Changes." *Journal of Communication* 32 (1982): 161–72.

Breines, W., and L. Gordon. "The New Scholarship on Family Violence." *Signs* 8 (1983): 490–531.

Broderick, Carlfred. "Fathers." *The Family Coordinator* 26 (1977): 269–71.

Brommel, Bernard. "A Critical Analysis of Communication Instruction in Current Family Interaction Improvement Programs." Paper presented at Speech Communication Association Convention, November 1978.

Brutz, Judith L., and Bron B. Ingoldsby. "Conflict Resolution in Quaker Families." *Journal of Marriage and the Family* 46 (1984): 21–26.

Bubolz, Margaret M., and Alice P. Whiren. "The Family of the Handicapped: An Ecological Model for Policy and Practice." *Family Relations* 33 (1984): 5–12.

Buerkel-Rothfuss, N. L., et al. "Learning About the Family from Television." *Journal of Communication* 32 (1982): 191–202.

Burchinal, Lee G. "Characteristics of Adolescents from Unbroken, Broken, and Reconstituted Families." *Journal of Marriage and the Family* 26 (1964): 44–51.

Burgess, E. W., H. J. Locke, and M. M. Thomas. *The Family: From Institution to Companionship.* New York: American Book Company, 1963.

Burgess, Robert L., and Rand D. Conger. "Family Interaction in Abusive, Neglectful, and Normal Families." *Journal of Youth and Adolescence* 8 (1979): 1163–78.

Burke, Ronald, Tamara Weir, and Denise Harrison. "Disclosure of Problems and Tensions Experienced by Marital Partners." *Psychological Reports* 38 (1976): 531–42.

Burleson, Brant R. "Age, Social-Cognitive Development and the Use of Comforting Strategies." *Communication Monographs* 51 (1984): 140–51.

Buscaglia, Leo. "On Becoming Human." Videorecording transcript, Kent, OH, PTV Publications, 1977.

Carlson, John. "The Recreational Role." *Role Structure and Analysis of the Family.* F. Ivan Nye, ed. Beverly Hills: Sage Publications, 1976, 131–48.

—. "The Sexual Role." *Role Structure and Analysis of the Family.* F. Ivan Nye, ed. Beverly Hills: Sage Publications, 1976, 101–10.

Carnes, Patrick J. *Family Development I: Understanding Us.* Minneapolis, MN: Interpersonal Communication Program, 1981.

Carter, Elizabeth A., and Monica McGoldrick. "The Family Life Cycle and Family Therapy: An Overview." *The Family Life Cycle: A Framework for Family Therapy.* Elizabeth A. Carter and Monica McGoldrick, eds. New York: Gardner Press, Inc., 1980, 3–20.

Carter H., and P. C. Glick. *Marriage and Divorce: Social and Economic Study.* (revised edition) Cambridge, MA: Harvard University Press, 1976.

Centers, R., B. H. Raven, and A. Rodrigues. "Conjugal Power Structure: A Reexamination." *American Sociological Review* 36 (1971): 264–78.

Cherlin, Andrew J. *Marriage, Divorce, Remarriage.* Cambridge, MA: Harvard University Press, 1981.

Chilman, Catherine. "Habitat and American Families: A Social-Psychological Overview." *The Family Coordinator* 27, 2 (1978): 105–11.

Clausen, Peggy, et al. "Divorce American Style." *Newsweek* C111-103 (Jan. 10, 1983): 42–48.

Clinebell, Howard, and Charlotte Clinebell. *The Intimate Marriage.* New York: Harper and Row, 1970.

Collins, Glenn. "Study Says Teenagers Adopt Adult Values." *New York Times* February 6, 1984, 20.

Conger, John J. *Adolescence and Youth.* 2nd ed. New York: Harper and Row, 1977.

Conrad, Charles. "Power and Performance as Correlates of Supervisors' Choice of Modes of Managing Conflict: A Preliminary Investigation." *Western Journal of Speech Communication* 47 (1983): 218–28.

Constantine, Larry L. "Dysfunction and Failure in Open Family Systems, I: Application of a Unified Theory." *Journal of Marriage and the Family* 45 (1983): 725–38.

Cook, Alicia S., and Daniel J. Weigel. "Relocation and Crises: Perceived Sources of Support." *Family Relations* 32 (1983): 267–74.

Cook, Jacqueline. "Reminiscing: How It Can Help Confined Nursing Home Residents." *Social Casework* 65 (1984): 90–93.

Cooper, Pamela. "Issues of Concern in the Stepfamily." Paper presented at the SCA/Northwestern University Family Communication Research Conference, 1984.

Corder, Judy, and Stephan Cookie White. "Females' Combination of Work and Family Roles: Adolescents' Aspirations." *Journal of Marriage and the Family* 46 (1984): 391–402.

Cornfield, Noreen. "The Success of Urban Communes." *Journal of Marriage and the Family* 45 (1983): 114–25.

Corrales, Ramon G. "Power and Satisfaction in Early Marriage." *Power in Families.* Ronald E. Cromwell and David H. Olson, eds. New York: John Wiley & Sons, 1975, 197–216.

Coser, Lewis A. *Continuities in the Study of Social Conflict.* New York: The Free Press, 1967.

308

Courtright, John A., Frank E. Millar, and L. Edna Rogers-Millar. "Domineeringness and Dominance: Replication and Expansion." *Communication Monographs* 46 (1979): 179–92.

Cromwell, R. E., and David H. Olson, eds. *Power in Families.* New York: Halsted Press, 1975.

Cronen, Vernon, W. Barnett Pearce, and Linda Harris. "The Logic of the Coordinated Management of Meaning: A Rules-Based Approach to the First Course in Inter-Personal Communication." *Communication Education* 23 (1979): 22–38.

Crouter, Ann C. "Spillover from Family to Work: The Neglected Side of the Work-Family Interface." *Human Relations* 37 (1984): 425–42.

Curran, Dolores. *Traits of a Healthy Family.* Minneapolis: Winston Press, 1983.

Cushman, Donald P., and R. T. Craig. "Communication Systems, Interpersonal Implications." *Explorations in Interpersonal Communication.* G. R. Miller, ed., Beverly Hills: Sage Publications, 1976.

Cushman, Donald P., and C. Whiting Gordan. "An Approach to Communication Theory: Toward Consensus on Rules." *Journal of Communication* 22 (1972): 217–38.

Cutler, Beverly R., and William G. Dyer. "Initial Adjustment Processes in Young Married Couples." *Love, Marriage, Family: A Developmental Approach.* M. E. Lasswell and T. E. Lasswell, eds. Glenview, IL: Scott, Foresman and Co., 1973, 290–96.

Davis, E. Clifton, et al. "Effects of Weekend and Weekly Marriage Enrichment Program Formats." *Family Relations* 31 (1982): 85–90.

DeFrain, John. "Androgynous Parents Tell Who They Are and What They Need." *Family Coordinator* 28 (1979): 237–43.

Dell, Paul F. "Beyond Homeostasis: Toward a Concept of Coherence." *Family Process* 21 (1982): 21–42.

DeLong, Alton. "Environments for the Elderly." *Journal of Communication* 24, 4 (1974): 101–12.

Demaris, Alfred, and Gerald R. Leslie. "Cohabitation with Future Spouse: Its Influence Upon Marital Satisfaction and Communication." *Journal of Marriage and the Family* 46 (1984): 79–84.

Demott, Benjamin. "Grouping in the 80s." *Psychology Today* 17 (1983): 26.

DeVito, Joseph. "Educational Responsibilities to the Gay and Lesbian Student." Paper presented at the Speech Communication Association Convention, 1979.

DeYoung, Alan J. "Marriage Encounter: A Critical Examination." *Journal of Marital and Family Therapy* 5 (1979): 27–41.

Doherty, William J. "Locus of Control Differences and Marital Dissatisfaction." *Journal of Marriage and the Family* 43 (1981): 369–77.

Doherty, William J., Patricia McCabe, and Robert G. Ryder. "Marriage Encounter: A Critical Appraisal." *Journal of Marriage and Family Counseling* 4 (1978): 99–106.

Doster, J. A., and B. R. Strickland. "Perceived Childhood Practices and Self-Disclosure Patterns." *Journal of Consulting and Clinical Psychology* 33 (1969): 382.

Douglas, Susan P., and Yoram Wind. "Examining Family Role and Authority Patterns: Two Methodological Issues." *Journal of Marriage and the Family* 40 (1978): 35–47.

Dreikurs, Rudolf. *Children: The Challenge.* New York: Hawthorn Books, 1964.

Dreyer, Cecily, and Albert Dreyer. "Family Dinner Time as a Unique Behavior Habitat." *Family Process* 12 (1973): 291–302.

Duck, Steve, Dorothy Miell, and David Miell. "Relationship Growth and Decline." *Communication by Children and Adults.* Howard Sypher and Jones Applegate, eds. Beverly Hills: Sage Publications, 1984, 292–312.

Dumazedier, Jafre. *Toward a Society of Leisure.* New York: The Free Press, 1967.

Duncan, O. D. "Social Organization and the Ecosystem." *Handbook of Modern Sociology.* R. Farris and L. Farris, eds. Chicago: Rand McNally, 1964.

Dunlop, Richard S. *Helping the Bereaved.* Bowie, MD: Charles Press Publishers, Inc., 1978.

Duvall, Evelyn Ruth (Millis). *Family Development.* 5th ed. Philadelphia: J. B. Lippincott, 1977.

D'Zurilla, T. J., and M. R. Goldfried. "Problem Solving and Behavior Modification." *Journal of Abnormal Psychology* 78 (1971): 107–26.

Easterlin, Richard A. "The Changing Circumstances of Child-Rearing." *Journal of Communication* 32 (1982): 86–98.

Edwards, John N., and Janice M. Saunders. "Coming Apart: A Model of the Marital Dissolution Decision." *Journal of Marriage and the Family* 43 (1981): 379–89.

Einstein, Elizabeth. "Stepfamily: Chaotic, Complex, Challenging." *Stepfamily Bulletin* 1 (1980): 1–2.

——. *The Stepfamily: Living, Loving, Learning.* New York: Macmillan, 1982.

Ellis, Titia. "The Marriage Enrichment Weekend: A Qualitative Study of a Particular Weekend Experience." Unpublished dissertation, Northwestern University, 1982.

Elman, Margaret R., and Lucia A. Gilbert. "Coping Strategies for Role Conflict in Married Professional Women with Children." *Family Relations* 33 (1984): 317–27.

Emmerich, H. J. "The Influence of Parents and Peers on Choices Made by Adolescents." *Journal of Youth and Adolescence* 7 (1978): 175–80.

Epstein, Nathan B., Duane S. Bishop, and Lawrence M. Baldwin. "McMaster Model of Family Functioning." *Normal Family Processes.* Froma Walsh, ed. New York: Guilford Press, 1982.

Epstein, Nathan B., Duane S. Bishop, and S. Levin. "The McMaster Model of Family Functioning." *Journal of Marriage and Family Counseling* 4 (1978): 19–31.

Erikson, Erik H. *Identity, Youth, and Crisis.* New York: W. W. Norton & Co., 1968.

Eshbach, Ellen. "Your Dream House Could Give a Family Nightmares." *Chicago Tribune,* May 16, 1976: Sec. 5, p. 3.

Falicov, Celia. "Mexican Families." *Ethnicity and Family Therapy.* Monica McGoldrick, Joseph Giordano, and John Pearce, eds. New York: Guilford Press, 1983, 134–63.

Falicov, Celia, and Betty Karrer. "Cultural Variations in the Family Life Cycle: The Mexican-American Family." *The Family Life Cycle: A Framework for Family Therapy.* Elizabeth Carter and Monica McGoldrick, eds. New York: Gardner Press, 1980, 383–425.

Family Guidebook. Salt Lake City, Utah. The Church of Jesus Christ of Latter-day Saints, 1980. See also the journals *Dialogue* and *Ensign,* 1985.

Family Home Evening: Love Makes Our House a Home. Salt Lake City: The Church of Jesus Christ of Latter-day Saints Press, 1974.

Family Home Evening Resource Book. Salt Lake City, Utah. The Church of Jesus Christ of Latter-day Saints, 1983.

"Father's Priesthood—To Be Used, but Not Abused." *Family Home Evening: Love Makes Our House a Home.* Salt Lake City: The Church of Jesus Christ of Latter-day Saints Press 3 (1974): 224.

Feifel, Herman. *New Meaning of Death.* New York: McGraw-Hill Book Co., 1977.

Feldman, Larry B., "Marital Conflict and Marital Intimacy: An Integrative Psychodynamic-Behavioral Systemic Model." *Family Process* 18 (1979): 69–78.

—. "Sex Roles and Family Dynamics." *Normal Family Process.* Froma Walsh, ed. New York: The Guilford Press, 1982, 354–82.

Festinger, Leon. "Architecture and Group Membership." *Journal of Social Issues* 1 (1951): 152–59.

Festinger, Leon, S. Schachter, and K. Beck. *Social Pressures in Informal Groups: A Study of Human Factors in Housing.* New York: Harper & Row, 1950.

Filley, Allan C. *Interpersonal Conflict Resolution.* Glenview, IL: Scott, Foresman and Co., 1975.

Fitzpatrick, Mary Anne. "A Typological Approach to Communication in Relationships." *Communication Yearbook I.* Brent Rubin, ed. New Brunswick, NJ: Transaction Press (1977b): 263–75.

—. "Dyadic Adjustment in Traditional, Independent, and Separate Relationship: A Validation Study." University of Wisconsin-Milwaukee. Paper presented at Speech Communication Association, Dec. 1977a.

Fitzpatrick, Mary Anne, and Patricia Best. "Dyadic Adjustment in Relational Types: Consensus, Cohesion, Affectional Expression, and Satisfaction in Enduring Relationships." *Communication Monographs* 46 (1979): 165–78.

Fitzpatrick, Mary Anne, Susan Fallis, and Leslie Vance. "Multifunctional Coding of Conflict Resolution Strategies in Marital Dyads." *Family Relations* 31 (1982): 61–70.

Floyd, Frank J., and Howard J. Markman. "An Economical Observational Measure of Couples' Communication Skill." *Journal of Consulting and Clinical Psychology* 52 (1984): 97–103.

Foley, Vincent D. *An Introduction to Family Therapy.* New York: Grune & Stratton, Inc., 1974.

Fombyron, Charles J. "Attributions of Power Across a Social Network." *Human Relations* 36 (1983): 493–508.

Ford, David A. "Wife Battery and Criminal Justice: A Study of Victim Decision-Making." *Family Relations* 32 (1983).

Ford, Fredrick. "Rules: The Invisible Family." *Family Process* 22 (1983): 135–46.

Fortier, Laurie M., and Richard L. Wanlass. "Family Crisis Following the Diagnosis of a Handicapped Child." *Family Relations* 34 (1984): 13–24.

Framo, James L. "Family of Origin as a Therapeutic Resource for Adults in Marital and Family Therapy: You Can and Should Go Home Again." *Family Process* 15 (1976): 193–209.

French, J. R. P., Jr., and B. H. Raven. "The Bases of Social Power." D. Cartwright and A. Zander, eds. *Group Dynamics.* Evanston, IL: Row Peterson, 1962, 607–23.

Frey, Joseph. "A Family/Systems Approach to Illness-Maintaining Behaviors in Chronically Ill Adolescents." *Family Process* 23 (1984): 251–60.

Gagnon, John. *Human Sexuality.* Glenview, IL: Scott, Foresman and Co., 1977.

Galper, Marian. *Co-Parenting: A Sourcebook for the Separated or Divorced Family.* Philadelphia: Running Press, 1978.

Galvin, Kathleen M. "An Analysis of Communication Instruction in Current Marital Interaction Programs." Paper presented at the Speech Communication Association Convention, 1978.
—. "Exploring the Teaching of Intimate Communication Within Church-Sponsored Programs." Paper presented at the Religious Speech Communication Association Convention, 1983.
—. "Family Communication Workshops." Annandale, VA: SCA/ERIC. 1985.
—. "Pishogues and Paddywhackery: Transmission of Communication Patterns and Values Through Three Generations of an Extended Irish-American Family." Paper presented at the Speech Communication Association Convention, 1982.

Gantman, Carol. "A Closer Look at Families that Work Well." *International Journal of Family Therapy* 2 (1980): 106–19.

Garcia-Preto, Nydia. "Puerto Rican Families." *Ethnicity and Family Therapy.* Monica McGoldrick, Joseph Giordano, and John Pearce, eds. New York: Guilford Press, 1983, 164–86.

Garland, Diana S. *Working with Couples for Marriage Enrichment.* San Francisco: Jossey-Bass, 1983.

Gaylin, Jody. "Family Policy—Our Endangered Children: It's a Matter of Money." *Psychology Today* 11 (1977): 94–95.

Gecas, Viktor. "The Socialization and Child Care Roles." *Structure and Analysis of the Family.* F. Ivan Nye, ed. Beverly Hills: Sage Publications, 1976, 33–60.

Gibb, Jack R. "Defensive Communication." *Journal of Communication* 11 (1961): 141–48.

Gilbert, Lucia A., Gary R. Hanson, and Beverly Davis. "Perceptions of Parental Role Responsibilities: Differences Between Mothers and Fathers." *Family Relations* 31 (1982): 261–70.

Gilbert, Shirley. "Empirical and Theoretical Extensions of Self-Disclosure." *Explorations in Interpersonal Communication.* Gerald Miller, ed. Beverly Hills: Sage Publications, 1976b; 197–215.
—. "Self-Disclosure, Intimacy, and Communication in Families." *Family Coordinator* 25 (1976a): 221–29.

Gilbert, Shirley, and Gale Whiteneck. "Toward a Multidimensional Approach to the Study of Self-Disclosure." *Human Communication Research* 2 (1976): 347–55.

Gilford, Rosalie, and Vern Bengtson. "Measuring Marital Satisfaction in Three Generations: Positive and Negative Dimensions." *Journal of Marriage and the Family* 41 (1979): 387–98.

Gillespie, Dair L. "Who Has the Power? The Marital Struggle." *Journal of Marriage and the Family* 33 (1971): 445–58.

Goetting, Ann. "The Six Stations of Remarriage: Developmental Tasks of Remarriage After Divorce." *Family Relations* 31 (1982): 213–22.

Golanty, E., and B. B. Harris. *Marriage and Family Life.* Boston: Houghton Mifflin, 1982.

Goldberg, Lee. "They Stole Our Childhood." *Newsweek on Campus* March 1983, 32.

Goldenberg, Irene, and Herbert Goldenberg. *Family Therapy: An Overview.* Belmont, CA: Wadsworth, 1980.

Gongla, Patricia. "Single Parent Families: A Look at Families of Mothers and Children." *Marriage and Family Review* vol. 5, no. 2, New York: Haworth Press, 1982.

Gordon, Thomas. *Parent Effectiveness Training.* New York: New American Library, 1975.

Gottman, John M. "Emotional Responsiveness in Marital Conversations." *Journal of Communication* 32 (1982): 108–120.
—. "Temporal Form: Toward a New Language for Describing Relationships." *Journal of Marriage and the Family* 44 (1982): 942–62.

Gottman, John M., Howard Markham, and Cliff Notarius. "The Topography of Marital Conflict: A Sequential Analysis of Verbal and Nonverbal Behavior." *Journal of Marriage and the Family* 39 (1977): 461–77.

Greene, Bernard. *A Clinical Approach to Marital Problems.* Springfield, IL: Charles C Thomas, 1970.

Grote, Douglas F., and Jeffery P. Weinstein. "Joint Custody: A Visible and Ideal Alternative." *Journal of Divorce* 1 (1977): 43–54.

Guenther, Robert. Real estate column. *Wall Street Journal.* April 11, 1984.
—. "Stress on the Single Bath." *Wall Street Journal.* September 5, 1984.

Guerney, Bernard G. *Relationship Enhancement: Skill Training Programs for Therapy, Problem Prevention, and Enrichment.* San Francisco: Jossey-Bass, 1977.

Guion, Edward. "Elder Cottages." *Aging* 342 (Dec. 1983–Jan. 1984): 9–11.

Gurman, Alan, and David Kniskern. "Enriching Research on Marital Enrichment Programs." *Journal of Marriage and Family Counseling* 3 (1977): 3–10.
—. *Handbook of Family Therapy.* New York: Brunner-Mazel, 1981.

Haley, Jay. "Establishment of an Interpersonal Relationship." *Interpersonal Communication: Basic Text and Readings.* B. R. Patton and Kim Giffin, eds. New York: Harper and Row, 1974, 368–73.

Hall, Edward T. *The Hidden Dimension.* Garden City, NY: Doubleday, 1966.

Harevan, Tamara. "American Families in Transition: Historical Perspectives on Change." *Normal Family Processes.* Froma Walsh, ed. New York: Guilford Press, 1982, 446–65.

Harisingh, Maskay Manish, and Anne McCreary Juhasz. "The Decision-Making Process Model: Design and Use for Adolescent Sexual Decisions." *Family Relations* 32 (1983): 111.

Harkins, Elizabeth Bates. "Effects of Empty Nest Transition on Self-Report of Psychological and Physical Well Being." *Gerontologist* 15 (1975): 43.

Hartley, Ruth E. "Sex Role Pressures and the Socialization of the Male Child." *Men and Masculinity.* Joseph Pleck and Jack Sawyer, eds. Englewood Cliffs, NJ: Prentice-Hall, 1974, 7–13.

Hawkins, Leo F. "The Impact of Policy Decisions on Families." *Family Coordinator* 28 (1979): 264–72.

Heiss, Jerold. "An Introduction to the Elements of Role Theory." *Family Roles and Interaction.* Jerold Heiss, ed. Chicago: Rand McNally, 1968, 3–27.

Herbst, P. G. "The Measurement of Family Relationships." *Human Relations* 5 (1952): 3–35.

Herz, Fredda. "The Impact of Death and Serious Illness on the Family Life Cycle." *The Family Life Cycle: A Framework for Family Therapy.* Elizabeth Carter and Monica McGoldrick, eds. New York: Gardner Press, 1980, 223–40.

Hess, Robert, and Gerald Handel. *Family Worlds.* Chicago: University of Chicago Press, 1959.

Hetherington, E. Mavis. "Girls Without Fathers." *Psychology Today* 7 (1973): 49–52.

Hetherington, E. Mavis, Martha Cox, and Roger Cox. "Divorced Fathers." *The Family Coordinator* 25 (1976): 417–28.

Hill, Reuben. *Families Under Stress.* New York: Harper & Brothers, 1949.

—. *Family Development in Three Generations.* Cambridge, MA: Schenkman, 1970.

—. "Methodological Issues in Family Development Research." *Family Process.* Nathan Akerman, ed. New York: Basic Books, Inc., 1970, 294–314.

Hill, Reuben, and Joan Aldous. "Socialization from Marriage and Parenthood." *Handbook of Socialization Theory and Research.* D. A. Goslin, ed. Chicago: Rand McNally, 1969, 885–950.

Hill, Wayne, and John Scanzoni. "An Approach for Assessing Marital Decision-Making Processes." *Journal of Marriage and the Family* 44 (1982): 927–40.

Hof, Larry, and William R. Miller. *Marriage Enrichment.* Bowie, MD: Brady/Prentice-Hall, 1983.

—. *Marriage Enrichment: Philosophy, Process, and Program.* Bowie, MD: Brady/Prentice-Hall, 1981.

Hoffman, L. W. "Changes in Family Roles, Socialization and Sex Differences." *American Psychologist* 32 (1977): 644–57.

Hoffman, Lois W. "Effects of the Employment of Mothers on Parental Power Relations and the Division of Household Tasks." *Marriage and Family Living* 22 (1960): 27–35.

Hoffman, Lynn. "Enmeshment and the Too Richly Cross-Joined System." *Family Process* 14 (1975): 457–68.

—. "The Family Life Cycle and Discontinuous Change." *The Family Life Cycle: A Framework for Family Therapy.* Elizabeth Carter and Monica McGoldrick, eds. New York: Gardner Press, 1980, 53–68.

Holmes, T. H., and R. H. Rahe. "The Social Readjustment Rating Scale." *Journal of Psychosomatic Research* 2 (1967): 213–18.

Hopkins, La Donna, et al. *Toward Better Marriages.* Winston-Salem: ACME, 1978.

Hopkins, Paul, and La Donna Hopkins. "Marriage Communication Labs." *Marriage and Family Enrichment.* Herbert Otto, ed. Nashville: Abingdon Press, 1976, 229.

Hopper, Robert, Mark L. Knapp, and Lorel Scott. "Couples' Personal Idioms: Exploring Intimate Talk." *Journal of Communication* 31 (1981): 23–33.

Horwitz, Jaime, and Jerome Tognoli. "Role of Home in Adult Development: Women and Men Living Alone Describe Their Residential Histories." *Family Relations* 31 (1982): 335–41.

Howard, Jane. *Families.* New York: Berkley Books, Simon & Schuster, 1978.

Huber, Charles H. "Cognitive Considerations in Coping with Marital Conflict." *American Mental Health Counselors Association Journal* (1984): 71–78.

Hurvitz, Nathan, and Mirra Komarovsky. "Husbands and Wives: Middle Class and Working Class." *The Marriage Game,* 2nd ed. Cathy Greenblatt et al., eds. New York: Random House, 1977.

Indvik, Julie. "Bringing the Job Home: Some Proposed Effects of Work on Marital Communication." Paper presented at the Central States Speech Association Convention, 1983.

Indvik, Julie, and Mary Anne Fitzpatrick. "If You Could Read My Mind Love. . . . Understanding and Misunderstanding in the Marital Dyads." *Family Relations* 31 (1982): 43–52.

Jackson, Don D. "The Question of Family Homeostasis." *Psychiatric Quarterly* 31 (1957): 79–90.

—. "The Study of the Family." *Family Process* 4 (1965): 1–20.

Johnson, Fern. "Communication with Children: Toward a Healthy Construction of Communicative Roles." Paper presented at Central States Speech Association, Chicago, 1978.

Johnson, Richard. "Conflict Management in Established Gay Male Dyads; A Qualitative Study." Paper presented at the Speech Communication Association Convention, 1984.

Jordon, Joe. "The Challenge: Designing Buildings for Older Americans." *Aging* 342 (Dec. 1983–Jan. 1984): 18–21.

Jourard, Sidney. "Some Lethal Aspects of the Male Role." *Men and Masculinity.* Joseph Pleck and Jack Sawyer, eds. Englewood Cliffs, NJ: Prentice-Hall, 1974, 21–29.

—. *The Transparent Self.* New York: Van Nostrand Reinhold Co., 1971.

Kahana, R., and B. Kahana. "The Theoretical and Research Perspectives on Grandparenthood." Paper presented at American Psychological Association Meeting, 1970.

Kalmuss, Debra S. "The Intergenerational Transmission of Marital Aggression." *Journal of Marriage and the Family* 46 (1984): 11–19.

Kalmuss, Debra S., and Murray A. Straus. "Wife's Marital Dependency and Wife Abuse." *Journal of Marriage and the Family* 44 (1982): 277–86.

Kantor, David, and William Lehr. *Inside the Family.* San Francisco: Jossey-Bass, 1976.

Kennedy, Robert W. *The House and the Art of Its Design.* New York: Reinhold Publishing Co., 1953.

Kenniston, Kenneth. "The Search of Adulthood." *New York Times Book Review,* July 8, 1979, 7.

Kenniston, Kenneth, et al. *All Our Children.* New York: Harcourt Brace Jovanovich, 1977.

Kerr, Michael. "Family Systems Theory and Therapy." *Handbook of Family Therapy.* Alan Gurman and David Kniskern, eds. New York: Brunner-Mazel, 1981, 226–64.

Killmann, Ralph, and Kenneth Thomas. "Interpersonal Conflict Handling Behavior as Reflections of Jungian Personality Dimensions." *Psychological Reports* 37 (1975): 971–80.

Klinger-Vartabedian, Laurel, and Robert Vartabedian. "The Alcoholic Family: A Communication Perspective." Paper presented at the Speech Communication Association Convention, 1980.

Knapp, Mark L. *Interpersonal Communication and Human Relationships.* Boston: Allyn and Bacon, 1984.

—. *Nonverbal Communication in Human Interaction.* New York: Holt, Rinehart & Winston, 1972.

—. *Social Intercourse.* Boston: Allyn and Bacon, 1978.

Knapp, Mark L., D. G. Ellis, and B. A. Williams. "Perceptions of Communication Behavior Associated with Relational Terms." *Communication Monographs* 47 (1980): 262–78.

Koch, Joanne, and Lew Koch. "The Urgent Drive to Make Good Marriages Better." *Psychology Today* 10 (1976): 33–34, 85, 95.

Kohlberg, Lawrence. "Continuities in Childhood and Adult Moral Development Revisited." *Life-Span Developmental Psychology: Personality and Socialization.* P. Baltes and K. W. Schaie, eds. New York: Academic Press, 1973.

—. "Development of Moral Character and Moral Ideology." *Review of Child Development Research 1.* M. L. Hoffman and L. W. Hoffman, eds. New York: Russell Sage Foundation, 1964, 383–431.

Kolb, Trudy M., and Murray A. Straus. "Marital Power and Marital Happiness in Relation to Problem Solving Ability." *Journal of Marriage and the Family* 36 (1974): 756–66.

Komarovsky, Mirra. *Blue Collar Marriage.* New York: Vintage Books, Random House, 1967.

Korman, Sheila K. "Nontraditional Dating Behavior: Date-Initiation and Date Expense-Sharing Among Feminists and Nonfeminists." *Family Relations* 32 (1983): 575–81.

Kotlar, Sally L. "Middle Class Marital Role Perceptions and Marital Adjustment." *Sociological and Social Research* 49 (1965): 283–93.

Kramer, Charles H. *Becoming a Family Therapist.* New York: Human Sciences Press, 1980.

Kramer, Jeannette. *Family Interfaces: Transgenerational Patterns.* New York: Brunner-Mazel, 1985.

Krueger, Dorothy Lenk. "Pragmatics of Dyadic Decision Making: A Sequential Analysis of Communication Patterns." *Western Journal of Speech Communication* 47 (1983): 99–117.

Kübler-Ross, Elisabeth. *On Death and Dying.* New York: Macmillan, 1970.

Kübler-Ross, Elisabeth, ed. *Death: The Final Stage of Growth.* New York: Spectrum Books, 1975.

L'Abate, Luciano. "Skill Training Programs for Couples and Families." *Handbook of Family Therapy.* Alan Gurman and David Kniskern, eds. New York: Brunner-Mazel, 1981.

Laing, R. D. *The Politics of the Family.* New York: Vintage Books, 1972.

Lasswell, Marcia, and Thomas Lasswell, eds. *Love, Marriage, Family: A Developmental Approach.* Glenview, IL: Scott, Foresman and Co., 1973.

Lederer, William, and Don D. Jackson. *The Mirages of Marriage.* New York: W. W. Norton and Co., 1968.

Lee, Gary R. "Marriage and Morale in Later Life." *Journal of Marriage and the Family* 40 (1978): 131–39.

Lennard, Suzanne, and Henry Lennard. "Architecture: Effect of Territory, Boundary, and Orientation on Family Functioning." *Family Process* 16 (1977): 49–66.

Levinger, G., and D. J. Senn. "Disclosure of Feelings in Marriage." *Merrill Palmer Quarterly* 13 (1967): 237–49.

Levinson, Daniel, et al. *The Seasons of a Man's Life.* New York: Ballantine Books, 1978.

Levitin, Teresa E. "Children of Divorce: An Introduction." *Journal of Social Issues* 35 (1979): 1–23.

Lewis, Robert A. "Emotional Intimacy Among Men." *Journal of Social Issues* 34 (1978): 108–21.

Lewis, Robert A., Phillip J. Freneau, and Craig R. Roberts. "Fathers and the Postparental Tradition." *The Family Coordinator* 28 (1979): 514–20.

Lewis, Robert A., and Joseph H. Pleck. "Men's Roles in the Family." *The Family Coordinator* 29 (1979): 429–32.

Lieberman, Stuart. *Transgenerational Family Therapy.* London: Croom Helm Ltd., 1979.

Lindhan, Marsha M., et al. "Reasons for Staying Alive When You Are Thinking of Killing Yourself: The Reasons for Living Inventory." *Journal of Consulting and Clinical Psychology* 51 (1983): 276–86.

Linton, Ralph. *The Cultural Background of Personality.* New York: Appleton-Century-Crofts, 1945.

Littlejohn, Stephen. *Theories of Human Communication.* Columbus, OH: Charles Merrill, 1978.

Lomrantz, J. "Cultural Variations in Personal Space." *Journal of Social Psychology* 99 (1976): 21–27.

Longini, Muriel. "The Delicate One—Transferring a Childhood Role into Married Life Can Cause Problems." *Marriage and Family Living* 61 (1979): 8–9.

Lopata, H. Z. *Widowhood in an American City.* Cambridge, MA: Schenkman, 1973.

Luepnitz, Deborah A. "Which Aspects of Divorce Affect Children?" *Family Coordinator* 28 (1979): 79–85.

Lutz, Patricia L. "The Stepfamily: An Adolescent Perspective." *Family Relations* 32 (1983): 367–76.

McAdoo, Harriette P. "Stress Absorbing Systems in Black Families." *Family Relations* 31 (1982): 479–88.

McClelland, David, et al. "Making It to Maturity." *Psychology Today* 12 (1978): 42–54.

McCubbin, Hamilton I., and Barbara Dahl Blum. *Marriage and Family: Individuals and Life Cycles.* New York: John Wiley and Sons, 1985.

McCubbin, Hamilton I., et al. "Chip-Coping Health Inventory for Parents: An Assessment of Parental Coping Patterns in the Case of the Chronically Ill." *Journal of Marriage and the Family* 45 (1983): 359–70.

McCullough, Paulina. "Launching Children and Moving On." *The Family Life Cycle: A Framework for Family Therapy.* Elizabeth Carter and Monica McGoldrick, eds. New York: Gardner Press, 1980, 171–96.

McDonald, Gerald W. "Family Power: The Assessment of a Decade of Theory and Research, 1970–1979." *Journal of Marriage and the Family* 42 (1980): 841–52.

—. "Parental Power and Adolescents' Parental Identification: A Reexamination." *Journal of Marriage and the Family* 42 (1980): 289–96.

—. "Structural Exchange and Marital Interaction." *Journal of Marriage and the Family* 43 (1981): 825–40.

McGillicuddy-DeList, Ann V. "The Role of Parental Beliefs in the Family as a System of Mutual Influences." *Family Relations* 29 (1980): 317–24.

McGinnis, Kathleen, and James McGinnis. *Parenting for Peace and Justice.* Maryknoll, NY: Orbis Books, 1981.

McGoldrick, Monica. "Normal Families: An Ethnic Perspective." *Normal Family Processes.* Froma Walsh, ed. New York: Guilford Press, 1982, 399–424.

McGoldrick, Monica, and Elizabeth A. Carter. "Forming a Remarried Family." *The Family Life Cycle: A Framework for Family Therapy.* Elizabeth A. Carter and Monica McGoldrick, eds. New York: Gardner Press, 1980, 265–329.

—. "The Family Life Cycle." *Normal Family Processes.* Froma Walsh, ed. New York: The Guilford Press, 1982, 167–95.

McIlroy, Joan Hartzke. "Midlife in the 1980s: Philosophy, Economy, and Psychology." *The Personnel and Guidance Journal* 62 (1984): 623–27.

Macklin, E. "Nontraditional Family Forms: A Decade of Research." *Journal of Marriage and the Family* 42 (1980): 905–22.

McLanahan, Sara A. "Family Structure and Stress: A Longitudinal Comparison of Two-Parent and Female Headed Families." *Journal of Marriage and the Family* 45 (1983): 347–58.

McWhirter, D. P., and A. M. Mattison. *The Male Couple.* Englewood Cliffs, NJ: Prentice-Hall, 1984.

Majors, Randall. "A Comparison of Phase Models in Gay Male Primary Relationship Development." Paper presented at the Speech Communication Association Convention, 1983.

Manz, Charles C., and Dennis A. Gioia. "The Interrelationship of Power and Control." *Human Relations* 36 (1983): 459–76.

Maret, Elizabeth, and Barbara Finlay. "The Distribution of Household Labor Among Women in Dual-Earner Families." *Journal of Marriage and the Family* 46 (1984): 357–64.

May, Robert. *Sex and Fantasy Patterns of Male and Female Development.* New York: W. W. Norton and Co., 1980.

Mederer, Helen, and Reuben Hill. "Cultural Transitions over the Family Life Span: Theory and Research." *Social Stress and the Family.* H. McCubbin, et al., eds. New York: Hayworth Press, 1983, 39–60.

Mehrabian, Albert. *Silent Messages.* Belmont, CA: Wadsworth, 1971.

Menaghan, Elizabeth. "Marital Stress and Family Transitions: A Panel Analysis." *Journal of Marriage and the Family* 45 (1983): 371–86.

Meyers, C. E., Andrea Zetlin, and Jan Blacher-Dixon. "The Family as Affected by Schooling for Severely Retarded Children." *Journal of Community Psychology* 9 (1981): 306–15.

Midelfort, C. F., and H. C. Midelfort. "Norwegian Families." *Ethnicity and Family Therapy.* Monica McGoldrick, Joseph Giordano, and John Pearce, eds. New York: Guilford Press, 1983.

Millar, Frank, L. E. Rogers-Millar, and Kenneth Villard. "A Proposed Model of Relational Communication and Family Functioning." Paper presented at the Central States Speech Association Convention, April 1978.

Miller, Brian. "Gay Fathers and Their Children." *Family Coordinator* 28 (1979): 544–52.

Miller, Sherod, Ramon Corrales, and Daniel B. Wackman. "Recent Progress in Understanding and Facilitating Marital Communication." *The Family Coordinator* 24 (1975): 143–51.

Mills, Carol J., and Harvey L. Noyes. "Patterns and Correlates of Initial and Subsequent Drug Use Among Adolescents." *Journal of Consulting and Clinical Psychology* 52 (1984): 231–43.

Mills, David. "A Model for Stepfamily Development." *Family Relations* 33 (1984): 365–72.

Minuchin, Salvador. *Families and Family Therapy.* Cambridge, MA: Harvard University Press, 1974.

Minuchin, Salvador, et al. *Families of the Slums.* New York: Basic Books, 1967.

Mishler, E. G., and N. E. Waxler. *Interaction in Families, An Experimental Study of Family Process in Schizophrenia.* New York: John Wiley & Sons, 1968.

Montagu, Ashley. *Touching: The Human Significance of the Skin.* New York: Harper & Row, 1978.

Montgomery, Barbara M. "The Form and Function of Quality Communication in Marriage." *Family Relations* 30 (1981): 21–30.

Moses, Kenneth. "Effects of the Developmental Disability in Parenting the Handicapped Child." *First and Second Annual Early Childhood Symposia: Patterns of Emotional Growth in the Developmentally Disabled Child.* Margaret Rieff, ed. Morton Grove, IL: Julia S. Malloy Education Center, 1978: 31–62.

Muchmore, John. "Role Context and Speech Communication Education: Approach to Instruction Demonstrated by Application to the Occupational Category of Dental Hygienist." Unpublished Dissertation, Northwestern University, 1974.

Murphy, Wendy. "Albert Hadley—The Search for Right Clues." *Architectural Digest* 41 (1984): 98–98J.

Murray, Ellen M. "Channels to the Top: An Exploration of Sex Role and Information Source." *Communication Quarterly* 31 (1983): 156–57.

Murstein, Bernard I. "Self-Ideal—Self-Discrepancy and the Choice of Marital Partner." *Love, Marriage, Family: A Developmental Approach.* M. E. Lasswell and T. E. Lasswell, eds. Glenview, IL: Scott, Foresman and Co., 1973, 246–49.

Myers, J. E., H. Wass, and M. Murphy. "Ethnic Differences in Death Anxiety Among the Elderly." *Death Education* 4 (1980): 237–44.

Napier, Augustus, with Carl Whitaker. *The Family Crucible.* New York: Harper and Row, 1978.

Nash, John. "The Father in Contemporary Culture." *Love, Marriage, Family: A Developmental Approach.* M. E. Lasswell and T. E. Lasswell, eds. Glenview, IL: Scott, Foresman and Co., 1973, 352–62.

Nehls, N., and S. Morgenbesser. "Joint Custody: An Exploration of Issues." *Family Process* 19 (1980): 117–24.

Neugarten, B., and K. K. Weinstein. "The Changing American Grandparent." *Journal of Marriage and the Family* 26 (1964): 119–204.

Nock, Steven L. "Family Life-Cycle Transitions: Longitudinal Effects on Family Members." *Journal of Marriage and the Family* 43 (1981): 703–14.

Nock, Steven L., and Paul William Kingston. "The Family Work Day." *Journal of Marriage and the Family* 45 (1983): 267–76.

Nussbaum, Jon F. "Relational Closeness of Elderly Interaction: Implications for Life Satisfaction." *Western Journal of Speech Communication* 47 (1983): 229–43.

Nye, F. Ivan. "Family Mini-Theories as Special Instances of Choice and Exchange Theory." *Journal of Marriage and the Family* 42 (1980): 479–90.

—. *Role Structure and Analysis of the Family.* Beverly Hills: Sage Publications, 1976.

Nye, F. Ivan, and Viktor Gecas. "The Role Concept: Review and Delineation." *Role Structure and Analysis of the Family.* F. Ivan Nye, ed. Beverly Hills: Sage Publications, 1976, 3–15.

Offer, Daniel, and Judith Baskin, with the assistance of Eric Ostrov. *From Teenage to Young Manhood: A Psychological Study.* New York: Basic Books, 1975.

Offer, Daniel, and Melvin Sabshin. *Normality and the Life Cycle.* New York: Basic Books, 1984.

O'Flaherty, K. W. "Evaluation of a Coaching Procedure for Marital Decision Making." Unpublished Dissertation, University of Michigan, 1974.

Oliveri, Mary Ellen, and David Reiss. "Family Concepts and Their Measurement: Things Are Seldom What They Seem." *Family Process* 23 (1984): 33–48.

Olson, David H. "The Measurement of Family Power by Self-Report and Behavioral Methods." *Journal of Marriage and the Family* 31 (1969): 545–50.

Olson, David H. and Hamilton McCubbin and Associates. *Families: What Makes Them Work.* Beverly Hills: Sage Publications, 1983.

Olson, David H., Candyce S. Russell, and Douglas H. Sprenkle. "Circumplex Model of Marital and Family Systems: VI Theoretical Update." *Family Process* 22 (1983): 69–84.

Olson, David H., D. H. Sprenkle, and C. S. Russell. "Circumplex Model of Marital and Family Systems: Cohesion and Adaptability Dimensions, Family Types, and Clinical Applications." *Family Process* 18 (1979): 3–28.

O'Neill, Nena, and George O'Neill. *Open Marriage.* New York: Avon Books, 1972.

Osmond, Harry. "Function as the Basis of Psychiatric Ward Design." *Environmental Psychology.* H. Proshansky, W. Ittleson, and L. Rivlin, eds. New York: Holt, Rinehart & Winston, 1970.

Otto, Herbert. "Marriage and Family Enrichment Programs in North America: Report and Analysis." *The Family Coordinator* 24 (1975): 137–42.

—. *More Joy in Marriage: Developing Your Marriage Potential.* New York: Hawthorn, 1969.

Papernow, Patricia. "The Stepfamily Cycle: An Experiential Model of Stepfamily Development." *Family Relations* 33 (1984): 335–63.

Papp, Peggy. *The Process of Change.* New York: The Guilford Press, 1983.

Parkes, Collin Murray. *Bereavement.* New York: International Universities Press, 1972.

Pasley, Kay, and Viktor Gecas. "Stresses and Satisfactions of the Parental Role." *The Personnel and Guidance Journal* 62 (1984): 400–404.

Patterson, Joan M., and Hamilton I. McCubbin. "Gender Roles and Coping." *Journal of Marriage and the Family* 46 (1984): 95–104.

Pearce, W. Barnett, and Stewart M. Sharp. "Self-Disclosing Communication." *Journal of Communication* 23 (1973): 409–25.

Phillips, Richard. "Exploding the Myths of Adolescence." *Chicago Tribune.* May 6, 1979, Sec. 12.

Pleck, Joseph H., and Jack Sawyer. *Men and Masculinity.* Englewood Cliffs, NJ: Prentice-Hall, 1974.

Pollard, W. E., and T. R. Mitchell. "Decision Theory Analysis of Social Power." *Psychological Bulletin* 78 (1972): 433–46.

Powell, Gleam S., and Karen Smith Wampler. "Marriage Enrichment Participants: Levels of Marital Satisfaction." *Family Relations* 31 (1982): 389–94.

Price-Bonham, Sharon. "A Comparison of Weighted and Unweighted Decision-Making Scores." *Journal of Marriage and the Family* 38 (1976): 629–40.

Rapoport, Rhona. "The Transition from Engagement to Marriage." *Love, Marriage, Family: A Developmental Approach.* M. E. Lasswell and T. E. Lasswell, eds. Glenview, IL: Scott, Foresman and Co., 1973, 250–58.

Raschke, Helen J., and Vernon J. Raschke. "Family Conflict and Children's Self-Concepts: A Comparison of Intact and Single-Parent Families." *Journal of Marriage and the Family* 41 (1979): 367–74.

Raush, H. L., et al. *Communication Conflict and Marriage.* San Francisco: Jossey-Bass, 1974.

Raven, B., C. Centers, and A. Rodriges. "The Bases of Conjugal Power." *Power in Families.* R. E. Cromwell and D. H. Olson, eds. New York: Halsted Press, 1975, 217–34.

Reinhardt-Kompara, Diane. "Difficulties in the Socialization Process of Stepparenting." *Family Relations* 29 (1980): 69–73.

Reiss, David. *The Family's Construction of Reality.* Cambridge, MA: Harvard University Press, 1981.

Reiss, David, and Mary Ellen Oliveri. "Family Paradigm and Family Coping: A Proposal for Linking the Family's Intrinsic Adaptive Capacities to Its Responses to Stress." *Family Relations* 29 (1980): 431–44.

—. "Sensory Experience and Family Process: Perceptual Styles Tend to Run In but Not Necessarily Run Families." *Family Process* 22 (1983): 289–308.

—. "The Family's Construction of Social Reality and Its Ties to Its Kin Network: An Exploration of Causal Direction." *Journal of Marriage and the Family* 45 (1983): 81–90.

Remer, Rory. "The Effects of Interpersonal Confrontation on Males." *American Mental Health Association Journal* 6 (1984): 56–69.

Ridley, C. A., D. J. Peterman, and A. W. Avery. "Cohabitation: Does It Make for a Better Marriage?" *The Family Coordinator* 27 (1978): 129–36.

Ritter, Ellen. "Social Perspective-Taking Ability, Cognitive Complexity and Listener-Adopted Communication in Early and Late Adolescence." *Communication Monographs* 46 (1979): 42–50.

Rivenbark, W. H. "Self-Disclosure Patterns Among Adolescents." *Psychological Reports* 28 (1971): 35–42.

Rogers, Carl R. *Becoming Partners: Marriage and Its Alternatives*. New York: Delta Books, 1972.

Rogers, Edna. "Potentials in Family Communication Research." Paper presented at the SCA/Northwestern University Research Conference on Family Communication, 1984.

Rogers-Millar, L. Edna, and Frank E. Millar. "Domineeringness and Dominance: A Transactional View." *Human Communication Research* 5 (1979): 238–46.

Rollins, Boyd C., and Harold Feldman. "Marital Satisfaction Over the Family Life Cycle." *Love, Marriage, Family: A Developmental Approach*. M. E. Lasswell and T. E. Lasswell, eds. Glenview, IL: Scott, Foresman and Co., 1973, 381–83.

Rollins, Boyd C., and Darwin L. Thomas. "A Theory of Parental Power and Child Compliance." *Power in Families*. R. E. Cromwell and D. H. Olson, eds. New York: Halsted Press, 1975, 38–60.

Rosenblatt, Paul C., Sandra L. Titus, and Michael R. Cunningham. "Disrespect, Tension, and Togetherness-Apartness in Marriage." *Journal of Marital and Family Therapy* 5 (1979): 47–54.

Rossi, Alice S. "Transition to Parenthood." *Journal of Marriage and the Family* 30 (1968): 26–39.

—. "Transition to Parenthood." *Love, Marriage, Family: A Developmental Approach*. M. E. Lasswell and T. E. Lasswell, eds. Glenview, IL: Scott, Foresman and Co., 1973, 334–43.

Rotunno, Marie, and Monica McGoldrick. "Italian Families." *Ethnicity and Family Therapy*. Monica McGoldrick, Joseph Giordano, and John Pearce, eds. New York: Guilford Press, 1983.

Rubin, Lillian. *Women of a Certain Age: The Midlife Search for Self*. New York: Harper & Row, 1979.

Rubin, J. Z., and B. R. Brown. *The Social Psychology of Bargaining and Negotiation*. New York: Academic Press, 1975.

Russell, Candyce S. "Circumplex Model of Marital and Family Systems: III. Empirical Evaluation with Families." *Family Process* 18 (1979): 29–45.

Ryan, Kevin, and Marilyn Ryan. *Making a Marriage*. New York: St. Martin's Press, 1982.

Safilios-Rothschild, Constantina. "A Macro- and Micro-Examination of Family Power and Love: An Exchange Model." *Journal of Marriage and the Family* 37 (1975): 335–62.

—. "The Study of Family Power Structure: 1960–1969." *Journal of Marriage and the Family* 32 (1970): 539–52.

Satir, Virginia. *Conjoint Family Therapy*. Palo Alto, CA: Science & Behavior Books, 1967.

—. *Peoplemaking*. Palo Alto, CA: Science & Behavior Books, 1972.

Satir, Virginia, James Stachowiak, and Harvey Taschman. *Helping Families to Change*. New York: Jason Aronson, 1975.

Sawin, Douglas B., and Ross D. Parke. "Fathers' Affectionate Stimulation and Caregiving Behaviors with Newborn Infants." *Family Coordinator* 28 (1979): 509–19.

Sawin, Margaret. *Family Enrichment with Family Clusters*. Valley Forge, PA: Judson Press, 1979.

Sawyer, Jack. "On Male Liberation." *Liberation* 15 (1970): 6–8.

Scanzoni, John. *Sexual Bargaining*. Englewood Cliffs, NJ: Prentice-Hall, 1972.

—. "Strategies for Changing Male Family Roles: Research and Practice Implications." *Family Coordinator* 28 (1979): 435–44.

Scanzoni, John, and Karen Polonko. "A Conceptual Approach to Explicit Marital Negotiation." *Journal of Marriage and the Family* 42 (1980): 31–44.

Scanzoni, J., and M. Szinovacz. *Family Decision Making: A Developmental Sex Role Model*. Beverly Hills: Sage Publications, 1980.

Schaefer, Robert B., and Patricia M. Keith. "Equity in Marital Roles Across the Family Life Cycle." *Journal of Marriage and the Family* 43 (1981): 359–67.

Scheflen, Albert. "Living Space in an Urban Ghetto." *Family Process* 10 (1971): 429–49.

Scheiner, Lillian C., Andrew P. Musetto, and David M. Cordier. "Custody and Visitation Counseling: A Report of an Innovative Program. *Family Relations* 31 (1982): 99–108.

Schrag, Keith G. "Relationship Therapy with Same-Gender Couples." *Family Relations* 33 (1984): 283–91.

Schram, Rosalyn Weinman. "Marital Satisfaction over the Family Life Cycle: A Critique and Proposal." *Journal of Marriage and the Family* 41 (1979): 7–14.

Scoresby, A. Lynn. *The Marriage Dialogue.* Reading, MA: Addison-Wesley, 1977.

Scott, Joseph. "Comfort and Seating Distance in Living Rooms: The Relationship of Interactants and Topic of Conversation." *Environment and Behavior* 16 (1984): 35–54.

Sheehy, Gail. *Passages.* New York: Bantam Publishing Co., 1976.

Shepard, W. "Mothers and Fathers, Sons and Daughters: Perceptions of Young Adults." *Sex Roles* 6 (1980): 421–33.

Shimanoff, Susan. "The Role of Gender in Linguistic References to Emotive States." *Communication Quarterly* 30 (1983): 174–77.

Shon, Steven, and Jan Davis. "Asian Families." *Ethnicity and Family Therapy.* Monica McGoldrick, Joseph Giordano, and John Pearce, eds. New York: Guilford Press, 1983, 208–28.

Sieburg, Evelyn. "Interpersonal Confirmation: A Paradigm for Conceptualization and Measurement." Paper presented at International Communication Association, Montreal, Quebec, 1973. ERIC document No. ED 098 634 1975.

Sillars, Alan L., et al. "Communication and Conflict in Marriage." *Communication Yearbook 7.* Robert Bostrom, ed. Beverly Hills: Sage Publications, 1983, 414–29.

Slevin, K. F., and J. Balswick. "Children's Perceptions of Parental Expressiveness." *Sex Roles* 6 (1980): 293–99.

Slocum, Walter L., and F. Ivan Nye. "Provider and Housekeeper Roles." *Role Structure and Analysis of the Family.* F. Ivan Nye, ed. Beverly Hills: Sage Publications, 1976, 81–99.

Spanier, Graham B., and Paul C. Glick. "The Life Cycle of American Families: An Expanded Analysis." *Journal of Family History* 5 (1980): 97–111.

Spooner, Susan. "Intimacy in Adults: A Developmental Model for Counselors and Helpers." *The Personnel and Guidance Journal* 60 (1982): 168–70.

Sporakowski, Michael J., and George Hughston. "Prescriptions for Happy Marriage: Adjustments and Satisfactions of Couples Married 50 or More Years." *The Family Coordinator* 27 (1978): 321–28.

Stachowiak, James. "Functional and Dysfunctional Families." *Helping Families to Change.* Satir et al., eds. New York: Jason Aronson, 1975.

Steffenmeier, Renee Hoffman. "A Role Model of the Transition to Parenthood." *Journal of Marriage and the Family* 44 (1982): 319–34.

Steinglass, P. "The Home Observation Assessment Method (HOAM): Real-Time Naturalistic Observation of Families in Their Homes." *Family Process* 18 (1979): 337–54.

Steinmetz, S. K. "The Use of Force for Resolving Family Conflict: The Training Ground for Abuse." *Family Coordinator* 26 (1977): 19–26.

Steinmetz, S. K., and M. A. Straus. *Violence in the Family.* New York: Harper & Row, 1974.

Steinor, Claude. "Problems of Power." Lecture at National Group Leaders Conference, Chicago, March 22, 1978.

Stephen, Timothy D. "A Symbolic Exchange Framework for the Development of Intimate Relationships." *Human Relations* 37 (1984): 393–408.

Stevens, Joseph H., Jr. "Child Development Knowledge and Parenting Skills." *Family Relations* 33 (1984): 237–44.

Stinnett, Nick, James Walters, and Evelyn Kay. *Relationships in Marriage and the Family.* 2nd ed. New York: Macmillan, 1984.

Straus, Murray A. "Leveling, Civility, and Violence in the Family." *Journal of Marriage and the Family* 36 (1974): 13–29, and "Addendum" 36 (Aug.): 442–45.

Strodbeck, F. L. "Husband-Wife Interaction over Revealed Differences." *American Sociological Review* 16 (1951): 468–73.

Taylor, A. B. "Role Perception, Empathy, and Marital Adjustment." *Sociology and Social Research* 52 (1967): 22–34.

Taylor, Denny. "Reflections on Parenting: A Multigenerational Perspective." *Family Process* 22 (1983): 341–46.

Terkelsen, Kenneth G. "Toward a Theory of the Family Life Cycle." *The Family Life Cycle: A Framework for Family Therapy.* Elizabeth A. Carter and Monica McGoldrick, eds. New York: Gardner Press, Inc., 1980, 21–52.

Toffler, Alvin. *Future Shock.* New York: Bantam Books, 1971.

Troll, Lillian E. *Early and Middle Adulthood.* Monterey, CA: Brooks-Cole Publishing Co., 1975.

Troll, Lillian E., Sheila Miller, and Robert Atchley. *Families in Later Life.* Belmont, CA: Wadsworth Publishing Co., 1979.

True, Michael. *Homemade Social Justice: Teaching Peace and Justice in the House.* Mystic, CT: Twenty-Third Publications, 1982.

318

Turk, James. "Power as the Achievement of Ends: A Problematic Approach in Family and Small Group Research." *Family Process* 13 (1974): 39–52.

Turnbull, Sharon K., and James M. Turnbull. "To Dream the Impossible Dream: An Agenda for Discussion with Stepparents." *Family Relations* 32 (1983): 227–30.

Turner, Lynn H. "Family Communication: Toward the Development of Androgyny." Paper presented at the Central States Speech Association Convention, 1982.

Uhlenberg, Peter. "Death and the Family." *Journal of Family History* 5 (1980): 313–20.

U.S. Bureau of the Census. "Marital Status and Living Arrangements: March 1983." *Current Population Reports, Series P20. No. 389* Washington, DC: U.S. Government Printing Office, 1984.

U.S. Bureau of the Census. *Statistical Abstract of the United States: 1984.* 104th ed. Washington, DC: U.S. Government Printing Office, 1983.

Villard, Kenneth, and Leland Whipple. *Beginnings in Relational Communication.* New York: John Wiley and Sons, 1976.

Vines, Neville R. "Adult Unfolding and Marital Conflict." *Journal of Marital and Family Therapy* 5 (1979): 5–14.

Visher, John, and Emily Visher. "Stepfamilies and Stepparenting." *Normal Family Processes.* Froma Walsh, ed. New York: Guilford Press, 1982.

Wackman, Daniel. "Communication Training in Marriage and Family Living." Paper presented at Speech Communication Association Convention, 1978.

Wallerstein, J. G., and J. B. Kelley. "The Effects of Parental Divorce: Experiences of the Pre-School Child." *Journal of the American Academy of Child Psychiatry* 14 (1975): 600–16.

Walsh, Froma. *Normal Family Processes.* New York: The Guilford Press, 1982.

Walters, J., and N. Stinnett. "Parent-Child Relationships: A Decade Review of Research." *A Decade of Family Research and Action.* C. Broderick, ed. Minneapolis: National Council on Family Relations, 1971.

Wampler, Karen Smith. "The Effectiveness of the Minnesota Couple Communication Program: A Review of Research." *Journal of Marital and Family Therapy* 8 (1982): 345–55.

Wampler, Karen Smith, and Gleam S. Powell. "The Barret-Lennard Relationship Inventory as a Measure of Marital Satisfaction." *Family Relations* 31 (1982): 139–46.

Wampler, Karen Smith, and Douglas H. Sprenkle. "The Minnesota Couple Communication Program." *Journal of Marriage and the Family* 42 (1980): 577–84.

Ward, Allan. "The Influence on Family Communication of a Specific Belief System: The Baha'i Faith." Paper presented at Southern Speech Communication Association, Birmingham, 1980.

Wass, Hannelore, and Jane E. Myers. "Psychosocial Aspects of Death Among the Elderly: A Review of the Literature." *The Personnel and Guidance Journal* 60 (1982): 131–45.

Waterman, Jill. "Family Patterns of Self-Disclosure." *Self-Disclosure.* Gordon Chelune and Associates, eds. San Francisco: Jossey-Bass, 1979, 225–42.

Watson, John J., and Rory Remer. "The Effects of Interpersonal Confrontation on Females." *The Personnel and Guidance Journal* 62 (1984): 607–11.

Watson, Roy E. "Premarital Cohabitation vs. Traditional Courtship: Their Effects on Subsequent Marital Adjustment." *Family Relations* 32 (1983): 139–48.

Watzlawick, P., J. Beavin, and D. D. Jackson. *Pragmatics of Human Communication.* New York: W. W. Norton & Co., 1967.

Weaver, Carl, and Jean Mayhew. "The Use of the Family Council as a Technique in Reducing a Communication Barrier." *Journal of Communication* 9 (1959): 68–76.

Westin, Alan. *Privacy and Freedom.* New York: Atheneum, 1967.

Westman, J. C. "Effects of Divorce on a Child's Personality Development." *Medical Aspects of Human Sexuality* 6 (1972): 38–55.

White, Burton. *The First Three Years of Life.* Englewood Cliffs, NJ: Prentice-Hall, 1975.

Wilmot, William W. *Dyadic Communication: A Transactional Perspective.* Reading, MA: Addison-Wesley, 1975. Revised 1979.

Wilmot-Hocker, Joyce, and William W. Wilmot. *Interpersonal Conflict.* Dubuque, IA: Wm. C. Brown Company, 1978.

Wolfe, D. M. "Power and Authority in the Family." *Studies in Social Power.* D. Cartwright, ed. Ann Arbor: University of Michigan, Institute for Social Research, 1959.

Wood, Barbara. *Children and Communication.* Englewood Cliffs, NJ: Prentice-Hall, 1976.

Yelsma, Paul. "Functional Conflict Management in Effective Marital Adjustment." *Communication Quarterly* 32 (1984): 56–62.

Yerby, Janet, and Nancy L. Buerkel-Rothfuss. "Communication Patterns, Contradictions, and Family Functions." Paper presented at the Speech Communication Association Convention, 1982.

Author Index

Subject Index

323

ACKNOWLEDGMENTS

pp. 44–46, 68–71. From *Social Penetration* by Irwin Altman and Dalmus Taylor. Copyright © 1973 by Holt, Rinehart and Winston, Inc. Reprinted by permission of the authors.

pp. 64, 91. From "Marital Conflict and Marital Intimacy" by Larry B. Feldman, *Family Process*, Vol. 18, March 1979, p. 70. © 1979 Family Process, Inc. Reprinted by permission.

pp. 96–97. From "Communication with Children: Toward a Healthy Construction of Communication Roles" by Fern Johnson. Paper presented at the Central States Speech Association Conference, April 14, 1978, Chicago, Illinois. Reprinted by permission.

p. 218. From "The Changing American Grandparent" by Bernice L. Neugarten and Karol K. Weinstein, *Journal of Marriage and the Family*, May 1964, pp. 202–203. Copyrighted © 1964 by the National Council of Family Relations. Reprinted by permission.

p. 226. Reprinted with permission from *Journal of Psychosomatic Research*, Vol. 11, Thomas H. Holmes and Richard H. Rahe, "The Social Readjustment Rating Scale." Copyright 1967, Pergamon Press, Ltd.

pp. 272, 275. From "Living Space in an Urban Ghetto" by Albert E. Scheflen, M.D. in *Family Process*, Vol. 10, 1971. © 1971 by Family Process, Inc. Reprinted by permission.

p. 285. Excerpts from "Healthy Family Systems" by Laurence R. Barnhill in *Family Coordinator*, Vol. 28, No. 1, January 1979, pp. 94–100. Copyright © 1979 by the National Council on Family Relations. Reprinted by permission.

pp. 287–88. From FAMILIES by Jane Howard. Copyright © 1978 by Jane Howard. Reprinted by permission of Simon & Schuster, Inc.

p. 298. From "Communication Training in Marriage and Family Living" by Daniel B. Wackman. Paper presented at the 64th annual meeting of the Speech Communication Association, Minneapolis, Minnesota, November 1978. Reprinted by permission.

p. 90. A. Lynn Scoresby, THE MARRIAGE DIALOGUE, © 1977, Random House, Inc., Chapter 4, pages 45–46; table 2, pages 64–65. Reprinted by permission.

p. 188. Excerpts adapted from pp. 162–165 in THE INTIMATE ENEMY by Dr. George R. Bach and Peter Wyden. Copyright © 1968, 1969 by George R. Bach and Peter Wyden. By permission of William Morrow & Company.

p. 102. "Psychological Dimensions of the Female and Male Roles" from NORMAL FAMILY PROCESSES ed. by Froma Walsh. Copyright © 1982 The Guilford Press. Reprinted by permission.

p. 72. "A Model of Interaction Stages" in INTERPERSONAL COMMUNICATION AND HUMAN RELATIONSHIPS by Mark L. Knapp. Reprinted by permission of Allyn & Bacon, Inc.

p. 126. From "Family Power: The Assessment of a Decade of Theory and Research, 1970–1979" by Gerald W. McDonald, JOURNAL OF MARRIAGE AND THE FAMILY, November 1980. Copyright © 1980 by the National Council on Family Relations. Reprinted by permission.

p. 147. From "A Conceptual Approach to Explicit Marital Negotiation" by John Scanzoni and Karen Polonko, JOURNAL OF MARRIAGE AND THE FAMILY, February 1980. Copyright © 1980 by the National Council on Family Relations. Reprinted by permission.

Photo Credits